WITHDRAWN

The
Vegetable Growers
Handbook

The Vegetable Growers Handbook

By

Frank Tozer

Green Man Publishing
Santa Cruz

Copyright © 2008 Frank Tozer

ISBN: 978 - 0 - 9773489 - 3 - 0

Library of Congress Control Number 2008900191

Green Man Publishing
Santa Cruz
P.O. Box 1546
Felton
CA 95018

Contact us online @ Greenmanpublishing.com

Contents

Introduction

Up until the twentieth century people in rural areas commonly produced a significant proportion of their own food in their vegetable gardens. This was an age old practice that dated back beyond memory; it was what people had always done. In those more uncertain times the garden was the most secure and reliable source of food. At many points in history it actually became a matter of life or death; it provided the food that kept people alive in times of crisis. Even when it wasn't essential for survival, the garden provided a margin of comfort and security, supplying its inhabitants with a better and more varied diet and making their lives easier. Indeed often the only difference between a comfortable family and an impoverished one was whether they had access to land for growing food.

In the twentieth century, industrialization and greater affluence broke the old bonds with the land. People moved to the cities and suburbs and the self-sufficient home vegetable garden became a thing of the past. To most people food is now just another commercial product, like shampoo or detergent. It is available year round, ready packaged from the supermarket. It is no longer our most vital link to the earth and as a result our view of nature has become distorted. We now see ourselves as so separate from nature that the health of the economy seems more important than the health of the planet.

The way our food is produced has also changed radically. We are often told that modern agriculture is the most efficient the world has ever seen, but it is really only efficient in terms of the amount of food produced relative to the amount of human labor expended. This has been made possible because massive amounts of fossil fuel energy have replaced human energy (as much as 10 calories of fossil fuel energy are now expended to produce 1 calorie of food energy). Industrial agriculture has undeniably made food cheaper, but this has come at a very high price. It requires an enormous amount of oil, electricity and natural gas, not only to run machinery and transport the food, but also to produce fertilizers, pesticides and other chemicals and to obtain irrigation water. Industrial agriculture also uses vast quantities of water and in many places this is being pumped from underground sources much more rapidly than it is being replenished (basically it is being mined). It also burns up so much topsoil that it's been said that we are already past the point of peak soil (if not peak oil). In parts of the plains over 50% of the topsoil has disappeared in less than 100 years. Not only does the loss of soil threaten future food production, but it also has another, more immediately damaging effect. When this soil vanishes, its organic matter is converted into huge quantities of greenhouse gases. When a tonne of soil disappears it liberates about three tonnes of carbon dioxide, along with nitrous oxide (which is much more powerful greenhouse gas), together the equivalent of about 33 tonnes of carbon dioxide. Many farms are losing several tonnes of soil per acre annually, so it's no surprise to learn that our system of industrial agriculture creates 40% of all greenhouse gases.

Cheap food has also cheapened the most essential human activity of all and made growing food into a menial task. The people who do the work of actually growing food are near the bottom of the heap in terms of status and wages. This is why they are often emigrants; doing work Americans consider to be beneath them. We live in a strange world when the activity that is most essential to human life is though to be beneath our dignity.

The industrial methods we have been using to produce food won't work for much longer. There is no alternative to eating, so how will our food be grown in the future? Do we increase out reliance on a brave new world of technology, machines, chemicals, genetically engineered organisms and multi-national corporations (whose primary responsibility is to their shareholders), or do we look to more sustainable and self reliant ways of producing food?

Part of the answer to this question is as close as your backyard. If you look at food production per acre (or in relation to the amount of energy, water and other inputs), home gardens are the most productive way of growing food that humans have ever devised. It is possible to produce a significant proportion of your own fruits and vegetables in the average backyard. If every house had its own productive vegetable garden, it could revolutionize the way food is grown in this country and how household wastes are disposed of. If we are ever to succeed in building a truly sustainable "Green economy", the organic home vegetable garden must become an essential component of every household. To quote Christopher Alexander "In a healthy town every family can grow vegetables for itself. The time is past to think of this as a hobby for enthusiasts; it is a fundamental part of human life".

Not only do we need a dramatic increase in the number of home vegetable gardens, we also need a new kind of urban and suburban farmer, growing food intensively on small plots of land, in and around our cities. Some imaginative pioneers have already done this successfully in various cities, as did our ancestors around all major cities, before cheap transportation became available. The Maraichers who worked the land around Paris during the nineteenth century are the best known of these.

The United States in a unique position to be at the forefront of a new green revolution, because it has a benevolent climate and plenty of space for anyone who wants to have a garden. In recent decades suburban sprawl has swallowed up vast tracts of prime farmland, so the land is often right where people live. Some estimates say there are 30 million acres of irrigated suburban lawn in this country, as well as enough small tractors to supply the third world. If some of this land were devoted to home food production, the changes could be awesome.

The benefits of a vegetable garden

Fine food
I love great food and have found that the best way to get it is to grow it myself. One of the greatest pleasures of growing a vegetable garden is in eating the best food that can be obtained anywhere. With a little effort you can grow foods that are of exceptional flavor and quality and often simply aren't available commercially. All serious home gardeners are familiar with the superior flavor of homegrown food; it can be so much better it doesn't even taste like the same thing. This superiority may be due to homegrown food being fresher, the use of superior tasting varieties, because the plant receives better nutrition or maybe occasionally just because you have grown it yourself.

Health
Organic food, fresh from your own garden, is the most nutritious you can get and it can improve your health significantly. It's been noticed that domestic animals will usually eat organic food in preference to that grown with chemicals. Obviously they know something that we don't. Organic foods commonly have more protein, vitamins and minerals to begin with, largely because they aren't bloated with water to make them bigger (the much vaunted high yields of chemically dependent agriculture are often simply extra water). When you are harvesting from your garden the food can be eaten at the peak of freshness, before their vitamins and other nutrients have started to break down.

Of course organic foods don't contain any pesticide residues, which is significant because we really don't know the long-term effects of pesticides in the body. This is particularly important for children, as they consume larger quantities of pesticides in relation to their body weight. Many conventional farmers have an organic garden for their own consumption.

Health is more than just good food of course and gardening helps here too. It is both a pleasant way to relax and one of the best forms of exercise, with benefits far greater than the simple burning of calories would suggest. Working out in the fresh air, creating a beautiful garden, working at your own pace, doing a meaningful activity you enjoy, growing the food that sustains you. All of these contribute to psychological health. It's even been suggested that a persons stress level is directly related to how close they are to plants; that plants are actually a biological need for humans.

Environmental

A home vegetable garden can significantly lessen your impact on the earth, by reducing your consumption of resources. Indirectly you will use less fossil fuel, because you will be eating food produced with only a fraction of the energy used by commercial agriculture and there are no transportation costs. It also has a significant impact on the amount of stuff you throw away. You can eliminate a lot of the packaging that comes from purchased foods and you can recycle a lot of the stuff you do acquire, by composting food waste, paper packaging, and most natural materials. Using rainwater catchment and waste gray water from the house could help to reduce the amount of water needed to grow food. An even bigger step would be to recycle human wastes though the garden. A system to safely do this would be a momentous step forward in reducing water use and pollution, and in recycling nutrients back to where they can be a valuable resource.

The vegetable garden can also teach you a significant lesson in how you don't always have to spend money to enjoy yourself. When you get down to the fundamentals, life can actually become richer and more satisfying when you consume less.

Financial

A vegetable garden can save you money. If you have a well paying job this may not seem like much, but if you are trying to raise a family on a limited income it can be significant. Many poor people, in this country and around the world, depend upon their home vegetable gardens to keep them well fed and they would be considerably poorer without them. Just because you are poor doesn't mean you have to eat badly. If you want to eat organic food and don't have much money, this is probably the only way to make it happen.

I have never thought of saving money as a big reason to have a vegetable garden, because food has always been relatively cheap in this country. However at the time I am finishing this book, food prices have risen more rapidly than at any time I can remember. Maybe in the future saving money will become an important reason.

Security

The ability to produce your own food also gives you a measure of psychological security. The number of Americans who remember the last serious economic upheaval is diminishing rapidly, but many will testify that their vegetable garden was an invaluable buffer against economic crisis. If food ever becomes scarce or very expensive you can always grow your own. Americans have rarely lived with the threat of not having anything to eat, but in other parts of the world it is an all too frequent reality. I recently read an account of how many city dwelling Russians survived the demise of communism and the resulting economic collapse. Many depended upon their gardening relatives in the country to supply them with food and without this lifeline they would have been in dire circumstances.

Spiritual

Working with the earth to fulfill the basic need for food is a fundamentally benevolent activity, that can help you to re-connect with nature. It can bring you back to the reality that we are totally and absolutely dependent on the earth for our well being, and that we should look after it a little more carefully.

For me gardening is about using human energy to make a place more productive, more diverse, and biologically richer than it would be otherwise. It's been said that "Gardening is the natural activity of man" and that pretty much sums it up. It is one of the most gratifying and fulfilling activities a person can engage in. I love to be out in the garden, nurturing the land and bringing crops to fruition. If you garden long enough you will begin to understand what is meant by the expression "the garden cultivates the gardener".

Amaranth
Amaranthus spp

Introduction: In this country the Amaranths are most familiar as weeds of disturbed soils, especially in gardens, but in other parts of the world they are important crop plants. They reached their greatest popularity in their native South and Central America and in Pre-Columbian times they were among the most important grain crops grown there.

Amaranth is a high protein grain that has considerable potential as a garden scale grain crop. It is sometimes referred to as a pseu-docereal (as are Buckwheat and Quinoa), as it is grown as a grain crop, but isn't a member of the grass family.

In some parts of the tropics the Amaranths are very important as heat tolerant potherbs (under the names Hinn Choy, Tampala, Calaloo, and others).

I have grown Amaranth as both a grain and a leaf crop and find it par-ticularly useful as a summer potherb. In recent years the leaves have become my main summer potherb (my wife says they are the best green vegetable she has ever had). They are not only tasty, but also easy to grow, very productive, fast growing and require almost no work. In fact I first started using them because there were so many volun-teers from a previous grain crop.

Amaranths even find their way into the ornamental garden and some varieties are grown purely for their beauty (these too are edible). Their appearance ranges from quite attractive to downright spectacular. If you are looking for a substitute for Spinach to grow in hot summer weather, I highly reccomend you try Amaranth.

About Amaranth

Seed facts
Germ temp: 50 (60 to 80) 90° F
Germ time: 5 to 14 days
Viability: 7 yrs
Germination percentage: 70%+
Weeks to grow transplants: 4

Planning facts
Hardiness: Tender
Ease of growing: Easy
Temp for growth: 68 to 80° F
Plants per person: 10 greens
Plants per sq ft: 1 grain
            4 leaf
Transplants:
Start: 2 wks before last frost
Plant out: 2 wks after last frost
Direct sow: 2 wks after last frost
Succession sow: every 6 weeks
Harvest: 95 to 150 days seed
30 to 60 days for greens

Harvest facts
Harvest period: 4 to 6 weeks
Yield: Grain 1 oz / sq ft
Leaf 1 lb / sq ft.
Yield per plant: 4 to 16 oz

Nutritional content
Leaves: These are high in vitamins A and C, as well as protein, iron and calcium.

Amaranth leaves also contain oxalic acid (though less than Spinach), which can react with calcium and make it less available to the body. Fortunately this is not a significant problem to anyone with a reason-able intake of calcium. It may also contribute to the formation of kidney stones, so anyone prone to them should probably avoid the leaves (and Spinach).

If used as a potherb, most of the oxalic acid will be leached out in the cooking water.

Seeds: These are rich in high quality protein and have a better amino acid balance than almost any other common vegetable protein. They even contain the lysine and methionine so often lacking in plant proteins. The seed also contains about 20% oil, as well as the minerals calcium, magnesium, phosphorus and iron.

Soil
pH 5.5 to 7.0
Leaf Amaranth can do well on soils that are too poor and dry for most crops. However for a good seed crop Amaranth needs a well-drained and fertile soil, similar to that for Corn. It doesn't need a great deal of nitrogen or phospho-rus, though it does like potassium. It doesn't mind acid soil.

Planning
Where: Plant Amaranth in a warm sheltered spot with full sun.

When: Amaranth is a tropical plant that uses C4 photosynthesis (like Corn and Sunflower), which makes it particularly efficient in high heat and light intensities. It grows best in hot weather and doesn't do well if it is cold. Don't plant it until the soil has warmed up a little, at least two weeks after the last frost date (nighttime temperatures should go no lower than 60° F). Of course you could just plant it when the weed Amaranth appears.

Early plants flower when they are big enough and have enough food reserves. A late planting will flower when it is triggered by short day length, so the plants won't get as big.

Succession sowing: Leaf Amaranth should be succession sown every 6 weeks.

Planting

Using transplants: In warm weather Amaranth germinates and grows so vigorously that there is little to be gained from starting it inside. However if the growing season is very short, you might start a grain crop indoors, in cell packs, soil blocks or plug trays. Plant it out when the transplants are about 3″ high and the soil has warmed up.

Direct sowing: Amaranth is sown ¼″ to ½″ deep, by broadcasting or planting in rows. It is easy to sow a lot of plants at a time, but you usually don't need many.

Spacing

Grain: Put the plants 12″ to 18″ apart each way, in offset rows. In large mechanized operations, plants may be grown in densely packed beds as close as 4″ apart. Appar-

ently this makes for more uniform head size and ripening.

Leaf: Broadcast the seeds and then harvest thin, until the plants stand 6″ to 8″ apart. To grow it in rows, plant it ½″ apart in the row, with 18″ between the rows. This is gradually harvest thinned to a final spacing of about 6″ apart (eat the plants as you remove them).

Care

Weed: Amaranth is a weed itself, so doesn't generally have much of a problem with weeds. In fact the biggest problem may be differentiating crop Amaranth from weed Amaranth (the former commonly have a purplish tint). Weed the young plants after they have all emerged and that should be enough.

Water: Grain Amaranth is relatively drought tolerant and doesn't like too much water (it may cause the roots to rot). However don't let it dry out too much as this may reduce the harvest. For maximum production leaf Amaranth should always be kept moist.

Mulch: Once the plants are growing well, they should be mulched to conserve moisture. They should then pretty much take care of themselves until harvest time.

Pests: The only pest I have encountered on grain Amaranth have been Leaf Miners, though commercial farmers have met several other

pests and diseases. The succulent leaf Amaranths are a favorite of slugs and snails and young seedlings may be destroyed if not protected.

Harvest

Grain: It generally takes from 3 to 5 months for the seed to fully ripen. As harvest time approaches, examine the flower heads regularly for ripe seed. You can tell if the seed is ripe by biting it; a fully ripe seed will be firm rather than chewy. Don't wait too long to harvest, or seed will begin to drop.

When the plants begin to wither, or frost threatens, gather the entire heads by hand. If you only have a few plants you can bend the heads over a bucket and rub them to loosen the seed. If you have a lot of plants, cut the whole heads and lay them on a tarp to dry. Then beat, crush or walk on the dry heads to loosen the seeds. Other than winnowing to remove debris, they need no other preparation for eating. It is important that the seed be dried thoroughly for storage. Small quantities can be dried in a paper grocery bag.

Vegetable: Start by harvest thinning extra plants, to get them to the correct spacing. Once the plants are growing strongly, pinch out (and eat) the growing tips. Amaranths have strong apical dominance, so this makes them branch out and get bushier with new growth. The leaves are best before the flowers appear.

In some tropical home gardens, harvesting of leaves doesn't start until the plants are 4 or 5 feet high. Then the tops are pinched out and eaten. After this the side shoots are harvested as they reach useful size. Any flower buds are removed promptly and eaten with their surrounding leaves. By harvesting frequently and preventing them flowering, the plants can be made to produce edible shoots for months.

After harvest: Heavily cropped plants will benefit from a liquid feed of seaweed, applied to their roots. Don't use compost or manure tea, as you will be harvesting again fairly soon (you don't want pathogenic bacteria on to the leaves).

Amaranth wilts quickly once harvested, so use promptly. The young leaves can be added to salads. If you have a large harvest, you can freeze the cooked leaves like Spinach.

Seed saving: This is pretty simple, just treat it like a grain crop and take seed from the best plants Amaranth is monoecious, with separate male and female flowers on the same plant. They are wind pollinated, so it's best to have only one variety growing within 1000 feet (and make sure there are no wild relatives nearby). Take seed from at least 5 plants to maintain some genetic variability.

Unusual growing ideas
Volunteers: Amaranth often self-sows and can become a weed. Last year I let an entire bed get taken over by volunteer grain Amaranth. The only thing I did was to thin out the stand, by harvesting some of the plants for greens. Some plants reached 8 feet in height and gave me as good a crop as if I had sown it deliberately. However I usually use volunteers as a mixed green leaf crop, as there usually isn't enough seed to make a worthwhile grain crop.

Ornamentals: Some Amaranth varieties (Love–Lies-Bleeding and Josephs Coat) are usually grown as ornamentals, but are also perfectly edible. The grain varieties are quite spectacular when flowering, especially the purplish red types and make great specimen plants. I wonder if anyone has crossed Love lies Bleeding with a tall grain Amaranth? The resulting edible offspring could be quite spectacular

Cuttings: Amaranth can easily be grown from cuttings, if you get a plant you particularly like.

Varieties:
Some botanists consider all of the species below to be variations of *A. hybridus*. I have found all of the grain varieties to be very productive. The main distinguishing features being their appearance, so I won't mention specific varieties.

Grain Amaranths: The pale colored seed tend to have a better flavor than the black seed.
A. hypochondriacus: The most vigorous species.
A. cruentus:
A. caudatus: This is sometimes grown as a garden ornamental under the name Love-Lies-Bleeding. It attracts a lot of attention with its bizarre appearance.

The grain Amaranths are also good as leaf crops.

Leaf Amaranths: The flowers of the leaf varieties are much smaller and less conspicuous, than those of grain types.
A. hybridus
A. tricolor (syn *A. gangeticus*): Often grown as an ornamental.

Cooking
Grain: The seed needs no preparation except for cleaning. Its flavor can be improved by toasting, which causes it to pop like popcorn. This can be done in a hot pan in the same way as for popcorn (if it won't pop try sprinkling a little water onto the seed). If you have a large quantity of seed, you could try popping it in the oven. Spread it a half inch deep in a pan, cover and roast it at 350° F for a half-hour. Stir occasionally to prevent it burning.

The toasted seed can be added whole to baked goods, ground to flour for baking (it's usually mixed with wheat flour), or boiled as a kind of porridge. The whole raw seed can be sprouted like alfalfa until about ¼″ long and used in salads and sandwiches. It can also be boiled like millet in salt water. Some people soak it in water overnight before cooking.

Leaf: Amaranths are mildly flavored, but very good. They can be steamed, or boiled, in a small amount of water (the latter may be better as it can reduce the amount of oxalic acid they contain). Don't cook them for more than a few minutes or they will get too watery. In Asia they are often stir-fried, or used in soups.

Recipe: A good way to cook the leaves is to sauté some onion and garlic in a pan and then add the washed greens. The water sticking to the leaves is enough to cook them.

Try using the recipes described under Chard and Spinach. They will be just as good with Amaranth.

Artichoke, Chinese

Stachys sieboldi

Introduction: This plant is grown for its small, oddly shaped tubers. These are quite popular in its native China and Japan, but are a rarity in North America. It is also grown as a crop in parts of Europe, notably France where the people know a good tasting plant when they find one. I don't really know how it got its name. It is from China, but has nothing to do with the Artichokes (it doesn't taste like them). In France it is known as Crosnes (named after the place where it was first grown) and in Japan it is called Chorogi.

Probably the hardest thing about growing this vigorous and hardy crop is finding some tubers to plant.

The Chinese Artichoke plant somewhat resembles Mint in appearance (it is related), but it doesn't have aromatic foliage.

Nutritional content:
The tubers contain an unusual carbohydrate called, appropriately enough, stachyose.

Soil: The soil should be light, but moisture retentive. The more fertile the soil, the better the harvest. It will grow well enough in fairly poor soils, but won't be very productive.

Soil preparation: Incorporate 2″ of compost or aged manure into the top 6″ of soil, along with some wood ashes. If you are growing them in a permanent bed, then you can apply this as a mulch.

Planning
When: This species needs a long time in the ground, taking 180 to 200 days from planting to harvest, so it's best to plant it early. Plant the tubers anytime from mid February to mid spring (they are very hardy). It tolerates hot weather well.

Where: Chinese Artichoke prefers full sun, but will also grow in light shade. It is a perennial root crop and any tuber remaining in the ground will grow again the following year. For this reason you might think about giving it a semi-permanent bed of its own, or grow it in a semi-wild garden. With its mint-like foliage and small pink flowers, it is not an unattractive plant and doesn't look out of place in the ornamental garden.

Planting
Vegetative: Chinese Artichoke is propagated vegetatively by means of the small tubers, planted 3″ to 6″ deep. If you plant them in a permanent bed, you should not have to plant them again, as they will come back again every year.

Spacing: Intensive bed spacing is 6″ to 12″ apart, in offset rows across the bed. They can also be spaced in rows 6″ to 10″ apart, with 18″ between the rows. In good soil they may grow to 18″ in height.

Care
They don't need a great deal of care, but a little attention will generally be repaid with a larger harvest.

Water: For maximum production of tubers, the soil should be kept well watered at all times.

Feed: Give them a liquid feed when the tubers begin to form, to increase yield.

Mulch: Apply a thick mulch when the soil has warmed up, to keep in moisture and keep down weeds.

Pruning: You might want to remove any flower stalks, to concentrate the plants energy on producing tubers.

Pests: It is rarely bothered by pests or disease.

Harvest
When: The mature tubers can be gathered after the tops die back, from late autumn until early spring. They are not very big, being anywhere from ½″ to 2″ in length and ½″ in diameter.

How: If you don't want a permanent bed, be careful to gather every fragment of tuber. They have the ability to sprout from even the tiniest tuber and can become a minor weed.

Storage: The best place to store the tubers is in the ground. Just dig them, as you need them. If the ground freezes regularly, cover them with a thick mulch, so you can harvest after it gets cold.

The tubers don't store well out of the ground, their beautiful pearly white color dulls quickly in the air and they shrivel up. If it is impossible to dig from your garden in winter, then store them in a root cellar in damp sand.

Seed Saving:
This species isn't normally grown from seed, though it probably could be. The best way to ensure you have plants next year is to replant a proportion of the tubers as soon as you dig them. Or if you have a permanent bed, just don't harvest them all.

Unusual growing Ideas
Naturalizing:
Because the plant is so independent, it can be naturalized as a semi-wild plant in any unused part of the garden. It can even become a minor weed.

Groundcover:
This creeping plant could probably be grown as a groundcover, though it would take a few years to get going. It wouldn't work where I live because Gophers would eat it all.

Cooking:
The white tubers have a pleasant nutty flavor and can be eaten raw, pickled or cooked. The only complaint about them is that they are so small and convoluted they are difficult to clean, or peel. Don't try to peel them, just scrub with a vegetable brush and trim off any damaged parts.

The tubers can be eaten raw, or cooked by steaming, stir frying, boiling (use the cooking water for soup or sauce) or frying (for a few minutes). Don't overcook them, as it will spoil their flavor.

Artichoke, Globe
Cynara scolymus

Introduction:
This perennial is native to the Mediterranean, where its flower buds have been a favored food since the time of ancient Greece. They are quite a unique vegetable, in that the part eaten is actually a part of the flower (the scales and swollen base).

Artichoke is considered to be one of the finest of all vegetable foods. I think it fully lives up to its reputation, no other vegetable is quite as decadently delicious when cooked fresh from the garden. This is somewhat ironic, when you consider that it is a kind of Thistle.

Artichokes are quite nutritious, but you don't eat them in sufficient quantity for them to be an important food source. Also the sprawling plants need a lot of space, so the yield per square foot is very low.

In the right climate Artichokes are quite low maintenance and need almost no attention. They are also perennial, often yielding for 5 years or more.

In very cold climates they are sometimes grown as an annual.

This can work out okay, but the harvest won't be very big.

Nutritional content:
Artichokes are a fair source of vitamins A and C, as well as niacin and folate (the natural form of folic acid). They also contain some powerful phytochemicals, including cynarin and luteolin.

Soil
pH 6.0
To produce the highest quality Artichoke hearts you need a deep, rich, well-drained, sandy soil. Drainage is particularly important in cold climates, because if the roots stay wet for long periods in winter, they will often rot.

About Globe Artichoke

Seed facts
Germ temp: 50 (65 to 70) 75° F
Germ time: 7 to 21 days
Viability: 6 to 10 yrs
Germination percentage: 60 +
Weeks to grow transplants: 10 to 12

Planning facts
Perennial
Hardiness: Hardy
Ease of growing: Moderate
Growing temp: 40 (60 to 65) 75° F
Plants per person: 3
Plants per sq ft: 1/9th
Transplants
Start: 6 weeks before last frost
Plant out: 2 weeks after last frost
Time to harvest to 1½ yrs

Harvest facts
Length of harvest: 8 to 12 weeks
Yield per sq ft: 1 head
Yield per plant: 12 heads

Soil preparation: Amend the soil generously before planting, maybe even double dig. Artichokes are a short term perennial and you won't be able to dig the soil again without disturbing them. Incorporate lots of compost or aged manure, along with greensand (for potassium), colloidal phosphate (for phosphorus) and Kelp (for trace elements).

Planning

Where: Artichokes need good growing conditions and if the climate isn't suitable they won't produce very large flower buds. They are quite frost tender and grow best in the mild, damp, maritime climate of coastal California.

The plants won't survive cold winters, so in northern areas they must either be grown as annuals, or protected over the winter. They should be sheltered from strong winds, as they are prone to being blown over. They need full sun.

These large plants need a lot of space for the amount of food they produce and this is probably the main reason they aren't more popular. They are just too big for the intensive vegetable garden beds and so are best planted individually in any odd vacant corner. There they can get as big as they want, without causing any problems. Once established they don't require much attention.

When: The roots are usually planted while they are dormant in winter. To grow Artichokes from seed you usually start them in late winter. The earlier you get them growing, the bigger they will get. This is particularly important if you are growing them as an annual and will harvest flower buds in the first year. Plant them out after all danger of frost has passed.

Planting

Artichokes are usually propagated vegetatively from offsets. They can be started from seed, but this doesn't breed very true, which means there will be a lot of variation in the offspring. If you really must use seed, choose the best seedlings to grow on and discard the rest. When they get big enough, you can propagate the chosen seedlings vegetatively.

Growing from seed: Start the seed indoors 6 weeks before the last frost date, in cell packs, soil blocks or individual 3″ pots. The seedlings grow quickly, so be prepared to pot them up to larger pots if necessary. Plant them out in their permanent position after all danger of frost is past. The plants grow rapidly once they get established in rich soil.

If any buds appear during the first year, they should be nipped off to encourage strong root growth. The following year you can begin harvesting. Obviously if you are growing it as an annual, you don't do this, you want all the buds you can get.

Growing from suckers:
What: Artichokes are normally grown from the suckers (offsets), that emerge all around the old root in spring. These are much better than growing from seed, the plants yield earlier, are more uniform and are much more productive. Rooted suckers are widely available in garden centers in spring, or you might be able to beg, steal or borrow some.

How: Suckers are taken from the parent plant in spring, when they are about 10″ tall. The normal practice is to dig down the side of the plant and cut off the sucker with a heel of old plant root attached. Trim off most of the leaves (the roots can't support them) and plant it immediately in a well-prepared site. Alternatively you could plant it in a 1 gallon pot, or in nursery bed, until well rooted (and then plant it out).

The suckers are pretty tough and even if they appear to die, don't give upon them. I had a batch of plants that lay dormant all summer (I thought they were dead) and then burst into life when cool moist fall weather arrived.

Spacing: Artichokes are too big to plant in the intensive beds. If you want to grow them in rows then space them 30″ to 36″ apart. Space the rows 48″ to 60″ apart.

Care

True to its Thistle nature, the Artichoke is a vigorous and robust plant that needs little attention once established. Its only real weakness is its minimal tolerance of cold.

Water: Though relatively drought tolerant, Artichokes yield better if the soil is kept evenly moist. Water is especially crucial when the buds are developing.

Fertilization: Artichokes yield best if grown without any check in their growth, which means they must get all the nutrients they need. They are usually fed annually with a mulch of compost or aged manure. You can also use an occasional foliar feed of compost tea or liquid Kelp.

Mulch: This is the main source of nutrients for these perennial plants. It also helps to retain moisture, keeps down weeds and keeps the soil cool in summer.

Support: Artichokes can get quite tall and top heavy and can be blown over by strong winds. You can prevent this by staking them firmly.

Pruning: If you cut off all of the lateral shoots, the main bud (known as the "King Head") will get bigger

In spring, most of the emerging offsets should be removed, even if you don't want them for propagation. If they are all allowed to grow, the plants will get overcrowded. It is common practice to leave 3 to 4 shoots to develop on a plant and remove the rest for transplanting, trading or eating.

Renewal: Commercial growers usually replace the plants after 2 or 3 harvests, before their vigor begins to decline. Home growers may also do this, replacing a portion (20% to 33%) of their Artichoke plants each year. In this way they always have vigorous young plants and will have replaced them all every 3 to 5 years. However this isn't necessary for the gardener who prizes low maintenance as much as high yield.

Frost: Artichokes will probably be killed by hard frosts if not well protected. If you want your plants to survive the winter where the soil freezes, you must protect them carefully. Cover them with a thick mulch and then cover this with a cold frame, cloche or box. If you just mulch them, there is a danger that they will rot from too much moisture. They can survive down to 20° F if protected in this way.

If it gets really cold, you can dig the roots and store them inside. This is no more difficult than it is for Dahlias, simply lift the root as the leaves die back, cut off all but a couple of inches of stem and brush off loose soil. Store them in a burlap sack, in the root cellar at 35 to 40° F. Alternatively you could plant them in 5 gallon pots and keep them in a root cellar or cold garage.

Pests: I haven't found Artichokes to be seriously bothered by disease or pests.

Harvest:

When: The terminal bud should be harvested as soon as it reaches full size (2" to 4" in diameter). Any smaller than this and it isn't really worth bothering with, except perhaps in soup. The bracts should still be tight against the bud; if they have started to open it is too late.

If you miss the right harvest time, you should still cut the head off, as this stimulates the plant to produce more useful secondary buds. After the top flower buds are removed, more will be produced on side shoots. In this way a single plant can produce quite a few buds over the course of the summer.

You need to remove all of the flower buds as they are produced, even if they are not usable. If you leave any on the plant, it will waste energy making seeds. This may even cause the plant to die.

Seed saving: Saving Artichoke seed is pretty easy, but it is rarely done because they are normally propagated vegetatively. If the flowers are allowed to mature, seed is produced readily, as one flower can pollinate another (though not itself) on the same plant. It sometimes self-sows itself so vigorously it can become a pest.

Unusual Growing Ideas
Ornamental: If space in the intensive beds is limited you might put them in the ornamental garden, as their blue/purple flowers are quite spectacular (if rarely allowed to appear).

Varieties:
Grande Beurre, Green Globe Improved: These varieties can both be grown as annuals, as they will produce useful buds in their first year.

Cooking: You probably already know how to eat an Artichoke, but you may not know how to cook them properly. Cut off the stem and the top of the head and then trim back the points of the scales. The heads are then boiled in salt water for about 30 minutes (don't overcook them). They are then left upside down to drain and are served with butter or other dressing. They can also be steamed or fried.

It was almost inevitable that such a sensuous food as an Artichoke heart would be considered an aphrodisiac.

Artichoke, Jerusalem

Helianthus tuberosus

Introduction: This tall perennial Sunflower produces edible tuberous roots. It is the only common (if you could call it that) vegetable crop that is native to North America. It is hardy, easily grown and very productive, though not particularly nutritious.

Nutritional content:

Like most members of the *Asteraceae,* Jerusalem Artichokes store their food in the form of inulin, rather than starch. Unfortunately we can't digest inulin very well, so their calorific value to us is only about 75 calories per pound. This is a lot less than the Potato, to which they are often compared (it is also why they sometimes cause flatulence). They do contain useful quantities of B vitamins, as well as iron. calcium and potassium however and are quite a substantial food.

Soil
pH 6.0 to 6.5

Jerusalem Artichoke will do well on almost any soil, but it is more productive in a rich, moist, fertile one. Like most root crops it doesn't need a lot of nitrogen, though it does like phosphorus and potassium. If you are growing it in a permanent bed, you should incorporate lots of compost or aged manure before planting. Also give it greensand, colloidal phosphate and perhaps some Kelp powder.

About Jerusalem Artichoke

Planning facts
Direct sow: On last frost date
Hardiness: Hardy
Ease of growing: Easy
Yield per plant: 2 lb
Plants per person: 5
Yield per sq ft: 1 to 3
Plants per sq ft: .75
Time to harvest: 6 months

Planning

Where: This plant can be grown as an annual in the intensive beds. However I prefer to give it a permanent bed, where it can grow for several years without interruption (except for harvesting). As a perennial it would naturally grow in the same place for years anyway.

These plants may grow up to 12 feet in height, so don't put them where they will cast shade on other important plants.

When: Jerusalem Artichoke is very hardy while dormant and can take hard frosts and even completely frozen ground. It doesn't grow well in cool weather though, it is a warm weather crop.

Planting

Vegetative: Jerusalem Artichokes are not grown from seed, but are propagated vegetatively from tubers (or pieces of tuber).

The tubers are totally hardy and can be planted from late winter to early spring. If you don't have many tubers, you can cut them into several pieces, so long as each

---

piece has at least one bud on it. I use a bulb planter to plant them, making holes 4" to 6″ deep.

Spacing: A plant can easily get 8 to 10 feet tall, so it needs lots of room. If you are planting in a bed, space the plants 15" to 24″ apart in offset rows.

It is probably better to grow Jerusalem Artichoke in a double row, spaced 12″ apart in the rows, with 30″ between the rows. The advantage of this is that it is easier to earth them up and to give them support. The row soon becomes a temporary screen and can even be used for decorative effect.

Care

Once these plants are established you don't need to pay much attention to them. They are native wild plants and can take care of themselves.

Watering: These plants are somewhat drought tolerant, but in very dry climates they will need regular irrigation. For maximum yields you should keep the soil evenly moist at all times.

Earthing up: Earth up the plants when they are about a foot high, by piling soil against the stems. This makes them more stable and less likely to get blown over by strong winds. Earthing up has other benefits too, it gets rid of weeds, it may increase the number of tubers produced and it makes them easier to harvest.

Mulch: This helps to make these independent plants even more independent, by conserving moisture and feeding the soil.

Fertilization: If you are growing Jerusalem Artichoke in a permanent bed, you should fertilize it annually. The best way to do this is by mulching with aged manure or compost. If you are harvesting annually (and feel the need to do some extra work) you could also incorporate it into the soil after harvest. Wood ashes are also good as they supply potassium.

Support: These plants can get very tall and in wind prone areas you may need to support them. Do this by putting strong 6 foot stakes in the ground at 6 foot intervals. Run string along these and tie the stems to the strings. Plants supported like this make a good windbreak.

Pests: This crop is just too tough to die. When I planted it in my garden in western Washington, slugs repeatedly ate the tubers. This happened every time they sent up new shoots, for about two months, yet by the end of the summer the plants were about nine feet high and produced well.

Gophers will eat the tubers, so if they are a problem you will have to grow it in a wired bed, or in wire baskets. This can also help in harvesting, just pull up the basket and empty it out.

Eradication. Some people say that this plant doesn't need any pests, because it is one. If any fragment of the persistent tubers is left in the ground, it will sprout and grow. I haven't found this to be too much of a problem however, as in spring the emerging shoots give away their location and can easily be pulled up.

Harvest: The plants flower in late summer and fall and are quite attractive at this time. The tubers mature about a month after the flowers have finished, when the plants start to die back. They can be harvested from this point on, right through the winter, until they start to grow again the following spring. They are actually much better later on, after exposure to cold weather has made them sweeter.

It is a good idea to cut down the stems after they die back, leaving about a foot sticking out of the ground (these make it easier to locate the tubers later on).

Storage: The best place to store these hardy tubers is in the ground. If the ground freezes, cover them with a thick mulch so digging will be easier. They can also be stored in damp sand like Carrots. When the tubers are stored for any length of time, the inulin slowly turns into sugar, so they become sweeter and more digestible.

Seed saving: Generally any seed that is produced is sterile. This doesn't matter because this crop is always propagated vegetatively. You don't usually have to save tubers, some will remain in the ground after harvest and grow themselves.

Unusual growing ideas
Screen: These tall plants have been planted in double or triple rows as a deciduous screen (they need support in windy areas).

Cut flowers: The clusters of small yellow Sunflowers can be used for cut flowers. Taking them won't affect tuber formation.

Wild garden: This plant is very independent. I grew it in my garden beds for a couple of years and then decided to stop growing it. Being soft hearted and not wanting to kill it, I transplanted the remaining tubers out into one of the wilder parts of my garden. With almost no watering and Gophers eating the whole plants, it was pretty much forgotten for a couple of years. It managed to hang on though, as I recently rediscovered a couple of plants and brought them back into my garden.

Emergency food: This plant could be grown as an ever-multi-plying source of emergency food by those who worry about the future.

Compost crop: This fast growing plant can also be grown as a perennial compost material crop. It can be cut several times in a season and will regenerate itself without replanting. Of course this will have an adverse effect on tuber production.

Ornamental: With its small Sunflowers, this plant is actually quite ornamental when grown en masse. Some varieties produce flowers very freely and make quite good cut flowers.

Varieties: If you want to grow a specific variety, you will probably have to buy the tubers from a mail order company, as they are not readily available. If you don't care, then it's easier (and much cheaper) to buy them in a produce market, where they are often labeled as Sunchokes. Commercial crops are almost always Improved Mammoth French.

Improved Mammoth French (American) is more uniform and easier to use.
Fuseau: less knobby
Golden Nugget
Stampede
Dwarf Sunray

Cooking: The tubers are sometimes eaten raw in salads, but more often they are lightly cooked.

They are good cooked for 10 minutes and then sauteed with chopped Onions.

Asparagus
Asparagus officinalis

Introduction: This native of Eurasia has been prized as a gourmet food since the Romans. The newly emerging spring shoots are regarded as one of the great delicacies of the vegetable garden.

Asparagus is a great perennial crop. It's low maintenance, easy to grow, expensive to buy and much better when home grown. As an added bonus it's available early in the growing season, when few other crops are producing.

Asparagus does have some significant drawbacks as well. It takes a long time from planting to first harvest. The harvest season itself is pretty short, usually only 6 weeks or so. Perhaps most importantly for the intensive gardener, a good sized planting takes up a lot of space. When you consider all of these factors, it's not surprising that Asparagus is one of the most expensive vegetables to buy.

Asparagus isn't very productive for the space it occupies, so isn't a good crop for small gardens, or intensive beds in general. Fortunately it is independent and attractive, so can be planted in any spare corner of the garden, or even grown as an ornamental. Birds eat the berries and sow the seeds, so given the right conditions it may escape from your garden and naturalize.

Nutritional content:
Asparagus has been called a superfood for its nutritional content. It is rich in vitamins A, B6 and C, as well as soluble fiber, selenium, folate and rutin (an antioxidant).

About Asparagus

Seed facts

Germ temp: 50 (60 to 85) 95° F
"   time: 7 to 21 days
53 days / 50° F
24 days / 59° F
15 days / 68° F
10 days / 77° * F Optimum
12 days / 86° F
Seed viability: 2 to 5 years
Germination percentage: 70%+
Weeks to grow transplants: 10 to 12

Planning facts
Hardiness: Hardy
Ease of growing: Easy
Growing temp: 45 (60 to 70) 85° F
Plants per person: 10
Plants per sq ft: ½
Transplants
Start: 11 wks before last frost
Plant out: 1 wk after last frost
Direct sow: 2 wks after last frost
Time to harvest: seed 3 years
                              roots 2 years

Harvest facts
Length of harvest: 6 weeks
Yield per plant: 1 lb (20 shoots)
Yield per sq ft: 12 oz sq ft

Soil
pH 6.5 (6.0 - 7.0) 7.5
Asparagus isn't a particularly fussy plant, but it will produce more food if given optimal soil conditions. The ideal soil is deep, fairly light, rich and well drained, with lots of organic matter to help it retain water. In poorly drained soils the roots may rot over the winter. If you want to grow Asparagus in soil that gets wet in winter, plant it in raised beds.

Soil preparation: It's

important to amend an Asparagus bed thoroughly prior to planting. Once the plants are in the ground, you can't incorporate anything else and any further fertilization must be as a top dressing or mulch.

It is not a bad idea to double dig an Asparagus bed before planting, especially in heavy soil. This loosens the soil to a depth of 24″ and enables you to remove all perennial weeds (very important), tree roots and other debris. It also allows you to incorporate fertilizers and organic matter evenly throughout the soil. Add as much aged manure or compost as you can spare, along with liberal quantities of colloidal phosphate (it loves phosphorus), greensand (for potassium) and Kelp (for trace elements).

Climate: Asparagus doesn't like
very hot humid areas, or very mild winters.

Planning

Where: An Asparagus bed may last 20, 30, even 50 years (100 year old beds have been known), which is longer than many fruit trees. Consequently it is important to choose the growing site carefully. The first criterion is that it should be in full sun. It will take some light shade, but won't be as productive. The bed should be sheltered from strong winds and well away from large trees or shrubs, with their vigorous feeder roots. Lastly it should be placed where it won't interfere with other everyday garden operations.

An Asparagus bed takes a lot of space. Each plant sends out roots several feet in all directions and

they must be spaced far enough apart to prevent competition. In addition the individual plants aren't particularly productive, so you need quite a few to get a reasonable harvest (ideally at least 10 plants per person). Taken together these factors can make for a pretty good size growing bed.

If you don't have the space for a full sized bed of Asparagus, you might be able to fit a dozen or so plants in various spots around the garden. You won't get a huge harvest, but it's better than nothing. Asparagus is quite pretty with its ferny foliage and can blend in to the perennial ornamental garden pretty well.

Planting
Planting options: To grow Asparagus you can either buy 2 year old roots, ready to go in the ground, or you can grow your own roots from seed. The seedlings are planted out in the permanent bed when they are one year old.

Seed: Growing Asparagus from seed is the least expensive way to

go. One year old seedlings will eventually out-produce two year old roots, because they suffer less from transplant shock (Asparagus doesn't really like transplanting). Consequently they establish themselves better and eventually surpass the older roots in size. They are also less troubled by disease, probably because of their healthier root system.

The drawback of growing from seed is having to wait 3 to 4 years to get a worthwhile harvest. However this isn't such a big deal if you consider that they may live for 20 or 30 years.

It is possible to direct sow Asparagus, as it is vigorous and fast growing enough. However it isn't very practical to plant a seed every 24″ and then wait for a couple of years.

Two-year-old roots: These
are available in garden centers every spring. These give the fastest return and do pretty well, but purists say they don't do as well as younger plants. They are also significantly more expensive.

Raising transplants
If you are patient, the best way to grow Asparagus, is to raise it from seed and plant it out when a year old.

Starting indoors: The seeds
are usually started indoors in late winter, about 3 months before the last frost date. This is to give them the maximum growing time in their first year. The seed is soaked for a few hours and then sown 2″ apart and 1″ deep, in deep 4″ flats.

They can also be sown directly into 4″ pots, just plant two seeds to a container initially and thin out the weakest one later. In about 3 months the seedlings should be 9 to 12″ tall and can be planted outside in a temporary nursery bed. By next spring the one year old roots will be ready to go out into their permanent position.

Starting outside: The seed may be started outside in a nursery bed, when the soil has warmed up a little (about 2 weeks after the last frost date). Plant the soaked seeds 3″ apart and 2″ deep. You might also plant a few Radish seeds to mark the row, as the Asparagus may take a while to germinate.

Weed the newly emerged seedlings carefully and when they are 6″ tall thin them out (you could try transplanting the thinnings) to stand 6″ apart. They are then left to grow for one year. They can put on a surprising amount of growth in this time. A one year old plant may have roots 6″ long.

Planting out:

Asparagus can be planted out in early spring, as soon as the soil is in workable condition. However there is no rush, as it will take up to three years before you get a good harvest. Some people say late spring is actually better, as the plants grow faster in the warmer soil, so there is less danger of rot. Transplant only the best individuals and discard weak or inferior ones.

If you are planting two year old roots, they should be soaked overnight in water prior to planting out. The planting method is the same, whether you are planting one or two year old roots.

Planting: The traditional procedure is to dig a hole or trench 18″ wide and 12″ deep. Put a small mound of compost in the trench and spread the root out flat over the mound. Cover the root with a 2″ layer of a soil mix (3 parts soil to 1 part compost) and water thoroughly. As the plants grow, slowly fill up the trench with more of the same mix. The books say don't bury them to the full depth right away, as this might cause rot.

I have planted Asparagus without knowing this procedure. I just dug a large hole, amended it with compost, spread the roots out over a mound of soil and refilled the hole. It worked fine (I guess ignorance sometimes is bliss).

Shallow planting: Researchers have found that Asparagus yields more and earlier, if planted at a depth of only 6", rather than the traditional 12". This fact might be used to give you more flexibility in harvesting, as you can have some early yielding (shallow planted) plants and some later yielding (deep planted) plants.

Spacing: The recommended spacing is 18″ to 24″ apart, depending upon the fertility of the soil. It has been found that wider spacing produces more shoots and they also tend to be larger. In tests it was found that plants spaced 24″ apart, produced twice as many spears as plants that were closer together. This can give you the same harvest while using less plants.

In a 5 foot wide bed you might plant three rows, with 18″ between the rows and 18″ between the plants.

Care

A well cared for Asparagus bed should last for thirty years or more, but it can deteriorate quickly if neglected or over-harvested.

Asparagus is an independent plant, but if given even a moderate amount of care, it will be much more productive.

Weeds: If you conscientiously removed all perennial weeds before planting your Asparagus, then weeds should not be a big problem. These vigorous perennials get tall and are thickly mulched, a combination that discourages most weeds. You should weed whenever necessary, as a matter of course, especially when the plants are young. Hand weeding is usually recommended, so as not to disturb the shallow feeder roots. Traditionally weeds were killed with salt water, as Asparagus is very salt tolerant, but I wouldn't recommend it.

Watering: It is important to keep the plants well watered when they are young. Water deeply, but infrequently, to encourage deep rooting.

Fertilization: Feeding is important for Asparagus, because you can't amend the soil when you re-plant. It is usually done by mulching (see below), but to encourage maximum production you can also give them a foliar feed, once or twice in the season. Use compost tea or liquid Kelp

Mulch: The best way to fertilize Asparagus is with a nitrogen rich mulch of compost, aged manure or seaweed (Asparagus loves seaweed), applied in fall. This works well because Asparagus is shallow rooted and most of its feeder roots are near the surface.

Pests: Asparagus Beetles and Cucumber Beetles Aphids, Thrips and Cutworms all like Asparagus, but aren't usually too serious. Slugs can be devastating to young plants. I once had a whole planting wiped out by slugs. Every time the plants re-sprouted they were cut down again.

Fusarium Wilt: Use resistant varieties.

Crown Rot, Verticillium Wilt and Asparagus Rust can also be a problem.

I once had a problem where entire fronds were disappearing, leaving just a stub. This perplexed me, I just couldn't figure out what would do that kind of localized damage. It turned out my girlfriend was taking the pretty ferns for use in flower arrangements.

Gophers: Apparently Gophers appreciate Asparagus as much as humans. If these are a problem, you will have to protect each individual plant with a good sized basket of Gopher wire. There is nothing more discouraging than finally having your plants start to produce after several years, and then see them disappear down a Gopher hole (or to not see them at all).

Control: Asparagus often self-sows all over the place and can become a minor pest. I don't mind as they can be a good source of plants for transplanting, bartering or giving away. These seedlings can be a significant problem for commercial growers however. They often stop the plants from self-seeding by cutting the tops in fall, when the foliage begins to turn yellow.

Harvesting

Avoid the temptation to harvest from a new bed too soon. Leave one year old roots until their 3rd year in the ground. Start harvesting 2 year old roots in their 2nd year in the ground. In both cases you should only harvest sparingly the first year (only for 2 weeks). The longer you wait, the stronger the plants will get.

When: The spears are best gathered when about 4″ to 6″ shows above the ground and they are still tightly closed (though you get more if you wait until they are 8″ long). Don't harvest too many spears from a single root in one season, as you can weaken it. Cut from a bed for 6 weeks and then leave it to regenerate. Stop harvesting earlier if the spears start to look thin.

How: Cut the spear underground, just above the crown with a sharp knife. Or snap them off as low down as they will break.

Storage: The spears can be stored in a plastic bag in the fridge, for up to a week. You might store the spears as you harvest them, until you have enough for a meal. For longer-term storage freezing works best.

Unusual growing methods
Ornamental use: Though Asparagus takes up a lot of space, it is quite an attractive plant and fairly undemanding. These traits make it well suited to growing in the ornamental garden. It also does well at the edge of a wild or forest garden.

Male plants: Asparagus plants are dioecious, which means there are separate male and female plants. It has been found that male plants produce up to 25% more spears than females, though they tend to be slightly smaller. Another benefit of male plants (for commercial growers at least) is that they don't self-seed. You can now get cultivars that produce all male plants.

Forcing: To get an earlier crop the roots can be forced in spring, as described under Rhubarb.

Intercrop: The big spaces between the plants just demand that another crop (such as Lettuce) be intercropped between them, especially early in the season. This crop should have a shallow root system, so as not to interfere with the Asparagus. Be careful not to damage the Asparagus plants however.

Delayed harvest: One way to get a longer Asparagus harvest is to initially harvest from only half of your bed. When this half begins to slow down after 6 weeks, cut down all the new growth on the other half and it will send up a fresh crop of shoots. You can then cut from this for a further 4 to 6 weeks.

It is also possible to get shoots later in the year, by cutting the plants right down to the ground, which forces them to send up more. This practice runs the risk of weakening the plants however.

Propagation: If you get plants that are unique in some way, it is possible to propagate them vegetatively be dividing the crowns.

Seed Saving: You don't really need to save Asparagus seed as it is a perennial, but it is easy enough to obtain. The plants are insect pollinated, so to keep a variety pure there should be no other Asparagus varieties (or wild plants) within a mile. The plants are dioecious and only the female plants produce the red berries, each containing 6 seeds.

Varieties: There are now quite a few hybrids available, that produce larger spears or all male plants. Generally I hesitate to grow hybrids, because I like to save my own seed, but as Asparagus is normally propagated vegetatively, this isn't as much of an issue.

All males: Include Jersey Giant, Supermale, Lucillus and Saxon

Traditional varieties: Connovers Colossal, Argenteuil. Martha Washington.

Cooking: The traditional way to cook Asparagus is to tie the spears together in a bundle and boil them upright. The tender tip is out of the water and is cooked by the rising steam (if under water it would be overcooked). They need about 10 minutes to cook sufficiently. Gourmets (with too much disposable income) can buy special tall Asparagus pans, specifically designed for cooking it to perfection.

The problem with boiling Asparagus is that it leaches out many of the valuable nutrients. It is better to steam or roast it.

Asparagus soup
This is a great way to use an overabundance of Asparagus.

1 lb asparagus
1 medium onion
1 ½ cups vegetable broth
1 cup soy milk
1 tbsp butter
2 tbsp flour
1 tsp salt
½ tsp black pepper

Simmer the asparagus and chopped onion with a ½ cup of vegetable broth until tender.

Put it in a blender and puree until completely smooth. Melt the butter in a pan, with the flour and salt and pepper and cook for 2 minutes, stirring to prevent it turning brown or burning. Add the rest of the stock and bring to the boil, stirring to make it smooth. Then add the soy milk and the asparagus puree and heat up thoroughly, stirring occasionally.

Basil
Ocimum basilicum

Introduction: Basil is a native of India and many kinds are grown there. It is without doubt the most important culinary herb in my kitchen, In fact I think of it more as a vegetable than as a flavoring herb and grow it like Spinach. I can use as much as I can grow because I make any surplus into pesto and freeze it for winter use. Pesto is always quite expensive to buy, so this can be a very valuable crop. Basil is a short lived perennial in tropical climates, but anywhere the temperature drops below 60° F it has to be grown as an annual. It is very easy to grow if the weather is warm, not so easy if it is cold.

Nutritional content: Basil contains some powerful antioxidants that give it anti-cancer activity. It may also help to lower cholesterol.

About Basil
Growing temp: 60 (75 to 85) 90° F
Germ temp: 70° F
Germ time: 5 to 10 days
Seed viability: 8 years
Time to harvest: 60 days
Weeks to grow transplant: 4 to 8
Yield: 4 oz per plant
Plants sq ft: 3 to 4

Soil
pH 5.0 to 8.0
Basil prefers a rich, light, well drained soil.

Soil preparation: Basil can produce a lot of foliage in the course of a summer, so needs fertilizing well. Incorporate 2″ of compost or aged manure into the top 6″ of soil before planting.

Planning

Where: Basil is very unhappy if it isn't warm, so in cooler areas it should be in the warmest spot in the garden. If this isn't warm enough, then grow it under cloches. It will tolerate some shade when growing in hot climates, but does better in full sun.

When: Basil is slow to get established if the weather is not warm, so it is usually started indoors, about 6 weeks before the last frost date. Don't plant it out until at least 2 weeks after the last frost, when the soil has warmed up. You could hasten this process with cloches or plastic mulch.

Succession sowing: It is a good idea to make several sowings of Basil over the summer, perhaps every six weeks or so (these later plantings can be direct sown). This will give you a continuous and abundant supply of new plants.

Planting

Indoors: For an early crop, Basil is usually started indoors, in flats, cell packs, soil blocks or plug trays. It transplants fairly easily.

Outdoors: In warm climates Basil can be direct sown. This is a lot less work than raising transplants, but you won't get a crop until a little later. I use both methods, growing my earliest plants from transplants and later ones by direct sowing. Try sowing some seed when you transplant your first Basil seedlings into the garden.

Spacing: Space Basil 6″ to 8″ apart in the beds. The plants can grow to 24″ in height, though mine rarely do because I pinch them off so frequently.

Care

Warmth: The biggest problem with Basil is its dislike of cold weather. It just won't thrive if it isn't warm. Fortunately this isn't a problem in most of North America.

Weed: Be sure to weed carefully while the plants are young.

Water: Basil likes evenly moist soil, so water if it gets dry (otherwise it may bolt). Mulch helps to keep the soil moist.

Fertilization: If you are repeatedly harvesting from the same plants, you should give them a liquid feed (compost tea, manure tea, or fish emulsion), every couple of weeks. It's probably best to use this as a soil drench, rather than as a foliar feed, as you probably shouldn't spray the leaves with manure.

Pruning: The growing tips should be pinched out when the plants are 6″ to 8″ tall (this is actually the first harvest). This causes them to send up two growing tips, making the plants bushier and larger. It may also delay flowering. If you carefully harvest prune the plants, you can harvest from them for weeks, or even months.

Frost: If frost threatens you can try protecting the plants, but they are very sensitive to cold. If it is late in the year and it's getting cold anyway, you should just harvest

it all the and freeze it. You might also try potting up some plants and putting them in the greenhouse, but it needs to be warm.

Pests and disease: Basil isn't much bothered by pests, though slugs may eat it when young.

Harvesting

When: The leaves are at their best before the flowers appear, though they are still worth gathering even if the plants are actually blooming. It pays to remove any flower stems as they appear, as this encourages more leafy growth. If done carefully you can get 3, 4 or even 5 harvests from one planting (and make them last for a good part of the summer).

How: Harvest by pinching off the growing tips. Always leave plenty of foliage on the bottom of the plant (at least 4 sets of leaves), so it can regenerate and give you another harvest later on.

Storage: Basil has thin leaves and wilts quickly once cut. It will keep for a few days in a plastic bag in the fridge. You can also extend its life by keeping it in water like cut flowers.

The easiest way to store Basil is to dry it in a warm shady place. This alters its flavor considerably, but it is still very good. It must be dried quickly though, if it takes too long, it will deteriorate and turn black.

It is possible to store the fresh leaves by packing them in a jar and covering with olive oil.

You can freeze the leaves whole in a plastic bag, but a better idea is to put the chopped leaves in ice cube trays and cover them with water. Once they are frozen you can transfer them to a plastic bag.

I usually make pesto (see below) and freeze it in meal-sized portions (so I don't have to saw up large frozen chunks). You can also put it in a plastic bag (flatten it so that it will break easily when frozen).

Unusual growing ideas
Cuttings: You can root cuttings of Basil in water, which can give you new plants faster than growing them from seed.

Micro-greens
Micro-greens: Basil seedlings have a strong fresh Basil flavor. See Micro-greens.

Multi-plant blocks:
Multi-planting works well with Basil. Sow 4 or 5 seeds in a block or cell pack and thin to the best 3. These are planted out together and grow together. Harvest the largest plant when it gets to be a suitable size, leaving the others with more room to grow. When the biggest of the remaining plants gets to a suitable size harvest that (you may have to do some judicious pruning to keep both plants growing well). Then harvest the last plant as it reaches a suitable size. Of course you could allow all three plants to grow and just keep harvesting the growing tips.

Seed saving: Bees love Basil flowers and will cross-pollinate any plants within 150 feet of each other. For this reason you should only have one variety flowering at one time. Basil sets seed very readily; all you have to do is leave it alone. Don't collect seeds from the first plants to flower (remove them), as you don't want to select an early bolting strain.

Varieties: There are many types of Basil, each with their own unique properties. They include Lemon, Licorice, Mexican, Purple, Opal, Thai, Sacred and Cinnamon.

I have tried quite a few varieties of Basil, but still depend on the large leaved types such as Lettuce Leaved Basil. This variety produces an abundance of large, tasty, succulent leaves ideal for pesto.

Cooking: Basil is traditionally used to flavor Tomatoes and eggs. Of course it is an essential ingredient of Italian cooking. Probably its best-known use is for making pesto (or the French equivalent pistou).

Pesto
1 clove garlic
1 cup basil
3 tbsp pine nuts (or almonds or sunflower seeds)
½ tsp salt
pepper
½ cup olive oil

Blend the oil and basil together in a food processor, then add the garlic, pine nuts and salt and pepper. It can then be frozen for storage. I think it tastes better if it is cooked for a few minutes before serving. It is traditional to add 2 oz grated parmesan, or romano, cheese before serving.

Beans, Bush and Pole
Phaseolus vulgaris

Introduction: This species has been cultivated for over 6000 years in Central and South America. It is now a very important crop around the world, as beans are the most important source of protein for many people on earth (Black beans, Kidney beans, Pinto beans and others). A number of other species also yield important beans crops (in the P*haseolus, Vigna, Vicia* and *Glycine* genera), but this is the most important.

When most gardeners talk about growing beans in the garden, they usually mean French, Snap, Wax or shell beans. Only rarely do they grow dry beans.

Beans are also important to gardeners for another reason, they (like most members of the *Fabaceae*) have a symbiotic relationship with nitrogen fixing bacteria. This means that Beans can actually add nitrogen to the soil they grow in.

Beans are highly nutritious, easy to grow, drought tolerant, need little attention and actually enrich the soil they grow in. What more could you ask for?

Nutritional content:

Green beans are rich in iron and potassium. Dry beans are very rich in protein, soluble fiber (which can lower cholesterol), complex carbohydrates and folate.

About Beans

Seed facts
Germ temp: 60 (80) 85° F
Germ time: 6 to 18 days
16 days / 59° F
11 days / 68° F
8 days / 77° F * Optimum
6 days / 86° F
Seed viability: 3 years
Germination percentage: 75+
Weeks to grow transplants: 3 to 4

Planning facts
Hardiness: Tender
Ease of growing: Easy
Growing temp: 50 (60 to 70) 80° F
Plants per person: 40
Plants per sq ft: 9
Transplants
Start: on the last frost date
Plant out: 4 wks after last frost
Direct sow: 4 wks after last frost
Succession sow: every 3 weeks
Time to harvest:
Dry beans: 100 days
Green beans: 60 days

Harvest facts
Length of harvest: 4 to 8 wks
Yield per plant: 1 oz
Yield per sq ft: ¾ lb green
1 oz dry

Soil
pH 6.0 - 7.5
Beans like a light, well-drained loamy soil, with lots of organic matter. It needn't be very rich in nitrogen, because the plants won't fix nitrogen if it is too abundant. It should have good quantities of potassium, phosphorus and other nutrients.

Soil preparation:
Incorporate any amendments into the top 6″ to 8″ of soil, where most of the plants feeder roots are located. Beans dislike acid soil, so add lime if necessary, or wood ashes (beans love wood ashes). They are sometimes planted after a crop that was heavily manured, or after a winter cover crop.

Inoculation

Bean plants don't fix nitrogen, it is the bacteria that grow in nodules on their roots that do that. If the right strain of bacteria isn't present in sufficient quantity, no nitrogen will be fixed and the bean plants will take it out of the soil for their own use. If you have grown beans in the past 3 to 5 years, there are probably sufficient bacteria already in the soil for good root nodulation and you don't need to inoculate. If you haven't grown them recently, you can ensure it is available in abundance by inoculating the seeds with the appropriate bacteria. Inoculation greatly increases nitrogen fixation and can boost yields by as much as 60%.

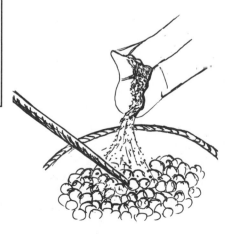

How:
The simplest way to inoculate the beans is to moisten them with water (some people add a little molasses to the water to help the inoculant adhere) and then roll them in the inoculant powder. Some gardeners then roll the inoculated seeds in bone meal, or colloidal phosphate, supposedly to supply phosphorus and to protect the inoculant.

Planning
Where: Beans like a warm sunny spot. Tall Pole Beans are vulnerable to being blown over, so should be sheltered from high winds. Bush Beans are sometimes interplanted between more space hungry crops.

When: Beans originated in the tropics and can't stand cold weather. Don't plant them out until all frost danger is past and the soil is warm (at least 60° F and ideally 80° F). This may be 4 weeks after the last frost date. If beans are planted in cold soil, they may rot. If you really want to get an early crop, you will have to warm the soil beforehand, with cloches or plastic mulch (or start them inside).

Succession sowing: Beans produce a lot of food in a short time, especially the Bush beans. This is fine if you want to freeze them for later use, but can also be something of a problem. For fresh eating you really need a modest and continuous harvest, preferably over a long period of time. The way to get this sustained yield is to sow small quantities of plants in succession every 2 to 3 weeks, until mid summer. Pole beans can bear for a longer period than Bush beans, so can be sown less frequently.

To grow dry beans you plant them all at once, as soon as the soil is warm enough. They need a longer period of warm weather to produce dry beans. They are not at all hardy and any frost will kill them.

Planting
Raising transplants

Beans are rarely grown from transplants, as they dislike transplanting and it is more work than direct sowing. The large seeds germinate easily and grow so fast in warm soil that direct sown plants often catch up to transplanted ones. It always surprises me to see six packs of bean plants for sale in the garden center, when it is better, much cheaper, and just as easy, to direct sow.

If you really feel you must start them inside, maybe to avoid hungry early birds, or to try and get a very early crop, it is simple enough. If the germination percentage of the seed is high, sow one seed in each soil block or cell pack. If germination is poor, plant two seeds and thin to the best one after they have both germinated. Don't forget to inoculate them.

Direct sowing

How: Some people soak the seed overnight prior to planting. Pole Beans are best sown in long rows down the bed, as it's easier to support them. Bush Beans are usually planted in offset rows across the bed, an equal distance apart.

I start planting by placing the seeds on top of the prepared seedbed, at the correct spacing. When I am satisfied that they are all correctly spaced, I simply push them down

into the soil with my finger and close up the small hole.

The depth they are planted varies according to the soil temperature. They should be planted 1″ deep in cold soil and 2″ (or even 3″) deep in warm soil. The deeper planting ensures they get enough moisture.

Sow roughly twice as many seeds as you need plants and thin to the approximate spacing, after they have all emerged. The best way to remove the extra plants is by pinching them out, as this doesn't disturb those remaining. Always try and remove the inferior plants and leave the best ones.

One way to improve and hasten emergence in cold soil is to pre-sprout the seeds indoors. This can be done in optimally warm conditions and could save you 10 days or more. You then plant out the already germinated seeds, being extremely careful not to damage the tender roots.

Spacing: The biggest factor in spacing the plants is whether they are bush or pole varieties.

Bush: Space the plants 4″ to 6″ apart both ways in the beds.

Pole: These are best grown in rows, down the middle of the bed, as this makes it easier to support them (you can interplant a low growing crop in the vacant space). You want the plants to be 4″ to 6″ apart, with 18″ between the rows. You could also space them like Bush Beans, 6″ to 8″ apart in offset rows across the beds, but this makes them harder to support.

If you plan on using a teepee of poles for support, then plant 5 to 6 seeds around each pole. When these have germinated, thin to leave the best 2 or 3 plants at each pole.

Care

Weeds: Young bean plants can't compete with weeds very well, so it's important to keep down weeds initially. They are also shallow rooted, so be very careful not to damage them if you use a hoe. Bush Beans are not usually mulched, as this tends to keep the soil cool. They eventually form a living mulch, which keeps down weeds very effectively.

Water: Keep the soil evenly moist, but don't over-water. A lack of water in hot weather will affect the set of the pods, so make sure they are well watered at this time. The most critical time is when they are flowering and sizing up their pods.

Try and avoid wetting the leaves when watering, as mildew and fungus diseases can be spread in this way. Drip or soaker hose is best way to irrigate them.

Dry beans do well as a dry farmed crop, (grown with no irrigation), though yields will be slightly lower. The plants should be spaced further apart (try 9″ to 12″), to lessen competition between plants and to give their roots more soil to extract water from.

Fertilization: Bush beans don't usually need feeding, as they aren't in the ground for very long. Pole Beans may benefit from a feed of compost tea or liquid seaweed, every 3 to 4 weeks. This is particularly helpful when they start to flower.

Pollination: Beans are normally self-pollinated, so it usually happens pretty much automatically. However if the temperature is much above 80° F the flowers may drop off instead of being fertilized.

Mulch: This is occasionally used for widely spaced pole beans, as it conserves moisture and keeps down weeds. Don't apply it until the soil is warm though.

Support: Pole beans often reach 8 feet or more in height so need a sturdy support. This should be put in place at the same time as planting, so you don't damage the young growing seedlings.

A traditional support is the bean tepee. Arrange this so the poles

Supports

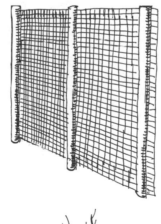

splay out a long way at the top. This ensures the growing tips of the plants don't get too congested.

Many other kinds of supports can be devised for supporting Pole Beans. Chicken wire, Bamboo canes, hog fencing and string have all been used. The important thing is to make sure the support is strong enough. I like to use wire fencing, simply because I can't be bothered with all that string and poles.

The traditional Native American support for Beans was Corn or Sunflowers. This was a brilliant solution for a pre-industrial people who didn't have access to string, wire or metal tools to cut poles. They simply grew the supports they needed and obtained food from them at the same time.

If you want to try this, you must make sure the Corn has made enough growth so that the Beans don't overwhelm it. They also planted Squash to make use of the open ground between the Corn hills. This very efficient growing system was known as the three sisters and was widely practiced by many tribes. (see **Corn** for more on this).

Pests and disease:
Anthracnose: Halo Blight and Bean Mosaic are serious diseases and may be seed borne, so watch out where your seed comes from.

Bacterial Blight: Curly Top virus, Downy Mildew Powdery Mildew and Rust can also be a problem under certain conditions.

Mexican Bean Beetles: These are a potentially serious pest and can quickly get out of control (watch for their yellow eggs). A traditional remedy was to interplant with Potatoes, Garlic or Nasturtium, but I can't vouch for their effectiveness. Hand picking works well for small numbers of plants.

Aphids: If these are a problem, blast them with a jet of water.

Bean Weevils, Wireworms, Leafhoppers, Tarnished Plant Bugs, Leaf Miners, Flea Beetles, Mites, Cucumber Beetles, Green Stink Bugs, Caterpillars all love beans.

Birds and mice will often go for the newly planted seeds or seedlings, especially in spring. Net the beds and get a cat or dog.

Harvest

Snap beans (Haricot Vert)
When: The pods take 18 to 21 days from pollination to full size. They are best gathered just as they are reaching full size, but before the beans start to swell. They should still snap in half easily. Many people prefer them when they are just slightly smaller in diameter than a pencil. You might try harvesting the pods at different sizes, to see which you like best.

How: The best time to harvest is in the early morning when it is still cool. Gather the pods carefully so you don't damage the plants. Hold on to the vine and pull down on the pod, so there is no danger of pulling the plant out of the ground.

The best way to harvest older beans is to break off the pod just below its stem and then break sideways and pull, leaving any strings attached to the plant. In humid areas, it's best not to harvest while the foliage is wet, as this can transmit disease.

You must gather the green beans conscientiously whether you want them or not, as the plants may stop producing when the first seed ripens. If you harvest Pole Beans every 2 to 3 days, it is possible to keep the plants producing for weeks.

The key to a large harvest is early and regular picking (just like life, the more you take the more you get).

If the harvest gets away from you, remove all the pods of any size. With luck this will encourage a new growth of pods.

Shell Beans: These are harvested as soon as the beans reach full size (4 to 8 days after the pods reach full size), but before they toughen up.

Dry Beans: These are gathered after the pods have shrivelled and dried on the vines (you can sometimes hear the seeds rattle). You can gather small quantities of pods individually, but for larger harvests pick the whole plants and lay them on a tarp to dry. Carefully thresh out the seeds to free them from the pods and then dry thoroughly.

A completely dry bean should shatter when crushed. If you can make a mark with your fingernail they aren't dry enough. An easy way to see if the beans are dry enough is to put a few in a closed jar for a few days. If condensation forms on the inside of the jar, they still contain too much moisture.

You can eat the immature pods of dry bean varieties as snap beans, if you get them early enough (they may have strings though).

Storage: Green beans may be stored in plastic bags in the fridge for a few days. This is usually done until you have harvested enough for a meal. For longer storage they can be dried, pickled or frozen. Shell beans can also be frozen. Fully dry beans store very well and will stay edible for several years.

Seed saving: Beans are amongst the easiest crops to save seed from, you just grow them like dry beans. They are mostly self-pollinating, though insects may cause some cross-pollination. For this reason it is best to have only one variety flowering at a time if possible. Be aware that some viruses may be transmitted through the seed and try not to gather from diseased plants.

Varieties:
The most obvious difference in bean varieties is between bush and pole types.

Pole Beans: These are generally more productive than Bush Beans, because there is more photosynthetic area for food production. They are also more interesting visually and take up less horizontal space in the garden They also bear for a longer period and there is less damage from pests such as slugs. They are particularly useful for very small gardens.

Bush Beans: These bear earlier than Pole types, though not so abundantly. They are more compact as a crop and easier to deal with.

Other differences mainly involve the final use of the beans, whether they will be used as dry beans, shell beans or green beans.

Snap Beans: Also known as
String Beans, French Beans or Green Beans, they are a mainstay of the traditional vegetable garden. Most modern varieties don't have strings. Varieties include:

Bush: Golden Wax, Jade, Provider, Romano, Royal Burgundy, Tender-green.

Pole: Blue Lake Pole, Kentucky Wonder, Romano

French Filet beans
(Haricot Verts): These are some of the best quality varieties of snap bean. The pods are harvested when very small (¼″ diameter or less) and tender. They are available as pole or bush varieties.

Fin De Bagnol, Nickel, Royalnel, Triomphe de Farcy, Vernandon.

Shell Beans (Flageolets):
These are gathered when the beans reach full size, but before they start to harden and mature. The soft beans are shelled out and cooked.

Lows Champion, Vernel

Dry Beans (Haricots):
These are unsurpassed from a nutritional and self-sufficiency viewpoint, as they are a major source of protein. They are also a great low maintenance crop.

Black Turtle, Pink, Hidatsa Shield Figure and Anasazi have all worked well for me.

Cooking:
Green beans: Trim the tops and bottoms off the pods and steam (or boil) them for a few minutes.

Ribollita
This Tuscan vegetable and bean soup has a lot of ingredients because it is made to use up leftovers.

½ cup olive oil
2 onion
6 leeks
3 celery stalks
3 zucchini
5 garlic cloves
4 carrots
4 zucchini
½ savoy cabbage
1 bunch Laciniato Kale
1 small bunch spinach
5 potatoes
1 cup green beans
2 ½ cups cannelloni beans
6 cups vegetable stock
5 sage leaves
4 tbsp tomato paste

Cover the beans with 2″ of water and soak overnight. Next day add the sage and simmer until cooked. Sauté the onion and leek in oil until cooked, then add the chopped garlic and sauté another minute or two. Then add the rest of vegetables (chopped), the stock and the beans (with their cooking water) and cook in a covered pot for 30 minutes. Stir occasionally. Add salt and pepper.

Traditionally this was eaten as soup on the day it was cooked. The following day the leftover soup was put in a casserole dish, covered with a layer of garlic bread (or bread with a layer of onion on top) and baked in the oven. If any was still left on the third day it was re-heated with a little olive oil.

Bean, Fava
Vicia faba

Introduction: Fava Beans originated in the Middle East, but has been grown in the colder parts of Europe as far back as the Iron Age. They have long been (no pun intended) a staple of Northern European peasants.

This species is unique among commonly cultivated beans in that it actually dislikes heat. It is a cool weather crop, with requirements more akin to the Pea than any other bean. If your climate is too cold for Snap Beans, this is the one to try. Most of the United States is too warm for Fava beans in summer, so it can only be grown in spring or fall (at the same time as Peas). In areas with mild winters, it is often grown as an over wintering crop. It does really well when planted in this way, which is how it became a favorite in Italy (Fava Bean is the Italian name).

Fava Bean isn't closely related to any other Bean and is actually a kind of Vetch (*Vicia*). It does resemble the other beans in being very rich in protein (it has been called the Soybean of the north) and because it is a nitrogen fixer. It is quite easy to grow and is often recommended as a good crop for beginning gardeners.

Nutritional content:
Fava Beans are very nutritious. A comparison of protein quality shows Soybean 68, Fava Bean 67, Kidney Bean 55 and Peanut 52. They also contain soluble fiber (which can lower cholesterol) and complex carbohydrates.

It has recently been found that Fava beans contain a substance called levodopa which is used in commercial medications to control Parkinsons Disease. Some people have been using Fava beans instead of the commercial drugs, apparently with some success.

Caution: Some people, particularly males of Mediterranean (and sometimes Asian) descent, are allergic to Fava Beans. It causes a serious (and sometimes even fatal) allergic reaction known as Favism. Favism occurs in people with a deficiency of a blood enzyme called G6PD and destroys red blood cells. If you have any reason to think you might be allergic then it is usually recommended, that you eat only a couple of beans initially (the first symptom is urinary bleeding).

Some people are even allergic to the foliage or pollen and get a rash when they come in contact with it.

Soil:
pH 6.0 - 7.0
Fava Beans do well in most soil types, so long as they aren't too acidic. Their preference is for a fertile, fairly heavy soil, with lots of organic matter to retain moisture. It is important that the soil be well drained, especially for an over-wintering crop, as their roots may rot in wet soil. The large seeds often rot if they stay wet for too long. Raised beds work well with Fava Beans.

Soil preparation: Fava Beans like organic matter, so incorporate 2″ of compost, or aged manure, into the top 6″ of soil. If they are following a crop that was heavily fertilized, you don't need to add

this. Fava Beans don't need a lot of nitrogen, because they contain nitrogen-fixing bacteria in nodules on their roots. If the pH is low, add lime, as they don't like acid soil.

About Fava Bean

Seed facts
Germ temp: 40 (40 to 75) 75° F
Germ time: 7 to 14 days
Viability: 2 to 6 yrs
Germination percentage: 75%+

Planning facts
Hardiness: Hardy
Ease of growing: Easy
Growing temp: 40 (60 to 65) 75° F
Plants per person: 20
Plants per sq ft: 3
Direct sow: 4 wks before last frost
Fall crop: sow 4 to 8 wks before first fall frost
Succession sow: every 2 to 3 wks
Time to harvest: 90 to 120 days

Harvest facts
Length of harvest: 6 to 8 wks
Yield per plant: 2 oz
Yield per sq ft:
 ¼ - 1 lb sq ft (green beans)
 1 oz sq ft (dry beans)

Planning
Where: Like most plants that grow in cool weather, Fava Beans prefer full sun. When growing in hot climates they often do better with light shade. They can get quite tall; so don't put them where they might cast shade on other crops.

When: Fava Beans are very hardy (they can survive temperatures down to 15° F) and don't mind cold soil, so long as it isn't actually frozen. They like the same growing

conditions as peas, 2 to 3 months of cool weather being ideal. The best time to plant them depends on the climate, there are several options.

Spring: In areas with many weeks of cool spring weather, they are often grown as a spring crop. They are planted out 4 weeks before the last frost (or as early as February if sown under cloches). These plants should be out of the ground by the end of June, leaving plenty of time for another crop.

Summer: In areas with cool summers, they can be succession sown every few weeks, for a continuous harvest all summer.

Fall: You can plant them in late summer for a fall, or winter crop.

Winter: In areas with mild winters they can be sown in fall, to grow right through the winter and mature in early spring. The trick is for the plants to be advanced enough when cold weather comes that they keep growing. Too small and they never really get started (they will then mature in the spring).

Early spring: If winter isn't mild enough for continuous growth, you can sow them in mid winter for an early spring crop. In England some particularly hardy varieties (the long pod types) are sown in winter, to emerge in early spring to a fast start. These plants bear a few weeks before spring planted ones. Much of North America is too cold for this however.

Planting

Inoculation: If you haven't grown this crop before, it will fix more nitrogen if inoculated with the appropriate nitrogen-fixing bacteria. By enhancing the health of the plants it may also increase yields. See Bush and Pole Beans for how to do this.

Indoors: Fava Beans aren't usually started inside, because they do so well when direct sown. The large seeds can germinate at low temperatures and grow quickly once they have germinated. I suppose you might want to start them inside to get a very early start, or if birds or rodents are a big problem. They can be started in flats, but (like most legumes) they dislike root disturbance. It is better to start them in large soil blocks or cell packs. The seedlings grow quickly and won't need to be inside for very long.

Outdoors: The seeds can germinate at temperatures as low as 40° F, so they can be direct sown into cold soil. You can hasten germination by pre-sprouting the seeds, though you have to be careful not to damage the delicate shoots.

The seeds are planted 1″ to 2 ½″ deep, using a dibber. It is a good idea to plant a few extra seeds at the end of the row, to fill in vacant spots where seeds fail to germinate.

If you give the earliest planting the protection of cloches, it will speed up germination and growth.

Succession sowing: To get a continuous harvest, you can make succession sowings every 2 to 3 weeks.

Spacing: This varies according to the fertility of the soil and the size of the variety. Dwarf varieties are planted closer together than the larger types.

Beds: Plant 6″ to 8″ apart in offset rows across the bed.

Rows: Taller varieties do best when planted in two rows, down the center of the bed. Space the plants 3″ to 4″ apart in the rows, with 18″ to 24″ between the rows.

It is possible to plant 2 double rows in a bed. Space the rows 9″ apart, with 6″ between plants in the row. Separate the 2 double rows by 24″.

Care

Weed: Fava Beans are robust plants and can handle almost any weeds when full grown. The young plants will need weeding at least once however.

Watering: Water regularly in dry weather, as lack of water can affect the set of pods (and so the size of the harvest) and their quality. Water is most critical when the flowers appear and they are setting pods. If water is in short supply, just give it when the flowers open and again when the pods begin to swell.

Support: Though these beans don't climb, they may get quite tall (to 4 feet or more). When they get a heavy load of pods they can become top heavy and fall over (especially in windy areas). Consequently they may benefit from some kind of support. The simplest support consists of Bamboo canes and garden twine. You could also earth up the stems to stop them falling over.

Pruning: It is a common practice to pinch out 4″ to 6″ of the growing tips, after the plants have set a half dozen pods. This not only helps the pods to develop, but also discourages Bean Aphids (these are attracted to the succulent new growth). If the tops aren't infested with aphids, they can be used as a potherb. If they are infested they should be removed from the garden.

Pests: Most pests and diseases aren't very active in the cool weather when Fava Beans are doing most of their growth, so they are relatively pest free. Cutworms may destroy the young seedlings as they appear. Slugs and snails can also be troublesome.

Bean Aphids are a common problem (though not really serious) and inevitably appear as soon as it gets warm. They tend to cluster on the growing tip of the plant, which is why this is often removed.

Harvest: The plants are indeterminate, so the lower pods ripen first and then those above. If temperatures get much above 70° F, the flowers may drop off instead of setting pods.

Pods: The very young (2″) pods can be used like green beans. They should be harvested before the beans start to enlarge and the interior of the pod gets cottony.

Shell Beans: These plants are most often harvested in the green shell stage, when they first reach full size, but before the skins start to toughen. At this time the pod will still be quite soft and the seed will be not much bigger than a penny. Gathered at this time, the seeds are tender and delicious.

Dry Beans: These (they are the largest seeds of any common vegetable) can be used in soups, stews and other dishes.

Greens: The succulent growing tips can be eaten like Spinach.

After harvest: Don't pull the plants out of the ground after the harvest is over, just cut them off at ground level. This leaves the nitrogen rich roots to decompose directly into the soil.

Storage: The pods can be stored in a plastic bag in the refrigerator, for up to 2 weeks.

Seed saving: Fava Beans are usually self- pollinated, but may occasionally be cross-pollinated by bees. To ensure purity, you should only grow one variety at a time. Allow the pods to ripen fully and dry out on the plant. Take seeds from 5 of the best plants. The seeds must be thoroughly dry for storage.

Unusual growing ideas
Second harvest: If you cut the plants down to the ground after harvest they will sometimes send up new suckers. These may actually produce more pods (not a lot, but some). Even if they don't, they will provide biomass for composting or green manure.

Green manure: Fava Bean is commonly used as a green manure or cover crop. In mild areas it will grow right through the winter and reach a height of 5 feet or more. It not only fixes nitrogen, but also produces a lot of compost material.

Varieties: Generally the small seeded types are used for green manure and animal feed (which could be why they are sometimes called Horse Beans). They are also good for humans however.

Foul Misri is a small seeded Egyptian variety that does well in warm weather. It is most often used as a green manure in warmer areas, but the seeds are also good to eat.

The larger seeded types are usually used as shell beans. There are varieties for autumn and spring sowing and its important to choose the right one, as they aren't the same.

Longpods: The pods on these varieties may be over a foot in length, with as many as 8 large kidney shaped seeds. They are very hardy and are often sown in fall, as a winter or early spring crop. Aquadulce, Bunyards Exhibition

Windsors: These varieties produce short pods with only 4 smallish round seeds per pod. They are not as hardy as the Longpods and so are usually sown in spring. Some people say these are the best-flavored types.

Broad Windsor, Express, The Sutton:

Cooking: Fava Beans are usually eaten as shell beans, either steamed, stir fried, or boiled for 5 minutes. If you are using older beans their tough skins must be removed before eating. This is done by snipping off the end with scissors and squeezing out the bean. The dry beans may be used like kidney beans in soups. Apparently they can also be popped like popcorn, though I have never tried it.

Falafel recipe
Though Falafel is usually made with Chick Peas in this country, in the Middle East, where it originated, it is usually made with Fava Beans.

1 lb dry fava beans
1/2 cup flat leaf parsley (chopped)
1/2 cup cilantro
8 green onions (chopped)
6 cloves of garlic
2 tsp ground coriander
2 tsp ground cumin
1 tsp baking powder
Salt and black pepper

Soak the beans for 24 hours and then boil them until tender (about an hour). Puree them to a paste in a food processor and then add the chopped parsley and onion and the rest of the seasonings. Leave for about an hour, then mold into 1½″ balls , coat in sesame seeds and fry. They are normally deep fried, but you can also saute them.

The balls are eaten with pita bread, tomatoes, lettuce, cucumber and a sauce made from tahini, lemon juice and garlic.

Bean Lima
Phaseolus lunatus

Introduction: It is believed that this South American bean was first cultivated almost 8000 years ago. It was brought to Europe from Peru, hence its common name and spread from there to tropical areas around the world

Lima Bean is very much a tropical plant and needs a warm climate to grow successfully. It is cultivated in much the same way as the Bush and Pole Beans described above. The main difference is its preference for warmer growing conditions

Nutrients. The beans contain protein, soluble fiber and complex carbohydrates. It is also rich in folate, thiamin, tryptophan, iron, manganese, molybdenum, phosphorus and potassium.

Caution: The early Lima Beans contained poisonous cyanogenic glycosides and had to be soaked before cooking to leach these out. Modern varieties don't contain these toxins, but some individuals are sensitive to Lima beans and can't eat them.

Soil
pH 5.0 to 6.0
Lima Beans are like most Beans in that they like a rich, well-drained loamy soil, with lots of organic matter. They like phosphorus and potassium (especially wood ashes), but don't need a lot of nitrogen (otherwise they won't fix any).

Soil preparation: Incorporate 2″ of compost or aged manure into the top 6″ of soil, where most of the plants feeder roots are located.

They dislike acid soil, so add lime if necessary. They are sometimes planted after a crop that was heavily manured.

About Lima Beans

Seed facts
Germ temp: 65 (75 to 85) 90° F
Germ time: 7 to 18 days
31 days / 59° F
18 days / 68° F
7 days / 77° F * Optimum
7 days / 86° F
Germination percentage: 70+
Viability: 3 to 5 yrs
Weeks to grow transplants: 4 to 6

Planning facts
Hardiness: Very tender
Ease of growing: Easy
Growing temp: 65 to 75° F
Plants per sq ft: 2 to 3
Transplants
Start: On the last frost date
Plant out: 4 wks after last frost
Direct sow: 4 wks after last frost
Days to harvest: 60 to 80 Bush
                     80 to 90 Pole

Harvest facts
Length of harvest: up to 10 weeks
Yield per sq ft: 2 to 3 oz
Yield per plant: 1 oz

Planting
Inoculation: If you haven't grown this crop before, it will fix more nitrogen if inoculated with the appropriate nitrogen-fixing bacteria. See **Beans** for how to do this.

Transplants
The plants need warm weather, but take quite a long time to mature, so they are often started indoors. Sow the seeds on the last frost date and plant the seedlings out 4 weeks later.

Lima beans dislike transplanting, so use cell packs or soil blocks. If germination is good, plant one seed per cell, or block. If it is poor then plant two and thin to one later.

Direct sowing:
Lima Beans shouldn't be planted out until all frost danger is past and the soil is warm (a minimum of 60° F and preferably closer to 70 to 75° F.) If planted in soil that is too cold they may rot, so wait until at least 4 weeks after the last frost date. If you want to plant them earlier, you could warm the soil with plastic mulch or cloches. Plant them 1″ to 2″ deep, depending on how warm the soil is.

Spacing: The climbing types are usually planted 4″ apart in rows (or around a teepee of poles). Bush varieties can be planted in offset rows across the bed, 8″ apart.

Care
Watering: Lima Beans need a steady supply of water and may not set pods if the soil is too dry.

Support: The Pole varieties are vigorous climbers and need something to climb up. See **Pole Beans** for suggestions.

Pests: These are pretty much the same as Bush Beans.

Harvest: Shell beans are harvested when they have swollen in the pod and are plump and shiny. The pods turn a paler whitish green at this time.

Dry beans are harvested after the pods turn crisp and the seeds rattle inside.

Storage: You can keep the pods in the refrigerator for several days, but they are best used fresh.

Seed saving: Lima Beans are mostly self-pollinated, but the nectar rich flowers are very attractive to bees, so they do get cross-pollinated to some extent. For this reason it is best to have only one variety flowering at a time (it needs isolating by one mile). Gather and prepare the seed as for other beans.

Varieties: Lima Bean needs a long, hot summer for best production, so does best in the southern States. If you want to grow it in a more northerly location, you will need to use a fast maturing variety. This crop can be divided into the bush types and the pole types.

Bush
Fordhook 242, Henderson

Pole
Christmas, King of the Garden, Kingston

Cooking: Fresh Lima beans are one of the great treats of the summer garden. They shouldn't be eaten raw as they may contain toxins.

Shell beans: Bring water to a boil, add the shelled beans and simmer until tender. This will only take about 5 to 7 minutes.

Dry beans: Presoak the rinsed beans overnight before cooking. Discard this water, cover with fresh water and simmer for about 45 minutes. Add seasonings after they are cooked.

Bean, Mung
Phaseolus mungo

Syn P. aureus

Introduction: Mung Beans are almost unknown by name to Westerners, yet they are often familiar as Chinese bean sprouts. The plants are as easy to grow as any other beans.

Nutritional content:
The dry beans are high in protein. The bean sprouts are high in protein, vitamins B1 and C, pantothenic acid, folate and several amino acids.

About Mung Beans

Seed facts
Germ temp: 60 (80) 85° F
Germ time: 3 to 12 days
Seed viability: 4 years
Germination percentage: 75+

Planning facts
Hardiness: Tender
Ease of growing: Easy
Growing temp: 50 (60 to 70) 80° F
Plants per sq ft: 3 to 4
Direct sow: 3 wks after last frost
Time to harvest: 70 to 100 days

Soil: Any good garden soil will grow Mung beans. The plants fix their own nitrogen, especially if inoculated.

Planning
When: Mung Beans dislike cold weather, so are not planted out until the soil has warmed up (60° F minimum).

Where: A warm sunny spot is preferable.

Inoculation: If you haven't grown this crop before, it will fix more nitrogen if inoculated with the appropriate nitrogen-fixing bacteria. By enhancing the health of the plants it may also increase yields. See **Beans** for how to do this.

Planting
Direct sowing: There is no point in starting Mung Beans inside, because they germinate and grow, rapidly when the weather suits them. Plant the seeds ½″ deep once the soil has warmed up. If some plants don't germinate in a few days, plant more seed in the gaps (or transplant seedlings from the edges.)

Spacing: Space the plants 6″ to 8″ apart in beds, or 8″ x 24″ in rows.

Care:
Watering: For best production keep the soil evenly moist.

Mulch: This keeps the soil moist and keeps down annual weeds.

Support: Mung Beans are bushy, vigorous twining plants that can be grown with or without support. Their stems are firm enough that they can climb up each other. Keep them away from other small plants though, or they may smother them. They could be allowed to grow up Sunflowers or Corn.

Harvest
When: The green immature pods can be eaten like snap beans. They should be harvested when the beans first start to swell in the pod.

To get dry beans leave the pods to dry on the vine (the seed inside will rattle when they are ready). Don't wait too long, or they will split and release their seeds.

How: If you only have a few plants, you can gather the dry, brittle pods individually. If you have a lot then cut down the whole plants and dry them on a tarp.

Storage: Make sure the seeds are thoroughly dry and store like any other dry beans.

Seed saving: Just save some of the dry seed.

Cooking: Cook the green pods like snap beans. Cook the dry beans like Adzuki beans.

Bean Sprouts: Mung Beans are most often sprouted to make the familiar bean sprouts. The beans are soaked overnight in water, in a jar with a piece of muslin held over the end with a rubber band. They are then rinsed 2 to 3 times a day. They should be kept in the dark if you want long fat white sprouts.

Bean Scarlet Runner
Phaseolus coccineus

Introduction: This Central American bean has been grown as a crop for over 4000 years. It is vigorous and easy to grow crop that is as ornamental as it is useful. It is the most commonly grown green Bean in Britain, where it is much more popular than Bush or Pole Beans.

About Scarlet Runner Bean

Seed facts
Germ temp: 60 (80) 85° F
Germ time: 6 to 14 days
Seed viability: 4 years
Germination percentage: 75+
Weeks to grow transplants: 3 to 4

Planning facts
Hardiness: Half hardy
Ease of growing: Easy
Growing temp: 50 (60 to 70) 80° F
Plants per person: 10
Plants per sq ft: 3 to 4
Transplants:
Start: on last frost date
Plant out: 4 wks after last frost
Direct sow: 3 wks after last frost
Time to harvest: 70 to 100 days

Harvest facts
Length of harvest: 4 to 8 wks
Yield per plant: 1 to 2 lb
Yield per sq ft: 6 lb

Nutritional content:
The beans are rich in protein, soluble fiber (which can lower cholesterol) and complex carbohydrates.

Soil
pH 6.0 - 7.5
The Scarlet Runner Bean prefers a light, well-drained loam, with lots of organic matter. It doesn't need a lot of nitrogen, but it should have good quantities of potassium, phosphorus and other nutrients.

Where: Though this species is a perennial in the tropics, it is usually grown as an annual in northern climates, as it doesn't like cold weather. In cool climates it must be planted in a warm sheltered location. It can get quite tall and a solid wall of the plants casts a lot of shade, so put it where this won't be a problem. It makes a nice temporary screen.

Planting
Inoculation: If you haven't grown this crop before, it will fix more nitrogen if inoculated with the appropriate nitrogen-fixing bacteria. See **Bush Beans** for how to do this.

Transplants: Scarlet Runner is sometimes started indoors in cell packs or soil blocks, to get an early start and to minimize bird and rodent damage. They should be started on the last frost date and planted out a month later.

Direct sowing: These plants don't like cold weather and are not started outdoors until the soil has warmed up, about a month after the last frost. Planted 2″ deep, the large seeds germinate readily and quickly grow into vigorous seedlings. You should plant a few extra plants at the end of the row, to fill in any gaps where seeds don't germinate.

Spacing: This tall plant is usually grown in rows because these are easier to support. It can also be planted in a circle (6″ apart) to grow up a teepee of poles. Sow the seeds 2″ deep and 6 to 9″ apart. Double rows (12″ apart) work well.

Care

Watering: For best production the plants need constant moisture. This is especially important when the pods are forming and in hot weather. Never allow the soil to dry out at these times.

Fertilization: These plants put on a lot of growth in a short time and will benefit from an occasional feed of compost tea or liquid Kelp.

Mulch: This is helpful to keep the soil evenly moist and keep weeds down (which is important while they are young). Don't apply it until the soil has warmed up.

Support: These vining plants grow big and heavy, so it's essential that the supports are tall and strong enough to carry their weight and volume. It is a good idea to install the supports at the same time you plant the seeds, so you don't damage the new seedlings.

See Beans for some suggestions on possible supports. You could make a teepee of 8 ft poles, tied together at a height of 5 ft. When arranged like this the tops splay out at the top and the plants don't get so congested.

I read somewhere that Scarlet Runner Beans climb counterclockwise, whereas other beans climb clockwise. I don't think this has any great significance however (if it does I don't know what it is).

No support: This crop is occasionally grown without support, being allowed to sprawl and run along the ground.

Pruning: Some gardeners pinch out the tops of the plants when they get to the top of their supports. This is said to encourage the production of new side shoots lower down.

Pests: I have never had any problems when I have grown this crop, but it can be attacked by any of the pests that afflict Pole Beans.

Harvest: Gather the pods before the seeds start to swell inside. As with Pole Beans, you need to harvest them regularly to keep them producing well, so go over the plants every 2 to 3 days. If you find any old pods that you previously overlooked, remove them, as they can slow down flowering and pod production.

Storage: Ideally the pods should be picked in the cool of morning or evening. You can store them in a plastic bag in the fridge, until you have enough for a meal. For longer storage freezing works best.

Seed saving: This is much the same as with other beans. The flowers are pollinated by bees and Hummingbirds, or they can self-pollinate (but they still need to be visited by insects to trip them). It is best to have only one variety flowering at a time within a half-mile.

Unusual growing ideas

Ornamental: In this country these attractive vines are commonly grown purely as ornamentals. Often by people who don't even realize that they are edible.

Perennial roots: In mild winter areas the roots may survive the winter and sprout anew the following spring. These probably aren't worth growing as a crop for a second year, as the plants are so easy to grow from seed and so productive. However they are sometimes kept going as an ornamental for a second year. Some gardeners is cold climates actually dig the roots and store them like Dahlias over the winter. They replant them the following spring.

Varieties: Most varieties have red flowers, but some have white, red and white, or even pink. In this country not many improved edible cultivars are available, though more are now appearing.

Scarlet Emperor, Painted Lady (red and white flowers) Sunset (pink flowers).

Cooking: Use as green beans or dry beans.

Bean, Soy
Glycine max

Introduction: Soybeans have the highest protein content of any common crop and have been cultivated in China for over 5000 years. They are a major crop in North America, for human and animal food and for their oil (which has many industrial and food uses).

Soybeans can also be an important crop for people working towards control of their own food supply, as they are easily grown. Add Potatoes, Kale and Amaranth or Quinoa and you could have a pretty good (if not particularly interesting) diet.

The main drawback with soybeans is that they don't taste as good as most other beans. You should always beware of growing something you do not actually like to eat.

Nutritional content:
Soybeans are not only one of the best sources of protein; they also contain a whole range of valuable phytochemicals, with antioxidant and anti-cancer properties.

Soil
pH 6.5 - 7.0
A light, well-drained soil is ideal for Soybeans. It needn't be very rich in nitrogen (don't use fresh manure), as it fixes its own, but it should contain plenty of phosphorus, potassium and trace elements. Soybeans dislike acid soil so add lime if necessary.

Planning
Where: The more sun the plants receive, the faster they will grow and the higher the yield. They need warm growing conditions to perform well.

About Soybean

Seed facts
Germ temp: 65 to 75° F
Germ time: 7 to 14 days
Viability: 4 yrs
Germination percentage: 75 +

Planning facts
Hardiness: Tender
Ease of growing: Fairly easy
Growing temp: 60 (70 to 80) 90° F
Plants per sq ft: 3 to 4
Direct sow: 2 to 4 wks after last frost
Time to harvest: 70 to 120 days

Harvest facts
Yield per plant: ⅛ oz
Yield per sq ft: ½ oz

When: Soybeans are planted after the soil has warmed up in spring (60° F minimum), which is usually 2 to 4 weeks after the last frost. Soybeans love heat (they will tolerate temperatures up to 100° F) and must have warm weather for good growth. If you plant them too early they may well rot and certainly won't grow very much until the soil warms up. You can hasten the warming of the soil with cloches, or black plastic mulch, prior to planting. The young plants are quite frost tender.

How much: Soybeans aren't very productive, so you will have to plant quite a large area if you want to grow a significant quantity of the dry beans.

Planting
Inoculation: If you haven't grown Soybeans recently, the seeds should be inoculated with their specific inoculant (*Rhizobium japonicum*). A garden bean inoculant won't work very well.

Transplants: Like most Legumes, Soybeans resent transplanting, so are usually direct sown. They could be started indoors if you use cell packs, or soil blocks, to minimize root disturbance. However this isn't really very practical if you are growing dry beans, as you would need a lot of plants to make it worthwhile. You might think it worthwhile for growing early shell beans however. Start them inside on the last frost date and plant them out a month later.

Direct sowing: Plant the seeds 1″ to 4″ deep, depending upon the soil. The warmer and drier the soil, the greater the planting depth.

If the temperature of the soil is marginal for germination, you can pre-germinate the seed indoors before planting. In which case you need to plant out very carefully to avoid damaging the delicate sprouts.

Succession sowing: If you are growing them for shell beans, you should make a succession of sowings every 3 weeks to ensure a continuous harvest.

Spacing:
Soybeans may be planted in rows, spaced 4″ apart in the row, with 12″ to 15″ between the rows. However they are more often planted in solid beds. For maximum production you need to get them as close together

as they can tolerate. This is quite close, as they don't branch very much. Space them 6″ to 9″ apart in offset rows across the bed.

Care
Once established Soybeans need very little attention.

Weeds: Soybeans need weeding while young. Once they are well established their foliage makes a dense canopy that suppresses weeds and shades the soil.

Watering: In dry weather they need regular watering to ensure maximum productivity.

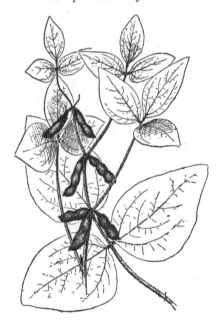

Support: Soybeans don't climb and don't usually need support. However some of the taller varieties may reach 36" in height and are prone to lodging (falling over). These may benefit from a few strategically placed stakes and string.

Pests: Soybeans may be affected by many of the same pests as Bush and Pole Beans. The biggest pest I have encountered was the Japanese

Beetle, though the damage wasn't too serious (I hand picked them off). Several fungus diseases may affect Soybeans, so the plants should be rotated annually.

You should protect the seeds and young seedlings from birds and rodents. Larger animals such as Rabbits may get a taste for the green beans if given the chance.

Harvest
When:
Shell beans: Gather the immature green beans as soon as they reach full size, but before they color up (and turn yellow or black). The harvest period is only about 2 to 3 weeks.

Dry beans: It takes another month for shell beans to turn into dry beans. By this time the whole plant is dying back and the dry pods shatter easily.

How: Gather dry beans by cutting the plants off at ground level and hanging them upside down to dry. The easiest way to deal with large quantities is to lay them on a tarp to dry. Walk on the dry plants to thresh out the ripe seeds.

Storage: Dry beans should have a moisture content of about 14% and should shatter when hit with a hammer. Store them in a cool dry place at 32 to 40° F. For a simple way to check their dryness see Bush and Pole Beans.

Seed saving: This is exactly the same as saving the dry seed for food. Soybeans are self-pollinated, in fact pollination usually occurs before the flowers even open.

Unusual growing ideas
Green manure: Soybeans have often been grown as a green manure crop to improve the soil. They could profitably be planted on land that will lie fallow for a full season. It's cheaper to buy bulk Soybeans from a food market for this. You don't care what variety they are, or even if they have time to mature.

Vacation planting:
Soybeans are a good crop to plant if you are going to be away from your garden for any length of time during the summer. As I already mentioned they need almost no attention once established. Simply weed when young to help them get established, then mulch and forget. They are quite drought tolerant, but will be more productive if you put them on a drip irrigation system with a timer.

Varieties:
Soybeans are day length sensitive, so you need to plant a variety that is adapted to growing in your area. Choose the longest season variety you can possible grow, as earliness comes at the expense of productivity. Like other beans, they can be divided into those grown for dry beans and those for use as shell beans (Edamame).

Dry beans:
Chico
Panther: Fine flavor
Fiskeby: Very early

Shell beans:
Envy
Kuromame
Black Pearl

Cooking:
Soybeans are very good when prepared as green shell beans. Known as Edamame in Japan, you boil the pods for 5 to 10 minutes, then shell out the green beans and cook for another 15 to 30 minutes. You can also cook them in the pods and shell them as you eat. The shelled cooked beans can be frozen for later use.

The dry beans can be sprouted, cooked in various soups, burgers, or made into tofu or tempeh (if you are really ambitious).

Beet
Beta vulgaris

Introduction: Beet still grows wild around the coasts of Western Europe. It is an old crop and has been used as food for humans and livestock since the time of the Romans.

Over the years Beet has been bred to produce several quite different crops. The best-known use is as human food, either for its leaves (as Chard), or for the edible root. It is also commonly grown in Northern Europe for winter animal feed. Another important use is as a source of sugar, in the form of Sugar Beet (which may contain up to 20% sugar). This is a very important commercial crop in temperate parts of the world.

Beets are a particularly useful garden crop because they produce both edible roots and leaves.

Nutritional content
Leaves: These are actually more nutritious than the roots, containing large amounts of vitamins A and C, as well as calcium, phosphorus, potassium and iron. They also contain oxalic acid, but this is no more of a problem than it is with spinach.

Roots: These are rich in carbohydrates and many beneficial phytochemicals, including folate, betacyanin and betaine.

Soil
pH 6.0 (6.5) 8.0
Beets do well in most soils, but the ideal is loose, sandy, well drained and close to neutral (they dislike acid soils). It should be quite fertile for the continuous uninterrupted growth that is necessary to produce good roots. If the soil is poor, growth will be irregular and the roots will show concentric growth rings (zoning).

About Beets

Seed facts
Germ temp: 50 (70 to 80) 85° F
Germ time: 5 to 21 days
42 days / 41° F
16 days / 50° F
9 days / 59° F
6 days / 68° F
5 days / 77° F * Optimum
5 days / 86° F
Viability: 5 years
Germination percentage: 60%+
Weeks to grow transplant: 3 to 4

Planning facts
Hardiness: Half hardy
Ease of growing: moderate
Growing temp: 45 (60 to 70) 75° F
Plants per person: 25
Plants per sq ft: 12
Transplants
Start: 3 to 4 wks before last frost
Plant out: On last frost date
Direct sow: On the last frost date
Fall crop: Direct sow mid-summer
Time to harvest: 50 to 100 days
35 to 45 days from transplanting

Harvest facts
Yield per plant: 8 oz
Yield per square foot: 3 lb sq ft

Soil preparation: Beets don't need a lot of nitrogen, as it encourages top growth and retards sugar storage. Like most root crops, they like phosphorus (colloidal phosphate, bone meal) and potassium (greensand or wood ashes). Kelp meal can be used to supply essential boron and other trace elements.

Fork 2″ of compost or aged manure (not fresh) into the top 6″ to 8″ of soil. This is where most of the plants feeder roots are found, though these deep rooted plants may go down to 24″ or more.

To grow good roots in heavy soil, dig a trench and fill it with a mix of compost (or aged manure), sifted soil and sand.

Planning

Where: The plants need full sun for best growth, especially when they are growing as a fall crop. In very hot climates they may do quite well in light shade.

When: Beets are quite fast growing, taking 50 to 80 days to maturity. They like cool weather and grow best with warm days (60 to 70° F) and cool nights. In most of the United States this means growing them as a spring or fall crop. They grow well enough in warm weather, but the high temperatures can cause the roots to be tough, unevenly colored (zoned), somewhat bitter (or lacking sweetness) and generally of poor quality.

Succession sowing: For a continuous supply of small, tender roots you should plant in succession every 3 to 4 weeks

Spring: Plant Beets 3 to 4 weeks before the last frost date and then in succession every 3 weeks. You won't need many plants at one time, unless you are really into pickling.

Fall: Beets can also be planted in midsummer as a fall crop (6 to 10 weeks before first fall frost date). This is the crop to store for winter.

Winter: In mild winter areas you can plant Beets in late summer, to mature in fall. They will continue to grow slowly over the winter and can be harvested as needed.

Planting

Each Beet "seed" is actually a cluster of flowers fused together, each one containing a single seed. This is why you end up with several plants from one "seed". It is possible to gently break up these clusters and get individual seeds to plant.

The seed clusters contain a water-soluble germination inhibitor. This can be leached out by soaking them overnight prior to planting. Don't simply soak them in a bowl of water overnight however, as they can absorb so much water they can be damaged. Instead they should be put on a damp paper towel, so they can absorb moisture slowly.

You could take this one step further and actually pre-germinate the seed.

Transplants

Starting inside: Beets can be grown from transplants, started inside 3 to 4 weeks before the last frost date. However this doesn't give you much advantage for the extra work involved (they would just be a little earlier). Cell packs or soil blocks work best as Beets don't like root disturbance. Plant one seed capsule in each cavity.

Planting out: Plant out the transplants no earlier than the last

frost date, as they aren't very hardy. To get an earlier start you could warm the soil with cloches before planting and cover the seedlings with cloches.

Vernalization: Don't start your transplants too early. If their stems are larger than ¼″ in diameter, exposure to cool temperatures (below 50° F) for 2 weeks may vernalize them. If this happens they will bolt as soon as the weather warms up and will never produce useful roots.

Direct sowing: Traditionally Beets are direct sown, starting on the last frost date. The soil should be at least 50° F for good germination. Plant the seed ¼″ to ½″ to ¾″ deep, depending on the warmth and dryness of soil. The cooler or wetter the soil, the shallower you should plant.

Broadcasting: Sow the seeds so they are spaced about 2″ apart. It's easier to get the proper spacing with these large seeds, than it is with smaller seed such as Carrot. The scattered seed is then covered with a layer of soil. If the soil in the bed has a tendency to crust, use a mixture of topsoil and compost to cover them.

Rows: The seed can also be sown in rows. Simply make shallow furrows across the bed, drop a seed every 2″ and re-fill the furrow (use cover soil if necessary).

Spacing:
The distance between plants has a direct effect on the final size of the root, the closer the spacing, the smaller the root. Spacing also affects the time they take to mature,

the more room they have, the faster they will mature. Suggested spacing:

5″ spacing: Large roots or poor soil.
4″ spacing: Main summer planting.
3″ spacing: Small roots for pickling.

Care

Beets need to grow quickly, so they can produce plenty of sugar to store in their roots. They can only do this if they get everything they need, when they need it.

Thinning: If germination is good, you will have a little clump of seedlings every 2″. These clumps thin themselves to some extent, the largest and most vigorous ones eventually crowding out the others. It is extremely important that the plants are thinned properly, as insufficient thinning is one of the commonest causes of failure to grow good Beets.

First thinning: Thin the plants soon after they all emerge, when they are about an inch tall. Do this at the same time you are weeding them, ideally in cool cloudy weather. The first thinning should give you a single plant every 2″. Don't thin them to the final spacing at this time, as some might not survive.

Second thinning: When the roots have swollen to an inch in diameter, thin them again. This time to the desired final spacing. The thinnings from this round are big enough to eat in salads or stir-fries.

Weeding: Beets won't grow well if they have to compete with weeds, so make sure they are weeded properly. This is particularly important when they are young and

don't have enough foliage to cover the ground. It is best to hand weed Beets as their raised shoulders are easily damaged by weeding tools.

Water: Consistent watering is essential for good root production.

Beets grown without sufficient water may have tough, woody roots and show concentric whitish zoning. They may also bolt prematurely.

Too much water may result in bushy, luxuriant tops and small roots. Irregular watering may cause splitting.

If water supplies are limited, keep the soil evenly moist while the plants are young. Then give them extra water when the roots are sizing up, to boost their final size.

Mulch: This helps to keep down weeds and conserves moisture. Wait until the soil is warm before applying it however.

Problems: The rounded shoulders of the root commonly stick out of the soil, exposed to the elements and this can result in cracking and woodiness. Cylindrical varieties are particularly prone to this. It can be prevented

by earthing up with soil, or using mulch. A good leaf canopy also helps.

Pests: The only significant pests I have encountered have been Leaf Miners. As you don't normally grow them for their leaves, this is only a problem if they get out of hand. You can crush them in the leaf and scrape off the white egg clusters, but it's easier to use row covers.

Beets may also suffer from aphids, Flea Beetles and caterpillars. Diseases include Cercospora Leaf Spot, Downy Mildew, Curly Top virus and Scab. Possible deficiencies include calcium, nitrogen, phosphorus, potassium and boron.

Harvest

When: You can start harvesting the roots as soon as they are large enough to bother with (1½″ to 2″), which should be in about 60 days or so. These are nice and tender at this stage, but not very sweet. The roots are sweeter, but still tender, when slightly larger (up to 4″). If they get much bigger than this they have a tendency to get rather woody. To some extent this depends on the variety, growing methods and time of year and, so it's not always the case.

How: Usually you can simply pull up the roots by the tops (if these are tender they can be used for greens, so don't waste them). If you are going to store the roots be very careful when harvesting them, as the slightest injury can lead to premature decay. To prevent moisture loss from the root, cut off the leaves to within an inch or two of the root. Don't cut too close to the crown as this may cause them to bleed. If you want to store them, leave the long stringy root tips in place and don't wash them.

Storage: The roots can be stored in a plastic bag in the fridge, for several weeks.

In mild climates the roots are best left in the ground, where they will grow slowly all winter. In colder climates they can be stored in the ground, if covered with a thick mulch to keep the ground from freezing.

In very cold climates they don't keep very well in the ground, so are usually dug and stored in the root cellar (or something similar). They are usually packed in a box filled with damp sand or sawdust. If stored at 32 to 40° F and 90%+ humidity, they will last for 4 to 6 months. On the farm they were once regularly stored in a clamp (see Potatoes).

Seed saving: Beets are cross-pollinated by the wind, so must be isolated from other varieties (and from Chard). This means having only one variety flowering at one time within a distance of two miles.

Beet is a biennial, which means the root has to survive the winter before it can produce seed. In mild climates, you can simply leave them in the ground (cover with mulch if necessary). In colder climates you may have to lift the roots and store them in a root cellar, as described above. Replant the best roots in spring and the seed will ripen by midsummer.

A flowering Beet plant may get to be 8 feet tall and can be quite top heavy, so is often staked to prevent it falling over. You will get a lot of seed from one plant, let alone 5 plants, which is the minimum number required to maintain some genetic variability.

Unusual growing ideas
Multi-planting: This works well with Beets. Simply sow two seed capsules per soil block (or plug tray) and thin to the best 3 or 4 plants (depending on the size required).

Varieties:
Bulls Blood: Has deep red leaves and is popular in salad mixes
Monogerm: Has only one seed per capsule.
Detroit Dark Red: Perhaps the commonest variety.
Chioggia: This Italian heirloom has red and white striations. It is very pretty, but not particularly tasty.
Burpees Golden: This species is very sweet because it contains some genes from sugar beet.
Formanova: A cylindrical beet with tasty tops and roots.

Cooking: The roots can be eaten
raw in salads, cooked as a vegetable (especially in soup), or pickled.

Don't forget about the leaves, as they are the most nutritious part. They may not be as good as Chard, but they are still useful as a potherb, or a colorful minor addition to salads.

The roots and tops are best steamed, or used in soups. Boiling leaches out many of their beneficial nutrients.

Grated sugar beet is sometimes used as a sweetener for cakes and other baked goods.

Broccoli
Brassica oleracea var *albo-glabra*

Introduction: Broccoli probably originated somewhere in Eastern Europe, but it spread throughout Europe via Italy, hence it is generally known by its Italian name. In the past 25 years Broccoli has come from relative obscurity, to become one of the most popular garden vegetables in America. This is good because Broccoli is not only delicious, but also one of the most nutritious of all common vegetables.

Much of what was written about Cabbage also applies to Broccoli, which is a close relative. I had a hard time growing Broccoli for a while. It would either bolt before it got large enough for the head to be useful, or it just kept growing and never produced a head before it was eventually killed by frost. I have since learned it is all to do with timing and Broccoli is actually pretty easy to grow, if you get the timing right.

Nutritional content:
The flower heads are rich in vitamins A and C, calcium, iron, potassium and folate. It is considered one of the very best anti-cancer vegetables, as it contains a whole range of beneficial phytochemicals, glucosinolates, luteine sulfuraphane and isothiocyanin.

Soil
pH 6.0 - 7.5
Broccoli needs to grow fast for best quality. To do this it needs a rich, moist, well-drained soil, with lots of organic matter and available nutrients. It is quite salt tolerant.

About Broccoli

Seed facts

Germ temp: 45 (60 to 65) 85° F
Germ time: 4 to 20 days
20 days / 50° F
9 days / 59° F
6 days / 68° F
5 days / 77° F * Optimum
4 days / 86° F
Seed viability: 3 to 4 yrs
Germination percentage: 75+
Weeks to grow transplants: 4 to 5

Planning facts

Hardiness: Half hardy
Ease of growing: Variable
Growing temp: 60 to 65° F
Plants per person: 5
Plants per sq ft: 1
Transplants:
Start: 2 to 3 wks before last frost
Plant out: 2 wks after last frost date
Direct sow: 2 wks after last frost
Fall crop: sow 10 to 12 wks before first frost
Time to harvest: 80 to 120 days
45 to 70 days from transplanting

Harvest facts

Length of harvest: 2 to 4 wks
Yield per plant: 1 lb
Yield per sq ft: ¼ to ½ lb sq ft

Soil preparation: Prepare the soil by incorporating 2″ to 3″ of aged manure, or compost, into the top 6″ to 8″ of soil (which is where most of the plants feeder roots are found). You might also add colloidal phosphate, wood ashes, Kelp and dolomitic limestone (Broccoli likes lots of calcium and magnesium and doesn't like acid soil).

Planning

Where: Broccoli likes full sun, especially when growing in cool weather. It will tolerate some shade, but this slows maturation. It takes up quite a bit of space, but this usually isn't an issue in cooler weather, as the winter garden is often half empty anyway.

Crop rotation: Ideally Broccoli should not be planted where another Brassica has been grown in the past 3 years.

When:

Spring: Broccoli isn't as hardy as Cabbage, so spring plants are usually set out in the garden about 2 weeks after the last frost date. The soil temperature should be at least 60° F.

Fall: Broccoli does best as a fall crop, as it prefers cooler temperatures, growing and heading up best at about 65° F. It is also less bothered by pests in cool weather and the heads stay in peak condition for longer. Mature plants can sit in the garden, ready to harvest, for weeks. They are quite hardy and can survive frost as low as 20° F.

Autumn Broccoli should be sown 2 to 3 months before the first fall frost date, so it is close to maturity by the time cold weather hits.

If you are growing a lot of Broccoli for freezing, you should plant it at the optimal time, which is late summer. It also means it will need to be frozen for a shorter time.

Winter: In very mild climates it can be sown in autumn, as a late winter / early spring crop. In harsher climates it won't survive the winter.

Succession sowing: You generally don't want a large amount of Broccoli to mature at one time (unless you are going to freeze it). For this reason it is usually sown in succession, every 3 to 4 weeks.

Planting

Transplants

Starting inside: Like most Brassicas, Broccoli doesn't mind transplanting, so is commonly started indoors. It can be sown in flats, cell packs, soil blocks or plug trays. Sow the seeds ⅛″ to ¼″ deep, 4 to 5 weeks before you need to plant out. By the time it goes outside, the plant should be 3″ to 4″ high, with 3 to 5 leaves and a stem diameter of about ⅛″.

Vernalization: In spring it is important to get transplants outside before they get too big. If their stems are over ¼″ diameter, they may be vernalized by cold temperatures. This happens when they are exposed to temperatures below 50° F for two weeks and will cause them to bolt as soon as it warms up. Of course you could just keep them inside until all risk of cold weather is past (or protect them with cloches or row covers). This is another reason Broccoli does best as a fall crop.

Planting out: If they are to go outside while it is still cold, the seedlings should be hardened off. They will then tolerate temperatures as low as 25° F. Plant them out slightly deeper than they grew in the flats, to the depth of their first true leaves.

Transplants

Starting outside: In warm weather Broccoli transplants can be started in an outdoor nursery bed. The seeds are sown in a small, protected area, pricked out into a slightly larger area and finally transplanted to their permanent position. This is much more efficient than direct sowing at their final spacing, as they don't take up any bed space for the first month or two of their lives.

Direct sowing: Though Broccoli is usually transplanted, it can also be direct sown. This works out best for an autumn crop, as the soil is warm in late summer so germination will be rapid. Simply plant twice as many seeds as you need plants, at a depth of ½". Thin to the required spacing, when they have their first set of true leaves. Of course you will probably have problems with pests when direct sowing at this time of year.

Spacing: The spacing you use depends on the fertility of the soil and how large you want the heads to grow. The wider the spacing, the larger the individual plants, (and their heads) can get. At 18" spacing, the heads may grow to be 10" in diameter. At 6" spacing they may only grow to 5". Closely spaced plants don't produce as many side shoots either.

12": Excellent soil, small heads
15": Good soil, medium heads
18": Poor soil, large heads

Care

The plants need looking after carefully. If there is a check in growth, they may never recover and may bolt prematurely.

Weed: Competition from weeds may also cause bolting, so keep them well weeded (especially when small).

Water: For optimal growth the soil must be moist at all times. Broccoli transpires quite a lot of water, but fortunately it grows in fairly cool weather, so watering isn't usually a problem. In hot weather it is critical that they receive sufficient moisture, as a lack of water may cause bolting.

Fertilization: If your soil is less than ideal, give your transplants a feed of compost tea, or liquid seaweed, 2 weeks after planting out. This will encourage early vegetative growth. You might also give them another feed a couple of weeks before harvest time, to encourage the production of side shoots.

Mulch: This is helpful to keep down weeds. Plastic mulch is sometimes used in spring, to warm the soil before planting. Organic mulch should be used in summer, to cool the soil and keep it moist. Broccoli loves seaweed mulch.

Pests and disease: Broccoli is the same species as Cabbage and is prone to the same pests and diseases (see **Cabbage**). You can avoid many Cabbage problems by covering the young plants with row covers. Aphids are a particular problem in warm weather and will often infest the flower heads.

Harvest

When: Harvest the mature heads as soon as they reach full size. You can eat them before this time, but you won't get as much food (this may not matter if you have a lot of plants). This can also help to extend the harvest.

The perfect time to harvest Broccoli is when the individual flower buds are visible and somewhat swollen. As the head gets over-mature, the individual florets start to separate and the yellow petals become visible. Broccoli is edible after the florets have separated and even when some of the flowers have opened, but it's not as good. If you miss the optimal harvest time you should still cut off the heads, as this will stimulate the plants to produce new side shoots

How: Cut the head off with a sharp knife. The standard for commercial harvesting is to leave about 5" of stem on the head, as they want the extra weight. However if you leave more stem on the plant, you may get more useful side shoots.

Side shoots: After the main head is cut, the plants will send out side shoots. On large healthy plants these can be 5" in diameter, so don't remove the plants after harvesting the first heads. After you cut the side shoots, the plant will send out yet more shoots and may continue to do this for several weeks (it really wants to flower and set seed). I keep cutting the side shoots until they get too small to bother with. In warm weather it can produce side shoots in only a few days, so keep on top of harvesting.

These side shoots greatly increase the size and duration of the harvest and make Broccoli a much more productive crop.

After the side shoots are finished, you might try cutting the plant right back, almost to the ground. This sometimes stimulates it to send up a new stem.

If a hard frost threatens, you should harvest any remaining heads and eat or freeze them. They won't survive a hard freeze.

Storage: Broccoli is quite perishable. It may keep for a week or so in a plastic bag in the fridge, but is best eaten as soon as possible. For longer term storage Broccoli freezes very well.

Seed saving: Broccoli is an annual. It is cross-pollinated by insects and will cross with any member of the Cabbage family. To keep the seed pure, it must be the only variety (of any *Brassica oleracea* species) growing within a mile. Otherwise it is fairly easy to save the seed (see Cabbage for more on this). To maintain some genetic variability, you should save seed from at least 6 plants.

Varieties: The choice of Broccoli varieties is fairly limited, but is increasing. It is important to grow a variety that suits your growing conditions.

The hybrid varieties have a high degree of uniformity in size and maturation date and often don't produce many side shoots. These traits may be desirable for commercial growers, but are not good for the home gardener. Unless you are growing for freezing, you don't want plants that all mature at the same time. You want plants that mature at different rates, over a long period and that produce lots of side shoots. Look for these traits in the variety descriptions.

Open pollinated:
De Cicco: Fine old Italian heirloom
Italian Green Sprouting: Heavy producer

Umpqua: Produces over a long period, ideal for home gardeners.

Romanesco - This unusual Italian Heirloom is becoming increasingly popular. It is actually one of the oldest Broccoli varieties and has a very attractive spiral pattern on its pale green head. It is quite variable, with about 20% of plants not heading up and the rest doing so over a long period.

Hybrids:
These have significant advantages.
Early Dividend F1: Very early, produces lots of side shoots
Green Comet F1: Early and heat resistant
Packman F1: Early, uniform fairly heat tolerant

Cooking: Fresh Broccoli is far superior to that you buy in the store.

If you heads are infested with aphids, try dipping them in warm water and vinegar. Don't soak them for too long though, or you will have vinegar flavored Broccoli.

The Interior of the stem can be used as a vegetable, somewhat like Kohlrabi.

Sprouting Broccoli

British gardening books sometimes talk about Sprouting Broccoli. This is somewhat different from the Broccoli described above, as it produces many small heads or shoots, rather than a single large one. These are cut with a long (5″) stem attached. The plants may continue to send up new small heads for weeks.

Sprouting Broccoli is hardier than Broccoli and is commonly sown in the fall, for a spring crop. Apparently it needs exposure to cold weather (below 50° F) before it will head up. It is otherwise grown and used, in the same ways as Broccoli. Varieties include Purple Sprouting and White Sprouting Broccoli. The biggest problem is finding seed to plant.

Chinese Broccoli
Gai Lohn
Introduction: This is the same species as the above and may have been developed from plants introduced into China by the Portuguese, some time in the sixteenth century. It differs from Broccoli in that the flower stems are quite slender, only ½″ to ¾″ in diameter.

This fast growing plant is cultivated in much the same way as Broccoli, but is easier and more forgiving. It deserves to be more widely grown in the West

When: This is a fairly easy crop to grow, tolerating cold and heat better than other Broccoli. In cool climates it can be grown in succession all summer, though late summer tends to give the best results, as it is less likely to bolt prematurely. In warm climates it is usually grown as a fall and winter, crop. It may also do well in spring, if you can get it going early enough.

Spacing: This varies from 6″ to 12″ depending upon the size of plants required. Larger spacing gives larger plants.

Harvest: The first flower shoots are followed by lots of side shoots, so the plants can be harvested 3 or 4 times. Check the plants every couple of days and cut all mature shoots. Don't let the flowers open.

Varieties: Green Lance is the most readily available variety.

Cooking: In China the shoots are usually stir fried or steamed.

Brussels Sprout

Brassica oleracea var *gemmifera*

Introduction: As the name suggests this crop originated in Belgium, sometime in the 18th century. It is a crop you either love (some people adore them) or hate, though don't be too quick to judge, until you have tried them fresh from your own garden. I have always disliked them, but with a little effort they have started growing on me recently.

Nutritional content:
The sprouts are rich in protein (for a green vegetable), vitamins A and C (much more than Cabbage), as well as potassium, iron, folate, riboflavin and several antioxidants.

Soil
pH. (6.0 to 6.5) to 7.5
Brussels Sprout likes a heavy, moisture retentive soil. It should be rich in organic matter and all nutrients for well balanced growth. It likes lots of potassium and phosphorus, but doesn't need too much nitrogen, as this can adversely affect the flavor of the sprouts.

Soil preparation: Prepare the soil by incorporating 2″ to 3″ of compost or aged manure, along with colloidal phosphate, wood ashes, Kelp and dolomitic limestone. Work all of this into the top 6″ to 8″ of soil, which is where most of the plants feeder roots are found.

Planning
Where: These plants get quite large and are in the ground for a long time, so you want to put them in the right place. If you are planting a winter crop, make sure they will get enough sun, are in a warm spot (not a frost pocket) and that the soil is well drained (important). Of course they should not be planted where another Brassica was grown the year before.

About Brussels Sprout

Seed facts
Germ temp: 45 to 85° F
Germ time: 4 to 20 days
20 days / 50° F
9 days / 59° F
6 days / 68° F
5 days / 77° F * Optimum
4 days / 86° F
Seed viability: 3 to 10 years
Germination percentage: 75+
Weeks to grow transplants: 4 to 6

Planning facts
Hardiness: Hardy
Ease of growing: Moderate
Growing temp 40 (60 to 65) 75° F
Plants per person: 5
Plants per sq ft: ½
Start transplants: 2 to 3 weeks before last frost date
Plant out transplants: 2 weeks after last frost date
Fall crop: Plant out in midsummer
Direct sow: 2 wks after last frost
Time to harvest: 140 to 250 days

Harvest facts
Length of harvest: 8 to 10 weeks
Yield per plant: 1 lb per plant
Yield per sq ft: ½ lb

When: Brussels Sprout doesn't do well in hot weather. It requires cool soil, cool weather and short days for best growth. It isn't recommended as a spring crop because the sprouts would have to mature in hot weather, which would seriously impair their flavor and quality.

Fall: Brussels Sprouts are almost always planted as a fall crop (in Britain they are a traditional Christmas "treat"). The sprouts then mature in the cool weather they prefer and so have much better flavor. They can be direct sown, or grown from transplants.

Brussels Sprouts are a very slow maturing crop (some varieties may take eight months), so are in the ground for a long time. This means that even a fall crop must go into the ground in early to mid summer (depending upon the climate and variety). In cool summer areas it is sometimes planted in the middle of spring.

Planting
Raising transplants: Like other Brassicas they don't mind transplanting, and may even like it.

Starting inside: They can be started indoors in flats, cell packs, soil blocks or plug trays. Sow the seeds 1/8″ to 1/4″ deep, 4 to 5 weeks before you want to plant out.

Starting outside: Brussels Sprouts are started during warm weather, so there is no need to start them in a greenhouse. An outdoor nursery bed will suit them just fine. Sow the seeds in a small protected area, prick the seedlings out into a slightly larger area and finally transplant the young plants into their permanent position. This saves bed space until it is really needed.

Planting out: The seedlings should be transplanted outside

when they are 4″ to 5″ high and have 5 to 6 true leaves. Don't wait too long to plant them out, or they may get deficient. Plant them a little deeper than they were in the flat, up to the first true leaves.

Direct sowing: There is no reason why you can't sow directly into the garden, except for the fact that they will be taking up bed space. You must take precautions to prevent them getting eaten though, otherwise there is a good chance they will end up as a snack for some of the many hungry pests that love Brassicas. Plant the seeds 1/2″ deep and keep well watered.

Spacing: The plants need a lot of space, so allow a minimum of 18″ to 24″ between the plants in the beds. Perhaps sow them in a row down the center of the bed. Another crop should be interplanted with them, to take advantage of the large vacant space between the plants.

Care
Weeds: It is important to weed the young plants carefully. This should be done by hand, as their shallow roots are easily damaged by careless hoeing.

Water: Keep the soil evenly moist at all times. Brussels Sprout absolutely must have enough water, especially if the weather is warm.

Mulch: This is very helpful for Brussels Sprouts, as otherwise there is a lot of bare soil between the plants. It keeps the soil cooler, suppresses weeds and conserves soil moisture.

Pests: This species is prone to the same pests as other members of the

Brassicaceae family. See Cabbage for more on these pests.

Harvest
When: Brussels sprouts are axillary buds and mature gradually from the bottom of the stem upwards, in the order they were formed. They do this because the apical dominance hormone produced by the growing top is only effective for a certain distance. The sprouts generally start to form when nighttime temperatures drop to 60° F. As the sprouts mature, the lower leaves may start to fade.

The hardy sprouts stay in good condition even with frost (down to 20° F). Their flavor actually improves with cold weather.

How: Start picking (actually cutting) when the sprouts are about an inch across, beginning at the bottom and working your way up to the top. Don't leave any mature sprouts on the plant, as this may affect further production.

When the plant is nearly finished, you can cut off the leafy top and eat the tender parts like Cabbage.

It is possible to speed up and even out the harvest by removing the leafy growing top. This ends its apical dominance and so all the sprouts start growing at once. You should do this about 6 weeks before you want to harvest, just as the first sprouts are starting to form on the bottom of the stem.

Storage: Brussels sprouts will store for a few weeks in a plastic bag in a refrigerator (don't wash them). For longer term storage they are usually frozen.

Seed saving: This is the same as for the related Cabbage.

Unusual growing ideas:
Edible flower buds: If the plant has any energy left after producing all those sprouts, it may produce an edible flower bud that can be used like Broccoli. If it isn't too woody, the stalk is also edible.

Varieties: This is one crop where hybrids are usually superior to open pollinated varieties (with a few exceptions). The only problem is that many hybrids are bred for commercial farmers and tend to produce all of their sprouts at once.

Open pollinated:
Roodnerf: One of best flavored varieties
Rubine: Sprouts are purple.
Hybrids:
Jade Cross F1
Bubbles

Cooking: Cut an x in the base of the stem and then steam them for 5 to 8 minutes. When cooked the stem end should barely be tender when you poke it with a knife. Don't overcook.

Buckwheat
Fagopyrum esculentum

Introduction: The name is derived from the similarity of the seeds to the larger seeds of the Beech (Boek) tree. This annual was once commonly grown as a home scale grain crop, especially in Eastern Europe. It is sometimes categorized as a pseudo-cereal as it is grown as a grain crop, yet isn't a member of the grass family. It was widely grown in the United States in the 18th and 19th centuries, but it almost disappeared along with the self-sufficient small farmer.

Nutritional content:
The high protein grain has a better amino acid composition than most cereals and is especially high in lysine. It is also rich in complex carbohydrates.

Buckwheat is a rich sources of rutin, a potent anti-cancer agent that also lowers "bad" cholesterol.

Soil:
pH: **4.0 to 6.0**
Buckwheat will grow in almost any soil (even very acid ones), so long as it is well-drained. Traditionally it was grown on soils that were too poor for more valuable crops.

Planning
When: Buckwheat is a cool season crop and grows best when the weather isn't too hot. However it doesn't like cold weather and can't stand frost. Plant it after the soil has warmed up in spring (2 weeks after the last frost date). More commonly it is planted in mid to late summer, so it can mature its seed in cooler weather

Buckwheat has the shortest growing season of any "grain" crop, as little as 2 months. In ideal conditions it may flower within 5 weeks of planting. This means it can be planted over quite a long period in summer and will still have time to mature before cold weather arrives.

Planting
Direct sowing: The easiest way to plant Buckwheat is to broadcast the seeds onto the bed and then rake them into the soil. If your supply of seed is limited, you will waste less seed if you sow in rows (make the furrows ½″ to 1″ deep).

Care
Watering: The seeds need moist soil for good germination, so keep them well watered. Buckwheat is quite drought tolerant, but gives higher yields if watered regularly.

Pests: Few insect pests bother Buckwheat, though birds and slugs will eat the newly planted seeds and emerging seedlings. They may also go for the ripening grain.

Harvest: Cut the seed heads with a sickle and dry them on a large tarp. Then thresh out the seeds and dry to 12% moisture for storage.

Processing: The thick seed coat (pericarp) comes off fairly easily when grinding the seed to make flour. Sift them out of the flour before using it.

Seed saving: Just save some of the seed you collect.

Unusual growing ideas
Green manure: This tender annual is most familiar to modern gardeners as a green manure crop. It is one of the best short-term soil improving crops for the summer garden. It produces a dense fibrous root system, thrives on poor soils, adds organic matter, improves structure and is very fast growing. It can be grown in a few weeks, in between crops. When incorporated as a green manure it is very effective at feeding and stimulating soil life. It also accumulates phosphorus and makes it more available.

Weed suppression:
Buckwheat can grow up to four feet in height in only a few weeks and grows so densely it can be an effective smother crop. It actually has an allelopathic effect on many weeds and can suppress weed growth for up to 2 months. This works best when the plants are simply cut down, within a week of flowering and left as a mulch.

A good way to establish a new garden is to plant and incorporate, two consecutive crops of Buckwheat.

Buckwheat flowers are very attractive to Hoverflies (important predatory insects that prey on aphids).

Buckwheat Lettuce: Some people use Buckwheat as an indoor Micro-green salad crop. The seeds are soaked for 3 hours and then spread out on a tray of soil, vermiculite, felt or wet paper. They are then put in a warm place and misted daily. When the seeds begin to germinate the tray is moved it into full light. The greens will be ready in 1 to 3 weeks, depending upon the temperature. The plants are harvested with scissors when they are 3 to 6″ tall, leaving about an inch of stem behind.

Caution: There is a potential problem with the frequent use of Buckwheat greens. The green plant contains a toxin called fagopyrin, which can cause the skin of some individuals to become hypersensitive to sunlight. For this reason I don't recommend that you use any green parts.

Buckwheat honey: This is considered to have a very fine flavor. Buckwheat is sometimes planted to provide forage for bees.

Varieties: This isn't a very important commercial crop, so there aren't very many improved varieties available. I have just used the seed available locally for use as a green manure crop.
Giant American, Mancan, Spanky

Cooking: Buckwheat has been an important peasant food in many parts of the world. In Japan it is used to make Soba noodles, in Eastern Europe it was used to make a porridge called Kasha and in North America it was used for Buckwheat pancakes. More recently it has been used to make gluten free beer.

Cabbage
Brassica oleracea var *capitata*

Wild Cabbage (*Brassica oleracea ssp oleracea*) is native to the coastal areas of Western Europe and is still found growing wild there. An impressive variety of cool weather garden crops have been bred from this unimpressive looking plant, including Kale, Collards, Cabbage, Broccoli, Cauliflower, Brussels Sprout and Kohlrabi. Cabbage was probably refined into the familiar crop we know in Germany and Italy. The word Cole is an old name for cabbage (hence coleslaw).

For centuries Cabbage was a staple food of northern European peasants. It is an ideal crop for self-sufficiency for many reasons. It is easy to grow and store, nutritious, high yielding, hardy (it will survive 20° F) and can be harvested in cold weather, after most other crops are finished.

Cabbage was the crop to depend upon when all else failed and there are varieties for harvesting for most of the year. Perhaps because of this association with poor peasants, Cabbage has never been held in very high esteem by gourmets, even though it can be very good.

Nutritional content
Cabbage is rich in vitamin C and several cancer preventing phytochemicals (anthocyanins, sulforaphane, isothiocyanates, dithiolethiones). It has been found that people who eat lots of Brassicas, have lower cancer rates than those who don't.

About Cabbage

Seed facts
Germ temp: 45 to 85° F
Germ time: 4 to 20 days
15 days / 50° F
9 days / 59° F
6 days / 68° F
5 days / 77° F * Optimum
4 days / 86° F
Seed viability: 3 to 10 years
Germination percentage: 75+
Weeks to grow transplant: 5 to 6

About Cabbage
Hardiness: Hardy
Ease of growing: Fairly easy
Growing temp: 40 (60 to 65) 75° F
Plants per person: 5
Plants per sq ft: 1
Transplants:
Start: 6 wks before last frost
Plant out: 2 wks before last frost
Direct sow: 2 wks before last frost
Fall crop: Sow in late summer
Time to harvest: 70 to 200 days
50 to 150 days from transplants.

Harvest facts
Yield per plant: 1 to 2 lb
Yield per sq ft: 1 to 3 lb sq ft

Soil
pH: (6.0 to 6.5) to 7.5
Cabbages are hungry plants and must have rich soil if they are to produce well. They prefer heavy soil, with lots of organic matter to retain moisture and lots of available nutrients (especially potassium and phosphorus). They don't need a lot of nitrogen however, as this can lead to sappy growth that isn't very hardy.

Cabbage doesn't like poorly drained soil. Early crops may do better in lighter soils that warm up more rapidly, or in raised beds.

Clubroot can be a problem in acid soil, so try to keep the pH above 7.0. Low pH may also lock up molybdenum, potentially causing a deficiency. Raising the pH with a liming agent will also add calcium, which is good for Cabbage.

Potential micronutrient deficiencies include boron and manganese.

Soil preparation: Cabbages love organic matter, so incorporate 2″ of compost or aged manure, into the top 6″ of soil. This is often applied the previous fall, in which case fresh manure can also be used.

Planning
Where: If you are growing Cabbages in cold weather, they should be planted in a warm sheltered place, with full sun.

Crop rotation: Cabbage should not be planted where another Brassica has been grown in the past 3 years.

When: Cabbage doesn't do well in hot weather, as it causes excessive transpiration from the large leaves. It really needs cool weather and short days to head up satisfactorily. This means that it does best when planted early (to mature before midsummer), or late (to mature in fall).

Spring: The first Cabbage plants can be started 6 to 8 weeks before the last spring frost and planted out 4 to 6 weeks later. They should still be small enough that they won't be vernalized by a late cold snap, which would cause them to bolt (see Broccoli for more on Vernalization). If you plant early and feed them well, the first plants should be mature by July.

Summer: In places with cool summers it can be grown almost year round, by succession sowing and using different varieties.

Fall: Start a fall crop 12 to 16 weeks before the first fall frost. This can be planted in a nursery bed, or in any vacant spot, so long as you give them protection from slugs and other predators. Plants grown at this time of year tend to be much better flavored than those grown in warmer weather.

Winter: In mild winter areas cabbage is a good winter crop, planted in late summer or early autumn. This will mature in late autumn and then stand right through the winter in good condition. Such plants can get very big.

Cabbage can also be planted in autumn, to over-winter and mature the following spring. In milder areas it might also be planted in January for a spring crop.

With all the options of when to plant, it is important to choose a variety that is appropriate for the season in which it will be grown.

Succession: Plant Cabbage in succession every 3 to 4 weeks. Generally you only need a few plants to mature at any one time, so you should only plant a few seeds (a dozen or so) at each sowing.

Planting

Transplants: Cabbage is hardy enough to be direct sown, but it actually seems to like being transplanted, so is often started indoors in early spring. This also had the advantage of avoiding the early Flea Beetles that can riddle direct sown Brassicas with holes.

Starting inside: The first spring Cabbages are usually started indoors and transplanted out 4 to 6 weeks later. Plant the seeds ½″ deep and keep them warm (60 to 80° F) for fastest germination. Once they are growing, reduce the temperature to between 50 and 70° F, as they grow better in cooler conditions. If necessary prick out the seedlings to a larger container when they have 2 sets of leaves.

Planting out: The seedlings will be ready to go in the ground when they have 4 or 5 true leaves and are about 4″ high. Be sure to plant them outside as soon as they are of sufficient size. If they sit around in containers for too long, they will get stressed and deficient.

In cold weather the plants should be hardened off before they are planted outside.

Transplanting is pretty straightforward; just bury the stems up to their first set of true leaves. Press down gently around the plant, to firm the soil and leave a slight depression. Water immediately to help the plant recover.

Starting transplants outside: Cabbage transplants are often started in an outdoor nursery bed. The seeds are sown in a small, protected area, pricked out into a slightly larger area and finally transplanted to their permanent position. This is a much more efficient use of space than direct sowing, as the plants don't take up any bed space for the first 4 to 6 weeks of their lives.

Direct sowing: As the weather warms up, Cabbage can be sown directly outdoors. The plants grow well when direct sown, though there is a danger that they may end up as dinner for some of the many hungry pests that love Brassicas. Some people sow Turnip seed along with the Cabbage, as many pests seem to prefer it, and will leave the Cabbage alone. You can also plant a lot more seed than you need, to compensate for some losses. This problem of predation is one reason it is common for them to be started indoors, where they are more easily protected.

Plant the seeds ¼″ deep in cool soil, up to 1″ deep in warm soil. Space them 2″ apart, to be thinned to the desired spacing when they get big enough.

Spacing: This varies according to variety, fertility, the time of year and how large you want the plants to get. You can control the final size of the plants by the spacing, a wider spacing means larger (but fewer plants).

12″ spacing is for very fertile soil, summer and small heads.

15″ spacing is for average soil, summer and average heads.

18″ spacing is for poor soil, winter and large heads.

If you want to plant them in rows, the traditional spacing is 12″ to 18″ apart in the row, with 24″ between the rows.

Care

For best quality the plants must grow continuously, with no check from lack of water or nutrients, or competition from weeds.

Weed: Keep down weeds around the plants. This is particularly important when the plants are young, as they can't compete very well.

Water: Cabbages need a regular water supply to grow well. They are quite shallow rooted, so make sure there is plenty of moisture in the soil at all times. This is particularly important in hot weather.

Consistent watering is also important. Lack of water can result in strongly flavored plants and thicker, tougher leaves. If plants are suddenly soaked after being very dry, the resulting burst in growth can cause the head to split.

It is best if the leaves don't get wet when watering, as several diseases can be spread in this way.

Fertilization: A liquid feed of compost tea is helpful in early spring, while the soil is cool and nitrogen is not readily available. A second feed may be given as they are heading up, to help them grow bigger.

Mulch: These widely spaced plants benefit from a mulch, to keep down weeds, keep the soil cool and to conserve moisture

Heading up: Before a Cabbage begins to head up it stores nutrients in its outer leaves. These are then used during the heading up phase when more nutrients are needed in a short time than the roots can easily supply.

Pests: Plants of the *Brassicaceae* family have developed a pungent and toxic oil to protect themselves from insect predators. This is very effective in most cases, however a number of insects have not only evolved some resistance to it, but are now actually attracted by it. These are serious pests of Brassicas and can make growing them much more difficult than it should be. These pests include:

Aphids: These are the ever-present pests of Brassicas. Blasting them off with a strong jet (I mean strong) of water makes a big difference. It pays to have lots of insectory plants (P*hacelia, Asteraceae. Apiaceae*) around, to feed the predators that prey on aphids.

Caterpillars: Several types of caterpillar live only of Brassicas

and can strip a young plant to the midribs in a short time. If you have only a few plants, hand picking is the best way to go. If you have a whole field then a spray of Bacillus thuringensis is most often recommended. Parasitic wasps can kill a lot of caterpillars if given the chance, but not if you start spraying poisons. Red Cabbage is not as attractive to caterpillars as the green, though it is more attractive to aphids.

Flea Beetles: These tiny insects are common in spring and pepper the young plants with tiny holes. Transplants can usually take this damage without too much problem, they just keep putting out new leaves, but newly germinated seedlings may be killed. You could use row covers, or plant some Turnip seed as a trap crop.

Clubroot: (*Plasmodiophora brassicae*): This serious root disease is a big problem in some areas. It causes the roots to swell up like clubs and can kill the plant. Clubroot likes acid soil, so the closer your soil is to neutral the better. If this disease gets into your soil it can stay there for years, even without any Brassicas to infect.

Cabbage Root Fly : This fly is the worst Brassica problem I have encountered. It lays its eggs at the base of the plant and the newly hatched larvae work their way down to the roots and eat them. When enough of the maggots get big enough, they pretty much destroy the roots and kill the plant. Often the first symptom you notice is when a plant wilts in sunny weather. If this occurs, examine the root for the small white maggots, which look like small grains of rice. If you find affected plants, remove

and kill the maggots to stop them maturing and reproducing (or just to make you feel better).

The easiest way to deal with these pests is to use row covers, which prevents the fly getting near enough to the plant to lay eggs.

Another effective control is to use 6″ squares (or disks) of foam carpet backing. You cut a slit to the center of the square and put them around the stem. These work very well, because the foam can expand as the stem enlarges. These disks not only make it harder for the fly larvae to get into the root, but also provide refuges for the predatory beetles that eat the eggs and larvae. These disks have achieved 70% control, which is as good as most pesticides.

You might also deter these creatures by spreading wood ashes around the plant and in the planting hole.

You don't have to eliminate all of these maggots. Some damage is tolerable, so long as it doesn't seriously affect the crop.

Other pests: Harlequin Bugs, Thrips, Root Knot Nematodes.

Other diseases: Alternaria Blight, Black Leg, Downy Mildew, Fusarium Wilt, Wirestem.

Boron deficiency: Brassicas generally are quite susceptible to boron deficiency, which manifests itself as hollow stems

Harvest

When: Harvest the first cabbage heads as soon as they are big and solid enough to be worthwhile. You can harvest the un-hearted (heartless) plants before this, but they will be less productive.

If a mature head begins to crack (this may be caused by excess nitrogen, aging or irregular water supply) harvest it and use promptly. This doesn't affect edibility, but it does affect storage life.

Delaying maturation: If too many Cabbages are maturing at once, you can slow their growth by cutting through some of their roots with a spade. You can also twist the head a quarter turn, to break some of the roots.

How: Harvest by cutting through the base of the stem with a knife. When you harvest early cabbage, you might want to leave a few leaves on the root (this is the fastest way to get a clean cabbage anyway). These will keep the root alive and may enable it to produce a new crop of mini cabbages. If you harvest all but one of these, the remaining one might even grow into another small head

Remove the roots after harvest and compost or burn them, to help prevent the buildup of disease.

Storage: The fleshy leaves of cabbage are intended as food storage organs, so they are one of the easiest crops to store. They can be stored in plastic bags in a refrigerator (for weeks), or in a root cellar at 32 to 40° F and 90 to 95%

humidity (for months). Don't wash them until you use them.

In mild winter areas, it is easier to leave them growing in the garden until you need them. Protect with mulch if necessary.

Seed saving: Cabbage is a biennial and takes two years to produce seed. Don't save seed from plants that flower in their first year, as you don't want to raise an annual strain that bolts quickly.

In harsh climates you will have to protect the plants over the winter. You can do this with a thick mulch of straw, cold frames, cloches or hay bales (half grown plants sometimes survive better than larger ones). You may also dig them up (leave 12″ of root attached) and store in a root cellar in damp sand.

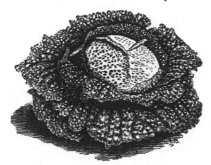

Cabbage is usually self-incompatible and must be cross-pollinated by insects. This means there must be a number of plants flowering at the same time.

All of the Cole crops are the same species and will cross with each other. To maintain racial purity you have to ensure that only one type flowers at once. The alternative is to isolate them, either by distance (1000 yards for different varieties, 1500 yards for different crops), or by caging them (don't forget they need insects for pollination).

Save the seed from at least 5 plants to maintain some genetic diversity.

Cabbages flower in the spring of their second year. If the head is very dense the flower stalk might have a hard time emerging. If this is the case you can cut a 2″ deep cross in the top of the head to help it get out.

A Cabbage plant may produce a half-pound of seed. This can get quite heavy, so a plant may need support if it is not to break under the weight.

The seed is produced in long pods and should be gathered when the older bottom pods first start to split open. Watch them carefully as they shatter easily when they are fully ripe. Cut the seedpod bearing stems and dry them in a warm place (I put small quantities in a paper grocery bag, so I don't lose any seeds). The large seeds are easily handled and cleaned. Of course it is essential that they are thoroughly dry before storage.

Unusual growing ideas

Intercrop: The plants need a lot of space when mature, but not when young. Use this vacant space by interplanting a fast maturing crop such as lettuce.

Spring Greens: This is over-wintered Cabbage, planted very close together (only 6″ apart). When the plants begin to touch, every other plant is harvested and eaten. The remaining plants are left to head up to full size

Sprouting: If you save all of the seed from 5 plants, you will have far more seed than you actually need for planting. A good way to use this is to sprout it like Alfalfa. Cabbage sprouts have a nice spicy Cabbage flavor and are very nutritious.

Micro-greens: The seed can also be used to grow tasty micro-green salads materials (see Micro-greens).

Varieties: There are a number of different kinds of Cabbage, grown for different purposes and at different times. Red, green, almost white, curly, crinkled, spherical, lettuce-like, summer, autumn, winter, mammoth and tiny. The most important differences are; the time of harvest, time needed to maturity, length of time they can be stored and their hardiness. If you choose the wrong variety for your needs, it may not respond as you would like.

Early: 60 to 80 days Copenhagen Market, Early Jersey Wakefield, Primo

Mid-season: 80 to 90 days Brunswick, Early Flat Dutch

Late: 90 to 110 days (these are bigger, have thicker leaves and store better) Danish Ballhead, Late Flat Dutch

Savoy: Very hardy and attractive, it is usually grown over the winter. Melissa, Best-of-All

Red: These are the least hardy, but are the most appealing visually. Red Danish

Cooking: A home grown cabbage, grown in cold weather and cooked really well, can be very good.

Cabbage, Chinese
Brassica rapa var pekinensis
Syn *B. pekinensis*

Introduction: This species is actually more closely related to the Turnip than the Cabbage. It is a very important vegetable in China (just as Cabbage was in Northern Europe) and in some poorer areas, it still makes up 80% of the vegetable diet. It has been grown in the cooler parts of eastern Asia for over 1500 years, but has only recently become popular in the West.

The name Chinese Cabbage is a fairly loose term, that may be applied to several different crops and causes some confusion. This is the sub-species that produces the densely packed heading varieties (as well as some non-heading types).

Chinese Cabbage has a reputation of being rather difficult to grow. This is because of its tendency to bolt prematurely if exposed to almost any kind of interruption in its growth.

Nutritional content:
Similar to Cabbage

Soil
pH 6.0 to 7.0
Chinese Cabbage prefers a rich, moist, well drained soil with lots of nitrogen (it is a fairly hungry crop). It dislikes acid soil.

Soil preparation: Incorporate 2″ of compost or aged manure into the top 6″ of soil, before planting. If the soil is acidic add lime to raise the pH.

About Chinese Cabbage

Seed facts
Germ temp: 45 to 80° F
Germ time: 3 to 10 days
5 days at 50° F
3 days at 59° F
2 days at 68° F
1 day at 77° F * Optimum
Germination percentage: 75+
Viability: 5 to 9 yrs
Weeks to grow transplants: 4 to 6

Planning facts
Hardiness: Hardy
Ease of growing: Difficult
Growing temp: 60 to 65° F (ideal)
Plants per person: 2
Plants per sq ft: 1.2
Transplants:
Start: 2 weeks before last frost
Plant out: 2 weeks after last frost
Direct sow: 4 wks before last frost
Sow a fall crop: 8 to 10 weeks before first fall frost
Time to harvest: 60 to 100 days

Harvest facts
Yield per plant: 1 to 2 lb
Yield per sq ft: 1 to 3 lb sq ft

Planning

Where: In cool weather Chinese Cabbage should be planted in a sunny location that is sheltered from cold winds. Don't plant it where any other Brassicas were grown the year before.

When: Chinese Cabbage is notorious for bolting in warm weather. This may be caused by the young plant being exposed to cold weather, exposure to long days (over 14 hours), or some kind of interruption in growth (lack of water, transplanting, high temperatures). This tendency to bolt varies according to cultivar, some are much more prone to it than others. It is the reason Chinese Cabbage is usually grown as a fall crop.

Spring: This plant can be made to work as a spring crop, by starting it indoors, but don't say you haven't been warned. Plant the seeds 2 to 4 weeks before the last spring frost and plant out 2 weeks after it. It is hardy enough to be planted much earlier than this (it can survive temperatures as low as 20° F), but the danger of vernalization and subsequent bolting is very great. It also helps to use an early maturing variety, that doesn't bolt easily.

Fall: Chinese Cabbage does much better as a fall crop, because it is less likely to bolt in the shorter days. It is started in mid to late summer, 2 to 3 months before the first fall frost.

Planting

Indoors: Chinese Cabbage doesn't really like transplanting (it may contribute to bolting) so plant it in cell packs or soil blocks and be very careful. If the weather gets very cold after planting out, protect the young plants with cloches, until temperatures are well above 50° F.

Outdoors: Chinese Cabbages can be direct sown in mid summer, for a fall crop. Sow the seeds ½″

deep and about 3″ to 4″ apart. Start thinning when the plants have 4 to 5 leaves. As plants get bigger you can harvest thin, to leave the plants at their final spacing of 10″ to 12″. Use the thinnings in the kitchen. It can also be started in an outdoor nursery bed, though it doesn't like transplanting very much (it must be young to transplant successfully).

Spacing: Plant in offset rows across the bed, 10″ to 12″ apart each way.

Care: Chinese Cabbage will only be successful if it is able to grow without any interruption. If it doesn't get everything it needs it will probably bolt.

Weeds: Keep down weeds while the plants are young, as they don't compete for nutrients very well.

Watering: If this shallow rooted crop is to get all the water it needs, it must have evenly moist soil. Never let it dry out.

Blanching: The heads are sometimes bound together with string (or tape) to blanch the inside leaves and make their flavor milder. If you do this make sure you don't trap water or slugs inside the plant.

Mulch: This is helpful to keep down weeds, conserve moisture and keep the plants cleaner.

Pests: Most of the pests and diseases that attack Cabbages may also attack these plants. If anything, they are even more susceptible. See **Cabbage** for more on these.

Harvest
When: Gather the heads as they start to firm up and feel solid to the touch. Given enough time some heads may get quite large. In warm weather they don't stay in peak condition for very long, so take them when they are ready. In winter they stay in good condition for much longer, sometimes several weeks. If they start to bolt, you can still eat them and should do so promptly (or you can use the resulting flower stalks instead).

How: You can gather individual leaves any time, but this may reduce the final yield. A better idea is to harvest thin every other plant in a bed, leaving the rest to grow to full size.

If you leave a few leaves attached to the root when harvesting, it may put out new shoots and grow up again. This can be a good way to extend the harvest, especially in winter when it would be hard to get another crop established.

Flower stem: If a plant gets away from you completely and sends up a flower stalk, harvest it before the flower buds open and use it like Broccoli. It will then make more attempts to flower and all can be eaten.

Storage: Store the heads in the refrigerator for up to 2 weeks. They may keep for several months in a root cellar at 34 to 38° F, with 90 to 95% humidity. You can also store them in the ground, under a cold frame filled with straw

Seed saving: This is done in pretty much the same way as for Turnip and Cabbage. It is cross-pollinated by insects and will cross with any other *B. rapa* crop (which includes Turnip, Broccoli Raab and Pak Choy) as well as other Chinese Cabbage varieties. You should save the seed from at least 6 plants to ensure some genetic variability.

These plants will produce more seed than you need for propagation. The surplus can be used for growing cut and come again salad greens and micro-greens, or for sprouting like Alfalfa.

Varieties: This is another crop where F1 hybrids are generally superior and so open pollinated varieties are disappearing from seed catalogs. Some varieties have been bred to be less day length sensitive and these do well as a spring crop. Chinese Cabbage can be roughly divided into three different types.

Cylindrical heading: Michihli, Jade Pagoda F1, Green Rocket F1, Monument F1

Round heading: The heading types do best in cool conditions.

Orient Express, Nozaki Early, China Express F1, Two Seasons F1,

Non-heading: These can stand more heat or cold than the heading types. They are also less prone to bolting. Most are open pollinated, but they are not so readily available.

Santo, Hiroshimana

Tyfon is a cross between a Chinese Cabbage and a Turnip. It grows very quickly and is most often used as a green manure. It can also be used as a food crop however, especially as a mild flavored cut and come again salad crop.

Cooking: These species are commonly used in Chinese cooking, for stir-fries, soups and more. They should only be very lightly cooked, by steaming or stir-frying. They are also good raw in salads and sandwiches.

Pak Choy, Bok Choy
Brassica rapa var chinensis

This ancient crop has been grown in China for over 7000 years. It is sometimes known as Loose Leaf Chinese Cabbage, because it doesn't form a tight head. Generally these types can be identified by the characteristic broad white midribs on their leaves.

This crop is exceptionally rich in beta-carotene (much more than Cabbage), which gives it powerful anti-cancer properties.

Pak Choy is cultivated in much the same way as Chinese Cabbage. Like that crop is grows best as a fall or over-wintering, crop. It isn't as temperamental as the above, but is still prone to bolting in warm weather.

Stages of use: This versatile and fast growing plant can be eaten at various stages of growth. It can be sown quite densely (1″ apart) and then gradually harvest thinned.

The first thinning takes place after all the seeds have germinated and evens out the plants. These seedlings are the first harvest and can be used in salads.

Thin the plants again (to 2″ to 3″ apart) when they only have a couple of leaves and no thickened midrib. These are good raw in salads. They are so good at this stage, that they are sometimes grown purely as a cut and come again crop.

When the larger seedlings reach 5″ to 6″ tall and have 5 or 6 leaves, thin them yet again. This time to their final spacing of 4″ to 8″ (depending upon variety). These larger thinnings are also very good.

The next harvest consists of the mature, fully grown plants.

If any plants bolt prematurely you can eat the flower stems like Broccoli (before the flowers open). If the flowers have already opened, you can let them produce seed and start the cycle all over again.

Varieties: These vary considerably, in their tolerance of heat and cold, so choose the variety carefully. Not many varieties are available in the west.

Pac Choi, Joi Choi, Ching Chiang, Tatsoi (try saying those names quickly).

Flowering Purple Pak Choy: This variety is grown for its edible flower stems, which are used like Broccoli. It is usually sown in fall, for a winter, or early spring crop.

Mizuna
Brassica rapa var japonica

This Japanese biennial is very popular in its native land. It is a versatile plant, hardy enough to be grown as a cold weather green vegetable, but also tolerant of warm weather and resistant to bolting. It stays edible for a long time and doesn't get tough or highly pungent, as many Brassicas do. These virtues put Mizuna on my list of indispensable, low work green vegetables.

Mizuna has a milder flavor than most Mustards and is generally quite bland. It is a great addition to salads and is found in most commercial salad mixes. The flower stems are also edible.

There are several types of Mizuna, some are more tender and mildly flavored than others.

Other species
There are yet more crops that have been derived from *B. rapa* in Asia, Choy Sum, Mibuna and more. Most are grown as described above and their uses are similar.

Carrot
Daucus carota var sativus

This cool season biennial was probably first domesticated somewhere in the region of Afghanistan. It didn't get its familiar orange color until it arrived in Holland however. As you probably know the orange color is caused by carotene (a precursor of vitamin A), so the redder the root the more nutritious it is.

Carrots are a great crop for those seeking greater self-sufficiency. They are very nutritious, don't take up much space, are highly productive, store well and can be left in the ground for months.

Nutritional content:
Carrots are famous for their high content of beta carotene, which the body converts into vitamin A (it is also a powerful antioxidant). They are also a good source of potassium and contain calcium pectate, which can lower blood cholesterol. Eating 4 raw carrots daily has been known to reduce blood cholesterol level by 10% in only 4 weeks.

Soil:
pH 6.5 - 7.0
The ideal soil is a light, well-aerated, sandy loam. It should be free of stones, well drained, rich in humus and fairly neutral (they don't like acid soil).

The soil makes a big difference in how well Carrot will grow. The most critical factor is porosity; a loose soil can increase the size of the roots by as much as 100%. They don't like heavy clay, or compacted soils of any kind.

About Carrot
Seed facts
Germ temp: 45 (60 to 70) 85° F
Germ time: 7 to 21 days
50 days / 41° F
17 days / 50° F
10 days / 59° F
7 days / 68° F
6 days / 77° F * Optimum
6 days / 86° F
Seed viability: 2 to 5 years
Germination percentage: 50%+

Planning facts
Hardiness: Hardy
Ease of growing: Moderate
Growing temp: 55 (60 to 70) 75° F
Plants per person: 100
Plants per sq ft: 16
Direct sow: On last frost date
Fall crop: Plant 8 to 10 wks before first fall frost
Time to harvest: 70 to 180 days

Harvest facts
Yield per plant: 2 to 6 oz
Yield per sq ft: 1 to 2 lb per sq ft

Soil preparation: Prepare the soil by loosening it to a depth of 10″ (minimum) and removing any large stones (these may cause forking) and other debris. Incorporate organic matter (compost or aged manure), wood ashes or greensand (for potassium), colloidal phosphate or bone meal (for phosphorus) and kelp (for trace elements).

Though aged manure is good for Carrots, you should never use fresh manure, as it may cause them to fork. The excess nitrogen may also cause them to grow hairy feeder roots. If you must use fresh manure, then add it the previous fall so it can age over the winter.

If your soil is heavy, or compacted, the best solution is to double dig, incorporating lots of organic matter and then make raised beds. If this is too much work, you could grow your carrots in narrow trenches, filled with a special soil mix. If even this is too much, you could use a short stubby variety.

An easy way to ensure a good soil for Carrots is to precede them with Potatoes. The soil will have been heavily amended and deeply dug and any organic matter will be nicely aged. They can also follow Brassicas, or any other crop that was heavily manured.

Planning

Where: Carrots need full sun for best production, though they may do okay in part shade. They also like a fairly warm soil.

Crop rotation: Don't plant them where any member of the *Apiaceae* family has grown in the last 3 years.

When: It is possible to have Carrots year round if you plan carefully. They prefer fairly cool growing conditions and the conventional wisdom says they get bitter or acrid in hot weather (above 80° F). However I have left spring sown Touchon carrots in the ground right through the summer and they were excellent (the last few still are and it is November as I write this). A lot depends upon the variety.

Spring: Plant your first carrots as soon as the soil is ready to be worked in spring, perhaps 3 or 4 weeks before the last spring frost. You can start them a few weeks earlier, if you plant them under cloches. Just be careful they don't get so big they get vernalized.

Autumn: Fall Carrots should be sown from mid to late summer (a minimum of 8 to 10 weeks before the first frost) to give them plenty of time to mature before it gets too cold.

Winter: In mild climates the fall sown Carrots will continue to grow right through the winter. They must be started early though, so they are almost mature by the time the first frost hits. They will then continue growing right through the winter. If they are too small when cold weather arrives, they will simply sit in the ground until spring and will then bolt.

Make one large planting for winter use, as you will be eating them for months.

Succession sowing: Carrots are in demand for the kitchen at all times, so it's a good idea to succession sow them regularly, every 4 to 6 weeks. They stay in the ground in usable condition for a while, especially in winter.

Planting

Indoors: There is nothing to stop you starting Carrots indoors, in cell packs or soil blocks, but I can't think of a reason why you would.

Outdoors: A seedbed for Carrots should have a fairly fine tilth and no large stones or other debris. The seeds are pretty slow to germinate (1 to 3 weeks), which means you have to keep the soil moist for quite a long period. To make things worse, by the time the seeds germinate there is usually a healthy crop of weeds to deal with. See below for ways to handle them.

Broadcasting: You can broadcast the seeds ½″ apart and then cover them with a thin ⅛″ to ¼″ layer of soil. If your topsoil has a tendency to crust, you may want to use a mix of sifted soil and compost.

The main thing to remember when broadcasting is to sow the seeds at the right density. Beginners usually plant too thickly, which wastes seed and necessitates some tedious hand thinning.

Sowing Carrot seed is tricky because it is so small. You might try mixing the small seeds with sand, to make it easier to distribute them evenly. Pelleted seed is supposed to make it easier to get the right spacing, but I have never used it.

Rows: I favor planting short rows of Carrots across the bed. It wastes less seed, they are easier to thin and it is easier to deal with weeds.

Scrape ¼″ to ½″ deep furrows with a hoe and sow the seed at roughly half the desired spacing. Then close up the furrows (preferably with the same soil and compost mix used to cover the broadcast seeds).

Some people mix a little Radish seed in with the Carrot seed, to mark the rows and break up any soil crust.

Care of seed beds

Watering: It is crucial that the seedbed be watered regularly until all of the seeds have germinated. A general rule is to allow 50% of the surface of the bed to dry out and then water again.

Don't water too heavily, or the light seeds may be washed around, resulting in an uneven stand, with bare patches and very dense patches.

In hot weather you can reduce the frequency of watering (and save water) by temporarily covering the soil with burlap or cardboard. This keeps the soil cool and slows evaporation. Of course it must be removed as soon as the seedlings begin to emerge (ideally just before).

Pre-emergence weeding:

Because Carrot seedlings take so long to emerge, you usually have a problem with weed seedlings. There are a few ways to avoid a lot of tedious hand weeding.

A few days before you estimate the seedlings will start to emerge, you can lightly scrape a spring rake across the bed to kill any plants that have already emerged. This will give your soon-to-emerge seedlings a slight head start on the weeds.

A less invasive pre-emergence weeding technique is flame weeding. The only problem with this is that you need a special flame-weeding torch (and fuel). A couple of days before the seedlings emerge, you quickly (you don't want to burn the soil surface) move a flame across the bed, heating and killing all of the newly emerged weed seedlings. A significant benefit of this method is that the soil isn't disturbed, so no new weed seeds are brought to the surface, where they would germinate.

You can also sow seeds under paper tape. The seed is sown in rows in the usual way. The rows are then covered with a strip of opaque paper, such as cash register or drywall tape. This is weighted down with soil, to keep it in place. A day or so before you expect the seedlings to emerge, you remove the paper, which exposes any weed seedlings that have already germinated. These will be elongated and chlorotic from the darkness and will die when exposed to strong sunlight. This leaves a weed free strip of soil for your seedlings to emerge into. The areas between the strips are hoed in the usual way.

Spacing: The right spacing depends on the fertility of the soil, the type of Carrot and the size of the root you want. A wider spacing results in larger roots).

5″ (poor soil)
3″ (good soil)
1½″ (excellent soil)
1″ (Baby carrots)

Care

Prompt weeding and thinning are the keys to growing good carrots. Take care of these tasks and you should succeed, neglect them and you may well fail. Happily both of these tasks can be done at the same time.

Thinning: After all the seedlings have germinated and are growing well, you will have to thin them. If they are packed too closely together they simply won't produce swollen roots.

The earlier you thin (and weed) the easier it will be. The initial thinning is done when the seedlings are about 2″ tall and should leave the plants about an inch apart. If you have a large area to thin, this can be done with a wire rake (careful!) Simply rake out excess plants.

A second thinning (and weeding) should be done 2 to 4 weeks later. This time you thin to the desired spacing by hand. Some gardeners leave this last thinning until the carrots have begun to size up and then eat them. However this may damage the remaining plants, or attract the dreaded Carrot Rust Fly.

It is important to remove all of the uprooted plants from the area after thinning, as the smell of damaged foliage can attract the Carrot Rust Fly. Ideally you thin on cool cloudy days, or late evening and water afterward to reduce the smell of Carrot.

Weeding: If weeds are not removed promptly they will quickly smother the sparsely leafed seedlings. Your first priority must be to weed (and thin) the newly emerged plants. Weeds will have to be removed by hand from broadcast beds. Row plantings can be hoed if widely spaced, though some hand weeding is usually needed also.

Water: Carrots need a steady and even supply of moisture for good growth.

Too little water may result in excessively hairy roots (produced to search for water), or woody roots with marked rings.

Too much water may cause the roots to split, encourage too much top growth or result in poorly flavored roots.

You might want to give the plants extra water when the roots start to size up, as this can boost yields considerably.

Mulch: This conserves moisture and keeps down weeds. It also covers the shoulders of the root, preventing them turning green and inedible from exposure to light. It may also help to prevent them being heaved by frost.

Problems

Root fail to size up: You may have tried to grow Carrots and ended up with lush foliage, but only small spindly roots. This happens when the plant is growing in less than ideal conditions. It produces enough food to survive, but doesn't make enough of a surplus to store in the root. This may be caused by competition from weeds or other carrots (you neglected to thin sufficiently), insufficient light or water, or from an inadequate supply of nutrients.

Splitting: This is usually caused by irregular watering, too wet, too dry, too wet.

Forking: This is generally caused by fresh manure, or stony soil.

Bolting: Carrots are biennials and don't naturally flower until their second year. However they may bolt if they get vernalized. This happens when a root is sufficiently large (more than ¼" diameter) and is exposed to temperatures below 50° F for a period of two weeks. When warm days arrive it thinks winter is over and flowers.

Deficiency: A deficiency of boron or manganese may cause the center of the carrot to turn black.

Pests

Carrot Rust Fly (*Psila rosae*): This is easily the worst pest of carrots. The larvae (small maggots) tunnel into the root, causing rust colored lesions and rendering the root inedible. In some areas they make it almost impossible to grow Carrots without protection.

The first line of defense against this pest is hygiene. The flies are said to be able to detect the smell of damaged Carrot foliage from more than a mile away. Keep thinning and weeding (which bruises the foliage) to a minimum and never leave the foliage lying on the ground. Don't leave the remains of a Carrot crop in the ground right through the winter, as it can mean a big increase in the incidence of Carrot rust fly. Always dig and compost old carrots.

If the fly is severe some kind of barrier is probably the best way to go. Row covers are the commonest solution to this problem, but it's said that a simple plastic screen, 30" to 36" high, around the plants will work just as well. Apparently the  flies always stay close to the ground and will try to go around the screen, but they won't go over it (so long as the bed is no more than 36" wide).

There are two generations of flies each year, the first in late spring and another in late summer. It is possible to avoid them both by carefully timing the planting and harvesting.

Four rows of onions, to one row of carrots, is said to disguise their smell, as is a mulch of fresh grass, or fresh sawdust.

There are now some Carrot Fly resistant varieties available. Apparently these work best if some non-resistant Carrots are sown next to them, to act as a trap crop.

Other pests: Aphids, Nematodes, Carrot Weevils, Wireworms. We all know that cartoon rabbits love carrots; well gophers, groundhogs and deer do too.

Harvest

When: Start pulling the roots as soon as they are large enough to be worthwhile. The larger rooted plants tend to give themselves away by having darker foliage.

In the case of Carrots, small isn't necessarily beautiful. Immature carrots are the most tender, but generally have little flavor, as they haven't had the chance to store much sugar (they may even be quite acrid). Commercial baby carrots are really just varieties with naturally small roots, planted closely together. They are still harvested when mature.

Larger Carrots are sweeter and better flavored than small ones, but after they get over an inch in diameter they may start to get woody (again a lot depends on the variety). Mature roots are often a deeper orange color, which indicates that they contain more carotene.

How: If you plan on harvesting a large quantity of roots, you should water the soil beforehand to loosen it. In light soil you can simply pull up the roots by gently tugging on the tops. If you do this in heavy soil the tops will simply break off. You have to loosen them with a fork before pulling them. Any carrot debris remaining after the harvest should be removed and composted. Never leave it on the ground near the plants, as the smell of the damaged foliage may attract the Rust Fly.

Some people say you should start your harvest at one end of the bed and work your way down, rather than harvest thinning. I tend to pull the biggest roots as I need them and leave the rest to grow on. It works for me, but my garden isn't really troubled by Carrot Rust Flies (at least not yet).

If you aren't going to eat the roots quickly, you should remove all but 1″ of the tops, as these drain moisture from the root. If you are going to store the roots for any length of time, you should leave them in the sun for several hours, to kill the root hairs. Any damaged roots should be used immediately, as they won't store well. Don't wash any Carrots you intend to store.

Storage: The best place to store Carrots is in the ground. They keep better and it is a lot less work. In mild climates they will continue to grow through the winter and slowly get bigger. You just harvest them as needed. In colder climates the tops will die back when cold weather hits. When this happens cover them with 6″ to 12″ of mulch (this needs to be deep to prevent the ground from freezing).

The roots actually get sweeter in cold weather, as some of their starch is converted into sugar. You must dig them before growth starts again in spring, as this will make them woody and inedible. If you can't store them, then at least use them for juice, rather than wasting them

Mice can sometimes be a problem with in-ground storage (especially under mulch). If this is a problem you might try covering the bed with a wire mesh screen, before laying down the mulch.

It is possible to store carrots for up to 6 months in a root cellar, at 32 to 40° F and 90% humidity. Put the roots in a garbage can, or a wooden box. Make alternate layers of damp sand (or sawdust or peat moss) and carrots. Make sure the roots don't touch each other, or they may rot.

You can store Carrots in a plastic bag in the fridge for weeks.

Unusual growing ideas
Winter Carrots: French market gardeners used to grow Carrots right through the winter in the harsh climate around Paris. They did it by planting them on hotbeds of warm manure, covered with cold frames.

Giant Carrots: If you want to grow a giant carrot (why?), do it in a section of 4″ drainpipe, filled with a specially prepared mix of compost, soil and sand. Water it frequently.

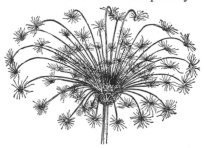

Seed saving: Carrot is a biennial, so stores food in its first year and flowers and produces seed the following year. Select some of your very best roots for seed production. Never gather seed from early flowering plants, uproot and get rid of them, before they have a chance to pollinate the rest.

In harsh climates you will have to protect the roots over the winter as described previously. Replant them in the spring and wait for them to flower.

The flowers are cross-pollinated by insects and will cross with any other Carrots (or Wild Carrot, Queen Annes Lace) within a half mile. The best seed is produced on the primary umbel, which is the first to ripen. The second umbel is pretty good too, so take it from these two. When the seed heads are ripe, cut them and leave in a paper grocery bag to dry thoroughly.

Varieties: There is considerable variation in carrots, some are 2″ spheres, others are huge tapered cylinders 10″ or more in length. Some red varieties are extremely rich in vitamin A. A few rare varieties are purple, red, yellow or even white. There are now quite a few hybrid Carrot varieties available, bred for uniformity, high carotene content, resistance to Carrot Rust Fly, or for extra sweetness.

The variety of carrot you choose will depend upon the soil, climate and the time of year you are planting. Some varieties do much better in cold, others do better in heat, some store better in the ground.

The most important factor in growing sweet carrots is genetic; some varieties are naturally much sweeter than others. If you want to grow sweet and tasty carrots, you are much more likely to be successful if you start with a sweet and tasty variety. A high quality cultivar, can also help you to overcome some of the other problems associated with growing Carrots.

Nantes: These long cylindrical varieties are some of the best flavored, but don't keep very well.

Touchon is my all time favorite variety. It is sweet, tender, very finely flavored and doesn't get woody.

Merida is a bolt resistant overwintering Carrot that can be planted in fall, for harvesting the following summer.

Scarlet Nantes

Danvers: These are also sweet.
Danvers Half Long

Chantenay: These are not as tasty as the above, but do better in cold soils and over-winter well.
Kuroda
Red Cored Chantenay

Imperator: These long carrots are bred for commercial use and are the carrots found in supermarkets. They store well and can be very tasty, but need a deep soil. They may be a cross of Chantenay and Nantes.
Gold Pak

Round: These are good for poor shallow soils and under cloches, but they don't usually have very good flavor.
Thumbelina

High vitamin A:
Juwarot, A-Plus F1, Healthmaster Beta III

Carrot Fly resistant:
Flyaway F1, Resistafly F1

Cooking: I don't have a good Carrot recipe because in my house no one wants to eat them cooked. They are almost always eaten raw.

Cauliflower
Brassica oleracea botrytis group

Introduction: Cauliflower was probably first grown somewhere in the Eastern Mediterranean. It is considered to be the most refined of the Brassicas, more of a delicacy than a staple. It isn't as nutritious as its cousin the Broccoli, or as productive.

This isn't a very forgiving crop and is generally considered to be the most difficult of the Brassicas to grow. It must have exactly the right growing conditions or it won't do well. It doesn't like extreme heat or cold and doesn't like being too wet or too dry. Cauliflower is even harder to grow organically. It is vulnerable to the legion of pests that attack the Cabbages and can be quite a test of the organic growers skill. However if you give it exactly what it wants, it isn't too hard to be successful.

Nutritional content:
A good source of vitamin C and potassium. It has the same valuable anti-cancer properties as the other Brassicas.

Soil
pH 6.0 - 7.0
Cauliflower must have rapid and uninterrupted growth if it is to perform well. It isn't particular as to what type of soil it grows in, so long as it is fertile and moisture retentive, with lots of organic matter. It doesn't like saline soil and is sensitive to a deficiency of micronutrients, especially molybdenum and boron.

About Cauliflower

Seed facts
Germ temp: 45 (55 to 85) 85° F
Germ time: 5 to 10 days
20 days / 50° F
10 days / 59° F
6 days / 68° F
5 days / 77° F * Optimum
5 days / 86° F
Seed viability: 5 to 10 years
Germination percentage: 75+
Weeks to grow transplant: 5 to 6

Planning facts
Hardiness: Half hardy
Ease of growing: Difficult
Growing temp: 45 (60 to 65) 75° F
Plants per person: 5
Plants per sq ft: ½
Transplants:
Start: 6 weeks before last frost
Plant out: on last frost date (to 2 wks after)
Direct sow 2 wks before last frost
Start fall crop: 12 to 14 weeks before first fall frost
Time to harvest: 60 to 160 days
45 to 80 days from transplant

Harvest facts
Yield per plant: 1 to 2 lb
Yield per sq ft: ½ to 1 lb sq ft

Soil Preparation: Prepare the soil by digging deeply and incorporating 2″ of compost or aged manure. If you are organized you could add fresh manure the previous fall. It does well if planted 2 weeks after incorporating a winter cover crop.

If the soil isn't very fertile, add colloidal phosphate (for phosphorus), wood ashes (for potassium) and kelp meal (to supply trace elements).

More than most Brassicas, Cauliflower doesn't like acid soils, as they can encourage Clubroot and make boron less available. Add lime if necessary, preferably dolomitic lime, as this supplies useful magnesium as well as calcium.

Planning

Where: Cauliflower needs quite a lot of space, which rules it out of many small gardens. It grows in the cooler part of the year, so also needs full sun.

Crop rotation: Ideally it should not be planted where another Brassica has been grown in the previous 3 years.

When: Cauliflower needs a long period of mild moist weather for best growth (it heads up best at 60 to 70° F). Hot weather can cause it to bolt prematurely and become unpleasantly flavored. This limits where and when it can be grown. It does well in the Pacific Northwest as a spring-sown crop, but in most areas spring is too short. It does well in California, as a fall/winter crop, but is not quite hardy enough to survive winters elsewhere. In most places it only does well as a fall crop. This is usually easier anyway and results in larger heads

Spring: For a spring crop, Cauliflower is usually started indoors, 6 weeks before the last frost date and planted out 2 to 3 weeks before the last frost date. Transplants should have no more than 4 or 5 true leaves, as larger plants don't transplant well and may be vernalized by a cold spell. It needs to be planted early, because it needs a long period of cool weather to mature. If the weather is very cold when planting,

you might want to protect the plants with cloches, or cold frames, until it warms up.

Summer: In mild climates, or areas with very short growing seasons, it can be grown as a summer crop.

Fall: To grow a fall crop, start the seeds 12 to 14 weeks before the average first frost date and plant out 9 weeks before. You could direct sow at this time, but they would take up bed space that can be used more efficiently by other crops. The problem with a fall crop is protecting the plants from pests during their early growth.

Winter: Over wintering, Cauliflower is planted out in early September and matures the following spring. It is important to use a variety that it appropriate for the time of year.

Planting
Generally a planting of Cauliflower doesn't mature very uniformly, so you don't have to make many sowings.

Transplants: Cauliflower needs quite a long period of cool weather to mature, yet is more sensitive to cold than most Brassicas (it can be injured by frost). If you want to grow it as a spring crop this usually means starting it indoors.

Starting inside: Cauliflower doesn't really like having its root disturbed, but it is can be transplanted while small. It is sometimes planted in flats (sow the seeds 1″ apart), but it is probably better to sow in cell packs or soil blocks (plant 2 seeds to a cell and later thin to the best one). Cauliflower needs more care than other Brassicas, so you have to pamper it.

Setting out: Cauliflower is transplanted like Cabbage, up to the first true leaves. It is somewhat more finicky however, so water after planting and every day thereafter until it looks good. You might need to put on cutworm collars or Cabbage Worm disks, provide shade if it's very sunny and protect it from late frosts. It is vital that growth is uninterrupted by transplanting, as this can be enough to make it bolt.

Direct sowing: Cauliflower can also be direct sown and in some cases these have been known to mature faster than transplants. Sow the seeds ¼″ to ½″ deep, with 2 to 3 seeds in each station. Thin to the best one when they are up and growing. This is most practical in climates that provide that ideal long cool growing season, or for use as a fall crop. Of course the drawback with direct sowing is that they take up space for a long time (maybe interplant it into another crop).

Spacing: Spacing has an effect upon the final size of the head.
15″ very good soil
18″ average soil
24″ poor soil

Care

Cauliflower must have everything it needs for fast, uninterrupted growth, without any checks, otherwise it may bolt prematurely.

Weeding: The plants don't compete with weeds very well, so weed regularly while they are small. Take care if using a hoe, as the shallow roots are easily damaged (this can cause bolting too).

Water: Cauliflower needs constant moisture, so it's important to keep the soil moist at all times (lack of water can cause bolting). The most critical watering time is when the head is developing; don't let it get water stressed at this time.

Fertilization: After the plants are established and growing well, feed them with a foliar feed of compost tea. Feed them again just before they start to head up. Cauliflower is one of the crops that is most susceptible to boron deficiency (which can be caused by acid soil).

Mulch: This not only keep weeds down, it can also help to keep the soil moist and cool.

Blanching: Some varieties of Cauliflower need to be blanched to prevent their turning brown from exposure to sunlight (and developing an off flavor). This is done when the head enlarges sufficiently that it is exposed to sunlight. Simply tie the top leaves together to cover the head (loosely so they don't trap water or suffocate the head). You could also crack the leaves and tuck them over the head, or cover the head with loose leaves. You could even make a cap of aluminum foil (if you wear one too, it may help to stop them bolting).

Not all Cauliflowers need blanching; some white types are self-blanching (their leaves protect the head). I would still wear the cap though.

Pests and disease: Cauliflower is attacked by all of the usual Brassica villains, especially root maggots (see Cabbage). If pests are a big problem in your area, you might want to protect the young plants with row covers.

Harvest

When: The optimal time to harvest Cauliflower is when the head has reached full size (6″ to 8″), but while it's still tight and firm. They are good later than this though and may be used until the flower clusters turn yellowish (rather than white) and start to separate (they are said to get ricey). In warm weather the plants don't stay in optimal condition for very long, in which case it's better to start harvesting a little too early, rather than too late.

How: Cut off the entire head with a knife. If you aren't going to use it immediately, leave some leaves on to protect it in storage.

Storage: Cauliflower will stay in good condition for several weeks if stored in the refrigerator. The curds freeze very well.

Seed saving: The process is much the same as for Broccoli. Cauliflower will cross with Cabbage, Kale and any other Brassicas. This could have interesting results, but it's probably not what you want. Take seed from the best, slow bolting plants. Be aware that the curds of Cauliflower are not flower buds like those of Broccoli, but mostly only fleshy receptacles that won't develop into flowers. In fact flower development in Cauliflower can be very erratic.

Unusual growing ideas
Mini-cauliflowers: This is a relatively new way to grow cauliflowers and results in miniature heads 2″ to 3″ in diameter (ideal for one serving). It can be a very productive way to grow Cauliflower.

Use a fast maturing summer variety for this method. Direct sow 2 seeds at each station, spacing them 6″ each way. When these are all up, thin to the strongest plant and care for them as usual. The closely spaced plants compete with each other and tend to keep each other all roughly the same size.

Varieties: The choice of varieties has traditionally been quite limited in North America, as has the areas in which it grows well. Some fine European and American varieties are now available however. This is good because choosing the right variety can be a big factor in your success. You will probably need to experiment to find out what works best for you at various times of the year.

Cauliflower is another crop where F1 hybrids are completely taking over. Some of these varieties are of very high quality and are worth trying. There are also some new varieties with spectacular orange, purple and green colors, however at $3.95 for 15 seeds I won't be growing them any time soon. Cauliflower can be divided into summer and winter varieties,

according to their hardiness. I'm not sure whether it is really worth naming any open pollinated varieties because most don't seem to be available anymore.

Winter: These are the easiest Cauliflowers to grow, because they are very hardy. They are planted out in early fall and form large heads the following spring. The Walcheren types are among the best known.

Summer: These include the common American varieties such as Snowball.

Purple: These resemble a cross between Broccoli and Cauliflower. They are somewhat easier to grow than Cauliflower because they don't need blanching.

Cooking: Use the curds raw in salads.

Celery
Apium graveolens

Introduction: This cool weather biennial is native to Europe and has been used as food at least since the time of the Romans (though this was probably Leaf Celery). There are three distinct types of Celery grown as crops. Stalk Celery is the most familiar to us, in fact it is the only one most of us even recognize. There is also root Celery, usually known as Celeriac, which is popular in Eastern Europe. Lastly there is Leaf Celery (sometimes knows as Chinese Celery), which is the type most commonly used in Asia.

Celery is notorious among home gardeners as being one of the hardest crops to grow well and it definitely isn't for the beginner. It is very particular about its requirements and must have all the nutrients it needs for fast, uninterrupted growth. It also needs a constant supply of moisture and a long period of cool weather. Celery is said to be even harder to grow organically and to be a true test of the organic gardeners skill.

Nutritional content:
Celery has barely any nutritional value, it is mostly water and fiber. I guess that's why it is associated with people who are trying to lose weight. It does contain some useful phytochemicals, including apigenin, which has anti-cancer properties.

Soil
pH 6.0 - 7.0
Wild Celery naturally grows near water and this is reflected in its preference for a rich, deep, moist (but not wet), fairly acid soil, with

lots of organic matter. It is a hungry crop, requiring a lot of nitrogen, potassium and phosphorus.

About Celery

Seed facts
Germ temp: 40 (60 to 70) 85° F
Germ time: 14 to 21 days
41 days / 41° F
16 days / 50° F
12 days / 59° F
7 days / 68° F * Optimum
8 days / 77° F
Viability: 5 yrs
Germination percentage: 55%+
Weeks to grow transplants: 8 to 12

Planning facts
Hardiness: Half hardy
Ease of growing: Difficult
Growing temp: 45 (60 to 65) 75° F
Plants per person: 6
Plants per sq ft: 1 to 1½
Transplants:
Start 8 to 10 wks before last frost
Plant out 2 weeks after last frost
Direct sow: 2 wks before last frost
Fall crop: Start 3 to 4 months before first fall frost
Time to harvest: 85 to 200 days
75 to 120 days from transplant

Harvest facts
Yield per plant: 1 to 2 lb
Yield per sq ft: 2 to 10 lb sq ft

Soil preparation: Incorporate a source of organic matter to supply nitrogen and to increase its water holding capacity (use 2″ of compost or aged manure). Add a source of phosphorus (colloidal phosphate), potassium (wood ashes or greensand) and micronutrients (kelp). If the soil is heavy, or compacted, you might also think about double digging. Add lime if the soil is acid.

The traditional way to grow Celery was in trenches 12″ deep by 12″ wide. These were filled with an enriched soil mix.

Planning
Celery must be planned carefully, because it takes so long to grow to maturity from seed. Then you get a large crop all at one time. It is possible to sow it in succession, but this is even more complicated.

Where: Celery is an upright, compact plant and doesn't take up a lot of space (which is good, as it is in the ground for quite a long time). In cool climates it prefers full sun, but in hotter climates it does best with light shade. It needs quite a lot of attention, so should be sited where it can be watched closely and tended frequently.

When: Celery needs a long period (3 months) of cool temperatures (60 to 70° F) for optimal quality. Temperatures above 80° F may make it fibrous and very strongly flavored.

Spring: In areas with long cool spring weather, it can be started inside 8 to 12 weeks before the last frost. It is planted out 2 weeks after the last frost.

Fall: Celery generally does better as a fall crop, planted in mid to late summer. It then gets to mature in the cool weather of fall.

Winter: In areas with mild winters, Celery does well as a winter crop, planted in early fall.

Planting
Celery seed is small, but germinates well when fresh.

Transplants
Starting inside: Celery is usually started indoors, because it is so slow growing initially. It doesn't mind transplanting when young, so is commonly started in flats. Some people pre-soak the seed in hot (120° F) water for a half hour before planting, or in manure tea overnight.

Purists say the seed must be scattered on the surface and left uncovered, as it needs light to germinate. I'm not sure though, I haven't always done this and have still had success.

Seed sitting on the surface must be kept moist at all times, otherwise it may die. Germination may take as little as a week, or as long as three weeks. Some books say it is important that the temperature fluctuates below 60° F at night during germination. Temperatures above 80° F may inhibit germination.

The seedlings prefer a fairly cool 60° F temperature for growth. Prick out the seedlings when they have their first true leaves, as they seem to benefit from transplanting at this stage. As always, take care to keep them moist. They should take 8 to 12 weeks to reach 5″ in height, which is the ideal transplant size.

Planting out
: The seedlings should be hardened off for a few days before planting out. When transplanting make sure you keep the root ball of each plant as intact as possible.

It is important not to expose the seedling to temperatures below 50° F, as it could vernalize them. They would then react to warmer weather by bolting prematurely. If cold weather returns you will have to protect them with cloches.

Direct sowing
: Celery can be direct sown, but this is so slow it is only practical in areas with very long, cool growing seasons, such as parts of coastal California. There it can be planted in spring to mature in late summer or fall. Of course you still run into the usual problem with direct sowing; the small plants take up bed space, that might be used more profitably for other crops.

The seed should be sown as early in spring as possible. Use cloches to warm the soil and protect the young seedlings during early growth. In cold soil germination may take up to a month. Usually it is sown quite thickly and harvest thinned several times (the thinnings can be used in the kitchen).

Spacing
: The plants are normally arranged in offset rows across the bed. The spacing varies from 9″ to 12″, depending upon the fertility of the soil. Plants have been spaced as close as 6″ to get a greater quantity of smaller plants

Care

Weed: Celery needs to be kept free of weeds at all times, but especially when young.

Water: Consistent watering is the single most important factor in growing good Celery, the soil should never be allowed to dry out. This may mean watering daily in dry weather, though every other day is more usual. Water is particularly critical as harvest time approaches, because this is the time of fastest growth (plants may double in size in their last month). Lack of water at this time can result in bitter, pungent, stringy plants with hollow stems. The best way to water Celery is with a drip system or soaker hose.

Fertilization: Celery needs lots of nitrogen to produce its succulent growth, so feed weekly with compost tea or liquid Kelp.

Mulch: This helps to conserve moisture, keeps down weeds and keeps the soil cooler.

Blanching: In England Celery is often blanched to improve its flavor (this makes it milder and nuttier, as well as less fibrous). Most modern American varieties don't need this, but a few are improved by it.

When Celery is planted in close blocks, it tends to self-blanch to some extent.

The usual way to blanch Celery is to remove the outer leaves to expose the tall stems and then wrap them in 12″ wide sheets of paper (newspaper isn't used as it may adversely affect the flavor). The paper is held in place by piling soil around the plant. Soil can be used by itself, but tends to get down between the stalks. This makes them gritty and hard to clean.

In cold climates Celery is sometimes blanched and protected from frost at the same time, by placing a board to each side of a row and filling it with dried leaves or straw.

Problems: The month before harvest is the most critical time for Celery growers, as the plants are growing very rapidly. They are prone to attacks by fungus disease, or they may bolt prematurely.

Pests and Disease: Celery Leaf Spot, Carrot Fly, Celery Fly, Leaf miners, slugs and snails can all be a problem at times.

Harvest: You can harvest individual stalks of Celery as soon as they are big enough to be worthwhile. This does adversely affect the final size of the plants, but also extends the harvest time. Harvest whole plants when the stems are 8″ to 10″ tall, by cutting them down at ground level.

Storage: If you want to store Celery for any length of time, pull it up with the root attached and re-plant it in moist sand in a root cellar. It likes to be kept at 32 to 40° F and 90% humidity.

Seed Saving: Celery is a biennial and doesn't produce flowers until its second spring (it sometimes produces flowers prematurely in its first year, but you don't want to save seed from those plants). The biggest problem with saving the seed is just getting the plants to survive the winter. In mild areas they will usually do this in the ground, perhaps under a mulch to protect them from frost. In very cold areas, they will have to be dug up and stored in a root cellar until spring (See **Storage**).

Celery flowers in the spring of its second year. The plants are cross-pollinated by insects, which makes it hard to save more than one variety at a time (unless you isolate by 1000 feet or more). Save the seed from at least 6 plants to ensure genetic variability. When most of the seed is ripe on the plant, cut the entire head and dry it in a paper bag. Be aware that some fungus diseases can be seed borne.

Unusual growing ideas
Multi-planting: It is possible to plant celery in multi-plant blocks. Plant 6 seeds per cell and thin to the best 3 plants, when they have all emerged.

Varieties:
There are varieties of Celery, with green, pink, yellow or red coloration. Some of the older varieties need blanching, but most modern ones are self-blanching.

Golden Self-Blanching
Giant Pascal
Giant Red: Has red stalks
Utah 52:70R Improved

Cooking:

Celery and Potato soup
3 tbsp olive oil
3 cups celery
1½ cups green onions
½ potatoes
½ tsp salt
½ cup soymilk
1 tsp salt
⅛ tsp black pepper
½ tsp thyme

Chop the celery stalks and tops finely (peel the stalks if they are stringy), then saute them with the green onions for 2 minutes. Add the potatoes, Thyme, salt, pepper and 3 cups of water. Cook for 15 minutes in a covered pot until the vegetables are tender. Allow the soup to cool slightly, add the soymilk and puree it until smooth in a blender. Reheat and serve.

Leaf Celery
As the name suggests, this type of Celery is grown for its leaves, rather than the stems or roots. It is almost identical to Wild Celery and has the vigor of a wild plant.

Leaf Celery is very popular in China, where it is grown as a flavoring for soups and many other dishes. I'm not going to devote much space to it here, because its cultivation is pretty much the same as for Celery (though it is not so demanding and is easier to grow). Be conscientious about keeping the soil moist, as this not only affects growth, but also its flavor. Well-watered plants are milder and better flavored.

Varieties: There aren't many available, normally it is just Leaf Celery.

Parcel: The only cultivar I know of. It actually looks very much like Parsley (hence the name). I believe it is a very old variety from Germany. It is easy to grow and has lived for several years in my garden.

Cooking: The leaves and stems are used as flavoring for soups and other dishes. Small amounts may be added to salads, but it is quite strongly flavored.

Celeriac
Apium graveolens var *rapaceum*

Introduction: This is the same species as Celery, but is grown for its roots (actually a swollen stem base, or corm) rather than its stems. It has pretty much the same requirements as Celery and is grown in the same way. It is easier to grow though, because you don't really care about the quality of the stems. The main edible part is the root.

Nutritional content: The root contains carbohydrates, as well as apigenin, which has anti-cancer properties.

Soil: The same as Celery.

Planning
When: Celeriac needs about 100 days of cool (60 to 70)° F weather to grow to perfection. If there is a long period of cool weather in spring it can be grown at this time (this works better than Celery). However it usually does best as a fall crop.

Where: A sunny spot is best.

Planting

Indoors: Unlike most root crops Celeriac can be started indoors. See Celery for instructions on raising seedlings. Start spring transplants 10 weeks before the last frost date. For a fall crop, it is started in the greenhouse or nursery bed, in mid summer. Transplant it to its permanent position 8 to 10 weeks later.

Outdoors: Celeriac produces a better root system when direct sown (most of its roots are within a couple of inches of the surface). For a spring crop this is done when hard frosts are past. For a fall crop it is done in mid summer. Simply scatter the seed on the soil surface and keep moist until it germinates. Thin when all of the plants have emerged and they have a set of true leaves.

Spacing

Space the plants 12″ to 15″ apart in the beds, depending upon the soil.

Care

To produce the best roots Celeriac needs to grow quickly, without a check in its growth. To do this it must get everything it needs.

Watering: Keep the soil moist at all times.

Fertilization: If the soil isn't very fertile, give the plants a liquid feed every two weeks.

Mulch: This is useful to conserve moisture and suppress weeds (hoeing can damage the shallow roots.)

Pruning: Any new shoots that appear on the root should be removed, as you want the plant to devote all of its energy to sizing up the root, not growing more foliage.

Pests: These are the same as for Celery.

Harvest: You can gather the first roots when only 2″ in diameter. They start to expand rapidly at this point, so the longer you wait the bigger they will get. However harvesting some roots while young does extend the harvest season.

Storage: The roots are best left in the ground under mulch, if this is possible. Otherwise dig them and store in a cool place at 32 to 40° F.

Seed saving: As for Celery.

Varieties: The choice of varieties is very limited.
Brilliant
Monarch

Cooking: The green leafy tops and stems can be used as flavoring. The knobby root looks a little formidable, but is easily peeled to leave a tasty white core. They are most often used in soups or like Potato, but they are also good raw in salads.

Celtuce
Stem Lettuce
Lactuca sativa var angustata

Introduction: If you know your botanical Latin you have probably noticed that Celtuce is actually a kind of Lettuce. Instead of being grown for its leaves (which are edible, if not always very good), it is grown for its succulent edible flower stems, which are supposed to resemble Celery (Cel - tuce Celery - Lettuce). It has been a popular crop in China for a long time, but was only introduced into America by Burpee in the 1940's. This explains why the name sounds like something an ad agency came up with (it probably is).

Though rarely grown in American gardens, Celtuce is a fast growing and useful plant and deserves be more widely grown. It makes a virtue of the problem faced by many Lettuce growers; that of bolting.

It has pretty much the same cultivation requirements as Lettuce, so I won't go into great detail here.

Nutritional content:
The leaves are richer in vitamin C than Lettuce.

Seed facts: Same as Lettuce

Soil
pH 6.0 - 6.8
Celtuce isn't too fussy as to soil, but does best in a fertile, moisture retentive one. It likes compost or aged manure.

Planning

When: The plant is treated in much the same way as Lettuce and like that plant it doesn't do well in hot weather.

Spring: In spring it is started indoors 4 weeks before the last frost date and planted out a month later.

Fall: In hot climates Celtuce is usually grown as a fall crop. Plant two months before the first fall frost (you can succession sow).

Winter: This hardy plant can be grown for winter use in mild areas.

Succession sow: In spring you may be able to make several succession sowings (every 2 weeks) before the weather gets too warm. Start succession sowing again, 2 months before the first frost.

Planting

Indoors: Celtuce transplants are grow in the same way as Lettuce. Plant the seedlings out when they are about 4 weeks old, which should be around the last frost date. They should be about 2″ tall and have 3 true leaves by this time.

Outdoors: Sow the seeds ¼″ to ½″ deep, about 6 weeks before the last frost date. When they are a couple of inches tall, thin the seedlings to stand 12″ apart (use the thinnings in salads.)

Spacing:
Rows: Space them 12″ apart in the rows, with 18″ between the rows.

Beds: Space them 12″ apart, in offset rows.

Care

Weeds: The young plants are vulnerable to weeds, so keep them well weeded. They are quite shallow rooted so be careful with the hoe.

Water: In warm weather the leaves can get too bitter to use. This may be caused by lack of moisture, so keep the soil moist at all times. Lack of water can also encourage premature bolting.

Feeding: Give the plants compost tea or liquid kelp at about 30 days and again at 60 days. You want the plants to grow as large as possible before they bolt, so you will get larger stems and more edible material.

Pests: Celtuce is affected by the same pests as Lettuce but generally seems to be less bothered. Slugs are the main problem.

Harvest: You can gather the very young leaves for salads, but the older leaves are often very bitter. Use the thinnings for salad material. Don't take leaves from plants you are growing for their stalks, they should be putting all their energy into producing large and juicy stems. These are harvested when about 1″ diameter. Use as soon as possible as they don't store very well.

Harvest for greens in 60 days, or stems in 90 days.

Seed saving: As for **Lettuce**.

Cooking: Peel the stems to remove the bitter outer layer. The heart of the stalk is good raw in salads. They can also be used in stir-fries and soups.

Chard
Beta vulgaris var cicla

Introduction: Chard is the same species as Beet, but is grown for its foliage rather than the root. It is one of the easiest vegetables to grow, very productive, little bothered by pests or disease and resistant to both heat and cold. I highly recommend it, as an almost foolproof cool weather potherb for the small garden.

Chard is cultivated in much the same way as Beet, though it is somewhat easier to grow, as it only has to produce edible foliage.

Nutritional content:
The leaves contain large amounts of vitamins A and C, as well as calcium, phosphorus, potassium and iron. They also contain oxalic acid, which can inhibits the absorption of calcium to some degree (see **Spinach** for more on this).

Soil
pH 6.0 - 6.8
Chard has a deep, strong root system and is able to seek out the nutrients it needs, consequently it can grow well on fairly poor soil. However for highest yield it does best in a fertile garden soil, rich in humus, well drained and not too acidic.

Soil preparation: Incorporate 2″ of compost or aged manure into the top 6″ of soil. Add dolomitic lime (to raise the pH and to supply magnesium) and wood ashes (to raise the pH and supply potassium).

About Chard

Seed facts
Germ temp: 50 to 85° F
Germ time: 5 to 21 days
42 days / 41° F
16 days / 50° F
9 days / 59° F
6 days / 68° F
5 days / 77° F * Optimum
5 days / 86° F
Viability: 5 years
Germination percentage: 60%+
Weeks to grow transplants: 3 to 4

Planning facts
Hardiness: Hardy
Ease of growing: Easy
Growing temp: 45 (60 to 70) 75° F
Plants per person: 10
Plants per sq ft: 4
Transplants:
Start: 4 wks before last frost date
Plant out: on last frost date
Direct sow on the last frost date
Fall: Plant 10 to 12 wks before
first fall frost
Time to harvest: 50 to 60 days

Harvest facts
Length of harvest: up to 30 weeks
Yield per plant: 10 oz (or more)
Yield per sq ft: 2 to 8 lb sq ft

Where: Chard doesn't like heat, so in hot climates it should be grown in part shade. It is one of the most shade tolerant of common crops. In cool climates it needs full sun for maximum production of foliage.

Planting

Each "seed" is actually a cluster of flowers fused together, each containing a single seed. This is why you end up with several plants, when you plant one seed. You can gently break up these clusters and get individual seeds to plant.

The seed clusters contain a water-soluble germination inhibitor, which can be leached out by soaking the seed overnight prior to planting. Don't simply soak them in a glass of water overnight however, as they may absorb so much water, so quickly, they can be damaged. Instead they should be put on a damp paper towel, so they can absorb moisture slowly. You could take this one step further and actually pre-sprout the seeds before planting.

Transplants

Starting inside: Chard doesn't really like root disturbance, though it will tolerate it when very young. For this reason it is usually grown in cell packs, plug trays or soil blocks. Germination is quite uneven, so seeds may continue to emerge for a week or more.

Planting out: Set out the transplants on the last frost date. Don't let them get too large inside, otherwise exposure to temperatures below 50° F (for two weeks), could vernalize them. They will then bolt as soon as it gets warmer. If cold weather threatens, you could protect them with cloches or row covers.

Direct sowing

This is pretty straightforward and is the preferred method of growing Chard.

Broadcasting: Scatter the seeds so they are spaced about 2″ to 3″ apart and cover with a ½″ of cover soil.

Rows: Make the furrows ½″ to ¾″ deep, plant the seeds 1½″ apart and re-fill with topsoil. If the soil isn't very good, you could cover with a mix of half soil and half compost.

Thinning: When all of the seeds have germinated, you can start thinning. Don't start too early though, as some may be damaged by cutworms, slugs, or other pests. Thinning is best done in several stages, as the plants get larger. You can use the thinnings for food, or as transplants (they transplant fairly well if less than 3″ tall). The clusters don't need much thinning, as the strongest plant tends to take over.

Spacing: Chard grows fast and gets quite large, so needs plenty of space. Plant it 8″ to 12″ apart, depending upon the fertility of the soil and the growing methods.

Care

Chard is a robust and undemanding plant. Keep it well fed and watered and it should produce abundantly.

Water: Chard is relatively drought tolerant, though for highest quality and yields it should be well supplied with water. It is particularly important to keep the soil evenly moist in hot weather, as lack of water can encourage bolting.

Fertilization: If you are going to be harvesting intensively, you should feed the plants regularly with compost tea or liquid Kelp.

Mulch: This helps to keep down weeds while the plants are young (older plants can take care of themselves). It also helps to keep the soil cool and conserves moisture.

Bolting: Chard is a biennial, but sometimes it will bolt in its first year. This is most often caused by vernalization (see **Broccoli**), but may also be caused by drought, crowding or other stress. If a plant bolts, there's not much you can do but pull it up.

Pests: Chard is little bothered by pests and disease generally. My biggest problem has been leaf miners. You can crush them in the leaf and scrape off the small white egg clusters, but row covers are the best solution. Slugs and snails will eat Chard if there is nothing more to their liking.

Seed saving: The process is the same as for the related Beet. Chard and Beet will cross-pollinate so you can only save one type at a time. The seed is produced abundantly, especially if you are saving it from 5 plants to ensure some genetic diversity.

Harvest

When: You can start pinching off the individual leaves as soon as they get big enough to use. I usually harvest the individual outer leaves, just as they are reaching full size (which may be 8″ to 12″).

How: Chard is a great "cut and come again" crop. Keep harvesting the outer leaves as they get big enough and more will be produced. Harvest freely, but take care not to take too many from a single plant at one time. Give them a chance to recover.

You may be able to rejuvenate a tired old plant, by cutting it down to within 3″ to 4″ of the ground. It should sprout tender new growth.

Storage: Use the leaves immediately after harvest, as they are thin and don't keep for very long (only a few days in the fridge in a plastic bag). For longer term storage, Chard can be frozen like Spinach. This is useful for those times when it is producing far more than you can use immediately.

Unusual growing ideas

Spring greens: If you protect the roots over the winter, they will start growing again as the weather warms up in spring. This new growth can be harvested several times before the plants bolt.

Ornamental: The spectacularly colored Chard varieties (red, white, orange, yellow) are highly photogenic and are a favorite of upscale magazine garden photos. They can be used as foliage plants for ornamental garden beds.

Varieties:
Ruby Chard, Rhubarb Chard: These varieties have beautiful red stems.

Bright Lights, Rainbow Chard: These both have a combination of red, yellow, green and white stems and are beautiful enough for the ornamental garden.

Perpetual Spinach: This is an old variety with thin tender stems, that more resemble Spinach than other Chards (it is also known as Spinach Beet). It isn't as attractive as some of the other varieties, but is very productive and bolt resistant. It can even be perennial in mild climates. It is my favorite variety.

Green Lucullus: One of commonest green varieties.

Cooking: Use the leaves like Spinach. Supposedly the thick stems are sometimes prepared as a separate vegetable, though I imagine they would be pretty bland

Sag Aloo
This Indian curry is normally made with spinach, but chard works just as well.

20 oz chard leaves
1 onion chopped
5 tbsp vegetable oil
1 cup water
½ tsp black pepper
2 tbsp Black Mustard seed
2 cardamom seeds
2 cloves garlic chopped
20 oz potatoes in small cubes
1 small hot pepper, chopped
1 tsp ground cumin
1 tsp ground coriander
1 tsp salt

Toast the cardamom and mustard seeds in the hot oil (don't let it overheat) until they start to pop. Add the onions and garlic and fry for 2 minutes, then add the rest of the spices and cook for another 2 minutes. Then add the potatoes, hot pepper, chard, salt and water. Cook a further 30 minutes until potatoes are cooked.

Chicory
Cichorium intybus

Introduction: This perennial has a history of cultivation dating back to the ancient Egyptians. It has long been a popular salad plant in France, Belgium and Italy. It was introduced into North America as a food plant by early European settlers and is now naturalized across most of the country.

Chicory is cultivated for three quite different foods, greens, roots (for coffee) and shoots (known as chicons) and specific varieties have been bred for each purpose.

About Chicory

Seed facts
Germ temp: 45 (60 to 65) 75° F
Germ time: 7 to 14 days
Germination percentage: 70+
Viability: 4 to 6 to 8 yrs
Weeks to grow transplants: 4

Planning facts
Hardiness: Hardy
Ease of growing: Easy
Growing temp: 45 (60 to 65) 75° F
Plants per person: 5
Plants per sq ft: 1
Direct sow: 2 to 4 wks before last frost date.
Fall crop: Sow 8 to 12 wks before first fall frost
Time to harvest: 90 days +

Harvest facts
Yield per plant: 6 to 12 oz
Yield per sq ft: 6 to 12 oz

Nutritional content:
Chicory leaves contain lots of vitamins A and C, as well as some vitamin E and folate. They are also rich in minerals, including iron, potassium, calcium and phosphorus.

Soil
pH 5.0 to 6.8
Chicory thrives in most soil types, but for the largest roots and easier harvesting, a loose, rich and fairly moist soil is best.

Soil preparation: Fork in a 2″ layer of compost, or aged manure, to supply organic matter. Add wood ashes (for potassium) and colloidal phosphate (for phosphorus).

Planning
When
Spring: In areas with cool summers Chicory can be treated like Lettuce. Plant it 2 to 4 weeks before the last spring frost.

Fall: Hot weather makes Chicory leaves intensely bitter, so in warm climates it is normally grown as a fall crop. It is started 8 to 12 weeks (depending upon the variety) before the first fall frost.

Roots: To grow the roots for forcing, or coffee, a suitable variety is planted some time in spring. It doesn't need to be started very early, as it is quite fast growing and has all season to mature.

Planting
Direct sowing: Chicory is usually sown like the related Lettuce. Plant the seed ¼″ to ½″ deep.

Spacing:
Roots: To grow roots for forcing plant it 4″ to 5″ apart, in rows 18″ apart. This maximizes the number of roots.

Leaf: As a salad plant Chicory is spaced 6″ to 9″ apart, depending upon the variety.

Care
Weeds: It is important to keep the young plants free of weeds.

Water: This deep rooted plant is very drought resistant. However a lack of water makes the plants even more bitter and increases their chances of bolting. Keep the soil evenly moist at all times.

Mulch: This is useful to keep down weeds and conserve moisture.

Blanching: The plants are often blanched like those of Endive, to make them less bitter.

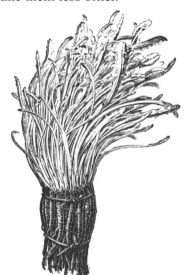

Growing chicons
Forcing the shoots: The roots are forced indoors to provide the tasty white shoots called *chicons*. This has become a major industry in Belgium and they are sometimes available in supermarkets under the name Belgian Endive. They provide a fresh green vegetable in the middle of winter, when few others are available.

The roots are dug in late fall, after the tops have died down and they have been vernalized by cold weather. By this time they should be as big as Parsnips. Cut off the dead top, leaving only an inch of stem. Also trim off the bottom of the root, so they are a uniform length of about 8". These are then stored in a cool root cellar, or in a trench in the ground, until needed.

To force the roots, they are planted in a deep plant pot, (as many as can easily fit, after leaving about 2" between them). To start them growing they are watered and moved to a warm (50 to 60° F) dark place.

The pale shoots take about 4 weeks to grow and are harvested when about 6" tall. The roots will usually produce 2 crops if well cared for. In large commercial operations they are now often forced hydroponically.

Pests: Chicory retains a lot of its wild vigor and isn't bothered by many problems. Slugs, snails and cutworms may attack it when young.

Tip burn: As the name suggests, the tips of leaves look like they have been burned. It is usually caused by excessively hot weather.

Harvest: You can harvest the whole heads, or just individual leaves, as soon as they are of sufficient size. Continue harvesting individual leaves until they get too bitter. They are always somewhat bitter, but in hot weather they become so bitter they are uneatable.

Storage: Store the leafy heads like lettuce, in a plastic bag in the fridge for up to a week. Store the chicons in a plastic bag in the fridge for up to 4 weeks.

Seed saving: Chicory sets seed very easily if allowed to. The flowers are pollinated by insects and will cross-pollinate with Endive or Wild Chicory (which is a common wild flower). To keep a variety pure you must isolate it by a ½ mile, or cage it. It is quite hard to separate the individual seeds from the flowers, so they are often stored in the dried flower heads. You have to crush the dry flower heads to release the seeds.

Unusual growing ideas
Volunteer: Chicory self-sows readily and might be considered a weed if it weren't so useful. Not only is it edible and of medicinal value, but its bright blue flowers attract many beneficial insects.

Varieties
Sugar Loaf: You can eat the leaves like Lettuce, or use the roots for forcing.

Witloof: This variety is grown for forcing.

Catalogna: Has long strap-like leaves. It has been naturalized in my garden for at least 5 years.

Magdeburg: This is grown for its edible roots (for coffee).

Puntarelle: In Italy this variety is prized for the edible flower shoot that appears in spring.

Cooking
Greens: The tender new spring leaves can be used in the same ways as the related Dandelion (See *Taraxacum*), as salad greens, or as a potherb. As the plant matures they become impossibly bitter. Blanching reduces this considerably and this probably led to the forcing of the roots.

Coffee: Chicory root has been widely used as a coffee substitute or extender and many people say it actually improves the flavor of coffee. It may also reduce its harmful effect on the liver.

To make Chicory 'coffee' the cleaned roots are dried thoroughly, until they are so brittle they snap easily. They are then ground to a powder and roasted in an oven until uniformly brown.

The drink is prepared by mixing a teaspoon of the roasted powder with a cup of boiling water. You can also add roasted sprouted Barley, Carob, Cinnamon, or other goodies. It is sometimes mixed with an equal amount of coffee.

Radicchio

Originally bred in Italy, this is another type of Chicory entirely and has become very fashionable in recent years. It is prized for its small dense head of colorful and somewhat bitter, leaves.

Radicchio is cultivated in the same way as Chicory.

From the gardeners viewpoint Radicchio can be divided into two types, the forcing and non-forcing.

Forcing types:

Red Verona, Treviso: These varieties need cold weather to stimulate them to produce a compact head. Cold weather may kill the outer leaves, but the colorful head will emerge from underneath them.

Non-Forcing types: Castelfranco. Palla Rossa, Giulio: These varieties produce a head even without cold weather. However you might have to stimulate them to head up, by cutting off most of the top growth (leave only 2″ of leaves). The resulting new growth should then form a head

A significant percentage of the plants in a bed won't produce the desired Cabbage-like heads.

I should add that Radicchio tastes much better when grown in cold weather. Plants grown when it isn't cold enough have been called Rad-yuck-io.

Coriander
Coriandrum sativum

Introduction: This annual provides two distinct quite foods. The leaves are better known by their Spanish name Cilantro, though they are also called Chinese Parsley. They have a distinctive aromatic flavor you either love or hate (I have an old English gardening book that described the foliage as "foul smelling"). I am in a position to appreciate both sides of this argument, as I used to be one of the people who really disliked it. However over the years, through its use in Mexican foods, I have grown to love it.

The large ripe seeds (pods) are known as Coriander and have an aromatic orange-like flavor and smell. They are particularly popular in Middle Eastern and Southeast Asian foods.

I really like the immature green seeds also. They have an intriguing flavor that is somewhere between that of the leaf and the ripe seed.

About Coriander

Seed facts:
Germ time: 7 to 10 days
Harvest time: 50 days Leaf
                  90 days Seed

Nutrients: The leaves contain cancer fighting phytochemicals.

Soil: Cilantro will do well in any garden soil that is fertile, well-drained and moisture retentive. It likes full sun.

When: Cilantro doesn't like heat and bolts quickly once the weather warms up (or is it the longer day length that is primarily responsible?) It does best in the cool weather of spring or early fall. In mild winter areas it may continue to grow right through the winter. It can also be sown in autumn for an early spring crop.

Planting: This annual is easily grown from seed (more than most members of the *Apiaceae*). It doesn't like transplanting, so is usually direct sown. However it can also be started indoors in plug trays or cell packs. The seed is a capsule and contains more than one seed.

Weeding: Cilantro isn't very vigorous when young and needs to be kept free of weeds.

Watering: It prefers moist soil and needs watering regularly in dry weather. Dry soil may contribute to bolting.

Saving seed: If left alone this insect pollinated plant will eventually produce seed and may even self-sow. There aren't many varieties, so you probably don't have to worry too much about cross-pollination.

Harvest: Gather the seed heads as the seeds start to turn brown and leave them to dry in a paper bag in a warm place.

Other plants:
The frustrating thing about Cilantro is that it doesn't grow very well in hot weather, when you have all those Tomatoes and Peppers and Onions crying out to be made into salsa. Fortunately there are a number of other plants that can be grown instead. These include:

Culantro (*Eryngium foetidum*)
This small tender plant has a slightly stronger flavor than Cilantro. Usually grown from seed, it takes up to 21 days to germinate. It is a fairly slow growing plant and takes about 75 days to start producing. It is normally started indoors early and planted out after the weather has warmed up.

Papalo (*Porophyllum ruderale*)
This species is commonly used in its native Mexico as a warm weather substitute for Cilantro. It eventually grow up to 4 feet in height, but is best harvested when about 12″ tall.

Vietnamese Coriander
(*Polygonum odoratum*) This sub-tropical plant needs constant moisture and can even be grown in water gardens. The first time I grew it I never realized this and gave it water only sparingly. It survived but didn't really thrive. In ideal conditions it can be very vigorous and can grow like a weed.

This tender perennial isn't very hardy, but survived at least one winter in my garden (if I had looked after it better it would probably have lasted more). It can be propagated from cuttings.

Corn
Zea mays

Introduction: This warm weather annual differs from all other common garden vegetables in being the only a member of the grass family (*Poaceae*). It is thought to have originated somewhere in Central America, though it is no longer found there as a wild plant (it may be descended from the closely related Teosinte, which is still found in the wild in Mexico). Native Americans have cultivated Corn for over 5000 years and in many places it was not only a staple food, but also an integral part of their culture. Corn was introduced into Europe in the sixteenth century and spread from there to all suitable climates around the world. There are several different types of Corn (see Varieties), but all are grown in much the same way, only their uses differ.

Nutritional content:
Sweet Corn is rich in carbohydrate, as well as soluble fiber, folate niacin, thiamin and phosphorus. It also contains useful phytochemicals. Yellow Corn contains vitamin A.

Field Corn is rich in protein, carbohydrates, potassium, calcium and the amino acid leucine.

Soil
pH 5.5 (6.0 to 6.8)
Corn will grow well in a variety of soils, but it is a hungry plant and needs a lot of nutrients for maximum production. The ideal soil is rich, moisture retentive and well drained. Field Corn isn't quite as demanding as Sweet Corn, but the better the soil the better the crop.

Soil preparation: This vigorous and fast growing crop needs generous amounts of nitrogen, phosphorus and potassium, as well as all of the other plant nutrients.

Incorporate 2″ of compost or aged manure into the top 6″ of soil, along with bone meal (for phosphorus) and wood ashes (for potassium). Add Kelp to supply the necessary trace elements.

About Corn

Seed facts
Germ temp: 50 (60 to 75) to 95° F
Germ time: 3 to 10 days
22 days / 50° F
12 days / 59° F
7 days / 68° F
4 days / 77° F * Optimum
4 days / 86° F
3 days / 95° F
Seed viability:
       Sweet Corn 1 to 3 yrs
       Field Corn 3 to 5 yrs
Germination percentage: 75%+
Weeks to grow transplant: 3 to 4

Planning facts
Hardiness: Tender
Ease of growing: Easy
Growing temp: 50 (60 to 75) 95° F
Plants per person: 15
Plants per sq ft: ⅔
Transplants:
Start: 2 wks before last frost
Plant out: 2 wks after last frost
Direct sow: 2 wks after last frost
Time to harvest: 60 to 150 days

Harvest facts
Yield per plant: 2 to 4 ears
Yield per sq ft: 1 to 3 ears

Corn is sometimes planted into a bed 2 weeks after a nitrogen fixing winter cover crop (such as Bell Beans) is incorporated.

Legend has it that Native American planted a fish in each hill of Corn, to supply the necessary nutrients. This isn't true though, when soil fertility started to decline, they would just move their gardens to new ground.

Planning

Where: Corn is a sub-tropical plant and uses C4 photosynthesis, which enables it to grow more efficiently in high heat and light levels. It needs warm weather and as much sunlight as it can get.

Sweet Corn can be grown in an intensive bed, but it must be in a large block for best pollination. It is a tall growing plant, so must be planted where it won't shade other plants.

Field corn should probably be grown in its own separate patch, as you will need to plant quite a large area, if you want to produce a significant quantity of food. I advise you to try growing it in a 3 sisters polyculture, along with Squash and Beans (see below)

Crop rotation: Don't plant Corn in the same soil for at least 3 years. In a rotation it commonly follows a nitrogen-fixing legume.

When: Don't plant Corn until at least 2 weeks after the last frost date, when the soil has warmed up to a minimum of 60° F (75° F for the supersweet varieties). Native Americans traditionally waited until the Plums had bloomed, or the

Oak leaves were emerging before planting. In cold soil, the seed take a long time to germinate and there is a much greater chance of loss to rot or some hungry creature.

Early corn: If your growing season is very short, or you just want to get early Corn, start your seedlings indoors 3 to 4 weeks before the last frost date. Corn doesn't transplant well, so use cell packs, soil blocks or plug trays. It helps to warm the soil under black plastic for a couple of weeks before planting out. Plant the seedlings on the last frost date and cover with row covers, or cloches, to keep them warm until the weather warms up.

Succession sowing: In the home garden you don't want a lot of Corn ripening at once (unless you are going to freeze it). You can stagger the harvest, by succession sowing every 2 to 3 weeks, by planting varieties with different maturation times, or by a combination of the two methods.

Planting
Transplants
Starting inside: Corn can be started indoors, in cell packs, soil blocks or plug trays. However this is only worthwhile for very early Corn, in exceptionally short or cool growing seasons, or to avoid predators such as birds and mice. Sow 2 seeds in each cell or block and thin to the best one when they have all emerged. If germination is very good, you might just plant one seed per cell. The seedlings grow rapidly and will get root-bound if left in their containers for too long. Ideally they should be out of their pots and in the ground, within 3 to 4 weeks.

Direct sowing: Corn is usually direct sown, because it grows fast, doesn't like transplanting and it is less work. In spring, when the soil is cool, it should be planted only 1″ deep. Later in the year, when the soil is warm, it may be planted as deep as 4″. The less vigorous seed of hybrid varieties is usually planted only 1″ deep. Plant twice as many seeds as you need and thin to the desired spacing when they are several inches high.

To get the plants off to a good start, you might soak the seeds overnight prior to planting, For an even faster start you could pre-germinate them, but be careful not to break the brittle roots.

In some areas mice or birds can be a major problem in spring, in which case you can use rows covers (these also keep the seedlings warmer).

Hill planting
Hill planting: Native Americans used to plant their corn in hills. These were quite literally small flattened mounds about 18″ in diameter. They planted 6 to 8 seeds in each hill, at a depth of 2″ to 4″ and spaced evenly in a circle about 9″ in diameter. The hills were spaced about 4 feet apart in the rows and there was about 4 feet between the rows.

Row planting
Row planting: Corn is usually planted in rows, but to ensure good pollination (which means full ears) it is important that the rows be in blocks. These should consist of at least four rows each.

Spacing
Spacing:
Rows: Put the plants 6″ to 8″ apart in the rows, with 24″ to 36″ between the rows.

Beds: Plant in offsets rows across the bed. The distance apart depends upon the soil:
18″ (poor soil)
15″ (average soil)
12″ (excellent soil)

Care
Weeding: It is important to weed the plants carefully while they are young. After they reach 12″ in height they can deal with almost any weed. The young plants can be hoed quite closely, as they don't have shallow roots.

Water: Sweet Corn is a thirsty plant, so water it regularly. Water is especially crucial during tasselling and subsequent ear maturation.

The best method of irrigation is with soaker hose or a drip system. Overhead irrigation may interfere with fertilization during the pollen shedding stage.

Generally Field Corn needs significantly less water than Sweet Corn, especially those varieties bred for desert conditions. They are often dry farmed (grown without irrigation), using only the water that's held in the ground. They will be more productive if given some irrigation however.

Fertilization: It is a good idea to give the young plants a boost of nitrogen, such as compost tea, when the seedlings are about 12″ tall and growing rapidly. Give them another boost when the silks appear.

Pollination: Corn is wind-pollinated and getting good pollination is a critical aspect of Corn growing. If you don't get good pollination, the ears may be only half filled and you won't have a good crop. Overhead irrigation and wet weather can impede pollination

The male tassel on top of the plant gives off pollen for a couple of days before the female flowers (the silks) become receptive. When the silks are receptive, you can improve pollination by gently shaking the plants, so pollen comes cascading down from the tassels. This should be done on a still day of course.

In some cases the type of pollen a plant receives will determines its taste characteristics. This means you should ideally only have one kind of Corn flowering at one time (unless you are prepared to hand pollinate). Genetic purity is most important with the super sweet hybrids and they should probably be isolated from all other types of corn. It is not so important for Field Corn, unless you are saving the seed for planting (in which case you may want to hand pollinate).

Suckers: Corn plants often produce suckers, smaller stems, which if left alone may eventually flower and produce small ears. Some people believe theses drain energy from the plant and remove them as they appear. This isn't really necessary though..

Pests: Many pests attack Corn at various stages of growth. These include Cutworms, Corn Rootworms, Wireworms, Aphids, Flea Beetles, Corn Earworm, Corn Borers, Japanese Beetles, Root Rot, Sap Beetles, Raccoons, Squirrels and Jays.

Diseases: Bacterial Wilt, Maize Dwarf Mosaic, Corn Leaf Blight, Rust.

Corn Earworm: This is perhaps the most common Corn pest. It burrows down into the ear, eating the seeds and making quite a mess. It isn't usually a problem on early Corn, but can affect almost every ear of a late planting. Fortunately the damage is mostly cosmetic and is usually confined to the tip of the ear. All you have to do is chop this off and the person eating the corn won't even be aware there was a problem. Supposedly some varieties have tighter husks than others and so are less affected (i.e. Country Gentleman).

Corn Smut (*Ustilago maydis*): Corn Smut is a fungus disease that infects Corn plants, producing swollen growths on the ears. In the United States it is considered a pest and is destroyed whenever it occurs. In Mexico it is known as Huitlacoche and is considered a delicacy that is actually worth more than corn. It has an earthy, sweet mushroom-like flavor and is said to be very good (I have never been lucky enough to get any to try).

Attempts have been made to popularize Corn Smut as a food in the United States by re-naming it Mexican Truffle. Perhaps one day it will become a useful crop here.

For culinary use this fungus should be gathered while it is still moist and immature, about 2 to 3 weeks after the initial infection. The mature fungus eventually releases a cloud of brown spores. If you are lucky enough to have Corn Smut, you could try collecting some of the spores. The Aztecs used to deliberately infect their plants with them and you could try doing the same.

Harvesting Sweet Corn:

When: More than any other crop, it is important to gather Sweet Corn at the right time. The ears mature from 17 to 23 days after pollination (depending upon the weather) and there are many indicators of maturity.

How to tell when Corn is ripe:

The silks wither and turn dark brown.

The ear feels fat.

The end becomes rounded rather than pointed.

The ear tilts away from the stem.

To check if an ear is ripe, pull open the top of the husk and squeeze a kernel. If it is fat and spurts milky juice, it is ready. If it is dimpled and spurts watery juice, it's not yet ripe (just close up the husk). Be aware that the new super sweet varieties may have clear juice and still be ripe.

If the kernel is fat and tough, the ear is probably over-mature and will be starchy and not very good.

Corn ripens quickly in warm weather so watch it carefully and harvest when it is ready (it is only really good for a few days). If you can't use it immediately, freeze it, or give it away. If not harvested at the right time it will be wasted.

How: Snap the ripe ear from the plant by pulling it downwards. Be careful not to break the plant, or damage its neighbors.

Field Corn: Harvesting Field Corn is much easier than Sweet Corn; simply leave the ears until the entire plant turns brown and dry. Then remove the husks and dry the whole ears. The dry ears can be stored whole (they are quite decorative), but the seed takes up less space if you remove it from the ears. Make absolutely sure the seed is completely dry before storing it, otherwise it will go moldy.

Seed saving: Saving Corn seed is a little more complicated than most other crops, because you have to worry about inbreeding (Corn strains are very inbred). If you want to maintain a pure variety indefinitely you need to save seed from at least 50 plants (some say a minimum of 100), to keep sufficient genetic variability. This is quite a bit of work.

Of course Native Americans saved their own seed for thousands of years, but they didn't worry about the purity of a strain. In fact they encouraged diversity in their seeds, by collecting seed from a variety of plants, rather than simply the "best", as we tend to do

Corn plants are cross-pollinated by the wind and can cross easily. To keep a strain pure you must either hand pollinate, grow only one variety at a time, or separate it from other tasselling plants by at least 250 yards (1000 yards is better). You should also collect your seed from the center of the stand, where there is less chance of stray pollen coming in.

Hand pollination: This isn't
difficult, but takes some time, especially if you are pollinating 100 plants. The first step is to put a bag over the female flowers before the silks emerge, to prevent them being pollinated by any stray pollen. This must be taped shut, to prevent any pollen entering. The next morning, after the dew has dried, you go out and gently shake pollen from the newly opened tassels into a paper bag. Then simply transfer a little pollen onto the silks of each plant with a brush. You then replace the bags and leave them on until the silks go brown. Mark the ears carefully so they don't get eaten accidentally.

Unusual growing methods
Baby corn: These are the tiny immature cobs seen in Chinese restaurants. Any kind of sweet corn can be used, but there are special varieties (Baby Asian, Chires Baby Corn) that produce several ears per stem (Chires is said to produce up to 40 ears per plant).

Baby Corn is grown in exactly the same way as sweet corn, though you can plant it closer together (as close as 8″ in fertile soil). The ears are harvested a couple of days after the silks show. As you might imagine this isn't a very productive crop.

Three sisters

Field Corn takes up a lot of space, so you might want to interplant it with beans and squash. This is the system used by Native Americans to grow their three main crops. It is a way of growing Corn, Beans and Squash in a more symbiotic and efficient way. The Corn stalks give the beans support, the Squash creates a living mulch over the bare soil between the corn hills and the beans supply nitrogen. Even the foods they provide complement each other.

The Corn is planted as described above, with 5 to 6 seeds in each hill. These are left to grow for several weeks, until they are about 10″ tall and are then hilled up with soil to a height of about 6″ (this gives them more stability). After hilling, 10 to 12 pole beans are planted in a circle around the growing corn, a few inches away from them. These sprout within 7 to 10 days. A week after they have germinated, 5 Squash seeds are planted around them, about a foot further out.

Once everything is growing there is little left to do, except ensure that they aren't overtaken by weeds and have enough water. You may want to help the individual Pole Beans find corn stalks to climb up. The Squash will soon cover and shade the ground, though you might feel the need to direct them to bare spots, so they fill in more evenly.

Other uses: Corn has traditionally been used for bread, mush, beer, whiskey and animal feed. It is now a major industrial crop, with thousands of uses from cornstarch to ethanol based motor fuel.

Varieties: If you mention Corn to a gardener, she will almost certainly think of Sweet Corn, as most of the corn grown by American gardeners is of this type. Yet in the history of Corn as a food crop, Field Corn is actually far more important.

If you grow a lot of Corn, you can save money by buying your Corn seed in bulk from a farm store, rather in packets from the garden center.

Corn varieties: Field Corn varieties can be divided into several groups, according to the type of starch they produce. There is also considerable difference in color, with blue, white, red and yellow varieties.

Dent Corn: *Z mays var indentata*
The kernels of this Field Corn have a depression in the middle (hence the name) and their starch is a mixture of hard and soft. Almost 80% of commercial Field Corn is of this type. Depending upon when they are picked, the kernels can be used for cornmeal, hominy, roasting Corn or Sweet Corn.

Flint Corn: *Z. mays var indurata*
The very hard starch in the semi-translucent seeds earns this the name Flint Corn. It grows well in cooler climates than other Corns. It is used for cornmeal, though it is so hard it can be difficult to grind.

Soft Corn: *Z. mays var amylacea*
The seeds contain mostly soft

starch hence the name. This type of Corn is easily ground to meal and is commonly used for bread, tortillas and corn chips.

Pop Corn: *Z. mays var everata*

Pop Corn kernels have a very hard outer layer and a soft inner layer, a combination which makes them pop very well. They can also be used for cornmeal. Popcorn is a great crop for children to plant, as they get an extra special reward at the end of it. In my family there is never any doubt that the crop will get eaten.

Strawberry Popcorn is the easiest variety to find, but I have had better luck with Japanese Hulless.

Sweet Corn: *Z. mays var saccharata*

Sweet Corn differs from Field Corn in that it is harvested while immature and most of its food is in the form of sugar rather than starch. This is why it is so sweet and why the seeds shrink when dried. It also makes the seeds somewhat temperamental in their germination capacity and accounts for their short storage life. The earliest varieties can mature in less than 60 days. It comes in yellow, white, bicolor and blue varieties.

Hybrids: Corn is one of the few crops in which hybridization has made a big difference. Hybrids are superior to non-hybrids in that they mature more uniformly and are often sweeter. Unfortunately you can't save the seed of a hybrid, as they don't come true to type. This type is sometimes referred to as Normal Sugary or (su), to differentiate it from the other types now available.

Super Sweet Hybrids: These Corns were bred for commercial growers, as they remain sweet for much longer than conventional varieties. They are certainly sweet, but it is important that they be fully mature before use, as they don't develop much Corn flavor until this time. They are also more temperamental to grow and shouldn't even be planted until the soil is at least 70° F.

Hybrid Sugary Enhanced (se) (se+)

These contain a gene that enhances the normal sugary gene (su) and makes the kernels sweeter and more tender. In addition the sugar is only slowly converted to starch after picking, so they remain sweet for longer. These varieties don't require isolation from other varieties.
Silver Queen F1, Bodacious F1, Kandy Korn F1

Hybrid Shrunken (sh2)

These varieties contain a shrunken gene that makes them very sweet. However they need to be isolated from other varieties while tasselling, or the resulting kernels will be tough and starchy.
How-Sweet-It-Is

Synergistic

These varieties contain both (se) and (sh2) genes, which makes them very tender and sweet. They also need to be isolated from other varieties when tasselling.
Frisky, Montauk

Open pollinated varieties:

Some traditionalists maintain that sweetness isn't everything and that open pollinated varieties simply have a better Corn flavor. If you grow them, you have to be more on top of things, as they don't maintain their sweetness for very long. Country Gentleman, Golden Bantam.

Cooking: Traditional Sweet Corn begins to lose its sweetness as soon as it is harvested, because the sugar is gradually converted into starch. The sooner you cook it, the less sweetness will be lost. Corn epicures say you should have the water boiling before even picking your Corn. This tradition is dying out because the newer hybrids stay sweet much longer.

Corn chowder

2 carrots
1 stalk celery
1 onion
1 sweet pepper
2 cups corn kernels
2 cups vegetable broth or water
1 cup potatoes
1 cup soy milk
1 tbsp flour
1 tbsp olive oil
Salt and pepper

Saute the carrot, celery onion and pepper in the oil for a few minutes then add the water and potatoes and simmer 10 minutes. Add the corn and cook for another 10 minutes. Then mix the soymilk and flour and salt and pepper and add to mix. Simmer for another 10 minutes.

Cornsalad

Valerianella locusta
Syn *V. olitoria*

Introduction: This cool season salad plant gets its English name because it was a common edible weed of grain fields (all grain was once known as corn). It is also known by its French name Mache and as Lambs Lettuce (supposedly because sheep like to forage on the wild plants). It is a fairly small plant, but significant because it is one of the hardiest salad crops and can be harvested when few other crops are producing.

About Cornsalad

Viability: 5 to 10 yrs
Time to harvest:
50 to 60 days (summer)
60 to 90 days (winter)

Soil: Cornsalad will grow almost anywhere, but does best in a sandy well-drained soil that is rich in nitrogen.

Planning

Where: In winter Cornsalad should be put in a warm sheltered spot, where it will get full sun. In warmer weather it can be planted in part shade.

When: This is a cold weather plant and does best in cooler areas. I have had no success with it at all in hot weather, so it surprises me to hear some people say they have. It is one of the first crops you can plant in spring and should be planted early, as it bolts when warmer weather arrives. In cool climates it can be succession sown right through the summer, for a continuous harvest.

Because of its predilection for bolting, Cornsalad is most often grown as a fall and winter crop. It doesn't mind hard frost and in many areas it will keep growing right through the winter. It actually grows better in cold weather as it gets bigger without getting bitter or bolting.

Planting
Outside: Cornsalad is usually direct sown like spinach, either by broadcasting, or by sowing in rows. In my experience the seed doesn't have a very good germination rate, so sow fairly thickly. Plant the seed ¼″ to ½″ deep and keep moist until it germinates.

Spacing: Space the plants 4″ to 6″ apart in offset rows.

Care
Thinning: When all the plants have emerged, thin them to 2″ apart. Thin them again a few weeks later, when they are a few inches high. This time to 4″ to 6″ apart (you can eat the thinnings this time).

Weeds: This is a low and fairly slow growing plant (especially when young) and needs to be kept free of weeds.

Watering: Cornsalad needs a constant supply of moisture, but this is rarely a problem in cool weather.

Protection: In very cold climates it can be grown under cloches. In milder climates it will grow faster if given the protection of cloches.

Pests: Few pests are active in the cool weather that Cornsalad prefers. Slugs and birds are the ones you are most likely to encounter.

Harvest: These plants are not very long lived; so start harvesting the leaves as soon as they are large enough to be worthwhile. Though the individual leaves are small, some people harvest them singly and leave the plants to produce more (don't take too many from any one plant.) In this way you can extend the harvest for months. You can also harvest whole plants of course, perhaps start by taking every alternate plant. Some people blanch the plants for a few days prior to harvest, by covering with plant pots.

Seed saving: Cornsalad will produce an abundance of seed without any help from you and will often self-sow. It is cross-pollinated by insects, but there are few varieties available (and fewer being grown) so keeping it pure isn't usually a problem. It can also cross with wild Cornsalad, so you might want to check to see if it is growing nearby. Watch the plants carefully as the seed ripens, so you can gather it before it all falls.

Unusual growing ideas

Volunteers: Allow some plants to self-sow and they will produce new plants in autumn. Cornsalad has been growing by itself in my garden for at least 3 years now.

Shade: It may be possible to grow Cornsalad in summer, by interplanting it in the shade of tall growing crops like Corn or Sunflower.

Winter crop: Cornsalad is a good winter crop for growing in cold frames. It can also be planted in fall as a spring crop.

Varieties: When I first tried Cornsalad, the packet of seed just said "Cornsalad". In recent years a few more refined varieties are appearing. The Italian varieties aren't as hardy as the French or English types, because they are a different species (*V. eriocarpa).*

Cooking: Cornsalad is most popular in France and Italy. The flavor is mild and can be used instead of lettuce in salads. It can also be cooked like spinach as a potherb. The older leaves can get quite bitter in warm weather, but not as bitter as Chicory.

Wash the leaves carefully before use, as they often get splashed with soil.

Cucumber
Cucumis sativus

Introduction: This tropical species is thought to have come from India or thereabouts and it has long been cultivated there. It reached Europe quite early and was widely grown by the time of the Romans

Cucumbers take up quite a bit of space, but they are tasty, productive and have an extended harvest season.

Nutritional content:
Cucumbers are a good source of water (96%). They also contain potassium and antioxidants.

Soil
pH 6.0 to 7.0
Cucumbers grow rapidly once established and to sustain their high level of growth they need a rich soil. It should be loose, moisture retentive and well drained, with lots of organic matter. Raised beds are good for Cucumbers, because they help the soil warm up quickly and provide good drainage.

Soil preparation: Incorporate 2″ of compost or aged manure into the top 6″ of soil. Add lime if the soil is acidic, as they don't like a low pH. They don't like salt either, so watch what kinds of manure you use.

Planning
Where: Cucumbers can tolerate light shade, but for maximum production they need full sun (at least 8 hours daily).

About Cucumbers

Seed facts

Germ temp: 60 (70 to 85) 105° F
Germ time: 3 to 10 days
13 days / 59° F
6 days / 68° F
4 days / 77° F
3 days / 86° F * Optimum
3 days / 95° F
Germination percentage: 80%+
Viability: 2 to 5 years
Weeks to grow transplants: 3 to 4

Planning facts

Hardiness: Tender
Ease of growing: Easy
Growing temp: 60 to 75° F
Plants per person: 1
Plants per sq ft: ¾
Transplants:
Start: On last frost date
Plant out: 3 to 4 wks after last frost
Direct sow: 3 to 4 wks after last frost
Succession sow: 6 to 8 wks later
Time to harvest: 70 to 100 days

Harvest facts

Length of harvest: 8 to 12 wks
Yield per plant: 4 lb (10 to 15 fruit)
Yield per sq ft: 3 lb sq ft

When: Cucumbers are native to the tropics and absolutely must have warm soil (70° F minimum) for good germination and growth. Consequently they are among the last crops to be planted out in spring. Most varieties fruit better in short days, so tend to be more productive later in the summer.

Cucurbits in general (Squash, Melons, Cucumbers) are all easy to start from seed, though they don't like transplanting. Start the seeds inside on the last frost date (they grow fast) and plant out 3 or 4 weeks later. Don't start them too early, as you can't put them out until the soil is warm (60° F minimum). If they sit inside too long, they will get root bound. Plants set out at the right time will quickly outgrow those planted too early.

Support: If you are going to support your cucumbers, you should set it up before planting. This will minimize disturbance to the young plants.

Planting

Transplants

Starting inside: Early Cucumbers are usually started indoors, because the soil outside may not be warm enough for good germination (even though the air may be warm enough for their growth). You can hasten soil warming with a black plastic mulch.

Cucumbers dislike transplanting, so are usually started in individual 3″ or 4″ containers, 2 seeds to a pot (later thinned to the best one). Don't use smaller containers, as the seedlings grow so quickly you will soon have to re-pot them.

Planting out: Plant out the seedlings up to their first true leaves and water immediately. If the weather isn't warm, you might want to cover them with cloches.

Direct sowing: Once the soil has warmed up it is simpler to sow Cucumbers directly in the soil. In good conditions they grow very quickly and will often catch up with transplants, even though they were started several weeks later.

You might want to soak the seed overnight before planting to hasten germination. You can even pre-germinate them (this is easy because they are so large). Plant the seeds 2″ to 3″ deep.

In intensive beds, it is probably best to sow cucumbers in 2 alternate rows down the middle of the bed. You should probably interplant a fast growing crop at the same time, to take advantage of the temporarily vacant space.

Cucumbers were traditionally planted in hills. You can do this by digging a large hole 12″ in diameter and 12″ deep. Half fill this hole with compost and then return the soil to the hole. The result is a slightly raised mound that warms up quickly and provides good drainage. Several seeds (5 to 6) are then sown on top of the mound. When these have several leaves they are thinned to the best 2 or 3 plants.

The disadvantage of raised hills is that they dry out quickly, so don't work so well in dry climates. You can flatten the "hill" flat in such circumstances. In very dry areas you might even make it into a slight depression (an anti-hill).

If the weather is cool, cover the plants with row covers for the first few weeks.

Spacing: Intensive bed spacing varies from 15″ to 24″ apart, depending upon the soil and the variety. Trellised plants can be grown 12″ apart in the row, with 24″ to 36″ between the rows. Cucumber hills are planted 36″ apart.

Care

Support: Cucumbers take up a considerable amount of space if left to sprawl randomly across the ground. Fortunately they are very good climbers and will happily use vertical space instead of ground space. Trellised plants may take up only one tenth of the bed space of unsupported ones.

Trellising can increase yields by as much as 100%, because fewer fruits are lost to rot, disease or slugs and there is more light for photosynthesis. Fruits are also straighter and cleaner.

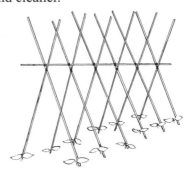

If building a trellis seems like a good idea, but too much work, you may be able to plant them along a wire fence. You can also use cages of 6″ mesh steel reinforcing wire, 3 ft in diameter and 6 ft high. These can work well, though the plants may eventually outgrow them. These cages can even be covered with plastic to protect the plants from late frost.

86

Many kinds of trellises have been used for supporting Cucumbers, including fencing wire, nylon netting and Bamboo canes. Be creative, but make sure it is strong enough to support the considerable weight of a fruiting crop.

In very dry areas it is better to leave the plants close to the ground, rather than trellising them. They can then create their own little humid microclimate and lose water less rapidly.

Watering: Cucumbers are mainly composed of water and need a constant and abundant supply of it for best growth. When they start producing, you should keep the soil evenly moist (but not wet) at all times. Ideally the water should be lukewarm (70° F), so it doesn't shock the plants, or cool the soil significantly.

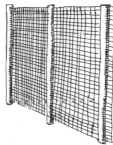

The best way to water Cucumbers is with a drip system or soaker hose. This keeps the leaves dry and so reduces the chance of disease problems. If you must get the leaves wet, water in the morning, or early evening, so they have a chance to dry out quickly. You don't want the leaves to stay wet all night.

Mulch: This is beneficial to conserve moisture and keep weeds under control. The soil must be warm before you put this on though, as mulches insulate the soil and prevent it from warming up.

Fertilization: When the seedlings have recovered from transplanting, give them a liquid feed of compost tea to give them a boost. If your soil isn't very fertile, give them a second feed when they are about 18″ high.

Pruning: Some people pinch out the growing tip of the young plant, to encourage branching. You might also pinch out the first few lateral shoots, to encourage the plant to grow larger before it starts producing fruit.

Pollination: Cucumbers are monoecious (they produce male and female flowers on the same plant) and the first few flowers to appear are usually males. These don't bear fruit of course. Female flowers are easily recognized by the tiny "cucumber" at the back of the petals. These appear soon after the first males and will begin to bear fruit if pollinated successfully. If the weather is cool this may not happen however and the flowers will drop off instead.

You can hand pollinate some of these if you are impatient (seed savers do it all the time), but there's usually no real need to. They will start to produce soon enough.

Apparently cold weather encourages the production of male flowers, while warm weather encourages female flowers.

Pests and diseases: I have found Cucumbers to be fairly free of pests, though they do have a few serious ones. It is a good idea to rotate Cucumbers regularly to minimize the potential for disease.

Cucumber Beetles: These insects not only eat the plants, but also spread bacterial wilt disease.

Other pests: Squash Bugs, Aphids, Squash Vine Borers.

Diseases: Alternaria Blight, Angular Leaf Spot, Anthracnose, Downy Mildew, Mosaic virus, Bacterial Wilt.

Harvesting

When: The fruit will be ready for harvest 15 to 18 days after pollination. The first fruits are usually quite small, simply because the plants themselves aren't very big.

For maximum yield you should harvest the fruits just before they reach full size. You can gather them when smaller than this, but you won't get as much food.

Once the plants start producing, you should check them every 2 to 3 days and harvest any fruits that are ready. Don't leave the fruits too long, as they will start to develop hard seeds and the skin will toughen. Definitely don't allow any fruits to mature on the vine, as they can stop the plant producing altogether. Pick the fruits regularly, even if you just throw them away. If you want small fruits for pickling, you can harvest ordinary cucumbers while they are still small, but the specially bred pickling varieties will be much more productive.

How: It's better to cut the fruit from the vine, rather than pulling it off. The stem is quite tough and it's easy to break off the vine accidentally. Ideally you should leave a short section of stem on each fruit, to prevent moisture loss. Brush any small spines off of the fruit with your hands.

Storage: Cucumbers should be stored in a cool place (40 to 50° F), but not as cold as a refrigerator. They don't keep for much more than a week, which is probably why pickling became popular.

Seed saving: Cucumbers are cross-pollinated by bees, so must either be isolated by at least 1000 yards or hand pollinated. Hand pollination is fairly straightforward because the flowers are so large. It is done in the same way as for Squash flowers (see **Squash**). Make sure you select the best and most typical plants for producing seed.

If you are saving seed, the fruit must be allowed to mature properly. It will turn yellow and start to wither when fully ripe. Separate the seeds from the pulp and ferment them for a couple of days, in the same way as you would for Tomato. Finally separate the cleaned seeds from the fermented mush and dry them thoroughly. Ideally they should have a moisture content of around 6% for storage. Be aware that a number of diseases can be seed borne.

Unusual growing ideas:
Ornamentals: The compact Bush cucumbers have been used

as ornamentals. The vining types are vigorous climbers and can be used to cover a wire fence or trellis, as a temporary screen. They are such good climbers they can even be trained over an arbor to provide summer shade.

Varieties: A lot of breeding work has gone into the Cucumber and the result is a lot of variation. The shape of the fruit varies considerably, from foot long green ones to tennis ball sized white or yellow ones. Some varieties are resistant to specific diseases. There are gynoecious varieties that produce all female flowers and so more fruit. There are even self-fertilizing (parthenocarpic) greenhouse varieties that don't need pollinating.

Bush Cucumbers are favored in small gardens because of their compact habit, though they aren't generally as productive as the vine types.

Vining Cucumbers are often preferred in warm moist climates as they get better air circulation, so are less vulnerable to disease. They may suffer more from sunburn however. They are also of more ornamental value.

Open pollinated:
Boothby's Blonde, Marketmore 97, Telegraph Improved

Lemon Cucumber, Crystal Apple: These round white varieties are an interesting change.

Hybrids:
Orient Express F1

All female greenhouse Cucumbers must be isolated from other varieties.
Cucino F1, Sweet Success F1

Pickling varieties: These produce a large number of small fruits, ideal for pickling. Wautoma, Parisian Pickling,

Cooking: Bitterness in Cucumbers is caused by chemicals known as cucurbitacins and is mostly genetic.

Pickle recipe

3 lb cucumbers (3″ to 4″)
8 cups water
¼ cup cider vinegar
⅓ cup salt
8 garlic cloves (peeled)
2 small fresh hot peppers
2 tbsp whole mustard seeds
2 tsp celery seeds
1 tsp turmeric
1 tsp freshly ground black pepper
6 to 8 seed heads dill

Thoroughly mix the vinegar, spices, garlic cloves, dill heads and salt (it should all dissolve) with the water and pour over the cucumbers into a large ceramic bowl. Put a plate over the bowl to push the cucumbers under the surface. Cover with a cloth and leave for 48 hours. Finally put the pickles into jars (about 5 or 6 in each), with a clove of garlic and cover with brine (remove the dill). They will keep in the fridge for about 3 months.

Edible Flowers

Edible flowers have become quite fashionable of late and for good reason. A handful of flowers will transform a mundane salad into a work of art. It makes you feel like Martha Stewart. These flowers don't only add color however; they can also add some unique and delicious flavors. I have a habit of picking a few flowers while I am out gathering salad materials.

You probably already grow edible flowers in your garden, so why not make use of them? I am not going to give any cultivation directions here; I just want to make you aware of what you might already have, or might choose to grow in the future.

Caution: The golden rule with eating anything is "know what you eat". Never put anything in your mouth that you don't know to be edible. Make sure you know exactly what species you are eating. Not all flowers are edible, a few are dangerously poisonous. Even some plants with edible flowers may have poisonous parts, so don't take anything for granted.

You should always be aware that flowers in other peoples gardens (or anywhere else) may have been sprayed with toxic chemicals.

On top of all of this, there is always the possibility that a plant can cause a reaction in one rare individual.

Always use these plants with caution, especially if you have never tried them before.

Cleaning: Clean your flowers carefully and make sure they don't contain hidden insects. Nothing spoils the dinner party like a guest crunching on an Earwig. You can be sure Martha Stewart doesn't have insects in her flowers.

Sometimes only the petals are good to eat, in which case you will have to remove the sepals, stamens and pistils (and sometimes even the white base of the petals). The simplest thing to do is taste the different parts and decide for yourself.

The best edible flowers include:

Anise Hyssop: Add a lovely blue color and Anise flavor.

Arugala: The flowers taste like Arugala.

Basil: The white flowers taste like Basil.

Brassicas: All Brassica flowers are edible and have a pleasantly pungent Mustard flavor.

Bee Balm: Beautiful and aromatic

Borage: Use the blue petals only, remove the hairy calyx

Calendula: A reliable standby if nothing else is available, Calendula flowers can be found almost year round in my garden. They don't have much flavor, but add a vivid orange or yellow color.

Chives: The purple, onion flavored florets are very good.

Cilantro: The small white flowers are good, but even better are the green seeds, which are a delightful combination of Cilantro and Coriander seed.

Ox Eye Daisy: The white ray flowers are good

Fennel: Yellow flowers, buds and immature seeds all have a delicious (and quite powerful) Anise flavor.

Garlic Chives: The pretty purple flowers have a nice Garlic flavor.

Leeks: The florets have a nice Onion flavor.

Nasturtium: One of the best edible flowers. Big and colorful with a delightful aromatic/pungent/sweet flavor all their own.

Radish: The flowers and green seed pods have a pungent Mustard flavor.

Roses: Not to everyone's taste, but some people love scented Rose petals in various dishes.

Salvias: Pineapple Sage, Common Sage and Clary Sage are all good.

Squash: The stuffed blossoms are a delicacy

Tagetes: Only a few varieties are good (Lemon Gem and others) so taste first

Violas: The flowers of the strongly scented Sweet Violet (*V. odorata*) are the best. Other kinds add color, but not much flavor.

Other edible flowers include:

Alliums Wild
Angelica
Apple
Black Locust: Flowers only, all other parts toxic.
Carrot
Chrysanthemum
Chamomile
Chervil
Chicory
Citrus: Taste first, some are not very pleasant.
Clover
Cornflower
Day Lily: Taste first, some are not very pleasant.
English Daisy (*Bellis perennis*)
Dandelion: Use individual petals
Dianthus
*D. caryophyllus (*Clove Pink): Best.
*D. plumarius (*Cottage Pink):
Dill
Elder
Fuchsia: Also has edible berries.
Garlic
Gladiolus: Taste first, some are not very pleasant.
Hawthorn
Hollyhock
Honeysuckle: (*L. japonica*)
Hibiscus
Hyssop
Impatiens

Jasmine
Lavender
Lemon Verbena
Lilac
Linden
Lovage
Mallows
Marjoram
Mints
Mullein
Okra: Flowers used like Hibiscus.
Oregano
Garden Pea: This is not the Sweet Pea (*Lathyrus odoratus)*, which is poisonous.
Pelargonium: Taste first, some are not very pleasant.
Peach
Pear
Pineapple Guava
Plum
Poppy: Petals add color.
Primulas
Sunflower: Use ray flowers.
Red Clover
Redbud
Rose of Sharon
Roselle (*Hibiscus sabdariffa*)
Rosemary
Safflower
Savory
Scarlet Runner Bean
Spiderwort
Strawberry
Sunflower
Sweet Rocket
Sweet Woodruff
Thyme
Red Valerian (*Centranthus ruber*)
Wisteria: Flowers only, all other parts are toxic.
Yucca

Eggplant
Solanum melongena

Introduction: This subtropical species was first cultivated by the great civilizations of China and India almost 6000 years ago. It traveled west to the Mediterranean with early traders and has been grown in the warmer countries of Europe since at least the 16th century. It is a tropical perennial, but is grown as an annual in temperate countries.

Eggplant isn't the easiest fruit to start from seed, as it is quite slow to get going. However once it is established it needs little care. The plant is of subtropical origin and so needs hot weather for best growth.

Soil
pH 5.5 to 6.8
Eggplant likes the same kind of soil as Peppers, fertile, well-drained, deep and loose. They like nitrogen and moderate amounts of phosphorus and potassium.

Soil preparation: Incorporate 2″ of compost or aged manure into the top 6″ of soil.

Planning
Where: Eggplant needs a warm, sunny spot, sheltered from cold winds.

Eggplant is quite slow growing, so plant a catch crop of Lettuce in between the transplants. The lettuce may even be beneficial, in that it can act as a living mulch.

When: The seed must be started indoors quite early (8 to 10 wks before setting out), so the plants have enough time to make good growth by transplanting time. They must have warm conditions if they are going to make much progress (80 to 90° F is ideal) and even then can take a long time to germinate. In cool climates you will have to grow them in a greenhouse.

About Eggplant

Seed facts
Germ temp: 60 (75 to 90) 95° F
Germ time: 14 to 21 days
13 days / 68° F
8 days / 77° F
5 days / 86° F * Optimum
Viability: 6 to 10 yrs
Germination percentage: 60%+
Weeks to grow transplants: 6 to 8

Planning facts
Hardiness: Tender
Ease of growing: Moderate
Growing temp: 65 (70 to 85) 95° F
Plants per person: 2
Plants per sq ft: ½
Transplants:
Start: 4 to 6 wks before last frost
Plant out: 4 wks after last frost
Time to harvest: 70 to 110 days
50 to 75 days from transplanting

Harvest facts
Yield per plant: 4 lb (5 to 10 fruits)
Yield per sq ft: ½ to 1½ lb sq ft

Planting
Eggplant seed is probably the most temperamental of all the common crops. Even at the optimal temperature of 86° F you should only expect about 60% of seeds to actually germinate. Soaking the seed overnight may hasten germination.

Transplants
Starting inside: Eggplants don't like root disturbance, so are best started in cell packs or soil blocks. Plant two per cell and when they have both emerged, thin to the best one. Be careful when transplanting, as any damage will show up as poor growth and delayed fruiting.

Planting out: Eggplants can't tolerate cold weather, so they are among the last plants to go outside in spring (usually a couple of weeks after Tomato). The soil temperature should be at least 60° F and the air temperature at least 70° F.

It is possible to set them out earlier, if the soil is warmed by black plastic mulch or cloches and they are protected by cloches.

I usually make a hole with a bulb planter, throw in a couple of handfuls of compost and plant the seedlings up to their first true leaves.

Direct sowing: If you have a very long growing season you can start the seed outdoors.

Spacing:
Rows: Space them 18″ to 24″ apart in the rows, with 24″ to 36″ between the rows.

Beds: Put transplants 18″ apart in the intensive beds.

Care
Weeds: Eggplants are quite shallow rooted, so don't use a hoe around them. Weed carefully by hand instead.

Water: The plants are fairly drought tolerant, but if they are to fruit well they need moist soil.

Fertilization: Once the seedlings have started growing well, give them a dose of compost tea or liquid Kelp (they especially need nitrogen and potassium). Repeat this every month for maximum production.

Mulch: A mulch can be applied after the soil is warm. This is useful to conserve moisture and keep down weeds.

Pruning: Pinch out the growing tip when the plants are about a foot high, to make them branch and get bushier. If you want large size fruit, don't let a plant produce more than a half dozen. Prevent this by pinching out new flowers and any lateral side shoots.

Problems: To produce well, Eggplant needs good soil, abundant moisture and warmth.

Planting out too early is a common cause of failure. If a young plant gets severely chilled it may be permanently retarded.

If it is too cold (especially at night) or too dry, the plant may drop its flowers instead of setting fruit.

Pests: Eggplant is a member of the *Solanaceae and* is susceptible to the same pests as Tomato and Potato.

Harvesting
When:
Big: Traditionally the fruits are harvested just as they reach full size, while their skin is still shiny. If the skin has turned dull and the seeds are brown it is too old.

Small: In Asia they pick the fruit while it is still small, the size of an egg, or only slightly larger. These young fruit are tastier and have a better texture than older ones. Picking smaller fruit increases the harvest, as a plant can produce many more of them. It also lengthens the harvest, as they will produce over a longer period of time. Harvest regularly and you may well be able to harvest as many fruits as you would from a Tomato plant.

How: Cut the fruit from the plant with a knife, without pulling on the plant too much. Leave an inch of stem attached to the fruit.

Storage: Eggplant should be treated like a Tomato and stored at room temperature, not in the fridge. The fruit will keep for a couple of weeks in a cool place, but no longer.

Seed saving: The plants are generally self-pollinated, but some cross pollination by insects also occurs. To keep a variety pure only one variety should be grown at one time, or it should be isolated by at least 50 feet. To ensure genetic variability, you should save the seed from at least 6 plants.

To get ripe seed, you need to let a fruit ripen completely. Separate the seed from the fruit by grating the seed bearing flesh and then mashing it in water. The seeds is then dried for storage. Eggplant seed is quite long lived if stored properly and may last for ten years.

Unusual growing ideas
Ornamental: With its mauve flowers and shiny fruits, Eggplant is one of the most attractive vegetables and can easily blend into the ornamental garden.

Varieties: The small Japanese Eggplants are considered to be tastier than the larger western varieties. They may also be more productive, as the fruits are picked when smaller (so more will form.) This is another crop where F1 hybrids are taking over the seed catalogs. However there are still some fantastically colored (orange, green yellow, purple) open pollinated varieties from Asia. The problem is finding them (try the Seed Savers Exchange).

Casper: A beautiful and tasty white variety. The white fruited varieties are less common than the colored types, but they are the reason this plant is known as Eggplant.

Black Beauty: An old favorite.

Ichiban: A good Oriental type

Thai Green:

Cooking: Probably more than any other common vegetable, cooking and recipe is all important with Eggplant. A badly cooked Eggplant is almost inedible; a well-cooked one is absolutely delicious. Garlic, Basil and Marjoram all go well with Eggplant.

Eggplant with Garlic

3 or 4 Oriental Eggplants chopped into 1″ cubes
2 cloves Garlic
4 green Onions chopped
1 tsp chopped fresh Ginger
1 tsp Chili sauce
1 tsp wine vinegar
1 tsp sugar
½ tsp ground black pepper
1 tbsp cornstarch
4 tbsp water
4 tbsp soy sauce
1 tbsp sesame oil

Mix the sugar, soy sauce, Chili sauce and pepper in a bowl. In another bowl mix cornstarch and water. Saute the Garlic, 2 green onions and ginger in a little oil for several minutes. Add the Eggplant and soy sauce mix and simmer 15 minutes. Finally add the cornstarch and rest of Onions

Endive
Cichorium endivia

Introduction: Endive (or Escarole) is a close relative of Chicory (which is sometimes called Endive). It is a useful green salad plant for cooler climates, though some people dislike its rather bitter flavor. The greens are particularly important in France and Italy and if they are popular in these famously epicurean countries there must be something to them.

Nutritional content: Similar to Chicory.

About Endive

Seed facts
Germ temp: 45 (60 to 65) 75° F
Germ time: 5 to 14 days
Germination percentage:
Viability: 5 to 7 to 10 yrs
Weeks to grow transplants: 4

Planning facts
Hardiness: Hardy
Ease of growing: Fairly easy
Growing temp: 45 (60-65) 75° F
Plants per person: 5
Plants per sq ft: 1
Transplants:
Start: 8 weeks before last frost
Plant out: 4 wks before last frost
Direct sow: 2 to 4 weeks before last frost date
Fall crop: Sow 12 weeks before first fall frost
Time to harvest: 100 to 140 days

Harvest facts
Yield per plant: 6 to 12 oz
Yield per sq ft: 6 to 12 oz

Soil
pH 5.0 to 6.8
Endive prefers a rich soil with lots of moisture retentive humus. It should be well drained (as with most cold weather crops), otherwise the roots may rot over the winter. It grows well in quite acid soil.

Soil preparation: Incorporate 2″ of compost or aged manure into the top 6″ of soil.

Planning
Where: Full sun is important when Endive is growing in cool weather. In warm conditions it will probably do better in light shade.

When: The plant is similar to Lettuce in many ways, including its tendency to turn bitter or bolt in hot weather.

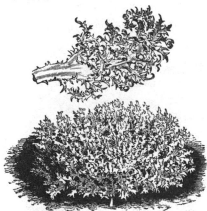

Spring: In cool climates Chicory can be grown as a spring crop. It is direct sown 2 to 4 weeks before the last frost, or started indoors earlier. It can be started earlier outdoors if protected by cloches.

Fall: Chicory is most successful as a fall crop, as it has less tendency to bolt in the cool short days. It also tastes better when grown in cool weather and may even be improved by light frost. Start the seeds about 12 weeks before the first fall frost. As with Lettuce, warm soil can hinder germination (see Lettuce for ways around this).

Over-Winter: The plants can be started in fall and over-wintered in the ground, for an early spring crop.

Planting
Transplants: Endive can be started up to 8 weeks before the last frost date and planted out 4 weeks before. Transplants are grown in the same way as Lettuce.

Direct sowing: Endive can be direct sown, using any of the techniques I have described for Lettuce. The seeds are usually planted ¼″ to ½″ deep. I plant quite thickly initially and slowly harvest thin to the desired spacing.

Spacing: Put the plants in offset rows across the bed. Space them 6″ to 9″ to 12″, depending upon the soil and variety.

Care
Water: The soil must be kept evenly moist, otherwise the plants may bolt.

Fertilization: For good growth the plants must have all the nutrients they need. If the soil is poor give them a liquid feed of compost tea, or liquid Kelp, every 3 weeks.

Blanching: The leaves are sometimes blanched to reduce their bitterness. This is done by tying the outer leaves together for 10 days before the harvest (or for up to 3 weeks in winter). Do this when the plants are dry, because if any water gets trapped inside the heart it may cause it to rot. Also don't tie slugs up inside the heart.

A simpler way to blanch them is to cover with an inverted flowerpot (close up the drainage hole). They have even been blanched by simply laying a board of wood on top of them. The inner leaves often get somewhat blanched naturally, just by being covered by the outer ones.

There is a downside to blanching. It not only reduces their bitterness, it also reduces their nutritional value. Of course you probably wouldn't eat them otherwise, because they would be too bitter (which invalidates this argument).

Pests: These are much the same as with Lettuce. Slugs can be a nuisance with young plants, or when blanching. Premature bolting is generally more of a problem than pests

Harvest: Harvest like Lettuce, taking the whole heads, individual leaves, or most of the heart (the part remaining will often re-sprout). Eat any thinnings in salads.

Storage: You can store the heads in a plastic bag in the fridge, for up to 10 days.

Seed saving: When Endive bolts in hot weather, it produces blue Chicory-like flowers. Don't save seed from any plants that bolt prematurely, as you don't want to produce a strain of quick bolting plants. The procedure for saving seed is the same as for Chicory. It is somewhat easier to save Endive seed however, as it can't be polli-nated by Chicory (or by the ubiquitous Wild Chicory).

Varieties: The Endives can be roughly divided into two types.

Broad-leaved: These varieties are sometimes known as Escarole and are the hardier of the two. They are usually grown as a fall or winter salad crop. Some people prefer their flavor.

Full Heart Batavian.

Curly leaved: These varieties are sometimes known as Curly Endive, or by the more chic French name of Chicory Frisee. These are more tolerant of hot weather, so are more often grown in spring and fall. They are much more visually appealing and find their way into many salad mixes.

Rhodos, Salad King, Tres Fin Maraichere.

Cooking: The pale heart is the best part of the Endive plant and is actually one of the best of all salad materials. Endive was originally used as a potherb (braising is good), but is now more generally eaten raw in salads.

Garlic
Allium sativum

Introduction: Garlic has been prized as a culinary flavoring for at least 5000 years. It was cultivated by almost every ancient civilization, from the Chinese, Indians and Egyptians onwards. Garlic probably originated in Central Asia, but no longer occurs there as a wild plant.

Garlic is a fairly easy crop to grow and one of the most satisfying. Harvesting the Garlic crop is one of the highlights of my gardening year.

Nutritional content:
Garlic isn't eaten in large quantities, but it contains so many valuable phytochemicals (including allicin, ajoene and allyl sulfide) that it is an important food. It has anti-carcinogenic, antioxidant, antifungal, anticlotting, antiseptic and antibiotic properties.

About Garlic

Plant: 8 wks before the first fall frost
Yield: ¾ to 2 lb sq ft.
Days to harvest: 90 to 220 days
Plants per sq ft: 4
Plants per person: 10 to 15
Ease of growing: Easy
Growing temp: 45 (55 to 75) 85° F

Soil
pH 5.5 (6.0) 7.0
Garlic will grow well enough on poor soil, but the bulbs won't get very big. For big beautiful bulbs it needs a light, rich, deep, well-drained loam with lots of organic matter. Drainage is important for this over-wintering crop, as the roots may rot if they stay wet and cold for too long.

Soil preparation: Garlic sends down roots 2 feet or more, so the ideal soil is deep, loose and friable. If the soil is at all heavy or compacted, then double digging and incorporating organic matter will help. Raised beds are also beneficial as they help to ensure good winter drainage.

Incorporate 2″ of compost or aged manure into the top 6″ of soil, along with a source of Potassium (wood ashes) and phosphorus (colloidal phosphate). Garlic has a particular liking for sulphur.

Garlic does well following a recently incorporated summer green manure crop, as it greatly benefits from the newly released nutrients. Wait two weeks for the crop to decompose a little, before planting the garlic.

Planning

Where: Garlic needs lots of sun at all times.

Crop rotation: Don't plant Garlic straight after any other Alliums, as it is subject to the same problems. Wait at least 3 years.

When: Garlic is very hardy and if the soil doesn't freeze, its roots will continue to grow right through the winter. The tops will also grow whenever the temperature is above 40° F.

In summer Garlic needs warm days (cool nights are fine) for good growth. Too much heat (above 95° F) can hasten maturation, which isn't good as it means the plant has less time to store food and so results in smaller bulbs. Rain while the bulbs are maturing isn't good either.

The most important factor in growing good Garlic is timing.

Spring: In areas with very cold winters, Garlic may not survive outside and so must be planted in spring. It can go in the ground as early as early as February if you protect it with cloches. If you plant Garlic too late, the cloves will merely get bigger and won't divide into the familiar bulbs. These are known as "rounds" and can be eaten, or left in the ground for the following year.

Fall: In most places Garlic will survive the winter outdoors and it does much better and gets larger when planted in fall. This gives it plenty of time to put on vegetative growth and store food, before the long days of the following summer trigger bulbing.

For fall planting set out your cloves from August onwards, at least 2 months before the first frost date. It should be well established before the onset of cold weather. In colder areas you should protect the young plants from frost, with a 4 to 6″ straw mulch.

Planting

How: Garlic is propagated vegetatively from individual cloves. The size of the bulb the cloves come from doesn't have any bearing on the size of next years bulbs, so use the largest bulbs for eating and use the smaller ones 2″ to 2 ½″ for planting. Gently break open the bulb, without bruising the cloves inside. Do this just before planting, as separating the cloves may initiate root growth.

Some people say larger cloves make larger bulbs. Others say it

doesn't matter much what size the clove you plant (within reason), the final bulbs will be about the same size. I say if you bought bulbs to plant, then plant them. Do you care if some of the resulting bulbs are slightly smaller than others?

Plant the cloves 2″ to 3″ deep (1″ in mild areas), making sure they are upright. This means planting them pointed side up and flat side down (planting them upside down does not help).

Spacing: Space the Garlic plants 4″ to 6″ apart, in short offset rows across the bed. If you want to be able to hoe between the rows, make the rows 8″ apart.

Bulbing: As with the related Onions, bulbing is determined by day length. Bulb formation is triggered by long days and once the right day length comes along, the plant will form a bulb, no matter what size the plant. Once bulbing starts, leaf growth comes to a halt.

Bulbing is also affected by temperature, plant size and vigor, but to a lesser extent

The bulb consists of specialized storage leaves. Bulbing occurs when the plant stops producing new leaves and starts to store food in the leaves it has. This causes their bases to expand, which creates the bulb. When the bulb is mature, all of the food has gone from the rest of the leaves, so they wither, fall over and die.

For large bulbs you want maximum leaf growth (in ideal conditions the plants may get two feet tall). Poor leaf growth means small bulbs, with small cloves that are so tedious to peel they often don't get used (don't throw them away, see Green Garlic below). It may also result in rounds, instead of divided cloves.

Care

Weed: These fairly small, strap-like plants don't compete with weeds very well, so it's important to keep them well weeded at all times. This is all the more important, as the plants grow for part of two seasons.

Water: This is another critical factor in growing good Garlic. The plants need to have a steady and constant supply of moisture when putting on leaf growth and bulbing up. Do not allow the soil to dry out at this time. Lack of water in fully grown plants, hastens maturation and starts the curing process.

About 2 to 3 weeks before the plants are ready to harvest, you should stop watering, to allow them to dry out.

Mulch: I like to lay down a straw mulch after planting, as it helps to deter birds and cats from digging in the freshly disturbed soil. It also conserves moisture and keeps down weeds. If thick enough it can also protect the cloves from cold weather.

Fertilization: Garlic isn't a very hungry plant, but it needs a steady supply of nutrients for best growth. If your soil isn't very fertile feed it with compost tea or seaweed. Start this when the plants are 3″ tall and repeat every 2 to 3 weeks during the growing season. Young plants need an adequate supply of nitrogen, so it's important to feed them while the soil is cool (not much nitrogen is available at this time).

The yellowing of some leaf tips is quite normal in Garlic; it doesn't necessarily indicate any kind of nutrient deficiency.

Bolting: This is undesirable because it diverts energy that could be used for enlarging the bulbs. If plants start to bolt, cut off the flower stalks as they appear, don't let them flower. Some people say that bulbs that have bolted, store better (even if they are smaller).

Don't throw the flower stalks away. In Asia they are highly prized as food and special varieties are grown to produce them. See Flower stems below for more on this.

Pests and diseases: Garlic is generally free of most pests and diseases, though it is more afflicted in cool wet climates. It is occasionally attacked by Onion Maggots (a relative of Cabbage Root Maggot) and of course Gophers will eat it (plant by plant, right down the row, if given the opportunity).

Harvest

When: Garlic is harvested when half of the top leaves have turned yellow (there should still be 5 or 6 green leaves). Pull up a bulb and inspect it carefully before harvest-

ing all of it. If Garlic is left too long the over-mature bulbs may split open. This may not look very nice, but doesn't affect its edibility or storage.

How: Sometimes you can simply uproot the plants by pulling on the tops. If the soil is very firm, you will have to loosen it with a fork first. Garlic bruises easily, so don't throw it around while harvesting.

Curing: Newly harvested Garlic should be cured before storage (curing also improves its flavor, as fresh Garlic may be somewhat bitter). If the weather is dry, you can cure the bulbs by leaving them in a shady place for a week or two. If it's wet, you will have to cure them inside (the greenhouse is a good place, as it's dry and warm). Don't leave the bulbs on the ground in the sun for too long, as they may get cooked. They then turn a trans-lucent yellow and are ruined.

The dry bulbs are prepared for sale by cutting off the shriveled tops (leave about 2″) and trimming the stringy roots (to ½″). They are cleaned by removing the outer wrapper layer.

If you want to make some Garlic braids, save the bulbs with the best tops (don't cut them off of course).

Storage: The bulbs must be thoroughly dry before storing them. They should be stored in a cool dry place, with 60 to 70% humidity and good air circulation. If the bulbs are to be used fairly quickly, they can be stored at 50 to 60° F. For longer-term storage (and for the bulbs that will be re-planted in fall) they should ideally be kept at 35 to 40° F. Store in wooden boxes, mesh bags, or the traditional Garlic braids. It is tempting to hang the attractive braids in the kitchen, but it is usually too warm and dry there. Some of the bulbs will probably dry out before you get around to using them all.

Seed saving

Seed saving: Garlic doesn't produce viable seed, it is propagated vegetatively from the same cloves you use in cooking. Simply save some of the bulbs for re-planting at the appropriate time. These must be stored carefully, otherwise they may dry out, or sprout prematurely.

If you use the same strain for long enough, it will eventually adapt to your climate.

Unusual growing ideas
Bulbils: You could grow Garlic from bulbils produced from the head, but you won't get mature bulbs for two years.

Green Garlic: In China a lot of Garlic is planted for use in the green stage. Any surplus, or unusually small cloves (such as the aforementioned ones that are too small to peel) can be planted in a couple of square feet of bed (like Green Onions). Single leaves can be cut off from the bulbs as needed (it will produce more). The whole young plants are also eaten. If you overlook a bulb and it sprouts in the garden, use the multiple stems in the kitchen.

Flower stems: In China and Japan when a bulb bolts it is considered to be an opportunity, rather than a loss. The flower stalks are highly prized and constitute an extra crop from the maturing bulbs.

The stems are cut off as they emerge and the bulb continues to mature. They even have special varieties that reliably bolt, but still produce good sized bulbs.

Variety: There are many more kinds of Garlic than you might expect, some adapted for long growing seasons, some for short ones. You can buy many strains by mail order, while a few may be available in local retail outlets. You should only need to buy a variety of Garlic once, as it's easy to save bulbs for next year.

You can grow Garlic from cloves purchased in a supermarket, but it will probably be adapted to the California (or Chinese) climate. You will do better with locally grown bulbs from a farmers market, as they should be of a variety that does well in your area. When buying bulbs intended for food use, you should be aware that some diseases can be spread vegetatively on the cloves.

Garlic can be (as always) divided into two types.

Hard neck varieties are said to be the best flavored, but bolt quite readily and don't store as well as the softnecks. They can be identified by their hard flower stalk.
Chesnok Red
Music
Spanish Roja

Soft neck varieties are the types commonly sold in supermarkets. They often do well when planted in spring.
Artichoke
Inchelium Red
Silverskin

Cooking: Garlic doesn't develop its characteristic flavor until the cell walls are ruptured. This releases as enzyme called alliinase which converts the alliin in the cells into the allicin (diallyl thiosulphinate) we all love.

The flavor of garlic varies according to how it is prepared. Some cooks insist that for best flavor Garlic cloves should be chopped rather than crushed. They say you should never use a garlic press.

Green Garlic: In China they don't just eat Garlic cloves. They eat the whole plant; young leaves, young plants, flower stalks. These can be used in the same ways as green Onions.

Garlic soup
You have to try this, it's a variation of the soup that earned me a marriage proposal. Not in any way pungent or harsh, it is rich and delicious. I believe it originated in Provence.

2 bulbs (not cloves) garlic peeled and chopped
4 tbsp olive oil
8 cups water
3 potatoes cut into small cubes
3 celery stalks (chop finely)
3 carrots sliced finely
1 tsp chopped parsley
1 tsp dried basil
1 bay leaf
Salt and pepper

Saute the garlic in the oil for a couple of minutes and then add everything else. Simmer until cooked.

Grass juice
Barley (*Hordeum* spp)

Wheat (*Triticum* spp)

I am including this rather unusual food, even though it is relatively unknown, because it has incredible nutritional value. The green juice expressed from the young leaves of cultivated Barley and Wheat plants is said to contain almost all of the nutrients humans require. It is packed with vitamins, minerals, antioxidants, chlorophyll and other nutrients and can make a significant contribution to your health.

You can buy these juices fresh or dried, but they are expensive and it is easy to grow your own. Many other grasses can also be used as a source of grass juice, but these are the easiest to grow, the most productive and maybe the most nutritious. They are one of the best, readily available and most overlooked survival foods.

Preparing indoor flats:
Wheatgrass can be grown indoors (or in the greenhouse) year round. You can even grow it without soil, just using paper towels to hold moisture, but it grows better in soil and the juice may be somewhat more nutritious.

The growing container may be anything of sufficient size that can hold an inch or two of soil. The best are probably ordinary garden flats, or large trays.

Scatter a thin layer of seed on to the tray, so the seeds just about touch one another and very little soil is visible underneath them. Put the tray in a warm, dark place until it starts to germinate. Once the seeds start to germinate they must be brought into full light and watered regularly.

Preparing outdoor beds:
The easiest way to grow wheatgrass in volume is to sow it out in the garden in an intensive bed (obviously this won't work in winter). For a continuous supply you might sow a few square feet every week or so.

Plant it as you would a cover crop, by scattering the seed on the bed. There should be a seed about every ¼" to ½" or so. It is then incorporated ½" to 1" deep into the soil with a rake. It will probably need protection from birds, mice and other predators (cats and dogs will chew it).

Care
The grass will grow rapidly if it is warm. It should be well watered for maximum growth and succulence, but shouldn't become waterlogged.

Harvest: The grass is harvested when 8" to 10" high, by cutting it off at the base with scissors. Leave a couple of inches on the plant to help it recover and you should get a second harvest.

Use: The juice can be extracted with any vegetable juicer, but the slower hand juicers are said to be the best. Apparently high speed juicers cause the juice to oxidize and deteriorate. The deep green juice is very strongly lawn flavored and quite nauseous to some people (though others like it). If you don't like it by itself, it can be disguised with other juices. For maximum nutritional content drink the sweet juice immediately.

Hamburg Parsley
Petroselintum crispum var *tuberosum*

Introduction: A little known and under used crop, this is a dual purpose plant, providing a swollen Parsnip-like root and tasty Parsley flavored foliage.

Nutritional content:
The green parts contains anti-cancer phytochemicals. The root is rich in carbohydrates.

About Hamburg Parsley

Seed facts
Germ temp: 40 (50 to 85) 90° F
Germ time: 2 to 4 weeks
29 days / 50° F
17 days / 59° F
14 days / 68° F
13 days / 77° F * Optimum
12 days / 86° F
Viability: 1 to 5 yrs
Germination percentage: 60%+
Weeks to grow transplant: 8 to 12

Planning facts
Hardiness: Hardy
Ease of growing: Easy
Growing temp: 45 (60 to 65) 75° F
Transplants:
Start: 6 wks before last frost
Plant out: on last frost date
Direct sow: 6 wks before last frost
Time to harvest: 85 to 150 days

Soil:
pH 6.0 - 7.0
This crop does well in most soils, so long as they are moisture retentive. Incorporate 2" of compost

or well-rotted manure (it doesn't like a lot of nitrogen, so don't use fresh manure). It also likes phosphorus, so add colloidal phosphate or bone meal.

Planning
When:

Spring: Hamburg Parsley is very hardy, but the seed takes a long time to germinate in cool soil. For reasonably prompt germination it needs fairly warm soil (around 70° F), so it is usually planted around the frost-free date. It can be started indoors about 6 weeks before the frost-free date and planted out on the frost-free date.

Fall: Hamburg Parsley does best when grown as a fall and winter crop, started in mid summer.

Where: This plant can tolerate more shade than most crops and still do quite well. However for best production it should be given full sun.

Planting
Indoors: Like most root crops it doesn't like transplanting, so must be started in soil blocks or plug trays to minimize root disturbance.

Outdoors: Sow the seed almost on the surface (⅛″ to ¼″ deep). It probably pays to soak the seed overnight prior to planting, or even pre-germinate it indoors on paper towels (fluid sowing makes this easier). It can be broadcast or sown in rows.

The seed is sometimes planted in fall, to germinate in early spring (this gives it plenty of time).

Spacing: Hamburg Parsley is sometimes spaced quite closely (3″ to 4″), to get a large quantity of small roots (these are eaten while they are still young and tender). Alternatively you can plant further apart (6″) and allow the roots to reach full size.

Care
Water: Though the plants are quite drought tolerant, you should keep them well watered for best growth and flavor.

Mulch: Mulch the established plants to conserve moisture and keep down weeds.

Weeds: The young plants don't compete with weeds very well, so must be weeded carefully. This should be done by hand, as hoes can easily damage the shoulders of the root. Older plants are better able to compete against weeds, as they produce an abundance of foliage.

Mulch: This is helpful to keep down weeds, conserve soil moisture and keep the soil cool.

Pests: Hamburg Parsley may be attacked by the same pests and diseases as Carrot, but is seldom bothered.

Harvesting
When: The roots can be used as soon as they are large enough to bother with, but taste best when 6″ to 8″ long.

The leaves can be used like Parsley, as soon as they are of sufficient size. Just don't take too much from any single plant, as the top growth is needed to provide food for the roots.

How: Dig the roots as you would Carrots or Parsnips.

Storage: The roots are best left in the ground under mulch until you need them. If this isn't possible store them in moist sand or sawdust in a root cellar at 32 to 40° F with 90%+ humidity.

Seed saving: Saving seed is quite simple, just leave the plants alone to flower and set seed. It is cross-pollinated by insects, so don't save seed from different varieties at the same time (not that there are many).

Unusual growing ideas
Naturalizing: You don't have to do anything to get this biennial to naturalize, just allow it to seed itself. Plants will germinate everywhere the seed falls. These will flower the following year and set seed of their own.

Ornament: Parsley foliage is attractive enough to warrant a place in the ornamental garden.

Varieties: I have never seen any, just plain old Hamburg Parsley.

Cooking: This plant is most widely used in Eastern European cooking. Cook the roots like Parsnips. Use the leaves in sauces, salads and as the all-purpose garnish.

Related species:
Parsley
Petroselintum crispum
Flat leaf Parsley is said to have the best flavor, but the curly varieties are more popular, as they are more attractive. Parsley is cultivated as described above, but is easier to grow, as you don't need to produce a large swollen root. You won't need a lot of plants, 3 or 4 should be plenty. I don't plant it anymore, as I have enough self sown plants.

Horseradish
Armoracia rusticana

Introduction: Horseradish is native to Eastern Europe, but it has been widely cultivated in temperate areas around the world and is now naturalized in most of them. This is typical of this persistent plant, where it is planted it stays.

Nutritional content:
Hardly a major source of nutrients, because it is too pungent to eat in quantity. It contains some phyto-chemicals with anti-cancer proper-ties, including allyl isothiocyanate.

Soil: Horseradish will grow in almost any well-drained soils, but gets bigger when growing in a rich, moist soil with lots of organic matter.

Planning
Where: This isn't an invasive plant, in that it doesn't spread, but it is very persistent. Once you plant Horseradish it can be difficult to remove, as any fragment of root left in the ground can grow into a new plant. For this reason it is best planted in a remote place, where it can be left to its own devices.

You can also plant it in a container, partly buried in the ground (it needs to be deep). The latter also makes harvesting easy, simply dig up the container and dump it out on to the ground.

Horseradish does best in a fairly cool climate and likes full sun.

Planting
Vegetative: Horseradish is not grown from seed, but is propagated vegetatively from pieces of root. Usually when a plant is harvested, the smaller rootlets are trimmed off from the large roots. These are saved for re-planting, while the larger roots are eaten. Very small rootlets take 2 years to produce usable roots. Larger roots will be ready to harvest in only 1 year.

Care
Mulch: This is helpful to keep down weeds and hold in moisture.

Water: Horseradish is somewhat drought tolerant, but gets bigger if watered regularly.

Pests: Gophers eat the roots. I haven't had any other problems.

Harvesting: The roots can be dug at any time of year, though they are at their best while dormant, from late fall until early spring (when they start growing again). In loose soil, the roots of older plants may grow to be three feet in length, but smaller roots are generally of better quality for food.

How: The brittle roots need to be dug carefully, as they break easily. Any fragment remaining in the ground will grow into a new plant, which can be good or bad.

Storage: In mild winter areas the roots can be gathered as needed through the winter. In cold areas, where the ground freezes, you should dig all you need in late fall and store them over the winter in damp sand.

Seed saving: Horseradish has been propagated vegetatively for so long that it doesn't usually produce seed. Of course it doesn't need to, it saves itself.

Unusual growing ideas: Horseradish doesn't need the pampered soil and growing condi-tions to be found in the intensive beds. It will be happy in almost any vacant spot in the garden.

Varieties: Maliner Kren is the commonest variety (in fact usually the only one). I originally bought my Horseradish root from a vegetable market (it was cheaper), so don't even know what variety it is.

Cooking:
An intact Horseradish root has no pungency at all, the acrid oil that gives it its characteristic flavor only appears when the root is damaged. Damage (such as grating) ruptures the cell walls, allowing an enzyme to react with a glycoside to form Mustard oil (allyl isothiocyanate). The relatively bland root then quickly develops enough pungency to take your breath away.

Like most plants that produce mustard oil, Horseradish irritates the kidneys and mucous membranes and so is toxic to some degree. However it is hard to eat enough to have any deleterious effect, beyond a sore tongue.

Horseradish is an acquired taste. A bite of the raw root may be the hottest thing you have ever eaten and this extreme pungency limits its use as food. It is far from insignificant however, as it is used to make the famous Horseradish sauce, as well as salad dressings.

Try making "Horseradish Bread" instead of garlic bread.

If you dislike the pungency of the raw root, try cooking it. This prevents the acrid mustard oil from forming and leaves you with a relatively bland root vegetable. The cooked root is a good addition to soup.

Horseradish Sauce

2 oz grated horseradish
1 oz sugar
pinch of sea salt
2 oz breadcrumbs
1/4 cup plain yogurt
1/2 cup mayonnaise
1 tbsp lemon juice

Mix together all the ingredients and then add enough wine vinegar to make a paste. Chill in the fridge.

Leaves: The first tender spring leaves can be added to salads, or cooked with other greens as a potherb. These are so good that the roots have actually been forced indoors like Chicory (*Cichorium*) to provide winter greens.

Kale, Scotch
Brassica oleracea var *acephala*

Introduction: This cool season biennial is the most primitive of the Brassica crops and is not very far removed from the wild *Brassica oleracea*. It is a relative rarity on the dinner table in this country, which is unfortunate as it is one of the most nutritious vegetables.

Kale grows quite well in warm weather, but so do lots of other potherbs. It really comes into its own in winter, as it can survive temperatures as low as 0° F (even lower under mulch). It will continue to produce food when most other crops are just frozen sticks. It can even be gathered from under the snow when frozen solid.

Kale was a staple winter food for many Northern European peasants (Scottish vegetable gardens were commonly known as Kale-yards). It was especially important during late winter and early spring, when it was one of the few fresh foods available. One cultivar was actually known as Hungry Gap.

Another benefit of kale is that it can be harvested repeatedly, often sending out new leaves for 6 months or more.

Many Americans see Kale as an attractive curly garnish (often used as a cheap substitute for Parsley), which isn't intended to be eaten. This is a shame because well-grown Kale, harvested in cold weather, is very good. At the same time I should add that poorly grown Kale, harvested in warm summer weather, can be tough and almost inedible.

About Kale

Seed facts
Germ temp: 40 (45 to 95) 100° F
Germ time: 7 to 12 days
15 days / 50° F
9 days / 59° F
6 days / 68° F
5 days / 77° F * Optimum
4 days / 86° F
Seed viability: 4 to 6 yrs
Germination percentage: 75+
Weeks to grow transplants 5 to 6

Planning facts
Hardiness: Very hardy
Ease of growing: Easy
Growing temp: 40 (60 to 65) 75° F
Plants per person: 10
Plants per sq ft: to 1
Transplants:
Start: 6 weeks before last frost
Plant out: 2 wks before last frost
Direct sow 4 wks before last frost
Fall planting: Sow 2 to 3 months before first frost
Time to harvest: 50 days

Harvest facts
Length of harvest: 16 to 26 wks
Yield per plant: 1 to 2 lb

Nutritional content:
Kale is rich in vitamins A, C and K, chlorophyll and important phytochemicals (including isothiocyanates, sulfuraphane, lutein and zeaxanthin).

Soil
pH 6.0 - 7.5
Kale is more tolerant of poor soil than any of the other Brassicas, but the most palatable leaves are produced by rapid uninterrupted growth. For this the soil must be rich and moisture retentive.

Moisture retention isn't usually a significant issue with a winter crop, in fact drainage is usually more of a concern. If the soil is too wet in winter the roots may rot.

Soil preparation: Kale likes organic matter, so amend the soil by digging in 2″ of compost or aged manure. It also likes a neutral pH, so add lime if necessary. Its nutritional requirements are similar to those of Cabbage, in that it needs a significant amount of phosphorus and potassium, but not a lot of nitrogen.

Planning

Where: Winter Kale will be growing in the coldest part of the year, so should be planted in the warmest, sunniest, most sheltered part of the garden. Late Kale can succeed a mid-season crop such as Potatoes or Beans.

Crop rotation: Kale should not be planted where another Brassica has been grown in the past 3 years.

When

Spring: Kale can be planted in spring for harvesting in early summer. It is started indoors 6 weeks before the last frost date and planted out 2 weeks before the last frost date.

Kale will actually grow right through the summer, but doesn't taste very good in warm weather. It really needs cool weather to make it tender and sweet.

Fall and Winter: As I already mentioned Kale is most useful as a fall and winter crop. It is planted in midsummer, at least 2 to 3 months before the first fall frost date. The plants need to be fairly big by the time of the first frost, so they are vigorous enough to keep growing. In mild climates Kale will continue to grow all winter without disruption and can be harvested continually for months (it will also be in peak condition in the cool weather).

It is a good idea to plant your autumn Kale as an intercrop, into an existing summer crop. It will gradually take over the space as the weather gets cooler.

Planting
Transplants

Starting inside: Kale is often started indoors for an early spring planting. Transplants may also be used where insects or other pests are a problem.

Kale doesn't mind transplanting so can be started in flats, as well as cell packs and soil blocks.

Planting out: The seedlings go outside when they have 4 or 5 true leaves and are about 5″ high.

Starting outside: In terms of bed space, a Kale seed takes up as much space as an 8-week-old transplant. To more efficiently use bed space, the plants can be started in a nursery bed in May or June and transplanted out at the full spacing in July or August.

Direct sowing: Kale germinates fast and grows quickly, so it is easily direct sown. Plant the seeds ¼″ to ½″ deep and 2″ apart. Start harvest thinning when all the seedlings have emerged.

Spacing: Kale plants can get quite big, so give them plenty of room:

12″ apart in excellent soil
15″ apart in good soil
18″ apart in poor soil.

Care

Weeds: Kale is pretty independent once established, so you only really need worry about weeds while it is young.

Watering: Kale has large leaves and can lose a lot of water in warm weather. For the best quality you must keep it well supplied with water.

Fertilization: If the soil isn't very fertile, feed the plants with compost tea or liquid Kelp. Start feeding them as soon as they have recovered from transplanting and every month thereafter. This is especially important if you are going to be harvesting for weeks on end.

Mulching: Use a mulch in summer to keep down weeds, keep the soil cool and conserve soil moisture. In winter a mulch protects plant roots by moderating soil temperature and preventing frost heaving.

Pests: Kale is less vulnerable to pests than other Brassicas, but it still has its share, especially in warm weather. See Cabbage for more on these pests and how to deal with them.

Aphids: These tiny pests are almost always present on Kale in my garden. The only time they disappear is when it gets very cold. The simplest way to deal with them is to blast them off the plants with a strong jet of water.

Quail: Where I live Quail seem to have a particular affection for Kale and in winter they may strip whole leaves from the plants. At my last house they got so bad I had to net the 3 ft tall plants.

Harvesting

When: Kale produces an abundance of foliage right through the growing season, but it is at its best during cold weather. This is because cold weather stimulates the conversion of starches in the leaves into sugars (a similar thing happens in Jerusalem Artichokes and Parsnips). A few nights of freezing temperatures are enough to make this happen. The cold also makes the leaves more tender.

You can gather Kale leaves for as long as they are produced, sometimes right through the winter. In extreme cold you might cover them with mulch for extra protection. Even the frozen leaves can be eaten and are actually very good.

The new shoots, produced when the plant first starts growing again in spring, are also good.

When Kale bolts in spring, the flower buds can (and should) be gathered and used like Broccoli. If they are not infested with aphids they are a nutritious and tasty treat, that is not to be missed

How: You can harvest entire plants, cutting out the growing center of the plant and leaving the rest to send up side shoots. However for a longer and bigger harvest it is best to gather single leaves, as they get large enough. Don't take them from the growing point and only take 1 or 2 leaves from a plant at one time. You may be able to stimulate an old plant to put out tender new growth, by stripping off all of its leaves.

Seed saving: Plants overwintered in the ground will flower the following spring. Kale will cross-pollinate with any other Brassica crop (Broccoli, Brussels Sprout, Cabbage, Collards), so only one variety can be flowering at one time. Save the seed in the same way as you would Cabbage.

The plants will produce an abundance of seed. In fact they sometimes get so top heavy with seed they need staking to stop them falling over.

If you save Kale seed you will end up with a lot, especially as you should save the seed from at least 5 plants to maintain some genetic variability. This is far more than you will ever need for planting. You can sprout most of it like Alfalfa, or use it to grow micro-greens.

Unusual growing ideas
Winter indoors: In very cold areas Kale can be grown in winter in an unheated greenhouse or cold frame. It has even been grown indoors as a winter houseplant.

Ornamental use: Some Kales have very attractive foliage and can be used in the flower garden. The specially bred ornamental Kales are supposedly edible, but are not very palatable.

Cover crop: Kale is sometimes planted as a green manure or winter cover crop. In areas with mild winters it will produce a lot of foliage over the winter and has the additional benefit that it is edible. In spring you can eat the tender new flower shoots, before incorporating the rest of the plants into the soil.

The drawback to using Kale as a cover crop, is that it is a member of the Brassica family and so prone to all of the same pests and diseases.

Varieties:
Dwarf Blue
Thousand Headed Kale: Very hardy.
Lacinato; This Italian variety is known in Italy as Cavolo Nero or Black Cabbage.

Tree Kale: Also known as Walking Stick Cabbage, because the woody stems have been used for making walking sticks. This variety was bred in the British Channel Islands for cattle feed and grows up to 10 feet tall. Humans can also eat the leaves. It is unusual in that it is a perennial and can be propagated from stem cuttings. It has been growing in my garden for several years.

Cooking: In cool weather the tender young leaves are good enough to eat raw. Older leaves can be steamed, stir-fried or used in soups. They are quite substantial and don't cook down nearly as much as Spinach, so you don't need to gather as much at one time.

Colcannon
This simple Irish peasant dish was traditionally eaten at Halloween.
1 lb kale (strip out any tough midribs and chop finely)
1 lb mashed potatoes
1 finely chopped onion or 2 small leeks or 4 chopped scallions
5 fl oz milk
butter
salt and pepper

Cook the kale until tender. At the same time simmer the onions in the milk for 5 minutes. Mix the finely chopped kale with the mashed potatoes and then add the milk. Reheat it for a few minutes then put in a dish. Sprinkle with salt and pepper and then make a well in the center for the butter.

Collards
Brassica oleracea var *acephala*

Introduction: Collards are the same sub-species as Scotch Kale, but differ in being more tolerant of hot weather. Their heat tolerance has made them an important crop in the southeastern States, where they are grown almost year round. Collards are cultivated and used in pretty much the same ways as Kale, so I won't repeat all of that information here.

How to grow: Collards are such a long season crop, they are usually direct sown 2″ to 3″ apart in mid spring. Wait until the cold weather has passed, so there is no chance of them being vernalized (which could cause them to bolt).

As the planting fills in, it is gradually harvest thinned, first to 6″, then to 12″ and then (if the plants get big enough) to a final spacing of 15″ to 18″. If conditions are right it will continue to grow right through the summer, fall and into winter. The fully grown plants are very tolerant of cold weather, smaller ones less so.

Harvest: Though Collards tolerate hot weather, the leaves taste better in cool weather and it is as a winter crop that it really comes into its own. If you only gather a couple of leaves from a plant each time, it will continue to grow strongly. Take them from the bottom of the plants and leave the growing heart alone.

Unusual growing ideas:
Like Kale this is an independent plant and does well in the wild or forest garden.

Varieties: Georgia, Vates and Florida are the most commonly available cultivars.

Siberian Kale
Brassica napus var *pabularia*

It is somewhat unfair that Scotch Kale gets a full heading, yet Siberian Kale only gets this small section, because this is actually a much more palatable plant. Most of the things I have said in praise of Scotch Kale apply here as well, except that it is less hardy. You would imagine that a Siberian would be hardier than the Scot, but in this case it isn't.

In Britain this species is sometimes called Rape Kale, which is a good name because it is actually a type of Rape (*B. napus*) and more closely related to Rutabaga than Kale. This species is good at any time, though it is at its best in cool weather. It is certainly most useful at that time, when fewer other crops are available.

This plant is one of the staple winter green vegetables in my garden and I can't praise it enough. It is a fantastic crop plant.

I have planted Red Russian Kale in late spring and it has fed us through the summer, fall, winter (in our mild winters it doesn't even slow down) and into early spring. It then bolts and produces an abundance of nutritious and tasty flower buds. If they are not infested with aphids, these can be used like Broccoli, Eventually the flowers start to open and go on to produce a lot of seed (often several ounces per plant). This can be used for sprouting, micro-greens and to grow future crops.

Siberian Kale is grown in exactly the same way as Scotch Kale. It differs from that plant in that it isn't as hardy and tastes better in warm weather. It won't cross-pollinate with any *B. oleracea* species, though it will cross with Rutabaga.

Varieties:

White Russian
Wild Kale
Red Russian: 60 days. This old heirloom variety is also known as Ragged Jack (because of its ragged frilled leaves). It grows well in heat and cold, though is not as hardy as some cultivars. It is one of the best-flavored varieties, with succulent and tender leaves.

Kohlrabi

Brassica oleracea var *gongylodes*

As the name suggests, Kohlrabi was developed in Germany. It is sometimes said to be a cross between a Cabbage and a Turnip, but that may be just because it seems like one.

Introduction: This somewhat bizarre looking vegetable is relatively rare in gardens and kitchens; in fact most people don't even know what it is. Those who are familiar with it, consider it one of the best tasting of all the Brassicas. The edible part of the Kohlrabi is not a root, but the swollen above ground portion of the stem, which tastes rather like a Turnip.

Kohlrabi is actually a very useful crop, fast growing, compact, nutritious and slightly more tolerant of warm weather than most Brassicas. Much that has been said about Cabbage also applies to Kohlrabi.

Nutritional content:
This is much the same as Cabbage.

Soil:
pH 6.0 - 7.0
Kohlrabi likes a light, rich, moisture retentive soil, with lots of organic matter. Incorporate 2″ of compost or aged manure into the top 6″ of soil (you could add fresh manure the previous fall). It is a light feeding crop and doesn't need a lot of nitrogen, but it does like potassium (add greensand or wood ashes). It also likes calcium.

Planning
Where: Kohlrabi needs full sun.

About Kohlrabi

Seed facts
Germ temp: 40 (45 to 95) 100° F
Germ time: 3 to 10 days
15 days / 50° F
9 days / 59° F
6 days / 68° F
5 days / 77° F * Optimum
4 days / 86° F
Seed viability: 4 yrs
Germination percentage: 75%+
Weeks to grow transplant: 5 to 6

Planning facts
Hardiness: Half hardy
Ease of growing: Fairly easy
Growing temp: 40 (60 to 65) 75°
Plants per person: 10
Plants per sq ft: 4
Transplants:
Start 4 to 6 wks before last frost
Plant out 2 to 4 wks before last frost
Succession sow: every 2 to 3 wks
Fall sow: 6 to 8 wks before first fall frost
Time to harvest: 55 to 90 days
30 to 40 days from transplanting

Harvest facts
Yield per sq ft: 1½
Yield per plant: 6 oz

Crop rotation: Kohlrabi should not be planted where another Brassica was grown in the previous 3 years, as it can lead to disease or pest problems.

When: Kohlrabi (like most Brassicas) grows best in the cool (40 to 70° F) weather of spring and fall.

Spring: Sow the first spring crop 4 to 6 weeks before the last frost date (it will grow at 40° F).

Fall: Kohlrabi generally does better as a fall crop, sown 6 to 8 weeks before the first autumn frost date. Autumn Kohlrabi can be allowed to get larger than 2" to 3", because cold weather seems to keep them tender (it also increases their sweetness).

Succession sowing: In spring you can make several succession sowings (very early sowings may be vernalized and bolt). In cool climates you can continue to succession sow all summer.

Planting

Transplants

Starting inside: Kohlrabi is such a fast growing crop, that starting it indoors is probably only worthwhile if your growing season is very short, or if space is limited. Sow the seeds 3 to 4 weeks before planting out. Use cell packs, soil blocks or plug trays, because it doesn't really like transplanting.

Planting out: Transplant the seedlings outside 2 to 4 weeks before the last frost date. Plant them to the depth of their first true leaves.

Direct sowing: Kohlrabi is usually direct sown, Sow the seed ¼" deep in rows or broadcast it. Sow quite thickly initially and thin when they are well established (eat the thinnings).

Spacing: You should plant Kohlrabi in offset rows across the bed. Space it 4" to 6" to 8" apart, depending on the fertility of the soil. Make sure the plants aren't crowded, or they won't size up properly.

Care

Kohlrabi must grow fast for best quality, so give the plants all the water and nutrients they need.

Thinning: It is important to thin (and weed) the plants properly, otherwise they won't bulb up.

Weeds: It is best to control weeds by hand weeding, as hoeing can easily damage the shallow roots and swollen stems. A mulch will also help.

Water: Keep the soil evenly moist, or the bulbous stems may turn woody. Fortunately this isn't often an issue with this cool weather crop. The plants have the greatest need for water when their bulbs are forming, so make sure you keep the soil moist at this time.

Fertilization: If the soil isn't very fertile, you should give the plants a liquid feed of compost tea once a month.

Pests: The same pests that attack Cabbage also go for Kohlrabi, but they aren't usually as bad (See **Cabbage**). In spring you may have to protect the seedlings from birds.

Harvesting

When: Start harvesting the bulbous stems when they are 1½" to 2" in diameter, as they are most tender at this stage. You can eat the larger 3" diameter roots, but in warm weather they often develop a woody core and their flavor deteriorates. In winter even the larger bulbs can be good.

How: Cut the stem an inch below the bulb, or simply uproot the entire plant if they aren't growing too close together (don't disturb neighboring plants). For storage you should cut off the leaves and roots.

Storage: Kohlrabi stores very well and will keep for several weeks in the fridge in a plastic bag. It may last for several months in a root cellar at 32 to 40° F and 90%+ humidity. It also freezes well.

Seed saving: This is the same as for Cabbage. In very cold climates you may have to lift the plants in fall and store them in a root cellar over the winter. Re-plant them in spring when it warms up.

Unusual growing ideas

Intercrop: This compact and fast growing plant can be very useful for intercropping.

Varieties: There aren't many varieties available, the commonest are:
Green Vienna (better flavored)
Purple Vienna (hardier)
Early White Vienna (what's this with Vienna?)
Gigante

Cooking: The bulbous stem is rich in protein and vitamin C. It is good cooked or eaten raw in salads. If the bulb is old, peel off the fibrous outer skin (this is easier after cooking). The young leaves can be used like Kale.

Leek
Allium porrum

Introduction: This non-bulbing relative of the onion was probably derived from *A. ampeloprasum*. It is native to Eurasia and was first cultivated somewhere in the Eastern Mediterranean. It has been a food of the common people since the ancient Egyptians.

One of the hardiest of common crops, Leek was very important for Northern European peasants. It could grow right through the winter and still be good in early spring, when little else is available. Its sweet and delicate onion flavor was widely used to flavor more bland staple foods.

The Leek is a satisfying and straightforward crop to grow. It is easier to grow than the onion, because you don't have to worry about bulbing and day length. Leeks grown in the summer can simply be left in the ground all winter, to be harvested as needed for the kitchen.

Nutritional content:
Similar to green Onions.

Soil
pH 6.0 - 7.0
Leeks need a deep, rich, fairly neutral soil. It should be well drained, because the plants will remain in the ground through much of the winter and are susceptible to rot in wet soil. Leeks do well in deep intensive beds

Soil preparation: A common practice is to plant Leeks in soil that was heavily amended and cultivated for a previous crop, such as Potatoes. If it is low in organic matter, or particularly heavy, incorporate 2″ of compost or aged manure, into the top 6″. If the soil is compacted, you might want to consider double digging, because Leeks like loose loam. They also like potassium and phosphorus, so add colloidal phosphate and greensand or wood ashes.

About Leek

Seed facts
Germ temp: 40 (60 to 75) 95° F
Germ time: 14 to 21 days
30 days / 41° F
13 days / 50° F
7 days / 59° F
5 days / 68° F * Optimum
4 days / 77° F
4 days / 86° F
Germination percentage: 75%+
Viability: 1 to 5 years
Weeks to grow transplants: 10 to 12

Planning facts
Hardiness: Hardy
Ease of growing: Easy
Growing temp: 45 (55 to 75) 85° F
Plants per person: 30 to 50
Plants per sq ft: 9
Transplants:
Start: 6 to 8 wks before last frost
Plant out: 4 weeks after last frost
Direct sow 4 weeks before last frost date
Sow fall crop 4 to 5 months before first fall frost
Time to harvest: 110 to 200 weeks
75 to 100 days from transplants

Harvest facts
Yield per plant: 8 oz per plant
Yield per sq ft: 2 to 9 lb sq ft

If your soil is poor, you might grow them in trenches, enriched with aged manure or compost. This is how they get those prize 9 lb Leeks.

Leeks can be planted fairly early in the spring, so gardeners often prepare the growing bed the previous fall.

Planning
Where: Leeks need full sun, especially if growing in winter.

Leeks take a long time to grow and will be in the ground for most of the growing season, so put them where they won't be in the way. Fortunately they don't take up much space and are good for inter-cropping, as their foliage is relatively sparse for much of their early growth.

When
Spring: Leeks like a long cool (not much above 70° F) growing season and are often the first spring vegetables to be started indoors. They grow so slowly they are usually started indoors, about three months before they are planted out (sometimes as early as December or

January). The earlier you start them, the larger they will get. Unlike many crops they don't get over-mature quickly, they just get bigger. The seedlings are transplanted outdoors 4 to 6 weeks after the last frost date (they should be hardened off first). This means you can get a lot of growth out of them before they even go into the ground.

Leeks can also be direct sown, about a month before the expected last frost, or as soon as the soil can be worked. Early Leeks may benefit from the protection of cloches. Some people start Leeks both indoors and outdoors. The transplants are for eating over the summer, while the direct sown ones are for using the following winter.

Fall: In areas with mild winters, Leeks are best grown as an overwintering crop. They are started in early summer (indoors or out).

Planting
Transplants:
Starting inside: Leeks transplant easily so are usually started in flats. They don't have much foliage, so can be planted quite close together and you can get a lot of plants in one flat. The seeds germinate and grow slowly, so start them early, water regularly, feed occasionally and be patient. They should be ready to plant out in 8 to 12 weeks when they are about 8″ tall. Some people advise trimming the tops and roots, but I don't.

Planting out: There is no point transplanting the seedlings outside before the soil has warmed up, they will grow faster inside. Wait until a month after the last frost date. In my opinion the only way to

plant Leek seedlings is with a dibber. In fact a desire to plant a lot of Leeks is a sufficient reason to get (or make) a dibber. Mark out the required 4″ to 6″ hole depth (depending on size of plants) on the side of the dibber, so you know how deep to go. Then you simply punch a series of holes in the soil, drop a plant into each hole and water them with a trickle of water. There is no need to fill the hole, enough soil will wash down into the bottom to cover the roots. It couldn't be easier, or quicker.

You can also transplant the seedlings into a 6″ to 8″ deep trench, but it's a lot more work. Dig the trench, lay the plants in it at the right spacing and then plant them almost up to the growing point. The trench is re-filled slowly to blanch the stems and provide a greater length of the most desirable white stem. If you fill the trench all at once, there is some danger that the stem may rot.

Leeks can also be planted in a row on level ground. They are then hilled up as they grow, to blanch the lower stems

Transplants:
Starting outside: Fall Leeks are often started outdoors in a nursery bed and later transplanted

to a permanent site. This is much more space efficient than direct sowing and the seedlings are more easily protected from pests.

Direct sowing: Summer Leeks can be direct sown in early spring at a depth of ¼″ to ½″. They rarely are though, because it is a waste of space. It's a much better use of space to start them in a nursery bed

Spacing: The spacing for Leeks ranges from 3″ to 6″ depending upon the fertility of the soil. They are usually planted in offset rows across the bed, so it's possible to hoe between them for weeding. To get the highest yield of large plants space them 6″ apart. You could initially plant Leeks closer together and thin as they get bigger. You can eat the thinnings or transplant them.

Care
Leeks need looking after carefully, because they grow slowly and don't have a lot of foliage. A newly planted Leek bed actually looks pretty pathetic.

Weeds: The lack of foliage makes young leeks very vulnerable to competition from weeds. It is very important to keep them well weeded, so they don't get overwhelmed. Leeks are quite shallow rooted, so be careful if weeding with a hoe (it's safer to hand weed).

Water: The lack of foliage also means that Leeks don't shade the ground very well, so the soil is prone to drying out in sunny weather. Leeks grow best in moist soil, so don't let this happen. Give the plants constant moisture and apply a mulch.

Fertilization: Leeks are often in the soil when it's cold. Many nutrients aren't easily available at this time, so it helps to give them a feed of compost tea or liquid Kelp, as soon as they are well established. If the soil isn't very fertile you should feed them again when they are about a foot tall and then every 4 weeks or so.

Mulch: Mulch is very beneficial for Leeks. It shades the soil and so helps it to retain moisture. It also helps to keep down weeds and is a source of nutrients for the soil.

Mulch is essential in areas where winter temperatures drop below 10° Fahrenheit. It not only protects the plants from cold, but also stabilizes the soil temperature. This prevents frost heaving, which can damage the roots. It's best to apply a mulch while the soil is still warm.

Blanching: Leeks are often blanched to get a longer area of white stem, as this is considered superior to the green part. Blanching is usually done with soil, either by earthing up the stems, or filling up the trench they are growing in. Some gardeners wrap corrugated cardboard collars around the plants before blanching, to prevent soil getting lodged between the leaves (no one likes gritty Leeks). You can also blanch the stems with a deep mulch, which has the advantage of not being gritty.

Pests: Leeks are susceptible to the same problems that afflict the related Onions, though generally they are fairly pest free. They are occasionally bothered by Onion Maggots or Thrips (see **Onions**).

Harvesting
When: Leeks can be harvested as soon as they reach sufficient size (about ¾″ diameter), their flavor and texture is almost always good. Winter Leeks can be dug as needed right through until spring, when they start to bolt.

How: You can often harvest Leeks by simply pulling them out of the ground. If the tops break off before they come free, you will have to loosen them with a garden fork first.

If you are harvesting Leeks before they reach full size, you should harvest alternate plants, as this gives the remaining plants more room to grow. Just be sure you don't disturb their roots. Alternatively you could take the largest plants first, leaving the others to size up.

Storage: Leeks are so hardy they are usually stored in the ground and harvested as needed (cover with mulch in cold climates). The outer skin may turn somewhat slimy in very cold weather, but the interior will be fine.

You can store leeks for several weeks in a plastic bag in the fridge. In very cold climates you can store them in a root cellar at 32 to 40° F. Trim off the excess tops and roots and plant them in a box of damp sand.

Seed saving: It's easy to save Leek seed, simply leave the best plants in the ground instead of eating them. Save the seed from at least 12 plants to ensure enough genetic variation. Leeks are biennial and will produce their spectacular flowers in their second spring. They are cross-pollinated by insects, so should be isolated by one mile from any other varieties (fortunately there are not likely to be any others nearby). These will produce seed in early summer.

It is a good idea to dig the seed-Leeks from their bed in early spring and move them to a convenient location. This frees up the bed they were growing in.

Unusual growing ideas
Multi-planting: You can plant Leeks in clusters, rather than as single plants, simply plant 4 or 6 seeds together. This is usually done in soil blocks, but could also work in flats or cell packs. These clusters must be spaced further apart than single plants to give their roots more room and prevent crowding.

Ornamental: Leek flowers resemble those of a number of ornamental Alliums and don't look out of place in the ornamental garden.

Vegetative propagation: If you allow plants to flower, watch for the offsets produced at the base of the stem. These are known as Leek pearls and can be used for propagation or eaten.

You can also grow Leeks from the plantlets that sometimes form on the flower head.

Competitive gardening: In parts of Britain the cultivation of the biggest and most perfect Leek is a very competitive activity. It results in monster Leeks weighing 9 lb or more. I find it amazing how humans can turn even the most unlikely activity into a competition!

Perennial: Leeks can be treated like perennials, as they propagate themselves vegetatively by means of offsets. They also self-sow.

Varieties: These differ in their hardiness, time to harvest, color and size of stem. In North America the choice of Leek varieties has been quite limited until recently. Fortunately many European varieties are now becoming more widely available. Leeks can be divided into two kinds (can't everything), according to their hardiness.

Summer Leeks: These tall, fast growing leeks aren't very hardy and don't store well. They are grown in summer for immediate consumption.

King Richard, Superschmelz.

Winter Leeks: These short stumpy leeks grow quite slowly, but are very hardy and can remain in the ground over the winter. They tend to have bluish foliage.

Alaska, Bleu Solaise, Carenton, Giant Musselburgh.

Cooking: Leeks are considered one of the finest flavored members of the Onion family and are especially highly esteemed in France. They are a main ingredient of the famous Leek and Potato soup (made from two peasant staples).

If they are sufficiently tender the green tops can be used as flavoring or added to salads.

Recipe:
Leek soup

4 leeks
1 onion
1 lb potatoes
½ tsp sea
4 cloves garlic
4 cups vegetable stock
2 tablespoon olive oil
2 tsp rosemary

Chop the leeks and onion and sauté until the onion go translucent. Add the chopped garlic and cook another minute. Add the potatoes (chopped into ½″ cubes) and the vegetable stock and simmer for 20 minutes in a covered pan. Allow the soup to cool so you can put it in a blender along with the rosemary and salt and blend until smooth. Reheat before serving.

Elephant Garlic
Allium scorodoprasum

This is actually a variety of Leek, rather than garlic, but in this case the Leek pearls have become true swollen bulbs. These have a mild garlic flavor and are used for flavoring like garlic

Lettuce
Lactuca sativa

Introduction: Lettuce is probably descended from *Lactuca serriola* and originated somewhere around the Mediterranean or Near East. Some types have been grown since the time of the ancient Egyptians.

Lettuce is almost synonymous with salad. It is easily the most popular salad ingredient, as countless restaurant salads consisting of a bowl of lettuce with a couple of Cherry Tomatoes will testify. The Lettuce available in supermarkets rarely measures up to those you can grow yourself.

Lettuce is easy to grow if you give it the right conditions, which means fairly cool weather. The challenge comes in getting it to grow when you want it, rather than when it wants to grow. It doesn't really like warm weather.

Nutritional content:
Despite its popularity Lettuce is not a particularly nutritious plant. The leaf and Romaine types are rich in vitamin A.

Soil
pH 6.0 - 7.5
Lettuce needs to grow fast for best quality, which requires a good soil. It should be fertile, moisture retentive, well drained and rich in organic matter. The pH isn't particularly important. Light soils that warm up quickly are good for early Lettuce.

About Lettuce

Seed facts
Germ temp: 35 to 80° F
Germ time: 2 to 15 days
49 days / 35° F (may rot)
15 days / 40° F
7 days / 50° F
3 days / 60° F * Optimum
2 days / 77° F
3 days / 86° F (only 12% germination)
Seed viability: 2 to 5 yrs
Germination percentage: 80%+
Time to grow transplant: 5 to 6 wks

Planning facts
Hardiness: Half hardy
Ease of growing: Easy
Growing temp: 45 (60 to 65) 75° F
Plants per person: 5 per sowing
Plants per sq ft: 4
Transplants:
Start: 6 wks before last frost
Plant out: 2 wks before last frost
Direct sow: 2 to 4 wks before last frost
Fall crop: 6 to 8 wks before first fall frost
Succession sow: every 2 to 3 wks
Time to harvest: 50 to 100 days

Harvest facts
Yield per plant: 6 to 12 oz
Yield per sq ft: 1 lb

Soil preparation: Lettuce has a weak root system and isn't a very efficient feeder, so the soil needs to be quite fertile. Its first requirement is for nitrogen (add compost or manure), but it also needs moderate amounts of potassium (add wood ashes or greensand) and phosphorus (add colloidal phosphate). It is sometimes deficient in calcium, so you might also want to give it some dolomitic limestone.

Prepare the soil by adding 2″ of compost or aged manure (unlike most plants it is also happy with fresh manure). This needn't be dug in very deeply as Lettuce is quite shallow rooted (the weak roots only penetrate about 4″ to 8″). For very early crops you might want to prepare the soil the previous fall.

Planning

Where: In cool climates Lettuce needs full sun, but in hotter climates it doesn't mind part shade (and may even benefit from it).

When: Lettuce will germinate quite well in cool (40° F) soil and will continue to do until it gets up to 75° F (after this it gets erratic). With careful planning and clever tricks, it is possible to have Lettuce for 6 to 9 months of the year, depending on the climate.

Spring: The first spring sowing should be of Leaf Lettuce, as this is the hardiest kind. It can be direct sown or transplanted as soon as the ground can be worked in spring (the same time as Peas, Spinach and Onion). Properly hardened seedlings can take frost down to 20° F. For the earliest crops you may want to warm the soil with cloches and use transplants.

Head lettuce is less hardy than the leaf types, so is usually started indoors 6 weeks before the last frost date. Seedlings can be planted out 2 weeks before the last frost date.

Summer: Lettuce doesn't like hot weather. At temperatures above 75° F only 50% of the seed may germinate and the plants may turn bitter and bolt quickly. To have lettuce through the warmest part of the growing season you have to be creative. Use a heat tolerant variety, water every day and plant it in the shade of a larger (but moisture loving) plant. See **Unusual Growing** ideas for more on this.

Autumn: Sow fall Lettuce 4 to 8 weeks before the first fall frost date. Pests are very active at this time, so you may want to start them inside or in a protected place.

Winter: Some hardy varieties of Lettuce can tolerate temperatures as low as 25° F and can be grown as a winter crop in milder areas. Start the plants (inside or out) about 4 to 6 weeks before you expect the first frost. Though they are quite hardy, they still do better when given protection from hard frost, or the additional warmth of a cold frame or cloche.

In very cold areas you can grow Lettuce in the greenhouse or cold frame. If you do this, make sure they stay cool (35 to 45° F), as low light levels and short days, combined with higher temperatures, can encourage bolting.

Succession sowing: Most Lettuce is only harvested once and then it is gone, so you need a constant supply of new plants. To get this constant supply you need to sow a small quantity of seeds every 10 days to 3 weeks (depending on time of year). There is only a short time between Lettuces maturing and Lettuce bolting, so you don't need to have many mature plants at one time.

You can plant different varieties with different maturation dates, to spread out the harvest. You can also harvest in different ways.

Planting

Transplants

Starting inside: Lettuce is commonly started as transplants, as this gives the fastest harvest and saves on bed space. Seedlings are easily raised and don't mind root disturbance, so you can use flats, cell packs, plug trays or soil blocks.

It is said that some kinds of Lettuce need light for germination. This is easy to arrange, just don't cover the seed with soil. Of course you must then take extra care to ensure it doesn't dry out.

Planting out: Lettuce transplants easily in cool weather. In hot dry weather you must take precautions to ensure that young plants are kept moist.

Direct sowing: Lettuce is commonly direct sown in drills, with 1″ between the plants and 5″ between the rows. Plant at a depth of ⅛″ in cold soil and up to ¾″ deep in warm soil.

When the plants are about 4″ high, they can be thinned to the required spacing. The thinnings can either be eaten, or replanted elsewhere at the final spacing. Transplanting will slow them down a little, which helps to extend the harvest. Careful sowing of seed can reduce the need for thinning.

You may run into problems when the soil gets warm, as often the seed doesn't germinate very well above 75° F. You then have to resort to various subterfuges such as cooling the soil with cold water and shade netting, chilling the seed in the fridge or putting the flats in a cooler place (maybe a root cellar).

Pre-germination: You can pre-germinate the seed in the fridge on a paper towel. You don't have to keep it in the fridge until it has germinated, just 5 days will be enough to break its dormancy. It will then germinate in warm soil.

Raising transplants

Outside: Lettuce germinates readily in cool soil, so you can easily start your transplants outdoors in a nursery bed. This saves on greenhouse or bed space. Just transplant the largest seedlings as space becomes available in the intensive beds.

Spacing: This varies depending upon the type of Lettuce and the variety grown. Crowded plants don't produce large heads and won't grow rapidly, which is important if you are to grow the best tasting lettuce. For variations on the standard spacing see **Unusual growing methods**.

Head Lettuce: Plant this in offset rows: 15″ to 12″ to 10″ apart, depending upon the variety and soil fertility.

Leaf Lettuce: Plant this in offset rows: 12″ to 8″ to 6″ apart, depending upon the variety and soil fertility.

Care

Lettuce needs to grow quickly for best quality. This can only be done by giving the plants everything they need.

Weeds: The young plants are vulnerable to weeds, so keep well weeded. Their roots are shallow so be careful with the hoe.

Water: Lettuce is largely composed of water and it responds to irrigation by giving a larger and better tasting harvest. If you think the plants might need water they probably do.

Good watering practices can help offset the negative effects of summer heat, so it is important to keep the soil constantly moist. In hot weather this may mean watering every other day.

Fertilization: If your soil is not as rich as it could be, give the plants a feed of compost tea or liquid Kelp about a month before harvest. This is especially important with the crisphead varieties.

Mulch: This helps to conserve soil moisture, keeps down weeds and helps to keep the plants clean. If you apply it early, it can also help to keep the soil cooler in hot weather. On the negative side, it may also harbor lettuce loving slugs.

Other problems

Bolting: Lettuce flowers when the day length gets up to 14 or 16 hours (the exact day length depends upon the variety), even if the weather is cool. Warm weather (above 75 to 80° F) frequently accompanies the long days of midsummer and may hasten bolting, but it isn't the primary cause.

Bolting will also occur when a plant reaches full size and has all the resources it needs to flower. When the plant has enough large leaves they signal the plant that it is ready to flower. It is possible to slow down bolting, by removing some of the larger leaves, but it won't stop it. The onset of bolting may be retarded somewhat by the frequent picking of single leaves.

When a plant starts to bolt, it turns bitter, the head elongates and the new leaves begin to take on an elongated shape. Then the flower stalk appears. Lettuce plants are quite beautiful at this stage and if left alone will soon produce an abundance of seed. I often allow them to produce seed, as I like to have plenty available for growing cut and come again salad or Microgreens (see below).

Vernalization: Lettuce will also bolt if the plants are vernalized while small. This happens if a plant with a stem diameter greater than ¼″ is exposed to temperatures below 50° F for two weeks. When the weather warms up it senses that winter has passed and so goes into flowering mode.

Bitterness: This is a characteristic sign of imminent bolting, but it may also be caused by water stress or unusually warm weather.

Tip burn: Burnt looking leaf tips may indicate a shortage of calcium, or night temperatures over 65° F.

Pests:
Lettuce can fall victim to quite a few pests and diseases, but they

are not usually too serious. These include Tarnished Plant Bugs, Thrips, Aphids, Leaf Miners, Flea Beetles. These small creatures can be controlled by using row covers.

Cutworms: These can be a real problem for young seedlings in spring. Some gardeners use individual Cutworm collars of cardboard. If you find plants laying on the ground, dig in the soil around them and you can usually locate the culprit. If you find it, you can prevent it doing further damage.

Slugs and snails: These molluscs love the tender young leaves and are the commonest problem you will face when growing Lettuce.

Mammals: Deer, Rabbits and Groundhogs can quickly devastate even a mature Lettuce patch. A fence may be necessary if you have these problems.

Harvesting

When: Lettuce is most nutritious if used fresh and doesn't keep well, so it's best to harvest it right before a meal.

You can start harvesting Lettuce only a few weeks after planting, as soon as there are enough leaves to be useful. Don't wait for them to reach full maturity, as they will bolt soon afterwards (picking indi-

vidual leaves may even slow down bolting). Better too early than never. Head Lettuce is harvested when the heads are firm, or at least have formed.

How: I commonly gather individual leaves as I need them for salads. This works out well, so long as you leave enough on the plant for it to recover.

Traditionally the whole Lettuce is cut off at the base. If you leave a few leaves on the stem, rather than cutting at actual ground level, the head will be cleaner. The stem remaining in the ground may then continue to grow and sprout new leaves. It may even grow some little Lettuces.

Storage:
Leaf lettuce has thin leaves and won't keep for much more than a week. Crisphead Lettuce has stiff, fleshy leaves and keeps very well, in fact that is why it is so popular with commercial growers. It will keep for several weeks in a plastic bag in a refrigerator. The other types are somewhere in between. Don't wash Lettuce until you are going to use it.

Seed saving: It is fairly easy to save Lettuce seed. The plants are mostly self-pollinated, though there may be some cross-pollination from insects. It is recommended that varieties be separated by 25 ft to keep them pure, which is simple enough.

If you save the seed from your best plants, you can develop better strains than you can buy (and have higher quality seed). I often save Lettuce seed with no thought for purity, as I want it in volume for growing cut and come again Lettuce. I don't really care if the variety is somewhat mixed up (I wouldn't even notice if it was).

Though I often gather seed from plants that have bolted, it is important not to gather it from the first plants to bolt. Early flowering is not a trait you want to perpetuate.

Head lettuce can present a problem when it comes to seed saving. The head may be so dense that the flower stalk may not be able to get out. If this is the case, you may have to cut an X in the top of the head, to enable the flower stem to emerge (as you would with a Cabbage). If the flower stem is very big, you may have to stake it, to prevent it from falling over when it gets loaded with seed.

The yellow flowers are followed, 2 to 3 weeks later, by fuzzy Dandelion-like seed heads. Gather the seed as it ripens by holding a paper bag over the head and shaking (I really dislike the smell the plants leave on your hands at this time). The seed ripens sequentially, so you must collect it every few days to get all the ripe seed. Keep on collecting until you have all the seed you need, or until it is blown away by the wind. Alternatively you can cut the entire head when about 50% of

the seed has ripened and dry it in a paper grocery bag. Clean the seed as much as possible, then dry and store it in a cool place.

Newly harvested seed usually won't germinate for a couple of months.

Lettuce Mosaic virus can be seed borne so watch out for it if you save your own seed, or swap seed with others.

Cut and come again:

What: If you have limited space, or want to grow Lettuce indoors, you can try growing it as a cut and come again crop.

When Lettuce is planted very closely together, the crowding inhibits heading, so the plants produce an abundance of single leaves instead. These are the perfect size for using in salads. When grown in this way Lettuce needs only about half the space it would for growing heads. I like this method so much, I have almost stopped growing individual Lettuce.

How: Simply broadcast the seed directly on to the bed, so there is a seed roughly every ½″. You may want to cover the seeds with a very light covering of soil.

If you want to grow it indoors, you can use 4″ flats, filled with a fairly rich soil mix.

Harvesting: Start harvesting when the leaves are 2″ to 3″ tall, leaving at least an inch of stem on the plant when cutting, so that it can regenerate. I like to make a small sowing every 3 weeks to maintain a steady supply of leaves. See **Salad Mix** for more on this.

Variations on salad mix:
Micro-greens: This is just a smaller version of the above. You plant the seeds ¼″ apart and harvest them when the first true leaves appear, which should be within 2 weeks. The end result is almost a Lettuce sprout.

Growing Micro-greens takes up so little space it can even be done in the kitchen. See **Micro-greens** for more on this.

Bigger leaves: You can also use the cut and come again technique with slightly larger plants. Plant as described above, but harvest thin them, to leave plants 2″ to 3″ apart. You can harvest the individual leaves from the remaining plants when they are 4″ long.

Unusual growing ideas
Intercrop: Lettuce is a compact and fast growing plant, perfect for intercropping between a slower maturing crop. They are so fast growing they will be out of the ground before the other crop needs the space. This works well with slow growing crops such as Parsnip Peppers or Tomato. If you have a ready supply of transplants, you can fit a few Lettuces into any small vacant space that appears.

Multi-planting: Leaf Lettuce can also be multi-planted. Sow 2 or 3 seeds in each block or plug tray and allow them all to grow to maturity. Plant the clusters out 12″ apart.

Hot weather growing: The best way to grow summer Lettuce is as a cut and come again crop. Use a heat tolerant variety and grow it in the shade (use shade netting or interplant under taller plants). Apply cold water daily to keep the soil moist and cool. Cut the leaves frequently, to make the most of the harvest and to slow down bolting.

Volunteers
: If you allow Lettuce to flower it will often self-sow. You can aid this process by scattering some of the abundantly produced seed in suitable places. In spring you can often simply transplant these seedlings to where you want them. If they are of different varieties, they can give quite an extended harvest period.

Varieties
: Four types of Lettuce are commonly grown, Looseleaf, Crisphead, Butterhead and semi-heads (Romaines). There is a lot of variation within these types, with many cultivars bred for specific purposes. Some are especially good for a specific season, some are for growing under glass and some have even been bred for container growing.

Crisphead / Iceberg
L. sativa var *capitata.*
These have dense heads of crisp leaves and need a long period of cool weather for best growth. Head lettuce is the most difficult to grow, the slowest, the most demanding and the least nutritious. It is very popular however, because of its crisp and crunchy texture. It is prized by industrial agriculture for its ability to survive handling, shipping and sitting on supermarket shelves.

Great Lakes, Iceberg

Butterhead / Bibbs
L. sativa var *capitata*
These have soft, loosely packed heads and very good flavor. They

are fairly easy to grow and tolerate some heat.

Buttercrunch, Tom Thumb, Merveille de Quatre Saisons

Romaine (Cos)
L. sativa var *longifolia*
These produce heads of tender green leaves with crisp midribs. They are better flavored and more heat tolerant than most other lettuces.

Little Gem, Paris Green Cos, Valmaine, Winter Density.

Looseleaf Lettuce
L. sativa
This is the easiest to grow, the most tolerant of heat or cold, the fastest to mature and the most nutritious.

Oakleaf (heat tolerant), Black Seeded Simpson, Deer Tongue, Salad Bowl, Red Sails.

Cooking:
Lettuce is usually eaten raw in salads and sandwiches, but it has other uses as well. It has been used as a potherb, added to soups and used as wrapping for other foods.

Luffa
Luffa species

Introduction: These vines are widely cultivated in the tropics for food and for their sponges. They are related to the Squash and their cultivation is quite similar.

About Luffa

Ease of growing: Fairly easy
Germ temp: 60 (70 to 95) 105° F
Germ time: 14 to 21 days
Seed viability: 2 to 5 years
Time to harvest: 70 to 100 days
Growing temp: 60 to 75° F

Soil: Incorporate 2″ of compost or aged manure into the top 6″ of soil. Luffa doesn't need a lot of nitrogen, (it may encourage excessive leaf growth), but it does like phosphorus (give it colloidal phosphate) and potassium (wood ashes).

Climate: These tropical plants needs a long, hot growing season, with full sun.

Planting
Starting inside: In northern climates the Luffa is treated in much the same way as the Melon. It is started in the greenhouse about a month before it can be planted out. The seeds have a hard seed coat that must be softened before they can germinate. You should probably soak the seed overnight prior to planting. They don't like having their roots disturbed, so should be started in cell packs or soil blocks.

Planting out: Plant them outside when they have at least 3 true leaves and all danger of frost has passed. Plant them up to their first true leaves.

Direct sowing: Luffas are slow to germinate and so can only be started outside in areas with long growing seasons. It is sown like Cucumber.

Spacing: Sow the plants in hills 36″ apart. Trellised plants can be grown 12″ apart, in two rows 36″ apart.

Care

Watering: They need even moisture for best fruit production, so water regularly.

Support: These vigorous sprawling vines produce better fruit when grown on a trellis. They also suffer less from pests and diseases.

Pests: They may be attacked by the same pests that bother Squash.

Harvest

Food: The flowers should appear about 6 weeks after transplanting. If you are using the immature fruit for food, you should gather them while they are under 6″ in length. As with Squash, regular harvesting will keep them producing well.

Sponges: The fruits are left to mature fully and turn pale green or yellow. If you want to get big sponges, don't allow too many to mature on one plant.

Processing sponges: Allow the ripe fruit to dry for a couple of weeks, then cut off the ends and shake out the dry seeds. Dry them thoroughly and keep them for next year. To remove the skin soak the

fruit overnight (or boil for a few minutes). The softened skin will then peel off. To get the familiar clean pale loofah soak it for a half hour in a dilute solution of bleach (it doesn't take much bleach).

Seed saving: This is easy, just save the seed when you process the mature fruit. Like other Cucurbits they are insect-pollinated, but there is little danger of cross-pollination, as few varieties exist.

Unusual growing ideas
Ornamental: This vine is quite ornamental and can be grown on a trellis as a deciduous screen.

Varieties:
L. acutangula: **Chinese Okra**
This species has 10 prominent ridges on the fruit. It is the best species for food, but not as good for sponges.

L. cylindrica: **Sponge Gourd**
(Syn. *L. aegyptiaca*)
This species has smooth skin. It is the best for sponges, but not as good for food.

Cooking
The immature fruit can be used like Summer Squash, or eaten raw in salads.

Apparently the leaves are also edible and can be used as a salad or potherb. I haven't tried them though.

Melon
Cucumis melo

Introduction: The melon has been called "The noblest production of the garden". It is a member of the Cucurbit family and is grown in much the same way as the related Cucumbers. It isn't quite as vigorous when young however.

This succulent tropical fruit originated in Africa and was first grown in Britain in the sixteenth century, in hotbeds made with manure. It is actually fairly easy to grow in a warm hospitable climate, less so in cooler areas.

Nutritional content:
The fruits contain vitamin C, beta-carotene, potassium, pectin and several beneficial phytochemicals, including lycopene and zeaxanthin.

Soil
pH 6.0 to 7. 0
The ideal soil for Melons is loose, moist, fertile and well drained. It should also be fairly neutral.

Soil preparation: Incorporate 2″ of compost or aged manure (they love old manure) into the top 6″ of soil. Melons don't need a lot of nitrogen, as this encourages leaf growth at the expense of fruit. They do like phosphorus (give them colloidal phosphate) and potassium (wood ashes), as well as boron and magnesium. They dislike acid soil so lime if necessary, using dolomitic lime (which also adds magnesium).

About Melon

Seed facts
Germ temp: 65 (70 to 95) 100° F
Germ time: 3 to 10 days
8 days / 68° F
4 days / 77° F
3 days / 86° F * Optimum
Germination percentage: 80+
Viability: 2 to 4
Weeks to grow transplants: 3 to 4

Planning facts
Hardiness: Tender
Ease of growing: Moderate if it's warm, harder if it is cool
Growing temp: 65 to 75° F
Plants per person: 4
Plants per sq ft: ¾
Transplants:
Start: on the last frost date
Plant out: 4 wks after last frost
Direct sow: 4 wks after last frost
Succession sow: about 4 to 6 wks after first sowing
Time to harvest: 70 to 150 days

Harvest facts
Length of harvest: 12 wks
Yield per plant: 2 lb (2 to 4 fruit)
Yield per sq ft: ½ to 1½ lb sq ft

Planning

Where: Melons must have hot weather (ideally 90° F) if they are to make the sugar needed to produce sweet fruits. In cooler areas you need to give them as much sun and heat as possible. They should also be sheltered from cool winds.

I must emphasize that if Melons don't get enough heat they won't taste very good (even if you do grow them successfully.) In very cool climates it's a waste of time trying to grow them outside, grow them in greenhouses, or under cloches or cold frames.

Crop rotation: Don't plant Cucurbits (Melons, Squash, Cucumbers) in the same soil more frequently than every 3 or 4 years.

When: Melons need warm weather, so don't plant them until all danger of frost is past and the soil temperature is at least 60° F. If you want to grow melons in areas with short growing seasons, start them indoors and warm the soil with black plastic, or cloches, before planting.

Planting
You might want to pre-soak the seeds overnight before planting, especially if you are sowing directly outside.

Succession sowing: If you want to have a continuous harvest of Melons. you will want to make several sowings, perhaps 3 to 4 weeks apart. You can also plant several varieties, with different maturation times.

Transplants
Starting inside: If your growing season is short, you will have to start your Melons indoors. Like most Cucurbits they dislike root disturbance, so should be started in cell packs, soil blocks or individual pots. Plant 2 seeds to a block and thin to the best one after both have emerged. The seedlings will be ready to plant out 3 to 4 weeks after sowing, when they have at least 3 or 4 true leaves.

Don't start your Melons too early, as you don't want them to get root-bound. If it is too cold to put them out when they are ready, you will have to move them into larger pots.

Planting out: Plant out the seedlings up to their first true leaves and water immediately. When they have recovered from transplanting, give them a liquid feed to get them growing again. In cool areas you might want to put them under row covers until the weather warms up.

Outdoors: If your growing season is long and hot enough, you may want to direct sow your Melons. They will germinate and grow rapidly in warm (75° F) soil.

Sow the seeds 1″ deep, with 4″ between the plants. When they have all germinated, thin the row to leave a plant every 18″. You may be able to transplant some of the thinnings if you do it very carefully.

Hills: Melons are often planted in hills, slightly elevated above the surrounding soil. This helps the soil to warm up faster and provides better drainage (melons rot easily in wet soil.

To make a hill remove 2 spadesful of soil, dump in 2 spadesful of compost or aged manure), then replace the soil. Mix it all together and shape it into a low mound. Plant the seeds on edge, ½″ to 1″ deep, sowing 5 to 6 seeds on each mound. When these are growing well, pinch out the inferior seedlings, to leave the best 3 plants to grow on.

Spacing:
Hills: Space the hills 3 to 5 ft apart, with 3 plants to a hill.

Rows: Space the plants 18″ to 24″ apart, in rows 72″ apart.

Beds: Intensive gardeners plant Melons 15″ to 18″ to 24″ apart, depending upon the soil and variety. They are usually planted in rows, to facilitate supporting them. If they grow upwards they take up a lot less space.

Care
Watering: Melons are quite shallow rooted, so need fairly constant water. This is most critical when the fruits are sizing up, and they should get all the water they can use at this time. In hot weather this can be up to 2 gallons a day for each plant. Ideally this should be lukewarm, so it doesn't cool the soil. When the fruits have reached full size you should ease up on watering, otherwise they may split.

The best way to water Melons is with a drip system, as they don't like having wet leaves (this encourages fungus disease).

No-watering: There is an alternative way to water Melons, you could not give them any water at all. You will get fewer and smaller fruits, but they will be sweeter. You have to space the plants further apart for this to work, so they have more volume of soil to extract water from.

Mulch: This helps to conserve moisture in the soil. Don't apply it until the soil has warmed up however

Fertilization: This should be done cautiously with melons, as you don't want to merely encourage foliage growth at the expense of fruiting. When the flowers start to set fruit, you might give the plants a feed of compost tea or liquid Kelp. Feed them again as the fruit begins to size up.

A low-tech way to feed Melons is to bury a 1 gallon plant pot alongside the plant and half fill it with vermicompost or manure. Just fill it with water every day and let the water slowly seep out.

Protection: In cool climates Melons should be covered with cloches until the weather warms up. They must have heat if they are going to have good flavor.

Pruning: The seedlings should be pinched back twice, so they produce four growing tips. These are then allowed to grow and flower.

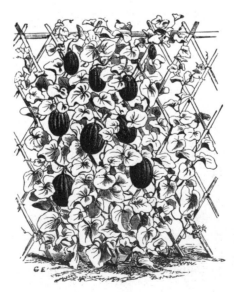

Support: The plants can be trained up trellises to save space, just as you would Cucumber. However the fruits are heavier than cucumbers and may need support (slings made from old panty-hose work well.)

Fruiting: The first flowers to appear are usually male and can't produce fruit. Female flowers follow soon afterwards and these will bear fruit, if they are pollinated.

If you want to make sure your plants are pollinated, you can do it by hand. This isn't normally necessary however, as insects will usually do the job. Hand pollination is most often done in greenhouses or cloches, where insects may not be able to get to them easily.

Growers often allow one fruit to develop on each branch and then pinch off any others that form. The more fruit you allow to develop, the smaller they will all be.

Care of fruit: As the melon swells it can get quite heavy. If it is growing on a trellis it should be supported in a sling. If it is growing on the ground you can insert a tin can, plant pot, tile or stone underneath it, to get it off the soil.

Pests: Melons are related to Cucumbers and suffer from many of the same afflictions. They are particularly vulnerable when small, so should be protected carefully at this time. Melon Aphids, Squash Bugs, Squash Vine Borers, Mites, Cucumber Beetles (which spread fusarium wilt) and more. Rabbits, raccoons and birds will eat the ripe fruit.

Diseases: Mosaic virus, Downy Mildew, Powdery Mildew, Alternaria Leaf Blight, Anthracnose, Fusarium Wilt, Bacterial Wilt.

Harvesting

When: The first fruits will be ready to harvest in mid to late summer, about 35 to 45 days after pollination. The key to great Melons is to pick them at the peak of ripeness, so don't pick a melon before its time. There are several ways to tell when a melon is ripe, though not all of these indicators may be present at the same time.

When a Melon is ripe:

It develops a very strong aroma.

The blossom end gets soft.

Most varieties develop cracks around the stem. Gently roll the fruit in your hand, if it separates from the vine it is ready.

The tendril closest to the fruit usually shrivels up.

The spot where the melon was resting on the ground will turn from white to yellow.

How: It is best to cut the fruit from the vine, leaving a couple of inches of stem attached. Handle the fruit carefully once it is harvested, as it will bruise very easily.

Storage: The fruits should be eaten as soon as possible. Otherwise they should be treated like Tomatoes and kept at room temperature. They can be stored in a fridge for a couple of weeks, but their flavor will slowly deteriorate.

Seed Saving: Melons are cross-pollinated by insects so you can grow only one variety at one time, isolate by a ½ mile, cage or hand pollinate.

Hand pollinating Melons isn't difficult, though the flowers are smaller than other Cucurbits. The flowers are most receptive to pollination before any fruit start growing. Once there are fruit maturing on the plant they become less inclined to produce more by pollinating successfully.

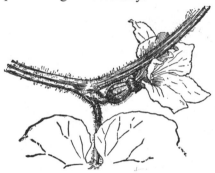

You need to prepare to pollinate the flowers the night before, by finding some male and female flowers (the female has a tiny "Melon" behind the flower) that are about to open the following day. Tape them shut with a little piece of masking tape (don't tape it too well or it will be hard to remove without damaging the flower). This prevents them from opening and being pollinated before you get to them.

The next day pick a male flower and remove its tape and petals. Then carefully open a female flower (from a different plant), being very careful to not damage the petals. Insert the male flower into a female flower and brush the pollen from the anthers on to stigma. Finally tape the female flower closed again. The petals will soon fall off and if pollination was successful the tiny fruit will begin to grow.

If you are adventurous, you could collect the seed from any ripe fruit as you eat it (so long as it isn't an f1 hybrid) and see what grows. In the case of Melons I would avoid hybrids for this reason, it seems a shame not to be able to use some of those seeds.

Unusual Growing Ideas
Salad greens: You can actually get salad greens from melons, by sprouting the seeds like those of Sunflower.

Varieties: Melons can be divided into several categories.

European Canteloupe Melons (*C. melo* var *cantalupensis*) These are not the familiar fruits we call Canteloupes and don't have netted skin. These are some of the hardiest varieties. Charentais, Boule d'Or

Muskmelons (*C. melo* var *reticulatus*) These are the fruits we know as Canteloupes and have the familiar netted skin. They need hot weather to ripen properly. Haogen, Jenny Lind, Blenheim Orange,

Honeydew and Casaba Melons (*C. melo* var *inodorus*). Earlidew F1, Honeyloupe

Japanese Melons Sakatas Sweet

Cooking: Melons should be eaten at room temperature, as chilling reduces their flavor.

Micro-greens

Introduction: Micro-greens are the seedlings of a variety of salad plants, gathered after they have formed their first true leaves. They have become one of the hottest trends in fashionable gourmet restaurants nationwide, but are not just a high priced gimmick. They are a great idea for a versatile and nutritious new fresh food, that bridges the gap between sprouted seeds from the kitchen and salad mix from the garden. They can be grown indoors or outside and are another way to grow highly nutritious salad materials year round. In restaurants the trays of seedlings sit in the kitchen, to be clipped as needed.

There is a precedent for micro-greens. In Britain inexpensive trays of "Mustard and Cress" have long been available in markets, to be clipped as needed for salads and sandwiches. In North America people have been growing trays of Buckwheat and Sunflower Lettuce for years. These are both used in the same way, cut when they produce their first true leaves (or even before). The idea of micro-greens takes this a step further and introduces a wide variety of new plants and flavors.

Growing micro-greens is a great way to use up some of those seeds you have been saving all summer. In fact it is a good reason to start saving seed.

Nutrients: The nutritious young plants are rich in vitamins A, B's, C, E and K as well as calcium, iron, magnesium, phosphorus and potassium. They also contain anti-oxidants, amino acids and many useful phytochemicals.

Time to harvest: This varies from 3 to 21 days, depending upon the crop and growing conditions.

When: One of the great things about micro-greens is that they can be grown inside or outside. This means you can have cheap fresh salad materials at any time of the year, no matter how cold or hot it gets outside.

In winter you can grow them in the house or greenhouse. In spring and fall you can grow them in the greenhouse, cold frame or garden. In summer you can grow them in the garden, or back in the house (to get cool weather crops started).

Indoors:
Where: Micro-greens can be grown in soil in flats or pots. They can also be grown in trays, with a layer of water absorbent material like vermiculite, peat moss, felt pads or paper towels.

Where: The seedlings don't last for very long, so it doesn't matter if they don't get full sunlight all of the time. In fact they don't need sunlight at all until they have germinated.

In hot weather you can start the seeds in a cool dark place and bring them into the light when they start to germinate.

If it is too cool to plant directly outside, you can grow them in a cold frame or greenhouse.

Planting: The seeds are scattered on the moist growing medium, keeping them very close together (¼" maximum). Keep the containers in a warm place (70° F is optimal for most salad crops). The tray is misted as necessary to keep the growing plants well supplied with moisture.

If you plant more than one kind of seed in a container it is important that they grow at roughly the same rate, so you can harvest at the same time.

Outdoors:
When: It is easiest to grow micro-greens outdoors in the cool weather of spring and fall, but with a little extra care you can often grow them right through the summer. They aren't in the ground long enough for the plants to react to heat or long days by bolting. The main constraint is soil temperature; some cool season plants won't germinate if the soil is too warm. Of course they won't germinate if it is too cool either.

Where: Any garden soil will work, you just have to make sure it is kept moist. In cool weather they will need full sun.

Planting: Seed is scattered on the soil ¼" apart and covered with ⅛" of cover soil. . If you plant more than one kind of seed it is important that they grow at roughly the same rate.

Succession sowing: This is a very short term crop and the frequency of succession sowing will depend upon how much you plant and how much you use. After a couple of sowings you will work this out for yourself.

Care: Micro-greens don't need much attention. The main thing is to keep the soil moist (this is particularly important outdoors in summer). Outdoor plants will also need to be protected from predators at all times, as the succulent little plants are very tempting. In hot weather you will probably want to provide some shade as well

Harvesting: The best time to harvest is about 5 minutes before sitting down to eat.

The plants are usually cut when they have their first true leaves and are about 1″ to 2″ tall. The best way to harvest is to cut them off with scissors, just above soil level. This minimizes the disturbance to the remaining plants. Rinse carefully and use straight away. You can leave them to grow a little longer if you want, so they can get a bit bigger. Just don't leave indoor plants in low light for too long, otherwise they will get chlorotic.

Cooking: These plants can be used as a salad in their own right, but are so precious they are usually used as a garnish for more mundane salads. They can also be combined with sprouted seeds or other salad materials from the garden. The more pungent or strong tasting ones will add interest to any meal. In posh restaurants they are commonly used as a garnish for soups, sandwiches and salads.

Varieties: Almost any edible green plant can be used in this way, most commonly used include:

Amaranth
Arugala (one of the best)
Basil
Beet
Broccoli (very high in antioxidants)
Buckwheat (caution see Buckwheat)
Cabbage (and any other Brassicas)
Celery
Chard
Chervil
Chicory
Clover
Cornsalad
Cress
Dill
Escarole
Fennel
Fenugreek (one of my favorites)
Flax
Kale
Mizuna
Mustards
Onion
Oriental Brassicas
Peas
Plantain
Purslane
Quinoa
Radicchio
Radish (spicy)
Sorrel
Spinach
Sunflower
Tatsoi
Turnip

Mustards
Brassica juncea

Introduction: This species is probably a hybrid of *B. rapa* and *B. nigra*. It has been most highly refined in China, where it is an important cool season vegetable. There are many different types and varieties available there.

This is the green leaf Mustard, not the condiment mustard, which is made from the ground seeds of *B. nigra* and *B. alba*. However this species can also be used for making mustard.

If given the right conditions Mustards are an easily grown and fast maturing crop. They produce heavily in a small area and require little effort to grow. They deserve to be more widely cultivated in the west, especially in small gardens where space is limited. They are the second commonest ingredients in many commercial salad mixes, for the reasons I just mentioned.

Nutritional content:
These are among the most nutritious of greens, rich in vitamins A and C, as well as calcium, iron and potassium. Like other Brassicas they also contain a variety of cancer preventing phytochemicals.

Soil:
pH 5.5 - 6.8
Mustards aren't particularly fussy about soils, but are most productive on rich moisture retentive ones.

Soil preparation: If the soil is poor, dig in 2″ of compost or aged manure, as well as wood ashes or greensand (for potassium), colloidal phosphate (for phosphorus) and Kelp (for trace elements).

About Mustards

Seed facts
Germ temp: 45 to 95° F
Germ time: 2 to 7 day
Viability: 3 to 8 yrs
Germination percentage: 75%+
Seed viability: 4 years
Weeks to grow transplant: 3 to 4

Planning facts
Hardiness: Hardy
Ease of growing: Easy
Growing temp: 45 (55 to 65) 75° F
Plants per person: 5
Plants per sq ft: 4
Transplants:
Start: 6 wks before last frost
Plant out 2 wks before last frost
Direct sow: 2 wks before last frost
Fall crop: Sow 6 to 8 weeks
before first frost
Succession sow: every 4 weeks
Time to harvest:
       20 to 40 days (summer)
       60 days (winter)

Harvest facts
Length of harvest: 8 to 10 wks
Yield per plant: 1 lb
Yield per sq ft: 2 to 4 lb

Planning
Where: The ideal spot for Mustards depends on the weather. If it's cool they should be planted on a sunny site. If it's warm then some shade is a good idea.

Mustards are in and out of the ground quickly, so are often used for intercropping between slower growing crops.

Crop rotation: They should not be planted where another Brassica has grown in the past 3 years.

When: These fast growing plants thrive in hot or cold weather, but taste better when it's cool.

Mustards can be planted at any time as a cut and come again crop. Just plant a small section of bed every two weeks (space the plants ½″ apart), keep cool and well watered and see how it goes.

Spring: Mustards can be started indoors 6 weeks before the last frost and planted out 2 to 3 weeks later. Start direct sowing about 2 weeks before the last frost date, so they have time to mature before it gets hot. They are somewhat prone to bolting when planted at this time however and definitely do better as a fall crop.

Summer: In cool climates, it is possible to succession sow Mustards all summer.

Fall: Mustards generally work best as a fall crop and (like many Brassicas) cold weather actually improves their flavor. Direct sow a fall crop at least 8 weeks before the first fall frost is expected.

Winter: Mustard thrives in cool weather and can even take some frost (some varieties will take temperatures as low as 18° F). In milder areas it will grow right through the winter and makes a great winter crop. In colder areas it may be grown under cold frames or cloches.

Planting
Mustards can be direct sown or transplanted.

Transplants
Starting inside: Mustard doesn't mind transplanting, so is easily started indoors in flats or soil blocks. However you gain little time by doing this, as it grows quickly anyway. I suppose it may be worthwhile in early spring to get a head start, or if you want to save bed space.

Direct sowing: Mustard is usually direct sown, by broadcasting and then covering with ¼″ to ½″ of soil (or a mix of half soil and half compost). It doesn't seem to mind crowding, but should eventually be thinned to the proper spacing (eat the thinnings). It can also be sown in rows, planted ½″ deep and ½″ apart.

Starting transplants outdoors: Mustards can also be started outside in a nursery bed. The largest individuals can then be transplanted into the intensive bed as space becomes available.

Spacing: Plant Mustard 6″ to 12″ apart in the intensive beds (depending upon variety).

Care

You want Mustard to grow as fast as possible, which means giving the plants everything they need.

Water: If the soil is too dry the plants will develop a bitter and pungent flavor. If you want tasty, mild flavored Mustard greens you must keep the soil moist at all times

Fertilization: If the soil is less than ideal, you may want to feed your plants with a foliar fertilizer such as compost tea. Do this after thinning them to their final spacing and again as necessary.

Mulch: This is primarily of value to keep down weed growth and keep the soil moist. It can also help to keep the soil cool, which may delay bolting.

Pests: Mustards suffer from the same pests as the other Brassicas, but especially Flea Beetles and Cabbage Root Maggots (see Cabbage for more on these). Slugs and snails can also be a serious problem in early spring, when there is not much else for them to eat. They can wipe out a new planting almost overnight.

Harvest: Harvest Mustards by cutting the whole plants, leaving several inches of stem behind. The remaining stem will then resprout and grow again (you can sometimes cut them several times).

Alternatively you can harvest single leaves, as soon as they get large enough (about 3″ high).

If the plants bolt before you get a chance to harvest them, all is not lost. If it is big enough the immature flower stalk can be eaten like Broccoli Raab. The flowers and green seedpods can be added to salads.

Seed saving: It's easy to save seed from these annuals. Just treat them like Kale and gather the seed at the appropriate time. Be careful not to let it self-seed, as it can become a weed if it gets established (though perhaps not an unwelcome one).

Mustard can produce far more seed than you need for propagation. You can use the surplus for growing cut and come again salad greens and micro-greens, or for sprouting like Alfalfa (they make excellent, slightly spicy sprouts). They can even be used for making the condiment mustard (see below).

Unusual growing ideas
Cut and come again salad

greens: Pungent Mustard leaves are a basic ingredient of salad mixes. The red types are particularly prized, as they add color as well as flavor. (See **Salad mix**).

Micro-greens: This is just a smaller version of the above. You plant the seeds ¼″ apart and harvest them when the first true leaves appear, which of often within 7 to 10 days. **See Micro-greens**

Winter crop: Some Mustard varieties are very hardy (especially the oriental types) and make excellent winter crops for mild climates. They can also be used in colder climates if protected by cloches, or grown in a cold frame or greenhouse. If it gets very cold they may stop growing, but they won't be damaged and will start growing again when the temperature rises sufficiently.

Ornamentals: Some Mustards have unusual foliage and are quite ornamental. These types may be planted in ornamental borders to fill any unsightly gaps. Start the seedlings inside, or in a nursery bed and transplant them as vacant spaces appear.

Green manures: These fast growing plants are often grown as green manures, as they produce a large amount of biomass in a short time. An advantage is that you can also eat them. A disadvantage is that they are members of the Brassica family and so subject to all of their afflictions.

Varieties: There is a lot of variation in this crop. The most commonly available types include:

Green-in-the-Snow: Very hardy (down to 20° F). It is best in cold weather, can get pungent with heat.

Osaka Purple: Great for salad mix.

Green Wave: This curly Mustard is very hardy, fast growing and resistant to pests.

Southern Giant:

Cooking: The tender leaves can be used raw in salads, cooked as a potherb, or in soups and stir-fries. If they are very pungent try cooking with blander greens, or change the cooking water half way through.

123

Prepared Mustard

1 tbsp coriander seeds
6 tbsp mustard seeds
1 tbsp black peppercorns
¼ cup chopped onion
½ tsp dried thyme
¾ cup water
2 tsp honey
¼ cup red wine vinegar
½ tsp. ground turmeric

Toast the coriander seeds in a skillet, then crush them with the mustard seeds, and peppercorns. Mix with the thyme, onion, turmeric and leave for three hours. Add water and vinegar and honey and simmer 10 minutes, being careful it doesn't burn. It will get thick.

New Zealand Spinach
Tetragonia tetragonioides

Introduction: This species is rarely available commercially as a vegetable, so you may not have heard of it. It is quite widely grown in home vegetable gardens however, as it is a good hot weather potherb. For various reasons I haven't had a huge amount of success with it (certainly not enough to give up Amaranth). The last time I tried it Quail ate it all. Apparently in Australia it is know as Warrigal.

About New Zealand Spinach

Germ temp: 50 (60 to 70) 90° F
Germ time: 14 to 21 days
Germination percentage: 40%+
Viability: 5 yrs
Weeks to grow transplants 3 to 4

Planning facts
Hardiness: Tender
Ease of growing: Easy
Growing temp: 60 to 80° F
Time to harvest: 60 to 90 days
Plants per person: 5
Plants per sq ft : 1
Transplants
Start: 4 wks before last frost
Plant out: 2 wks after last frost
Direct sow: 2 wks after last frost
Time to harvest: 60 to 90 days
Harvesting period: 12 to 20 wks

Harvest facts
Yield per sq ft: 1 to 2 lb
Yield per plant: 1 to 2 lb

Soil
pH 6.0 to 7.0
New Zealand Spinach does best in the ideal garden soil, moisture retentive, well drained and fertile. It is very tolerant of saline soils and actually grows wild along the coast of California

Where: In cool climates this plant needs full sun, but in hot weather it does better with light shade.

When: This is a warm weather crop and can't stand any frost. There is no point in starting it until all danger of frost has passed and the soil has warmed up (at least 2 weeks after the last frost date).

Planting: The seeds are a little temperamental in their germination and may take 3 weeks to emerge. They are often soaked overnight prior to planting. They are relatively large so this isn't difficult.

Transplants: If the growing season is short it should be started indoors about 4 weeks before the last frost date. Plant the seedlings out 2 weeks after the last frost

Direct sowing: In hot climates it is easier sow the seed directly in the garden. Plant them ¼″ deep.

Spacing: Space the plants 12″ apart in the beds or rows.

Watering: Though this succulent plant is quite drought tolerant, it tastes better if given plenty of water.

Pests: When I have grown this crop in other areas I had no trouble with pests. However at my present garden the plants are plagued by

Quail and stripped down to the stems (in summer they go for a number of succulent leaf crops). The best solution to this problem is to net them.

Harvest: Don't start harvesting until the plant is about a foot tall and has enough vigor to tolerate frequent cutting. If you only harvest the growing tips the plant will regenerate quickly and can be harvested for months. You can also cut it down almost to the ground and (hopefully) it will sprout up again.

Seed saving: This couldn't be simpler, just leave it alone.

Unusual growing ideas:
Groundcover: This species can be used as a groundcover or foliage plant in the ornamental garden. It is so independent it can also be planted in the wild or forest garden (though it doesn't like shade), or any vacant spot. If it likes the conditions it will self-sow.

Varieties: I haven't seen any.

Cooking: The leaves are not very good raw, but make a great Spinach substitute when cooked. Use them in any recipe calling for spinach.

Oat
Avena sativa

Introduction: This is one of the most useful grain crops for small scale growing. It contains very high quality protein, is fairly easy to grow and does well in cool climates.

Soil: Oats like a moist fertile soil. They don't need too much nitrogen as it can cause them to lodge (fall over).

When: This very hardy plant doesn't mind the cold. It will just take advantage of the warmth whenever it comes.

Spring: Oats can be planted in spring (as early as possible) to be harvested in early summer.

Fall: It can also be planted in fall as an over-wintering crop, to be harvested in spring. If the climate is right, this usually works out better.

Spacing: People think of grasses as being spaced closely together, like a lawn, but they should actually be quite far apart. Space the plants 5″ apart in the beds, to allow for the fact that they send up several stems.

Planting:
Transplants: This is a lot of work, but it can increase yields significantly. Start the seed indoors in flats, about 8 to 10 weeks before the last frost. When the plants are about 2″ high they are transplanted outside. They are quite hardy.

Direct sowing: The seed can be broadcast (if you have lots of seed) or sown in drills (if you don't).

Care
Weeding: The wide spacing means that the young plants can't compete against weeds very well. The young plants will need to be weeded thoroughly.

Watering: Oats like to have a steady supply of water, so don't allow the soil to get dry.

Pests: Few pests bother Oats when it is growing on a small scale.

Harvest: Harvest the plants before the seed is perfectly ripe and the stems have turned completely yellow. Bind the plants into bundles and store them in a dry place until they are completely ripe. When the seed is fully ripe it is somewhat crunchy. Thresh the seed from the plants by walking upon it on a hard floor. If you used hull-less oats that is all you need to do.

The straw remaining after threshing is a good source of bedding for chickens (they will find and eat any remaining seeds). It is also a good source of carbonaceous material for the compost pile.

Seed saving: Just reserve some of the seed you have grown to eat.

Varieties: Hull-less Oats (of the species *A. nuda*) have hulls that aren't well attached to the grain and so come off easily. This makes them much easier to process, if somewhat less productive. These types are recommended for small scale growers.

Cooking: The cleaned grain can be ground to flour for baking, or made into oatmeal.

Oca
Oxalis tuberosa

Introduction: Oca is an important root vegetable in its native Andes mountains, where it is second only to the potato. Unlike its compatriot the Potato, it has never been very popular outside its native range. This is somewhat surprising when you consider of its many virtues. It is a rugged and independent plant; it tolerates poor soil and harsh climates, is fairly easy to grow and can be very productive. I think its time is coming though and that it is going to become much more popular as a garden crop in the near future.

Nutritional content: The tubers are fairly nutritious, but also contain oxalic acid.

Oxalic acid is considered bad because it can combine with calcium and prevent it getting absorbed by the body. However this isn't a serious problem to anyone with a reasonable intake of calcium.

When: Oca is native to subtropical mountains and grows best with relatively cool growing conditions and short days. In northerly regions it doesn't produce tubers until fall, when the days start to get shorter. It doesn't do well in very cold climates, because by the time the right day length arrives it is too cold. This was once the case with Potatoes also, but longer day length varieties were eventually developed. This is now happening with Oca too.

Oca can be planted as an annual crop like the Potato, but I prefer to give it a permanent home in the semi-wild or forest garden. If you want to plant it in spring, don't do it too early, wait until the last frost date.

Spacing: Space the plants 9″ to 12″ apart. They can get quite large, sometimes reaching up to 24″ in height.

Soil: Oca is well known for it ability to grow and produce well in poor soils. However it will be more productive in a fertile one.

Planting: Plant the tubers 2″ deep and 2″ apart. If you plant them in rows they will be easier to earth up.

Care
Watering: Oca is somewhat drought tolerant, but for best production the soil should be kept evenly moist. It will be more productive if you give it extra water when the tubers start to form (not too much though).

Weeding: Keep the young plants well weeded. Established plants can compete with weeds quite well.

Hilling: If the plants are earthed up after 3 months, they will produce more tubers.

Pests: I haven't noticed any pests or diseases (which is a nice change from the Potato).

Harvest: The tubers develop 4 to 6 months after planting, when the days get shorter. They are harvested in late fall, after the tops have died down (or frost has killed them).

Storage: The best place to store the tubers is in the ground. In colder climates you should cover them with mulch to prevent the ground freezing. If it isn't practical to leave them in the ground, they can be stored like carrots, in a root cellar in damp sand or sawdust. They will keep in the fridge for several weeks.

Seed saving: I have never seen Oca flower, let alone produce seed. This doesn't matter though, as it is normally propagated vegetatively.

Unusual growing ideas
Ornamental: The plants have attractive clover-like foliage and are pretty enough to be grown as an ornamental border. Though of course they won't look so pretty when you dig them up.

Perennial: Oca will grow quite happily as a perennial if you leave it alone. Its foliage is attractive enough to earn it a place in the ornamental garden.

Varieties: There are pink, red, purple and yellow varieties. Some newer varieties may be lower in oxalic acid.

Finding Oca tubers to plant isn't easy, finding named cultivars is even harder.

Cooking: The root can be used in the same ways as the potato: boiled, baked, fried in soups and more. Unlike the potato it is also quite good raw (or pickled).

The tops are also edible and can be added to salads. However they should be used in moderation as they contain oxalic acid.

Okra

Abelmoschus esculentus
Syn *Hibiscus esculentus*

Introduction: This relative of Cotton is native to Africa and is still most closely associated with African cooking. Okra grows best in hot weather and in this country it is most popular in the southeastern states. It can easily be grown in cooler parts of the country however, if grown in the same way as the Tomato.

Nutritional content:
Okra contains vitamin A and calcium. The seeds are rich in protein and edible oil.

Soil
pH 6.0 to 8.0
Okra is a vigorous and fairly greedy plant, so the soil should be rich in all nutrients. It should also be well drained and have a fairly neutral pH (it doesn't like acid soil).

Soil preparation: Add organic matter in the form of 2″ of compost or aged manure. You might also add wood ashes to supply potassium and colloidal phosphate as a source of phosphorus.

Planning
Where: Okra can get quite tall, so make sure it doesn't shade other crops. Most varieties only get to 4 or 5 feet though. The flowers and leaves are quite attractive, so it could also be planted in the ornamental garden.

When: This tropical plant thrives in heat and can't stand any cold whatsoever (minimum air temp 75° F). It should not be planted until all frost danger is past and the soil has warmed up to at least 60° F. If the growing season is short, you might use cloches or black plastic to warm the soil. Because it is planted so late, it can go in the space previously occupied by an early crop, such as Peas or Fava Beans.

About Okra

Seed facts
Germ temp: 60 (70 to 95) 105° F
Germ time: 5 to 10 days
27 days / 59° F
17 days / 68° F
13 days / 77° F
7 days / 86° F * Optimum
6 days / 95° F
Seed viability: 4 to 5 yrs
Germination percentage: 50%+
Weeks to grow transplant: 5 to 7

Planning facts
Hardiness: Tender
Ease of growing: Moderate
Growing temp: 65 (70 to 85) 95° F
Plants per person: 3
Plants per sq ft: 1
Transplants:
Start: 2 to 3 wks before last frost
Plant out: 4 wks after last frost
Direct sow: 4 wks after last frost
Time to harvest: 100 to 130 days

Harvest facts
Length of harvest: 6 to 10 wks
Yield per plant: 8 oz
Yield per sq ft: 8 oz

Planting
Sowing: Soak the seed overnight before planting.

Transplants
Starting inside: In cool or short growing seasons you should start Okra inside to save time. It doesn't like root disturbance, so plant it in cell packs or soil blocks. Start the seed 2 to 3 weeks before the last frost date and plant out about a month later.

Direct sowing: In areas with long growing seasons, Okra is often direct sown. The soil should be warm before you plant (60° F minimum), as the seed will simply rot if planted in cold soil. Plant the seeds ½″ deep in heavy (or cool) soil, or 1″ deep in light (or warm) soil. Space the seeds 4″ to 6″ apart, to be thinned to the desired spacing later.

Spacing:
Rows: Plan on spacing the plants 12″ to 18″ apart (depending on the size of the variety), in rows 2 to 6 ft apart.

Beds: Space the plants 12″ to 18″ apart, depending upon the size of the variety.

Care
Water: Okra must be kept well watered at all times.

Fertilization: Okra is a hungry plant. If the soil isn't very rich, give them a liquid feed of compost tea or liquid Kelp, every 2 to 3 weeks. It especially loves nitrogen.

Mulch: Apply a 3″ mulch to keep the soil moist and keep down weeds.

Pruning: If the plants get too big, cut them down to within a foot of the ground. They will sprout vigorously and start producing again.

Pests and diseases: Okra is attacked by Aphids, Leafminers, nematodes, Stinkbugs and some caterpillars. Diseases include Southern Blight and various molds and fungi. It is rarely affected by insect pests when growing in cooler areas.

Harvesting

When: The flowers should appear about 60 days after planting, but cold weather, or lack of moisture, may cause them to drop off without being pollinated. The pods are ready about 5 days after fertilization. They are at their best when still soft and small (2″ to 3″ long), while they still snap easily. As they get bigger than this, they start to get tough and are not so good.

Caution: Okra plants are covered in tiny spines and cause skin irritation in some people.

How: Pick the new pods conscientiously every day or two. The more you pick, the more you get. If any pods mature on the plant, they may cause the plant to stop producing. The plants grow fast in warm weather and can produce a lot of pods. Use them as soon as possible after harvest, as their flavor deteriorates quickly.

Seed: If the pods get over mature, you can always shell out the green seeds and use them like Peas. The dry pods are rich in high quality protein and it has been suggested that they could be more valuable for their seeds than for the pods

Storage: Fresh Okra pods don't keep for very long, but they do freeze quite well. They can also be dried for storage, just put them in a warm dark place. The flavor of dried pods is quite different from that of fresh plants, but still good.

Seed saving: Okra will self-pollinate if no other plants are growing nearby. However the flowers are very attractive to bees and if any other Okra is growing within a mile, they will probably be cross-pollinated. For this reason you should only grow one variety at a time, or you must isolate the plants (in a cage, by bagging or by a distance of one mile). To ensure genetic variability you should save the seed from at least 5 plants. Of course you should also select the best plants to produce seed. The fruit will take about 4 or 5 weeks to fully ripen (and the plants may well stop producing new fruits).

The dry pods are even more irritating than the green pods, so wear gloves and long sleeves when harvesting. Separate the seeds from the pods carefully and dry thoroughly before storage.

Unusual growing ideas:
Ornamental: Okra is attractive enough for the ornamental garden, and works well as an edible ornamental.

Varieties: Some of the old varieties were as much as 12 feet in height, but more modern varieties are considerably smaller.

Clemson Spineless: The commonest variety.

Perkins Mammoth: Can get very big. Not easy to find.

Red Burgundy: Has red pods.

Cooking: Okra is related to the Mallows and has the same mucilaginous (slimy) quality that some people object to.

Fried Okra

1 lb Okra pods
1 egg
1 cup cornmeal
2 tbsp water
2 dashes hot sauce
oil

Wash and trim the Okra and cut into ½″ slices. Beat the egg and water in bowl, then add the Okra, hot sauce and cornmeal. Roll around to coat all pieces. sauté in a pan slowly so the Okra dries out in cooking. This southern dish was traditionally deep fried, but that is a little too much fat for me.

Onion

Allium cepa

Introduction: Onion is one of the essential kitchen ingredients, that no cook can do without. It probably originated somewhere in central Asia, but has been cultivated by every major civilization from the Egyptians, Greeks and Romans onward. Its use has spread around the world and it is prized as a flavoring by people everywhere.

Apparently the word onion comes from the Latin unio meaning one, because it only produces one bulb, unlike the related Garlic and Shallot

The most important thing to remember about growing this biennial is that it is day length sensitive. It is programmed to produce bulbs when the appropriate day length arrives, no matter how big or small it is.

It is your job as a gardener to get the plants as big as possible before the onset of bulbing. To do this you must use a variety that is appropriate for the day length of your location. You should also plant them as early as is safe, as this enables them to put on the maximum amount of vegetative growth, before bulbing. Temperature also affects bulbing, cool weather may slow it down, while warm weather may hasten it.

Nutritional content:

Onions are a good source of vitamin C, potassium and calcium. They also contain a variety of beneficial phytochemicals, including diallyl sulfide, kaempferol and quercitin.

About Onion

Seed facts

Germ temp: 50 (60 to 65) 85° F
Germ time: 7 to 28 days
136 days / 32° F
30 days / 41° F
13 days / 50° F
7 days / 59° F
5 days / 68° F * Optimum
4 days / 77° F
4 days / 86° F
13 days / 95° F
Seed viability: 1 to 4 years
Germination percentage: 70%+
Weeks to grow transplant: 10 to 12

Planning facts

Hardiness: Hardy
Ease of growing: Moderate
Growing temp: 70 to 80° F
Plants per person: 25
Plants per sq ft: 16
Transplants:
Start: 7 to 9 wks before last frost
Plant out: 3 wks after last frost
Direct sow: 4 to 6 weeks before the last frost date
Fall crop: Plant 6 to 12 weeks before the first frost
Time to harvest: 80 to 160 days

Harvest facts

Yield per plant: 4 oz
Yield per sq ft: 1 to 4 lb

The green leaves are rich in vitamin A.

Soil
pH: 6.0 - 7. 5

Onions are not very efficient feeders, because their roots are weak and shallow. Consequently they need a loose, rich, moisture retentive soil with lots of organic matter. They don't like compacted, heavy, dry, acid, salty, or poorly drained soils (their roots may rot if it is too wet).

Onions don't need a lot of nutrients, but you have make sure they have plenty available, because they aren't very efficient feeders. For example they only need about 150 pounds of nitrogen per acre, but you may have to add 300 pounds for them to get even that much.

Soil preparation: Prepare the soil by incorporating 2″ of compost or aged manure, into the top 6″ of soil, which is where most of their feeder roots are to be found. For an early spring planting you could do this in fall, using fresh manure if necessary.

Onions don't need a lot of nitrogen, but they do like potassium, so give them wood ashes or greensand. If the pH is low then add lime.

Planning
Where: Onions like a warm sunny site, protected from strong winds.

Crop rotation: Don't plant them where any other Alliums have been grown in the past 3 years.

When: Correct timing is vital with bulb Onions. If you don't plant them at the right time they won't do very well.

Spring: Onions must be started early if they are to grow large enough before long summer days trigger bulbing. This means putting sets or seedlings into the ground (or starting them inside) as early as January or February. They put on vegetative growth steadily through spring and early summer and then bulb up when the days get to be the right length. They need warm weather to ripen and cure the bulbs.

Fall: One way to give the plants more time for vegetative growth is to start them in autumn. This gives the plants longer to grow and so results in larger bulbs. Some varieties are specifically intended for over-wintering.

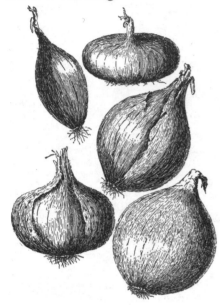

Planting

You have several choices when growing Onions; you can use seed, transplants or sets. All of these are fully hardy and can be planted as soon as the soil is workable in spring. When you first try growing onions it isn't a bad idea to use two different planting methods at the same time as extra insurance.

Seed

Growing your own Onions from seed gives you the greatest choice of varieties. The problem with Onion seeds is that they are slow, growing only half as fast as Lettuce.

Onion seed is the shortest lived of all common vegetables, so it is important that it is fresh.

You can use seed to grow sets or transplants, or to sow directly in the ground.

Onion sets

These are small Onion bulbs (⅜ to ¾″ in diameter) grown in crowded conditions, so as to induce premature bulbing (see below). They are the easiest way to grow Onions, as you don't have to worry about germination and are actually starting with a small bulb.

Buying sets: Every spring sets are readily available in every garden center, so they are probably the commonest way to grow onions. One problem with buying sets is that there are very few varieties available. In fact some packages don't even say what type they are.

Growing sets: This is easier than you might imagine and has the advantage in that you can grow whatever variety you want. Simply scatter the seed on a prepared bed in spring, ¼″ apart and cover with ¼″ to ½″ of sifted soil/compost. Don't feed the plants and go lightly on the watering. Because they are growing so close together they will crowd and stunt each other. When the tops turn brown, dig and dry the small bulbs for at least 10 days. Store your sets in the fridge or root cellar (below 40° F). Sets with a diameter of less than 1″ are the best, as they are less likely to bolt.

Planting sets: This is pretty straightforward, simply place them on the ground (right side up) at the proper spacing. You can then see the spacing easily and adjust it as necessary. Then just push the sets down into the soil, to the proper depth, with your finger and close up the hole.

Some gardeners sort out their sets and use the small ones for bulb onions and larger ones for scallions (these are more likely to bolt).

Transplants

Using transplants gives you the largest Onion bulbs and gives them a lot faster than by direct sowing.

Buying: Many people buy their transplants by mail order. They work well, but are a little too expensive for me, especially when you consider how easy it is to raise your own. They also have quite a big interruption in growth, while they are in transit to your garden.

Growing: Start the seeds about 8 to 12 weeks before planting out time. The longer the plants grow before bulbing, the bigger the bulb can get. Onions don't mind transplanting (it may even encourage good root growth), so are usually planted in flats, ¼″ apart and ½″ deep (cover with a sifted soil / compost mix). You can grow a lot of plants in a small area. The plants will germinate much quicker if you put them in a warm place (75 to 80° F). Once they have germinated they should be moved to a cool place (60 to 70° F), as this gives you stockier, hardier plants.

If the stems are smaller than ¼″ diameter when you plant them out, you won't have to worry about vernalization (see **Bolting** below). However you want them to be close to this size, so the bulbs will get bigger. If you don't plant them out until the weather has warmed up, you won't have to worry about this anyway.

Planting: The seedlings can be transplanted out 2 weeks before the

last frost date, but I prefer to wait a bit longer, to avoid the possibility of vernalization. Use only the largest, healthiest seedlings and plant them 1″ deep. Some people cut off part of the top and root before transplanting, but the logic of reducing their root and leaf area seems dubious and probably isn't a good idea.

Direct sowing: This is slower than transplanting of course, but easier and can work well in some situations. Onions are very hardy and can be direct sown in early spring, as soon as the ground can be worked (often 6 weeks before the last frost). You can either broadcast, or sow in drills (the seed should be planted ¼″ to ½″ deep). Keep the soil moist and free of crusting.

You can give the plants longer to grow, and so get larger bulbs, by sowing the seed in fall. Time your planting so the seedlings are well established before frost arrives. In cold areas, protect them with mulch over the winter.

Spacing: This has a direct effect on the final size of the bulbs. A wider spacing results in larger bulbs than a smaller spacing, but of course you get less of them. For maximum production of food you should plant fairly closely. The individual bulbs may be fairly small, but you will get a lot more of them.

Of course the fertility of the soil also affects spacing. In rich soil you can put the plants closer together. Close spacing can also result in faster maturation.

Large bulbs: 4″ to 5″ apart
Medium bulbs: 3″ to 4″ apart
Pickling bulbs: 2″ to 3″ apart
Green Onions: 2″ to 3″ apart

I like to plant Onions in offset rows across the bed, as it's easier to weed them with a hoe. Some gardeners initially plant at half the final spacing and remove each alternate plant for use as green Onions.

Care

You want Onions to grow as fast as possible, so by the time the day length is right for bulbing, they will be able to store enough food to produce large bulbs. This means spacing them properly and giving them all the nutrients and water they need.

Weeds: Onions don't produce much foliage and don't get very big, so they can't shade out, or outgrow, weeds as they mature. This means that competition from weeds can be a major problem, especially for direct sown crops. It is critical that they are weeded methodically, for at least their first two months in the ground. You need to be careful when weeding, as their shallow roots are easily damaged by careless hoeing. As the plants get bigger, a mulch is helpful to keep weeds down.

Water: Onions are quite drought tolerant, but a lack of water makes the bulb smaller and more pungent. For best flavor and largest bulbs, you should keep the soil moist at all times, so there is no interruption in growth. Give them water in the form of frequent shallow watering (there's no point watering these shallow rooted plants very deeply). It is best to water in the morning, so the tops dry out quickly, as this reduces the potential for downy mildew. Stop watering the bulbs when they stop enlarging, they need to be dry for curing.

Fertilization: If your soil isn't very fertile give the plants a feed of compost tea or liquid seaweed every 3 weeks.

Mulch: The sparse foliage doesn't shade the soil very much, so a mulch is helpful in dry weather, to conserve soil moisture. It will also help to keep down weeds. Mulch also insulates the soil, so don't apply it until the soil has warmed up.

Special problems
Day length: Onions don't always perform as expected, because of their sensitivity to day length. The days must be of a certain length to induce bulb formation and different varieties need different day lengths. If a long day variety is planted where the days are too short, it will grow well enough, but may never produce bulbs. If you plant a short day variety where the days get too long, it will bulb prematurely and the bulbs won't get very big. See Varieties below.

Short day: 11 to 12 hours
Intermediate day: 12 to 14 hours
Long day: 14 to 16 hours
Very long day: 16 or more hours
A few varieties are day neutral

Generally short and intermediate day varieties are grown below 40 degrees latitude, long day types above this line.

Bulbing: The onion bulb is a food storage organ comprised of layers of specialized leaves. Bulbing occurs when the plant stops producing new leaves and starts to store food in the leaves it has. This causes their bases to swell

The Vegetable Growers Handbook

and form the bulb. When the bulb is mature, all of the food has gone from the rest of the leaves, so they wither, fall over and die.

Bolting: Sometimes Onions will bolt instead of bulbing, or at the same time. This usually happens because the plants were vernalized. For a plant to be vernalized it must be at least ¼″ in diameter (smaller plants aren't usually affected) and must be exposed to temperatures below 50° F for two weeks. When warmer weather returns the plant thinks it has gone through a winter and so sets about following it's destiny, which is to produce seed. This phenomenon means you must be careful when planting Onions in fall or early spring. If they get too big (over ¼″ diameter) they may bolt.

Bolting doesn't affect edibility, you can just remove the woody stem core when chopping the bulb. However it causes the plant to waste energy trying to flower, so the bulb doesn't get as big as it could have.

Tip burn: A deficiency of potassium may cause the tips of older leaves to die back.

Pests and diseases: Alliums in general are rarely affected by pests, but there are quite a few potential disease problems. These include Fusarium rot, Downy Mildew, Onion Leaf Blight, Purple Blotch, Rust, Smut, Pink Root, Onion Smudge, Neck Rot (the people who named these diseases weren't very imaginative).

Onion Maggots: This small fly is found in the Northern United States and Canada. The larvae burrow into Onion bulbs and seedlings, stunting or killing them. I have had no experience with them, but row covers are an effective solution

Onion Thrips: These creatures suck juices from the plants. They over winter in weeds so keep the garden clean. Spanish Onions are resistant.

Harvesting

When

Bulbs: For immediate eating, you can gather bulbs as soon as they are big enough to be worth using. However if you want to store the bulbs for any length of time, they must be fully mature.

When bulbing is complete, the tops turn yellow and die back, as they have no more energy in them. Stop watering your Onions at this time, to allow them to dry out and cure. Some gardeners knock over any remaining green leaves at this point, to hasten their drying. Don't do this prematurely though, wait until at least a half of the tops have fallen by themselves and take care not to bruise the bulb. Leave the bulbs for another week to die back fully.

How: Lift the bulbs and leave them in the sun for a few days to dry out. If the sun is very hot, you should move them to a shady place, as they can be cooked by very strong sunlight. If there is danger of rain you should move them under cover. After the tops have dried out completely, cut them off, leaving 1″ on the bulb (obviously if you want to braid your onions don't do this). Finally put the bulbs in a warm, dry place for 2 to 3 weeks, to cure fully.

The bulbs are fairly delicate, so handle them carefully at all times

and don't throw them around. This is particularly important if you want to store them. Damaged or bruised bulbs will rot easily.

Greens: You can harvest individual leaves from your bulbing Onions at any time. Just don't take too many or it will affect bulb formation. Actually it is a better idea to leave the bulb Onions alone and plant extra plants for scallions (use the largest sets, or the weakest looking plants). Even better is to plant some perennial Welsh Onions or Egyptian Onions.

Storage: Before storing the bulbs, you should examine them carefully. The papery outer skin should be in good condition, there should be no bruising and the neck should be dry and papery. If the neck is still thick it didn't mature properly and won't store very well. These bulbs should be used first.

Store the bulbs in mesh bags (old panty hose works well), or make Onion braids. Keep them in a cool dry place, at 32 to 50° F and 60% humidity. Excessive moisture can encourage sprouting.

Onion braids look great hanging in the kitchen, but it is too warm and dry to store them there for any length of time (they will dry out). I suppose you could make small braids and bring them into the kitchen as you need them.

Seed saving: Onions are cross-pollinated by insects but this isn't usually a problem as there are no close wild relatives and most people don't let their Onions flower.

Onions are biennial and will flower in the spring of their second year.

132

In mild climates you can leave the bulbs in the ground over the winter, but in cold climates you will have to store them inside and re-plant them in spring.

Use the best Onions you have for seed. Larger bulbs produce larger flowers (they sometimes get to 4 feet in height) and more seed.

Make sure the flower heads are thoroughly dry before collecting seed. Finally remove the seed from the head and dry it thoroughly before storing. Onion seed doesn't remain viable for very long, 2 or 3 years at the most.

Unusual Growing Ideas
Interplanting: Onions are commonly interplanted with Carrots, but do well with many crops.

Green Onions:
These are varieties of bulbing onion, sown in fall (they may need protection in colder areas) and harvested as scallions in spring (which is why they are sometimes known as Spring Onions). They are planted very closely together, with as many as 30 plants per square foot.

Green Onions can also be multi-planted, with up to 10 seeds in one soil block, or plug tray (in this way you can grow a bunch of green Onions.

There are varieties specifically bred for this purpose (White Lisbon is one), or you can use any surplus Onion sets.

Latitudes for varieties

Ailsa Craig: 38 - 60°
Copra F1: 38 - 55°
Early Yellow Globe: 38 - 50°
New York Early: 38 - 50°
Red Creole: 24 - 28°
Yellow Granex: 20 - 36°
Walla Walla Sweet: 35 - 55°

Varieties: Even more than with most crops, the selection of the right variety for your location and purpose is extremely important. A given variety may perform quite differently in different areas, so you have to find out what does well in your areas.

I already described how Onion varieties are commonly classified according to the amount of daylight they require to produce bulbs. European varieties tend to be long day, because they come from more northerly latitudes. For some reason seed packets often don't contain day length information, which seems rather negligent. If you use varieties grown by local seed companies you should be okay.

Some varieties don't store well and must be used relatively quickly, others will keep for months.

Storage Onions:
Copra, F1, Ebenezer, Yellow Globe, Yellow Of Parma

Sweet Onions:
These have such a mild flavor they are often eaten raw. Their skins tend to be rather thin, so they can't be stored for very long.
Vidalia F1, Yellow Granex F1 Walla Walla

Cooking:
Onions resemble Garlic in that their pungent flavor only develops fully when cell walls are ruptured. If you bake a whole Onion this will inactivate the enzymes and the flavor won't be nearly so strong.

Onion Bhaji

1 large onion
1 small hot pepper (deseeded and chopped, the hotness is up to you
4 oz garbanzo bean Flour
1 oz cilantro
¼ tsp chili powder
½ tsp turmeric
½ tsp baking powder
½ tsp ground cumin
Salt
Water
Vegetable oil

Mix all the dry ingredients together in a bowl, then add enough water to make a batter (this should have the consistency of whipping cream). Let it sit for 15 minutes. Cut the onion into ¼″ thick slices and coat them with the batter. Then fry in 350° F oil (it needs to be hot) first on one side until crisp and then turn over (you can also deep fry, but this takes more oil).

Drain well on kitchen paper and serve hot with mango chutney.

Onion, Japanese

These are simply Japanese varieties of *A. cepa* that have been bred for growing in mild climates. They are planted in late summer or fall and harvested the following summer, slightly before other bulb onions. Start the seed in midsummer so you have seedlings for planting in fall. They can also be grown from sets, if you can find them, or are prepared to grow your own.

Japanese Onions are grown in exactly the same way as other Onions.

Varieties include Senshyu Semi-Globe, Imai Early Yellow

Onion, Welsh

A. fistulosum

Introduction: This perennial Onion has nothing to do with Wales. It's name is thought to come from the German *welsche* meaning foreign. It is the most important type of Onion in Asia and has been grown in China for thousands of years.

Welsh Onion doesn't produce a swollen bulb, but tillers and sends up several stems (it is also known as Bunching Onion). It can cross-pollinate with *A. cepa* and many varieties are actually crosses of the two species (these are often sterile however.) It is a very reliable and hardy crop plant and deserves a more prominent place in the vegetable garden. It has much the same cultural requirements as the bulb Onion.

Soil
pH 6.5 to 7.5
Like other Onions it has a shallow and not very vigorous root system, so needs to grow in rich, moist soil for best performance. Avoid fresh manure.

Planning

Where: With 12 to 16 plants per sq ft these Onions don't take up much space. The perennial clumping types can be planted in the ornamental, wild or forest garden.

When: This perennial plant can be harvested in spring and early summer, thus filling the gap between stored winter bulbs and the first summer crop.

Japanese Bunching Onions are usually grown as annuals. They are planted in autumn, to mature early the following summer. In very harsh climates they can also be started indoors in very early spring (8 to 12 weeks before last frost), to mature in late spring. They can also be grown over the winter in a cold frame.

Planting
Welsh Onions can be direct sown, but are more often started indoors (or in a nursery bed) and transplanted to their final position. Once you have a good stand, you can divide the clumps to multiply them.

Starting seedlings: In Asia these plants are not usually direct sown, but are started indoors or in a nursery bed. They transplant quite easily and in China they are sometimes transplanted several times, just to delay their maturation.

Sow the seed ¼″ deep in flats, cell packs or soil blocks (you can multi-plant them, sowing several seeds per station). It germinates best at a temperature of 60 to 65° F.

Spacing: Space the seedlings 3″ to 4″ apart.

Care
This is pretty much the same as for Onion.

Mulch: In colder areas protect them over the winter with a thick mulch.

Division: Divide Welsh Onions every couple of years, or when you want to start more colonies.

Pests: They are subject to the same problems as other Onions, but to a lesser extent. When grown as a perennial there is a greater chance of pests building up in the soil, so be watchful

Harvest: Bunching Onions can be eaten at several stages of growth. The very young plants can be thinned and eaten like Chives. The green leaves can be eaten anytime, as can the thickened white bases (these are sometimes blanched to make them longer).

In loose soil you can harvest by simply pulling on the tops. If you do this in heavy soil, they will just break off. In this situation you must loosen the soil with a trowel before harvesting.

Seed saving: Just allow the plants to flower and set seed. Cross-pollination probably won't be a problem. Of course as they are a perennial you don't need to save seed at all.

Unusual growing ideas:
Interplanting: Japanese Bunching Onions don't take up much space, so they are a good crop for interplanting between other crops.

Varieties: The Asian varieties are generally more vigorous and refined than the European types. There are attractive red and purple cultivars, varieties for cold winter growing and varieties for hot weather. This isn't really surprising as they are much more important there. At the same time many Asian types don't form clumps as well as the Welsh Onions, they are grown as annuals and just form single stems. I value this crop as a perennial and so like the clumping types.

He-Shi-Ko
Ishikura Long
Sakata Evergreen

Onion, Egyptian

Allium cepa var *viviparum proliferum* group

This unusual type of Onion grows like a green Onion, but then puts out a cluster of small bulbils instead of flowers. These in turn produce their own green onions and even more bulbils. Eventually the stem bends over and the bulbils take root. They then send up clusters of green shoots of their own. The plant is sometimes called the Walking Onion because it has the ability to move in this way.

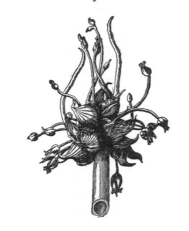

The plant is propagated vegetatively, by means of the bulbs or bulbils. It grows in most soils, so long as it gets full sun. I like this independent plant and often plant the entire bulb clusters in vacant spots around the garden. They soon grow into a new bunch of green onions. This is probably the most self-sufficient of all the Onion varieties and once established you can forget all about it, except for harvesting.

The plants can be used as green onions, the small bulbs can be eaten, as can the bulbils.

Varieties:
Catawissa: This is said to be an unusually vigorous type.

Orach

Atriplex hortensis

Introduction: Orach is native to the seacoasts of Northern Europe and is notable as being one of the first plants ever cultivated in Europe. It was an old potherb even to the ancient Greeks and Romans.

Soil: Orach does well on most soils, even quite alkaline ones. However for best results it should be grown in fertile, well-drained soil with lots of organic matter.

Planning
When: This annual prefers cool weather and bolts when it gets too hot. In areas with mild winters it can be grown as a winter crop.

Where: In hot climates Orach prefers to grow in light shade, so could be useful for forest gardens (especially as it is also very independent). It can cast quite a bit of shade itself, as it can grow to 6 ft or more. Don't plant it where it might shade sun loving neighbors.

Planting: Plant the first Orach in spring, 2 to 4 weeks before the average last frost date. Sow the seed directly into the garden ½″ to 1″ deep. The seeds normally germinate in 5 to 10 days.

Succession sowing: In cool climates you can sow every 2 to 3 weeks, from March until August

Spacing: Sow the plants 1″ apart, in rows 12″ apart. When they are a couple of inches high, they should be thinned to stand 6″ to 12″ apart. You can eat the thinnings or transplant them to another spot (they transplant quite easily).

Care: This independent plant doesn't need much attention.

Weeding: The young plants need weeding, but older ones can take care of themselves.

Water: Orach is quite drought resistant, but needs water if it is to produce an abundance of foliage.

Feed: An occasional liquid feed may help it to produce more plentiful and succulent growth.

Mulch: This helps to keep down weeds and conserve soil moisture.

Pruning: Pinch off the flowers as they appear unless you want to save seed. Regular picking encourages new growth and lengthens the harvest season.

When: Start gathering the leaves and growing tips about six weeks after planting. Gathering the growing tips causes them to get bushier. Older leaves aren't as good as younger ones, so you always want to encourage new growth.

Seed saving: Just allow them to flower and set seed. Your biggest concern is collecting it before it falls. Apparently the seed can live for up to 7 years, but I haven't had much luck with seed that wasn't fresh.

Varieties : White, Red, Yellow, green.

Cooking: The leaves are usually cooked as a potherb and in soups. The young leaves can also be eaten raw in salads.

Parsnip
Pastinaca sativa ssp *sativa*

Introduction: This European native has been cultivated since the time of the Romans. It hasn't changed a great deal from the wild form, except that the root is bigger and the woody core has disappeared.

The Parsnip was a staple root vegetable in Europe for centuries, but was eventually displaced by the Potato. It is still much more popular in Europe than it is in North America and is a common sight in vegetable gardens there. Parsnip has declined in importance in North America in recent years and is now relatively unusual.

The Parsnip is a useful crop for several reasons. It tastes good, is nutritious, is easy to store (you simply leave it in the ground) and it's quite easy to grow (easier than the Carrot). The main drawback is that it is slow growing and so is in the ground for quite a long time.

Nutritional content: The root contains vitamin C, folate, manganese, potassium and lots of fiber.

Soil
pH 6.0 to 7.0
The ideal soil for Parsnips is a fairly neutral, loose, well-drained, moderately rich loam. It should be deep because the roots may go down 2 feet and also fairly free of stones.

Soil preparation: Incorporate 2″ of compost or aged manure into the top 6″ of soil. Don't use fresh manure, as too much nitrogen encourages foliage growth, at the expense of the roots (it may

also make the roots fork). Like most root crops Parsnip needs lots of potassium (add greensand) and phosphorus (add colloidal phosphate or wood ashes), but relatively little nitrogen. Add lime if the soil is acidic.

If the soil is compacted double digging is beneficial, as it ensures the soil is loose and free of large stones. If the soil is really bad, you might consider growing the shorter varieties and planting in trenches filled with a special sifted topsoil / compost mix.

About Parsnip

Seed facts
Germ temp: 35 (50 to 70) 85° F
Germ time: 10 to 21
172 days / 32° F
57 days / 41° F
27 days / 50° F
19 days / 59° F
14 days / 68° F * Optimum
15 days / 77° F
32 days / 86° F
Viability: 1 yr
Germination percentage: 60%+

Planning facts
Hardiness: Hardy
Ease of growing: Easy
Growing temp: 40 (60 to 65) 75° F
Plants per person: 25
Plants per sq ft: 9
Direct sow in spring: 2 weeks before last frost
Direct sow for fall: Mid summer
Time to harvest: 120 to 200 days

Harvest facts
Yield per plant: 2 to 8 oz
Yield per sq ft: 1 to 4 lb sq ft

Planning

Where: Parsnips do better than most common crops in light shade, though they are more productive in full sun. They are in the ground for a long time, so should be located where they won't interfere with late garden operations, such as fall bed preparation.

Parsnips are a good crop to plant after potatoes. They like the deeply dug soil and the previous heavy fertilization.

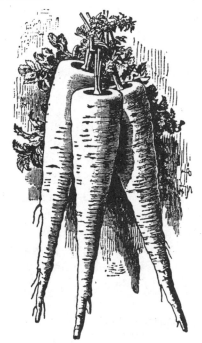

When:

Spring: In cool summer areas, you can plant Parsnips as a spring crop, putting them in the ground 2 weeks before the last spring frost date.

Fall: Parsnip doesn't grow very well above 75° F, so roots that mature in warm summer weather are generally inferior to those maturing in the cold weather of late autumn. For this reason Parsnips are really a fall crop. As an autumn crop there is no rush to get them in the ground, unless the growing season is very short. They are usually planted in mid summer, so as to mature around the time of the first fall frost. They will then sit in the ground until needed.

Planting

Direct sowing: Parsnip seed is considered to be temperamental and you often read warnings against using seed that is more than one year old. I have experienced little difficulty in getting it to germinate well and have used 2 year old seed on several occasions, with good results. However it is a good idea to use fresh seed where possible and to plant it all (don't save part of a packet for next year).

The seed is quite slow to germinate, taking almost 3 weeks at 60° F. It may not germinate well if the soil is very warm, which could be a problem if you are planting in mid summer. You could try cooling the soil a little, by repeated watering with cold water.

The most critical aspect of sowing is depth, as the seedlings aren't very vigorous and must not be sown too deeply. Some people plant a few Radishes along with the Parsnips. The theory is that the fast germinating Radishes break up the soil surface, making it easier for the Parsnips to emerge (they also mark the rows).

Broadcast sowing: Ideally you should broadcast the seed so there is an inch separating each one. Be careful of high winds when scattering these light seeds (they are designed to be scattered by the wind). Also make sure you sow enough seed, it might take a whole month before you know if your stand is too sparse. Cover the seed with a very thin ¼″ layer of soil, or a mix of sifted topsoil and compost.

Row sowing: Sow the seed ½″ to 1″ apart in ¼″ deep furrows. Then re-fill the furrows with a thin layer of sand, or a mix of sifted topsoil and compost. You can also sow it in wide rows.

Spacing: The distance between plants largely determines how big they can get. If you want very large roots space them 4″ or 5″ apart in the beds. For average sized roots space them 3″ apart.

Thinning: If the plants are to grow quickly, without competition from neighboring plants, they must be properly thinned. As with Carrots, this is one of the most crucial aspects of raising good Parsnips. When all of the seedlings are up and growing, thin them to the desired spacing, taking out the weakest plants where possible. Don't wait too long to do this, as their roots and tops will soon get tangled.

Care

Parsnip is a hardy and robust plant and once established it is perfectly capable of looking after itself.

Weeds: Young Parsnips don't compete with weeds very well, so must be weeded carefully. This should be done by hand, as hoes can easily damage the shoulders of the root. Older plants are better able to compete against most weeds, as they produce an abundance of foliage.

Watering: Parsnips need constant moisture (especially when the roots are sizing up), so don't let the soil get too dry.

Fertilization: If the soil isn't very fertile, give your plants a regular feed of compost tea or liquid seaweed every month.

Mulch: This is helpful to keep the soil moist, suppress weeds and to cover the shoulders of the roots.

Pests: The Parsnip may be affected by most of the pests that attack the related Carrot, but aren't usually as badly affected.

Leaf Miners: The only pest I have encountered has been Leaf Miners, but as we don't eat the leaves their damage is usually fairly inconsequential. If they get really bad, you might want to use row covers.

Canker: This disease is commonest in poorly drained, acid soils and causes the root to rot. Some varieties are resistant to it.

Harvesting

When: Parsnips can be dug any time they are large enough, but they are at their best in late autumn, after they have been touched by a few frosts. This is because cold temperatures cause the starch in the root to be converted into sugar, which makes them sweeter.

Generally the roots are gathered after the foliage has died down and it's getting cold. As with carrots the young roots are the most tender, but they are not as sweet or tasty as older roots.

How: If the soil is very loose, you can simply pull the roots up by the tops. If the soil is heavy they will just break off if you try this. You then have to loosen them with a fork before pulling.

Don't harvest any more roots than you can use in the next meal, as they store much better in the ground. If you still have roots in the ground in late winter, you should dig them all, as they turn woody and unpalatable once they start growing again.

Storage: Parsnips are one of the best crops for winter use. They are so hardy they can be stored in the ground all winter and dug as required. A thick mulch of straw can be used to prevent the ground from freezing so they are easier to dig (it may also protect the roots). If mice are a problem you may have to lay down wire mesh before you apply the mulch

The roots can be stored for several weeks in a plastic bag in the fridge.

For longer storage, treat them like Carrots and store them in a root cellar, in damp sand or peat moss. Large quantities can be stored in a clamp (see **Potato**).

Seed saving: It's easier to save Parsnip seed than most other biennials, because they are so hardy there is no problem getting them through the winter. You don't have to store the roots inside, or even protect them outside (though you might want to move them to a more convenient place).

Parsnips flower in the spring of their second year. They are cross-pollinated by insects, so you should grow only one variety at a time (or you could isolate them). They will also cross with Wild Parsnip, which is the wild form of this plant. (this is common in some areas). Save seed from at least a half dozen plants to maintain some genetic diversity.

Gather the ripe seeds from the umbels in summer (don't wait so long that they fall off) and dry thoroughly. They will need at least a month of after-ripening before they will germinate.

Unusual growing ideas

Intercrop: Plant a catch crop of fast growing Lettuce or Spinach, in between the rows of Parsnips. They will be gone before the roots need the room.

Greens: The tender new leafy growth of second year plants is sometimes eaten in salads. Surplus roots are sometimes forced indoors to supply early spring greens.

Varieties: Some Parsnip varieties can produce large, spindle shaped roots up to 18″ in length, with a diameter of 3″ at the top. These larger roots need a very deep and loose soil to perform well. Some varieties are resistant to Canker. The commonest varieties include: All American, Cobham Improved, Improved Hollow Crown

Cooking: Parsnips are best known for their use in winter stews and soups, but can be used in lots of other ways. Try roasted Parsnips, French-fried Parsnips, Stir-fried Parsnips, steamed Parsnips. When sugar was expensive they were sometimes used to sweeten cakes. In Britain they have been used to make a surprisingly palatable wine.

Pea

Pisum sativum

Introduction: This crop originated somewhere in central Asia about 8000 years ago and is now cultivated all around the world. In its dry state the pea is a highly nutritious, protein rich food and it was once a staple food of poor people in Northern Europe. Presently peas are more popular in their immature green stage and increasingly as edible green pods.

Peas are members of the *Fabaceae* and share the most important characteristic of many members of that family. They have a symbiotic relationship with nitrogen fixing bacteria that live in nodules on their roots. This makes them important for organic growers, because they can add nitrogen to the soil, rather than taking it out.

Don't take nitrogen fixation for granted. Growing Peas won't add nitrogen to the soil if the right nitrogen fixing bacteria aren't present (the plants don't fix nitrogen, bacteria do). If you are growing dry peas any nitrogen that is fixed may be converted into protein rich peas, rather than entering the soil.

Peas are an excellent home garden food crop, and have a delicious flavor that is far better than commercial peas. They can be very productive (especially of edible pods) and even improve the soil they grow in. As a cool weather spring crop they can be out of the ground by June, leaving time for a warm weather crop to succeed them (in enriched soil).

Nutritional content:
Peas contain Vitamins C and B6, along with folate, iron and several anticancer phytochemicals.

About Peas

Seed facts
Germ temp: 40 (60 to 75) 85
Germ time: 6 to 17 days
36 days / 41° F
14 days / 50° F
9 days / 59° F
8 days / 68° F
6 days / 77° F * Optimum
6 days / 86° F
Germination percentage: 80%+
Viability: 3 years
Weeks to grow transplant: 4

Planning facts
Hardiness: Hardy
Ease of growing: Easy
Growing temp: 55 (60 to 65) 70° F
Plants per person: 50
Plants per sq ft: 8
Transplants:
Start: 8 wks before last frost
Plant out: 4 wks before last frost
Direct sow: 4 wks before last frost
Fall crop: 8 to 12 wks before first frost
Succession sow: every 2 to 4 wks
Time to harvest: 55 to 120 days

Harvest facts
Length of harvest: 4 to 6 wks
Yield per plant: 2 oz
Yield per sq ft· 1 lb

Soil:
pH 5.5 (6.0 - 6.5) 7.5
The best soil for Peas is a loose well-drained loam. If the soil is compacted then double digging is beneficial. If it is poorly drained, use raised beds, especially for early plantings, as they don't like wet soil. In very poor soils it may pay to plant your peas in trenches, filled with a mixture of soil and compost.

Peas don't need a lot of nitrogen, as they can obtain their own. In fact if nitrogen is too easily available they won't bother to fix any. Peas do need phosphorus (colloidal phosphate) and potassium (wood ashes), as well as calcium and magnesium (use dolomitic limestone).

Soil preparation:
Dig in 2″ of compost or aged manure (it can be fresh if applied in fall), as well as colloidal phosphate and greensand.

Peas are one of the first crops to be planted in spring, so many gardeners prepare the soil the previous autumn and cover it with mulch. This must be removed several weeks before planting, to allow the soil to warm up.

Planning
Where: Peas need full sun and lots of space for good growth. The climbing habit of the pole varieties can be an advantage, as it keeps them up off the ground and so saves garden space. However it also makes the plants vulnerable to high winds, so they should be planted in a sheltered spot.

When: Peas are cool weather plants, hardy down to 20° (28° F when flowering). They prefer mild temperatures (60 to 75° F) and don't usually set pods above 80° F. In areas with hot summers they are grown as a spring or fall crop (fall planting presents its own problems however).

Spring: Peas can be started quite early, if the soil is warm enough for good germination (at least 40° F though preferably 60° F). If it is too cold they will just sit and rot (or be eaten by rodents or birds). You can speed up the warming of the soil with plastic mulch, or cloches, before planting.

It is important to plant your crop early enough, so that it has sufficient time to mature before hot weather sets in. Normally the first Peas are planted 2 to 4 weeks before the last frost date. Some gardeners plant their first Peas even earlier than this, but run the risk of their being killed or injured by frost. When this works out you get very early Peas, so it may be worth the risk.

Succession sowing: With peas it is hard to extend the harvest period by succession sowing, as later sowings usually catch up with the earlier ones. A better idea is to plant several varieties with different maturation times (or both bush and pole varieties).

Summer: In cool climates you can grow peas right through the summer. In warmer climates this won't work very well, as the plants have a hard time with heat and disease.

Fall: Plant a fall crop 8 to 12 weeks before the first fall frost, so they mature in cool weather.

The seed may be sown in autumn for an early spring crop, though it should be protected with mulch over the winter.

Planting

Inoculation: The nitrogen-fixing bacteria that live in Pea roots can survive in the soil for 3 to 5 years. If you haven't grown Peas within that time, you should inoculate your seeds with a commercial inoculant. This can make a big difference to the amount of nitrogen that is fixed. This in turn may increase the yield of pods by as much as 75%. See **Beans** for information on seed inoculation.

Transplants

Starting inside: Peas are traditionally direct sown because they are very hardy and dislike transplanting. However starting them indoors does have its advantages. It allows you to get a very early start on the season, which can help you to get an early harvest. Perhaps more importantly it is easier to protect the germinating seeds indoors, so you lose less to rodents and birds.

Peas don't like transplanting, so must be started in individual containers such as cell packs, or soil blocks, to minimize root disturbance. Start them about 3 to 4

weeks before planting out and don't forget to inoculate them. Don't keep them indoors any longer than necessary, or they will suffer.

Planting out: Take care to harden the plants off properly before planting them out in cold spring weather.

Direct sowing:
Pea seeds will germinate over a wide temperature range, but do so much faster in warm soil. At 40° F they may take over a month to germinate, if they don't rot, or get eaten, in the meantime. At 70° F they may take only a week.

You can speed up germination somewhat by pre-soaking the seeds overnight before sowing. The best way to do this is to put them between moist paper towels. Soaking them in a bowl of water can cause them to absorb water too rapidly and may actually injure them.

You can also pre-germinate the seeds, to improve emergence in cold soils. Sprout the seeds on paper towels in a warm place and plant them out as soon as the roots appear (don't wait too long).

It is a good idea to erect your supporting structure before you plant your seed, so you don't disturb the young plants later.

Peas are commonly planted in rows, as this simplifies the task of supporting them. The traditional way to do this is to make furrows, as deep and as far apart as required. Put the seed in the furrow at the required spacing and re-fill it with soil. Peas seed is quite vigorous and is not usually bothered by crusting. It's a good idea to sow a few extra seeds at the end of a row, so you have extra plants to fill in any gaps.

I don't usually bother with furrows, I just lay out the seeds on the surface at the required spacing. When I am happy with this, I just push the seeds down to the proper depth with my finger.

In early spring, when the soil is cold, plant your peas 1″ deep (it will be too cold down at 3"). For later plantings in warmer soil plant them 2″ to 3″ deep (where it is cooler and more evenly moist).

Spacing
This depends upon whether you are using Bush or Pole varieties.

Pole varieties
Pole varieties are usually grown in rows because it is easier to support them. They are best planted in double offset rows, with 6″ between the plants and 6″ between the rows. You can get two of these double rows in a 5-foot wide bed (space them 30″ apart).

Bush varieties
These short varieties don't need much support, so are commonly planted in offset rows across the beds, 6″ apart each way.

You can also plant them in rows down the bed. Put the seeds 4″ to 6″ apart in the rows, with 24″ in between the rows.

Care
Weeds
Weed the young plants carefully (preferably by hand), to avoid damaging their shallow roots. Older plants are usually vigorous enough to overwhelm most weeds.

Mulch
This is helpful to keep down weeds, keep the soil cool and conserve soil moisture.

Water
In cool spring weather Peas usually get enough water from rainfall, so you don't have to irrigate. Watering at this time may encourage mildew and can actually reduce yields. If the soil is dry by the time the flowers appear, you should give them extra water. This improves the set of pods and hastens their maturation.

Feed
In poor soil the young plants will benefit from a feed of compost tea or liquid Kelp.

Support
Just as with Beans there are both bush and pole varieties of Peas. Unlike beans however, even the bush types do better with some support and will repay the extra work with a larger harvest.

Peas climb by means of slender tendrils and can't grow up thick poles. This means they need a different kind of support from beans. A Pea tendril will take about an hour to curl around a slender twig.

Chicken wire (or any stiff wire) also works well, either as a fence or a cage of some kind. You can also use a trellis, which can later be used for Cucumbers or Melons. If you are creative, you can rig up something from poles and string or netting.

Tomato cages (which aren't needed so early in the season) can work well with Bush Peas.

In England peas were traditionally grown on the thinnings of Hazel shrubs, but any brushwood will do (fruit tree prunings are good). They

were trimmed to a flat 2 dimensional plane. You just stick the butt ends firmly into the ground.

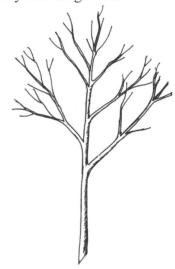

Whatever support you decide upon, it must be sufficiently tall and strong for the variety you will grow. The tangled full size vines and their load of peas can weigh quite a lot (especially when wet or when the wind is blowing).

Pests
Quite a few pests may attack Peas, including Aphids, Tarnished Plant Bugs, Cutworms, Mites, Leafminers, Leaf Hoppers, Cucumber Beetles, Pea Weevils and various caterpillars

Diseases
These include Fusarium Wilt, Mosaic Virus, Blight, Downy Mildew, Powdery Mildew, Pea Enation Virus.

Mice and Birds
These can be major pests and have been known to systematically eat whole plantings (birds break off the new sprouts, mice eat the seed in the ground). If mice are a problem there are repellent seed coatings available (kerosene was once commonly used). Netting can keep the plants safe from birds, but it's a real pain to deal with.

Slugs and snails: These are mostly a pest of unsupported plants. They don't really like Peas very much, but will eat them if there's nothing better available.

Deer, Rabbit, Groundhog
All of these animals like the young plants and must be kept out with fences or dogs.

Harvesting

When: Picking peas at the right time is almost as important as it is with Sweet Corn. Too early and they are very small, too late and they are starchy and not very good. You will have to experiment a little to find out the best time to harvest each particular type.

Peas mature quickly after pollination, so you have to check on the plants regularly (every day or so). You must pick the pods when they size up, even if you don't want to eat them, otherwise production will decline. In cool weather, a well managed planting may yield for as long as 6 weeks, though if the weather turns hot it may be as short as 2 weeks.

How: The pods start to ripen at the base of the plant first. Remove them from the plants carefully, so you don't damage the vines. Hold the plant with one hand, and pull down on the pod with the other.

Shell peas: Fresh shell peas seem to have disappeared from the diet of most Americans as too much trouble. This is unfortunate as fresh peas in their prime are one of the great treats of the spring garden. The peas are mature 3 to 4 weeks after blooming. They should be just

about full size in the pod (each pod should contain 4 to 10 peas) and should be very sweet (taste them). When the peas get over-mature the pod turns leathery.

Snap Peas: These should be picked as soon as the Peas reach full size and the pod is nice and fat and round. Taste them to see if they are ready, they should be sweet, crisp and succulent.

Snow peas: These should be picked after the pods have reached full size, but before the peas inside start to swell. Don't make the common mistake of harvesting smaller pods in the belief they will be better. They will be tender but they won't be very sweet.

If the pods have a string down each side, the best technique is to snap off the pod by bending it to one side. This breaks the pod but not the strings, so if you then pull on the pod, it will peel off the strings and leave them attached to the plant.

Dry Peas: To get dry peas simply allow the pods to ripen and dry fully on the vines. You can gather small quantities of pods individually, but for larger harvests pick the whole plants and lay them on a tarp to dry. Carefully thresh out the seeds to free them from the pods and then dry them thoroughly.

A dry pea should shatter when crushed. If you can make a mark with your fingernail it isn't dry enough. An easy way to see if they are dry enough is to put a few in a closed jar for a few days. If condensation forms on the inside of the jar, they are still too moist.

Storage: The sugar in the Peas begins to turn to starch soon after harvesting, so they don't store well. For this reason they should be used promptly for best flavor. If you have to store them, put them in the fridge in a plastic bag for up to 2 weeks. The best way to store them for any length of time is to freeze them.

You can store dry peas in any cool dry place.

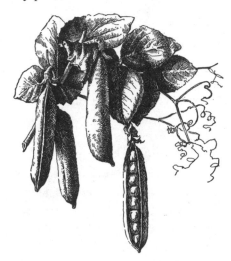

After harvest: Cut the plants down to ground level, leaving the nodulated roots in the ground to rot. You can compost the tops, or just dig them into the ground.

Seed saving: Peas are one of the easiest crops to save seed from. They are self-pollinating, though a small amount of insect pollination may also occur. Ideally you will isolate flowering varieties by at least 150 feet.

In dry weather all you have to do is leave the pods to mature and dry on the vine. In wet weather you may have to cut the vines and dry them under cover. When the pods are crisp and brown remove the seeds. These should be dried and stored in a cool dry place.

Unusual growing ideas

Green Manure: Peas are a very good green manure crop for soil enrichment.

Varieties: The cheapest place to buy Pea seed is at an agricultural supply store, where you can buy them in bulk by the pound.

Bush peas start to bear earlier than the pole types, but the latter give a more abundant and longer harvest. Many gardeners plant both types to get a longer harvest season.

Peas can be separated into several groups:

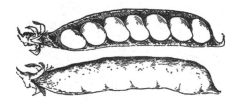

Soup or Field Peas: These varieties are hardier than the Garden Peas but aren't very sweet. They are grown as protein rich dry peas for soups.
Blue Pod

Garden Peas: These seeds are wrinkled when dry because they contain more sugar and less starch (like Sweet Corn). They are excellent as green fresh shell peas, though they can also be used as dried Peas. There are early, mid-season and late varieties.
Alderman, Wando, Maestro

Petit Pois: As the name suggests these originated in France and are the "gourmet Pea". They are green shell peas, harvested when still very small and sweet.

Sugar Peas: These originated in China and are the original edible podded peas.
Oregon Giant, Oregon Sugar Pod

Snap Peas: A more recently developed edible-podded Pea, this one originated in America. The pod is thicker and more succulent than that of the Snow Pea. These are probably now the most popular home garden Pea varieties, because there is no work in shelling and very little waste.

Super Sugar Snap is probably the best variety.

Amish Snap is an old heirloom from long before modern snap Peas were created.

Cooking: Green shell Peas, Snow Peas and Snap Peas are all excellent raw, steamed or stir-fried.

The tender growing tips may be eaten raw or cooked. The flowers can be added to salads.

My family prefer Snap Peas raw, rather than cooked. This simple recipe is good though.

1 lb snap peas
3 tbsp olive oil
1 clove garlic minced
⅛ cup soy sauce
¼ tsp sesame oil
1 tbsp tahini

Remove ends of pea pods and spread them on a baking tray pan. Mix the garlic into the oil and pour over the pods. Broil in oven for 5 minutes until cooked.

Mix the soy sauce, sesame oil and tahini to make a sauce to pour over the cooked pods.

Peanut
Arachis hypogaea

Introduction: Apparently also known as Goobers, though I have never heard anyone actually call them that (except in magazines attempting to be folksy). The Peanut is native to South America and has been cultivated for over 5000 years. It is an important crop in India, China, West Africa and the United States. The seeds are produced underground in the familiar leathery seedpods and are not really nuts.

About Peanut

Transplants:
Start 4 wks before last frost
Plant out: 2 weeks after last frost
Direct sow: Plant 2 weeks after the last frost date.
Time to harvest:
            90 to 100 days green
            110 to 140 days dry

Nutritional content:
We all know peanuts are very rich in protein (25g per 100g) and fat (48g per 100g). They are also a good source of niacin, thiamin, pantothenic acid, folate, magnesium, phosphorus and zinc.

Soil
pH 5.5 to 6.5
Light well-drained soil is good for Peanuts. It doesn't need to be very rich in nitrogen as the plant plays host to nitrogen fixing bacteria, but it should contain plenty of calcium. They don't like heavy or compacted soils (maybe the flowers can't penetrate them easily)

When: This South American plant likes a long hot growing season. However it is fairly hardy and can be grown in cooler northern areas. Don't plant it out until the soil has warmed up to at least 60° F (you can use black plastic or cloches to speed this up).

Where: Peanut is very much a warm weather crop and must be planted in a warm and sunny spot.

Inoculation: If you haven't grown this crop before, it will fix more nitrogen if inoculated with a suitable strain of nitrogen-fixing bacteria. See **Beans** for how to inoculate.

Planting:

Transplants: In cool climates, or where the growing season is short, they are often started inside in cell packs or soil blocks. Like most legumes they don't like root disturbance.

Direct sowing: In warm climates Peanuts are usually direct sown. Plant 1″ deep in cool soil, or 3″ deep in warm soil.

Spacing:

Beds: Space the plants 9″ to 12″ apart, in offset rows across the bed.

Rows: Put plants 6″ apart in rows 20″ apart.

Care

Weeding: The young plants should be kept well weeded (do this by hand to avoid damaging the shallow roots). A mulch helps while the plants are young.

Hilling: When the plants are 12″ tall they should be hilled like potatoes, to help bury the flowers and increase yields.

Mulch: This helps to keep down weeds and conserve moisture.

Watering: Water is most critical from the time the flowers appear until harvest. Water regularly during this period to keep the soil moist. Peanuts don't like wet leaves as it can contribute to disease.

Pests: I haven't had any problem with insect pests. There are a number of potentially serious diseases (Black Rot, Leaf Spot, Tomato Spotted Wilt Virus, White Mold and more).

Pod formation: The plants start to flower about 40 days after they emerge. They produce showy infertile flowers and inconspicuous fertile flowers. Once the latter are fertilized they send out a stalk (called a peg) that grows down into the soil to produce pods. These take a further 60 to 70 days to mature.

Harvest

When: You can harvest the pods after the leaves start to die back in September or October. Don't dig them too early, or the pods may be empty or not fully filled. The actual stage of harvest is a matter of personal preference, some people like them somewhat green, others prefer them to be fully ripe.

How: Harvest the plants like Potatoes, by lifting the whole plant and shaking off the loose soil. Hang the plants in a warm dry location for 2 months to allow the pods to dry thoroughly. It is very important that they be out of the reach of rodents, otherwise there won't be a single seed left (Mice love peanuts).

Seed saving: The plants are mostly self pollinating, so this is just the same as harvesting the seeds for eating. Make sure they are properly dry before storing, or they make go moldy. Save the seed from at least five plants to ensure sufficient genetic variation.

Unusual growing ideas
Peanuts can be grown in pots, or as an ornamental.

Varieties: Peanuts can be divided into two types.

Virginia (creeping with 2 seeds) These are the highest yielding and most versatile.

Valencia (upright with 3 to 4 seeds). Some people prefer their flavor

Cooking: Prepare the nuts by roasting them for 20 minutes at 300° F. They can also be boiled for 1½ hours in salt water.

Peppers Hot / Sweet

Capsicum annuum

Introduction: Peppers have been an important crop in Central and South America for over 5000 years. There are two quite distinct kinds of Peppers, with very different uses: the Hot Peppers and the Sweet Peppers. Though their flavor and uses differ considerably, they are both grown in the same way. They are interesting crops to grow and fairly easy if they have warm weather.

Hot Pepper is highly prized for its fiery flavor and after the colonization of the New World it quickly became an important spice all around the world. They were quickly accepted in China, India and Thailand and are now as important to those cuisines as any native spices.

Sweet Peppers are tasty and quite productive for the area they take up.

Nutritional content:

Peppers contain vitamin C and A (Beta carotene) as well as some important detoxifying phytochemicals, including, lutein, zeaxanthin and capsaicin (the chemical that puts the Hot in Peppers).

Capsaicin is most concentrated in the placenta, but as the fruit matures it seems to spread to the seeds and fruit itself. Humans can detect this fiery chemical in concentrations as low as 1 part per million. The Sweet Peppers don't contain any capsaicin (otherwise they would be Hot Peppers).

About Peppers

Seed facts
Germ temp: 60 (85) 95° F
Germ time: 7 to 28 days
25 days / 59° F
13 days / 68° F
8 days / 77° F
8 days / 86° F * Optimum
9 days / 95° F
Viability: 2 to 4 yrs
Germination percentage: 55%+
Weeks to grow transplant: 10 to 12

Planning facts
Hardiness: Tender
Ease of growing: Moderate
Growing temp: 75 to 85° F day
                55 to 65° F night
Plants per person: 4 Sweet
                   1 Hot
Plants per sq ft: ¾ to 1
Transplants:
Start: 8 weeks before last frost
Plant out: 4 weeks after last frost
Succession sow: after 6 to 8 wks
Time to harvest: 140 to 180 days
50 to 70 days from transplanting

Harvest facts
Length of harvest: 12 wks
Yield per plant: 1 to 2 lb
Yield per sq ft: ¼ to 1 lb sq ft

Soil
pH 5.5 - 7.0
Peppers like a deep, loose soil that is fairly rich in all of the plant nutrients, but especially magnesium. They don't mind acid soils and may even benefit from them. They don't like salt.

Soil preparation: Dig 2″ of compost or aged manure deeply into the soil, along with colloidal phosphate (for phosphorus), greensand or wood ashes (for potassium) and Kelp (for trace elements).

Planning
Where: All Peppers like a warm, sunny and sheltered spot.

Crop rotation: All members of the Solanum family (Eggplant, Potato, Tomato) are subject to the same pests and diseases. Don't plant Peppers where any related plant has grown in the last 3 years.

When: Peppers originated in the tropical highlands of Central and South America and grow best with warm (70 to 80° F) days, cool (55 to 65° F) nights and high humidity. If the soil gets above 85° F in summer it can slow growth. You can cool the soil by applying mulch and watering frequently with cold water.

In cool climates you have to grow Peppers under cloches or in the greenhouse. They won't grow if it's cold and may be permanently damaged by temperatures below 55° F. In cool weather, Sweet Peppers won't get as big or sweet, and Hot Peppers won't get as hot.

Peppers need to be started early, because they are slow to get going. Start them indoors about 6 to 8 weeks before the last frost date. They are generally one of the last crops to be planted out in late spring, a couple of weeks after Tomatoes (4 weeks after the last frost). If the weather turns cool cover them with cloches to protect them.

Succession sowing: In hot climates you might make a second sowing 6 to 8 weeks after the first one.

Planting

Transplants

Starting inside: I find Peppers to be one of the hardest of the common vegetable crops to raise successfully from seed. They vie with Celery for the title of slowest seedlings; consequently there is plenty of time for things to go wrong. The seed can be quite temperamental and hard to germinate (using fresh seed may help). My usual problem is that my greenhouse is too cold, they need warm temperatures for fastest growth

Soaking the seed overnight is said to help by removing germination inhibitors and so may speed germination. It is sometimes recommended that before planting you soak the seeds in a 10% bleach solution, for 10 minutes, to kill any disease spores (it should then be rinsed to remove the bleach). It is said that this treatment may also speed germination by several days.

Pepper seeds germinate best at a temperature of 85° F, which is higher than almost any common crop. If you want to speed them up, then give them the needed warmer temperature by starting them inside. If you can't put the whole container inside, you could pre-germinate the seeds, as described below (see **Direct sowing**).

Plant the seeds in a flat (they don't mind transplanting) or in cell packs or soil blocks. It is a good idea to water them with tepid water, to avoid cooling them. When the seedlings are about 2″ tall, prick them out into individual 4″ pots. You can bury them somewhat deeper each time you transplant, as they can form roots on their stems. Good transplants will be about 6″ tall when they go out.

Planting out: The soil must be warm (at least 65° F) before these tender plants are set out. If necessary you could use black plastic mulch to hasten warming. If the air temperature is still cool at this time, you should protect the plants with cloches to speed their growth.

If Cutworms are a problem, you can make protective collars of newspaper or aluminum foil.

Direct sowing: It is possible to direct sow Peppers, but it isn't very practical unless you have a long growing season. Plant the seed ½″ deep when the soil has warmed up sufficiently (the seed will rot if the soil is less than 60° F).

Pre-germination: To speed up growth you can pre-germinate the seeds. Place them on a strong (tear resistant) paper towel, roll this up and put it in a plastic bag. Place this in a warm place (85° F is best) and start checking it after 3 days. As soon as the seed starts to germinate, plant them out (even if you have to pick out individual seeds). If they don't germinate within 3 weeks, you should probably get new seed.

Spacing:
Space your Peppers 12″ to 15″ to 18″ apart, according to the fertility of the soil and the size of the variety. Some particularly large varieties may even need 24″ between the plants.

Care

Water: Peppers are somewhat drought tolerant (especially Hot Peppers), but lack of water can affect fruiting, so they need to be kept moist for best production. Sweet Peppers are particularly vulnerable to water stress, so keep the soil evenly moist. If not given enough water, the fruits can develop a slightly bitter flavor (and may get Blossom End Rot).

The plants should be given all the water they need, especially from the time the flowers appear until they reach full size.

Don't leave water on the leaves over night as this encourages disease. Drip irrigation works well with Peppers.

Fertilization: It's a good idea to feed the plants with compost tea or liquid Kelp, after they have recovered from transplanting. Feed them again as they start to flower to help in setting fruit. They need phosphorus and potassium, but not too much nitrogen (which may result in big vigorous plants, but few fruits).

Mulch: This is helpful to conserve moisture and to keep down weeds around these shallow rooted crops. Don't apply it until the soil is warm though; ideally wait until they are flowering. Ironically in very hot weather mulch is sometimes recommended to keep the soil cool.

In cooler areas people have been known to put flat rocks around the plants. The idea is that they will absorb heat during the daytime and radiate it back to the plants at night.

Pruning: Some gardeners pinch out the growing tip when the plant is about 6 inches tall to make it more bushy.

Pollination:
Peppers don't flower until they have produced about ten nodes on the stem. It is common for the first flowers to drop off without setting fruit, usually because nighttime temperatures drop below 50° F. Don't worry; as soon as it gets warmer they will set fruit. If the fruits drop off after they have started to swell it could be temperatures above 85° F, an excess of nitrogen or a deficiency of boron.

Pests: Peppers have more than their fair share of pests and diseases, as do other members of the *Solanaceae*. These include Aphids, Hornworms, Leafhoppers, Mites, Nematodes, Leaf Miners, Flea Beetles and Colorado Potato Beetles.

Fungus diseases: These are a common problem for Pepper plants, especially when they are young.

Tobacco mosaic virus: This often-fatal virus disease can be transmitted via cigarette smokers, so keep them out of the garden. Some varieties are resistant.

Boron deficiency: The fruits are often small and bitter. A deficiency usually shows up in light alkaline soils (high pH reduces its availability), as plants normally get enough boron from compost or other organic matter. Granite dust is another source.

If you are really sure your soil is deficient in Boron, you might try dissolving a teaspoon of borax in 10 gallons of water and spraying it over 100 square feet of bed. Be careful though, larger amounts may result in boron toxicity, which is worse than a deficiency.

Magnesium deficiency: The leaves drop off. Dolomitic limestone is the usual remedy, but is slow. A faster solution is a foliar spray, made from one teaspoon of Epsom salts (magnesium sulfate) in a pint of water. This should be enough to cover 100 sq ft.

Sunscald: This isn't a disease, but is literally caused by too much direct sun. It can be prevented quite simply, by putting the plants closer together. This gives the ripening fruit more shade.

Blossom End Rot: See Tomato.

Harvesting
When: Sweet Peppers take 4 or 5 weeks to reach full size from pollination and another 4 or 5 weeks to get fully ripe.

The fruits can be harvested anytime after they reach full size and this

is the way to get the highest yields (when fruit ripens, it invariably slows the plant down). It's useful that Peppers can be eaten while green, but unless you are very impatient I don't recommend it. Their flavor and nutritive value improves markedly as they ripen (in most countries they are never eaten green).

Remove all small fruit about a month before the first fall frost. These wouldn't have time to ripen anyway and removing them allows the plant to channel all of its energy into ripening the remaining larger ones. Once they reach full size the green fruit will ripen indoors like Tomatoes. You can even eat fruits that haven't reached full size, but they aren't very good.

How: Harvest Peppers by cutting the fruit from the plant, leaving a short stem on the fruit. You can break them off, but there is a greater risk of damaging the plant.

Storage: Sweet Peppers can be stored in a plastic bag in the fridge for several weeks. For longer term storage the fruits can be chopped and frozen.

Most Hot peppers can easily be dried for storage. However some of the fleshier types (like the Jalapeno) are traditionally smoked or pickled, as they hold too much moisture to dry easily.

Seed saving:

Though Peppers are mostly self-pollinated they do cross-pollinate to some extent. To ensure purity you should isolate them by 500 feet, or cover them with row covers. Ideally you will have a minimum of 5 plants to ensure genetic variation.

It's easy to save Pepper seed, simply allow the fruits to ripen. Just scrape out the seeds from the fruit before you eat it. Even the seed from green fruits may be viable, if not as good. Dry the seed thoroughly and store in a cool dry place. You must store Pepper seed carefully if it is to remain in good condition, ideally as close to freezing as possible, but not below.

Unusual Growing Ideas

Houseplants: Hot Peppers are often grown in pots and make attractive houseplants. You can often pot up them up in fall and bring them indoors for the winter. Plant them back outside the following spring. Hot Peppers may last for several years if not killed by frost.

Increasing light: Aluminum

foil mulch has apparently increased yields by 30%, by increasing light levels on the plant. However I'm not sure that would be good enough reason to have ugly sheets of shiny metal in my garden.

Unusual uses

Insecticide: Hot Pepper fruits have been used as an insecticide and repellent for many pests, as well as a fungicide. The purpose of capsaicin may be to prevent

the slow germinating seeds from rotting before they germinate.

Bleeding: Speaking of unusual

uses for the plant, how about to control bleeding? Powdered hot peppers are an excellent wound treatment and sprinkled on a cut they stop bleeding within minutes. People often think I'm joking when I suggest putting such a fiery substance on injured areas, but it really does work and doesn't sting any more than iodine.

Varieties:

In areas with long growing seasons you can grow any variety you choose. To successfully grow Peppers in cool climates it's best to use an early maturing variety. When reading catalogs remember that days to maturity usually means the time from the transplant being set out, to the green fruits reaching full size (but not turning red). Don't ask me why its not from seed to ripe fruit, I don't know.

Sweet Peppers:

If you are not interested in intentionally inflicting pain on yourself, then you may be more interested in these. There are now a lot of Hybrid varieties available.

California Wonder: This variety produces beautiful fruit, but it is a long season variety and doesn't always do well in cool climates.
Gypsy F1
Purple Beauty
Sweet Chocolate

Hot Peppers:

Like many people who love food, I find hot peppers much more interesting than Sweet Peppers.

In 1912 Wilbur Scoville devised a rating system for determining the hotness of Hot Peppers. This isn't an exact science, as the heat varies according to growing conditions and the hotter the climate the hotter the pepper. It is useful for comparing the relative difference between varieties however.

The Scoville scale

Sweet   (0 Scoville)
Banana   (100 to 500)
Anaheim (100 to 1000) mild
Ancho, Poblano (1000 to 1500)
This fairly mild Pepper is known Ancho when dried and Poblano when eaten green.

Jalapeno (2500 to 5000)
This is one of the most popular peppers, It can get pretty hot, but not ridiculously so, and it has an exceptional aromatic flavor.

Here we reach my limit, I don't really enjoy Peppers much hotter than this (wimp that I am).

Serrano (5 to 15,000) good flavor.
Cayenne (30 to 60,000)
Tabasco (30 to 50,000 (very hot)

Hot Hot Hot
Chiletepine (50 to 100,000)
Thai Dragon (150,000) Very hot
Habanero (200,000) The hottest common pepper. Here we enter the realm of the truly macho/masochistic. This is sometimes said to be a different species *C. chinense,* but it isn't.

Naga Jolokia (800 to 900,000)
A single seed of this almost mythical Indian variety will cause intense burning for 30 minutes.

Tabasco *(C. frutescens)*

This shrubby perennial is used to make hot sauce in Central America and of course the famous Tabasco sauce.

Cooking:

Sweet Peppers are most often used raw, as they have a unique flavor.

Hot Peppers are much more important than Sweet Peppers from a culinary standpoint. Their use often results in blisteringly hot foods fit to test the iron will of a warrior. This is a little unfortunate because Hot Peppers add more to cooking than just heat. They also have an intriguing flavor all of their own.

Capsaicin is very irritating to delicate skin and mucus membranes. This is especially noticeable when frying them, and when it comes to shedding tears some varieties can put Onions to shame. Some people are much more susceptible to their effects than others. If you've experienced this you won't be surprised to hear that capsaicin has been used as a bear and dog repellent and as a riot control agent.

Chile Rellenos

Poblano chiles (Anaheim will also work)
Cheese
Flour
Egg
Onion
Garlic
Tomatoes (chopped)
Olive oil

The first step is to peel the peppers. The best way to do this is to first blister their skins over a flame (you can also toast them in an oven, but this is quicker). You then put the blackened peppers in a plastic bag for 20 minutes (this steams them, so the skin comes off easily). Finally you peel off the tough outer skin.

Cut a slit in the side of the pepper and remove the seeds and white parts, being careful not to tear it. Rinse in water and roll them in flour. Next cut the cheese into strips and stuff the hollow peppers. Then close up the pepper (some people keep them closed with wooden toothpicks) and roll in more flour

Make a simple sauce by sautéing the onion and garlic in olive oil until translucent and then adding a pound of peeled chopped tomatoes, along with salt and pepper.

Beat 1 egg for every 2 chiles (normally this is separated and the whites are beaten first). Add 1 tablespoon of flour and some salt, then coat the pepper (hold the stalk end) with the egg mixture and then in flour. Fry them with the seam side down (to start with) until golden brown. When brown put it in the hot tomato sauce for at least 15 minutes to melt the cheese. Eat with rice.

Potato
Solanum tuberosum

Introduction: Potatoes originated in the mountains of Central and South America and have been cultivated for over 6000 years. There are still a huge number of varieties grown in that region.

Potato wasn't initially a success when brought to Europe, probably because they were short day varieties and didn't start to produce until late in the year. However it was eventually accepted, presumably as better varieties developed.

Potatoes are the most important vegetable crop in the world. They provide more usable protein per acre than any other crop (up to forty times more per acre than cows). They may yield from 10,000 to 30,000 pounds per acre.

Potatoes are unique as the only garden crop you could live on (at least for a while). At one time Irish peasants really did live on a diet of potatoes and milk and their population increased rapidly (until the Potato famine).

Many gardeners don't grow Potatoes because they believe they need a lot of space, are cheap to buy and don't taste much better than shop bought.

I disagree with that view and grow quite a lot of Potatoes. They are actually one of the most space efficient crops you can grow, considering the amount of nutrition they provide. A 10 square foot planting can yield 20 to 40 pounds of tubers. Organic potatoes are never cheap where I live; they generally range from $1 to 3 per pound. At those prices growing potatoes becomes a pretty good deal. Home grown Potatoes also taste better than those you buy and are one of the great treats of the summer garden.

I like growing Potatoes and find them to be one of the most rewarding crops of all. They emerge quickly, don't need much attention and harvesting is so much fun even my children like to help.

Potatoes are also a beneficial crop for the garden, as their growth and harvest improves the tilth of the soil and suppresses weeds. This feature makes them useful as pioneer plants for starting a garden, or for reclaiming rough land (see **Unusual growing methods**).

Nutritional content:
The humble Potato is a substantial and nutritious food. It contains important amounts of protein, vitamin C, several B vitamins and the minerals copper, iron and potassium. It makes an important contribution to the diet because it is eaten in quantity.

Soil
pH 4.8 (5.5 ideal) 6.5
Potatoes will grow in most soils, even those that are too acidic for most crops. For best results they prefer light, deep, well-drained sandy soils. They prefer a more acid soil than most vegetables, as it increases yield and decreases the incidence of Scab (a disease that mostly occurs in soils with a pH above 6.0). They don't like heavy wet clay, or very alkaline soil.

About Potatoes

Planning facts
Perennial
Hardiness: Half hardy
Ease of growing: Easy
Growing temp: 60 to 70° F day
                     45 to 50° F night
Plants per person: 30
Plants per sq ft: 1
Plant: 2 wks before last frost date
Time to harvest: 90 to 120 days

Harvest facts
Yield per plant: 1 to 2 lb
Yield per sq ft: 1 to 2 lb

Soil preparation: Potatoes aren't a fussy crop, but they respond well to any soil improvement. If the soil is heavy or compacted, deep cultivation such as double digging is very beneficial. It enables you to loosen the soil and add organic matter (use compost, aged manure or leaf mold). If the soil is too alkaline then add sulphur, pine needles or another acidifying agent. Never lime the soil when planting Potatoes

Fertilization:
Nitrogen: Too much nitrogen results in abundant top growth, but fewer (and inferior) tubers. Generally a potato rotation is scheduled to follow a heavy nitrogen user like Corn. They do need some nitrogen however, especially in the first few weeks, when they are putting on a lot of leaf growth. They use 75% of all the nitrogen they need in the first 4 weeks of growth. Too little nitrogen may result in the premature production of small tubers, so use your judgment.

Phosphorus: Potatoes should have a good supply of phosphorus, though they aren't heavy users. Use colloidal phosphate or bone meal.

Potassium: This is the most important primary nutrient for potatoes, increasing yield, improving quality and hastening maturation. Potatoes need a steady supply of potassium throughout their lives, but especially when their tubers are forming. Adding 5 pounds of wood ashes per 100 square feet of bed can increase yields by as much as 30%. If using wood ashes would raise the pH too much, you could use greensand, though this isn't as easily assimilated.

An old practice is to provide nutrients to Potatoes in the form of fresh plant material. Wilted Comfrey leaves or Seaweed were laid in the trench along with the tubers (up to a pound per tuber), to feed the plants as they decompose. You can also plant the tubers directly into a newly incorporated green manure or cover crop.

Planning
Crop rotation: Potatoes are susceptible to the host of diseases that affect members of the *Solanum* family. Don't plant them where Tomato, Pepper or Eggplant have been grown within the last 3 years.

When: Potatoes are native to tropical mountains and are easiest to grow in cool (below 70° F), dry weather. They can't stand any frost and don't like cold weather. In mild winter areas, with few frosts, they are sometimes grown in late fall or early spring. They don't do well in hot weather either. Soil temperatures above 70° F inhibit tuber formation and it stops altogether at 85° F. In hot summer areas they are usually grown as a spring or fall crop.

Early crop: The first crops can be started as early as 6 weeks before the last frost date, though you must take care to protect them from any frost. This is pretty easy when they are barely poking out of the ground; just cover them with soil or mulch (some varieties can even take mild frost).

Main crop: This is usually planted around the last frost date (2 weeks before to 2 weeks after).

Late crop: In many areas you can get two crops of potatoes a year. Time the second crop to mature around the time of the first fall frost. It can be a problem to find seed potatoes for this second planting, as they generally disappear from stores after the spring planting season. You might have to buy them in spring and store until required.

Planting
Planting from seed

Potatoes are not normally grown from seed, but are propagated vegetatively by means of their tubers. A few years ago there was much fanfare accompanying the introduction of true Potato seed, as the wave of the future, but it didn't really catch on. This is understandable as one of the big advantages of growing Potatoes is that you don't have to start with tiny seeds.

Potato seed does have its advantages however. Perhaps the most obvious is that the seed will be free of virus diseases. Of more significance is that you can start the seed at any time, whereas seed potatoes are only usually available in spring.

Certified disease free tubers:

You can grow perfectly good potatoes using old potatoes from the market (supposedly they are often sprayed to prevent them sprouting but they do sprout eventually). The problem is that these may be infected with virus diseases, which will then become established in your garden. Once a virus is established in your garden it is there to stay and can infect every subsequent crop (and maybe even Tomatoes, Peppers and Eggplants as well). Because of this problem most authorities recommend planting only certified disease free tubers. Its hard to get optimal yields from poor quality seed Potatoes, no matter how good your soil and cultural practices.

Selecting seed potatoes:

A tuber is not a root. It is a swollen stem adapted to be a food storage organ and has a small scar on one end where it was attached to the plant by the stolon. The other end of the tuber (the rose end) has a cluster of dormant buds known as eyes, which have the ability to grow into new plants. There are also eyes in other parts of the tuber and you can cut one tuber into several pieces. You just have to make sure that each piece has an eye that can grow (even a Potato peeling can grow if it has an eye). However the rose end contains the most vigorous shoots.

There is much debate over the ideal size of a seed potato (this is the kind of thing that makes gardening so exciting), but it is smaller than many people think. Most books recommend 2″ to 4″ (3 to 4 ounces) tubers, saying smaller ones produce smaller plants and hence smaller tubers and lower yields. They say that larger tubers produce bigger plants and hence larger tubers.

Agricultural researchers in England obtained their highest yields by planting very small (⅓ oz) tubers very close together (only 9″ apart). They found that larger tubers (spaced further apart) sent up several shoots that essentially became separate plants and eventually competed with each other. Using smaller tubers can also reduce seed potato costs significantly.

Of course many gardeners get the same results by cutting larger tubers into several pieces, each with 2 to 3 eyes. However cut pieces are more prone to rot unless they are left for a few days, so their cut surfaces can dry out and toughen. They can also be dusted with sulphur and left for 24 hours. These measures usually work out okay, but take time. You may as well just use smaller tubers in the first place.

Sets: If you buy seed Potatoes by mail order they may very well be in the form of sets. These consist of a single eye from a tuber with a small plug of potato attached. This is not a very satisfactory way to grow potatoes. Even if you are fortunate enough to get sets in good shape (which is not always the case), they won't perform as well as whole tubers, with their large reservoir of food to draw from. They may also be coated with fungicide for interstate shipment.

Chitting:

When you buy seed potatoes they shouldn't have started to sprout very much, as the brittle and delicate shoots are easily damaged once they start to elongate. To prevent premature sprouting store seed Potatoes at 40 to 50° F.

It is to your advantage to plant tubers that already have healthy shoots however, because it reduces the chance of rot and hastens maturation (the tubers may sprout very slowly in cool spring soil).

About 2 to 3 weeks before you wish to plant the tubers, you should start chitting (sprouting) them. Do this by setting them out, rose end up, in indirect light, at a temperature of 55 to 65° F (warmer temperatures will cause them to shrivel). The aim is to get 2 to 4 sprouts each 1″ to 2″ long on each tuber. If you can't plant them out as soon as they get to this stage, you should then return them to cooler conditions. Don't worry if the tubers turn green, the solanine produced may help to prevent them rotting.

You should rub off any excess sprouts (above the 2 to 4 required),

as soon as they start to sprout, so the tuber doesn't put too much energy into them.

Some gardeners allow the shoots to grow to 6″ to 8″ in length, claiming this increases yields by up to a third and reduces the time to harvest. However the long sprouts are easily damaged and must be handled carefully.

It is actually possible to remove the sprouts from the tuber and plant them separately (or leave one or two on the tuber and plant the others separately). This might be worth trying if you only have a couple of unusual tubers. It is also possible to eat part of the tuber and plant the peel, so long as it has some eyes on it. Of course with these techniques you will get lower yields and they will take longer to mature.

Planting depth

The top of the shoots should be planted under at least 3″ of soil (unless you are planting under mulch - see Unusual Growing Methods below). New tubers only form above the old one, so the deeper the tuber is set into the ground, the higher the potential yield. This is one reason potatoes were traditionally hilled up.

The actual planting depth varies according to soil and season. In England (where spring weather is cool) they tend to plant their potatoes quite shallowly (2″ to 3″) and hill them up later. They do this because the tubers can easily rot if planted too deeply in cool soil.

In warm soil you can plant the tubers much deeper. They might be 4″ deep in a heavy soil and up to 8″ deep in a light soil.

Planting

Rows: The traditional way to plant Potatoes is in trenches and this is probably still the best way. Begin by digging a trench one spades depth and one spade width. Put all of the amendments that Potatoes love (compost, wilted Comfrey leaves, seaweed, wood ashes, greensand) into the bottom of the trench. The tubers are then placed in the trench at the desired spacing and about 4″ of soil is pulled back into the trench to cover them. As the plants grow the trench is slowly filled up. One advantage of planting in rows is that it is easy to hill them up later.

Beds: If you don't want to use trenches you can simply dig holes in the wide beds, at the desired spacing (I use a bulb planter to speed this up). You then simply place your tubers in an upright position at the correct spacing and cover with 3″ to 4″ of a mix of compost and soil. If the soil is cold don't water the bed until the plants have emerged, to reduce potential rotting problems.

Spacing: This is the biggest factor affecting final tuber size. The closer the spacing, the more competition and the smaller the tubers (however you get more of them). Researchers have found the optimal spacing for highest yield (of fairly small tubers) is two plants per square foot, which averages out to be about 9″ apart. This could be worth trying, unless you really want large tubers.

Bed spacing: The traditional spacing ranges from 9″ to 12″ to 18″, depending upon variety, tuber size and soil fertility.

Row spacing: Traditionally they are planted 8″ to 12″ in the rows, with 18″ to 24″ between the rows.

Growth pattern
The growth of a Potato plant can be divided into four distinct stages.

1) Vegetative stage
For the first 30 to 70 days a Potato plant produces main shoots and lots of foliage. The larger the plant at the end of this stage, the larger the eventual yield can be. Watch out for pests such as Colorado Potato Beetle during this stage. Vegetative growth goes along best during the long days of early summer.

2) Tuber formation
After 70 to 90 days of vegetative growth the main shoots stop growing and side branching occurs. At this time tubers start to form on stolons coming from the feeder roots. A temperature of 60 to 65° F is said to be optimal for tuber formation and it slows down at temperatures above 70° F. This stage usually coincides with the onset of flowering and is a good indicator that tuber formation has begun. It is not physiologically related however and in some situations flowers may not appear at all.

3) Tuber enlargement
As the plants come into full bloom the tubers enlarge rapidly and the plant has its greatest need for potassium. This is also the most critical time for water and for maximum growth they need a steady supply. You can start digging new potatoes at this stage and mine often get no further than this. Fungus diseases often attack plants at this time.

4) Maturation
When the plants reach maturity the tops wither and die back and the skins on the tubers thicken (this is important for storage). When 75% of the foliage is dead, water them for the last time, wait 10 to 14 days and they are ready to dig.

Care
Hilling: If you planted the tubers at a shallow depth you will probably want to hill (or earth) them up. This increases the depth of soil for tuber formation and ensures they aren't exposed to the sun (which would turn them green). It is also a good way to eliminate weeds. Hill up the plants when they are 8″ to 10″ tall, leaving only the top 3 to 4 leaves above the ground. You might want to repeat this 3 to 4 weeks later and perhaps a third time several weeks after that. Hilling up is easy if you planted in widely spaced rows, but not possible if you planted in beds (use mulch instead).

Mulch: Potatoes are commonly mulched with compost, shredded leaves, hay or seaweed (Potatoes have a special affinity for seaweed). This conserves moisture and helps to keep the soil cool, which is important in warmer areas. A thick mulch can actually be used instead of hilling (see **Unusual growing methods**), though yields won't be as high. Of course you can't use mulch if you plan on hilling up the plants.

Feeding: The young plants need nitrogen for fast uninterrupted growth. Give them a foliar feed of compost tea, Comfrey tea or liquid Kelp, 3 to 4 weeks after the shoots emerge from the soil. This could also help to remedy any minor nutrient deficiency.

Water: It is important to keep the soil evenly moist (but not wet) for best growth, as lack of water results in smaller tubers. It is also important to water uniformly, making sure it penetrates through the dense foliage and down to the full root depth (or at least the top 12″ where the greatest proportion of roots are found).

If water is in short supply, just give them 4 gallons per square yard at the crucial time when the tubers start to form (when the flowers appear). In humid climates many gardeners stop watering when tuber formation starts, so they don't grow too fast. Excess water may cause Hollow Heart, where the interior grows so rapidly it cracks.

Pests: The Potato has more than its fair share of disease and insect pests. Fortunately these aren't found everywhere; in some favored areas Potatoes have few problems and are very easy to grow. The severity of potato pests also varies from year to year, with different growing conditions. In some years they do little harm, in other years they can be devastating. Warm humid conditions are the worst for Potatoes.

Colorado Potato Beetle
On a small scale you can simply hand pick off any beetles you find and scrape off the tiny orange egg

masses from under the leaves (and any newly hatched larvae). The larvae are eaten by many predators, though the adults are fairly poisonous.

Other pests: Aphids, Blister Beetles, Flea Beetles, Nematodes, Leafhoppers, Tuberworms, Wireworms.

Viruses

These aren't always an obvious problem, but they can reduce yields considerably. You may avoid them by using certified seed and not saving your own tubers for planting.

Removing viruses: It is possible to get a virus-free plant from an infected tuber. You plant the tuber in a container of sterile potting mix and keep it in a warm place to grow. When the shoot reaches 6″ to 8″ high you cut it off 2″ to 3″ above the soil line (it should never touch the soil or the rest of the tuber). The shoot can then be rooted in another container of sterile potting mix. It will then hopefully be virus-free, just hope that your garden is also, when you plant it out.

Verticillium wilt

This fungus shows itself by the tops dying off prematurely (it's also known as Early dying fungus). You may still get a small crop of potatoes from affected plants, but they won't store well. This disease may last for 7 years in the soil and to eliminate it you can't plant potatoes in the same spot for at least 4 years. Other members of the Solanum family are also affected, so they can't be grown either (except for a few resistant varieties).

Scab
(Streptomyces scabies)

Soil bacteria cause this very common disease. It is undetectable above ground and the damage is mainly cosmetic, so it is not very serious unless you are growing for market (it reduces their market-ability).

Alkaline soil (above 6.0 pH) and lack of moisture are the main causes of scab. It persists in the ground for several years and can also infect other root crops such as carrot, beet and turnip. The best ways to prevent scab are to rotate annually, keep the soil somewhat acid (don't lime it) and to use resistant varieties. Abundant water may reduce damage from Scab.

Late blight
(Phytopthora infestans)

This is the disease that caused the famine that depopulated Ireland, by killing one and a half million people and causing another million to emigrate. It is called Late Blight because it likes warmer weather and usually occurs after Tomatoes (which it also affects) have flowered. It doesn't much bother early crops.

This fungus first manifests itself as spots on the lower leaves in cool weather, but then the leaves die and brown patches appear on the tubers. The only thing you can do is dig the tubers 2 weeks after the tops die down and use them (then spores from tops won't be trans-ferred to the tubers). This disease affects yield, but doesn't affect stor-ability (of course you wouldn't use infected potatoes for seed). Many modern varieties have some resis-tance to Late Blight.

Early Blight
(Alternaria solanii)

Also produces spots on the leaves, which then die. If you recognize it early enough you may be able to treat with Bordeaux mixture.

Harvesting

When: You can start harvesting new potatoes 70 to 90 days after planting, after the plants have been flowering for a while. Just root around beneath the living plants until you find some sizeable tubers. This reduces the final yield (don't take more than 2 per plant), but they taste great. The skins of new Potatoes are very thin and they are high in sugar, so they don't store well. Some varieties don't have much flavor when immature.

The main Potato harvest occurs when the leaves start to lose their green color. If you want to store the tubers you should leave them in the ground for 2 weeks after the tops turn yellow and die down. This allows the skins to toughen up. If the skin rubs off easily with a finger they are not ready to store. Once the tubers are mature you should dig them, as otherwise they may eventually re-sprout.

How: Digging the tubers is a very rewarding activity. It feels like digging for treasure, but is a lot more fruitful. Dig the tubers with a spade or spading fork, starting at least a foot away from the plants to minimize accidental spearing. Tubers will always be found above the seed potato (which is usually still recognizable if rather mushy), but may be some distance to one side.

Some people like to dig a hole alongside the first plant and then pull the plant over into it. The second plant then goes into the hole left by the first one (this method ensures thorough soil cultivation).

Always handle the tubers gently to minimize damage. Even the slightest skin abrasion can cause a tuber to rot in storage and this can easily spread to nearby tubers. When you have finished digging, sort the tubers into three piles, badly damaged (speared or chopped) ones for immediate eating, grazed ones for use fairly quickly and perfect ones for storage. You will also sort out any green potatoes have been exposed to light and are toxic.

Storage: Careful storage is very important with Potatoes. If they are not given ideal conditions they will soon become inedible, due to rotting, turning green or sprouting.

Temperature is the most critical storage factor. If conditions are too warm (above 50° F) they will sprout as soon as their natural dormancy period is over in 2 or 3 months (of course this won't matter if you only have a 2 months supply of tubers to store). If it is too cold (below 40° F) their starch may turn to sugar and give them an off flavor.

Prepare the tubers by air-drying in a dark place for several days (don't wash) and then cure them at 60° F for 2 weeks. They should then be stored at 40 to 50° F with high humidity. Keep them in wooden boxes, or sacks, with good air cir-

culation (never in plastic bags) and check periodically for rot. Keep them in the dark of course, or they will turn green. If stored properly they can last up to 6 months.

Clamp: Large quantities of Potatoes can be stored over the winter in a clamp. This works best in light, well drained soil and should be in a sheltered position.

Start by digging out the soil in the area of the clamp to a depth of 10″ and then lay down a 3″ to 6″ layer of straw or dry leaves (you might first lay down a layer of Gopher wire to foil rodents). A piece of perforated pipe is arranged in the center and the roots are placed around it to form a cone or prism shaped pile (a vent can also be constructed from straw). The pile is then covered with a 6″ (more in very cold climates) layer of straw, or leaves. Finally the straw is covered with a 6″ layer of soil, which is packed down with a spade. Some of this soil comes from the original excavation; the rest is obtained by digging a drainage trench around the clamp. Keep the vent open on top of the clamp, unless it gets very cold, in which case it should be closed up with straw.

Seed saving: When we talk about seed saving with Potatoes we are usually talking about tubers, not seed. Saving your own tubers and re-planting them is frowned upon for the same reason as using supermarket tubers; it can lead to virus diseases. If you want to save your own seed Potatoes, just don't eat them (and store them very carefully).

You may want to experiment with actual Potato seed as well. Many varieties don't usually produce seed,

but some do. It can be gathered from any ripe fruits your plants produce. These take about 2 months to ripen and may be green or purple. Squeeze out the seeds into a bowl and wash them. The good seeds sink and bad ones float (like witches).

Companion plants: Some gardeners interplant Marigolds or Beans with Potatoes as a way to repel Colorado Beetles. Researchers have found that the presence of these plants in a stand of Potatoes does seem to confuse the insects (and most importantly there are fewer beetles to be found). Of course any time you plant anything among the potatoes, it is going to be disturbed and uprooted while harvesting.

Unusual growing ideas
Autumn planting: In mild areas any tubers overlooked during the harvest will survive the winter underground and volunteer the following year. This shows that (in mild areas at least) it is quite possible to plant Potatoes in autumn for a spring harvest. You might use some of the small tubers harvested earlier in the year.

Growing from seed: Potato seeds are grown in much the same way as Tomatoes. They won't come true to type, but will produce entirely new varieties. If you like any of them you can propagate them vegetatively.

Mulch planting: Some people prefer to plant potatoes under mulch. Just put the seed potatoes on the ground and lay a 3″ layer of mulch (compost, straw, chopped leaves, aged manure) on top of them. Add more mulch as the plants get taller, until it is 8″ to 12″ deep. This is necessary to keep light from turning the tubers green and because tubers only form above the seed potato.

Another mulch method: In fall pile chopped tree leaves where you want the Potato patch to be (do it as you clean them up). The following spring plant the sprouted tubers 6″ deep in the leaves. Hill up the plants with more mulch, as the pile settles and the plants grow.

Yet another mulch method: Lay the tubers at the bottom of a 12″ deep trench and cover with 3″ of chopped leaves. As the plants grow keep filling up the trench with more leaves.

These mulch methods works very well; the main problem is getting the large quantity of mulch materials needed. They make it easy to take a few new potatoes from the living plants, simply pull the mulch aside.

Land cleaning: These mulch growing techniques can be used to start a new garden on grass or weed infested land. Even many perennial weeds will succumb to the combination of a thick mulch, deep shade and the considerable soil disturbance of planting and harvesting.

Tubs: Apparently one can grow a single Potato to be enormously productive in the following way. Obtain a large garbage can, put drainage holes in the bottom and fill it with a foot of really good compost. Plant one large seed potato in the soil. As the plant grows, slowly fill the can with more fine compost. The most important thing is to water carefully,

too much, or too little, water will cause problems. With a little luck the end result will be one very large plant, completely filling the whole can with tubers. When the plant dies back, empty out the can and collect the tubers.

A refinement of this is to use tires (or slatted wooden bins). Start with one tire filled with soil and as the plant grows add more tires and soil. The advantage of this method is that the plant gets maximum light at all times and is never growing in the bottom of a can.

This might have a practical application, if you get one special tuber from somewhere and want to multiply it quickly.

Varieties: There are an enormous number of potato cultivars, with different shapes, sizes and colors (white, yellow, red blue) and other attributes. Some do better on heavy soils, some are more resistant to cold or disease, some are more nutritious, or contain less solanine, some taste better.

Generally the heavy yielding hybrids tend to contain more water, but farmer like them because they get paid just as much for the water as for potato. Older, lower yielding types are often more nutritious. Of course you can save seed potatoes from hybrid varieties just as easily as any others.

Russets: These have characteristic brown russeted skin and are best for baking.
Butte: (very high in vitamin C)
Russet Nugget

Fingerlings: Rose Finn Apple, French Fingerling, Russian Banana

Blue: I once grew some amazingly productive blue potatoes, but I never did find out what variety they were.

Caribe, Purple Peruvian, Purple Viking

Yellow: Yukon Gold, Yellow Finn

Red: All Red, Red Cloud, Red Norland

Cooking
Boiled, baked, fried, chipped, casseroled, stewed, roasted the list goes on. Remember that all green parts contain poisonous solanine and should never be eaten.

Potato latkes

8 potatoes
2 eggs
1 onion
1 tsp salt
½ cup flour
Oil

Grate the washed potatoes (don't peel) into a bowl. Beat the egg into another bowl, then mix in the grated onion, along with the flour and salt. Squeeze the excess moisture from the potatoes and add them to the egg mix.

Heat some oil in a skillet until it sizzles and drop in large tablespoonfuls of the mix. Flatten the mix and allow it to cook until golden brown. Then flip it over and cook the other side. Serve with apple sauce.

Quinoa
Chenopodium quinoa

Introduction: Quinoa (pronounced keen-wa) has been cultivated in the Andes mountains for centuries and was a staple food of the Incas. It grows at cooler temperatures than that other Incan staple: Amaranth, so was grown at higher altitudes. It is well adapted to high levels of U.V. light and daily temperature extremes.

Quinoa was a sacred grain to the Incas and was believed to give a person special endurance (and even heightened psychic abilities).

Quinoa is sometimes referred to as a pseudocereal (as are Amaranth and Buckwheat), as it is grown as a grain crop, but isn't a member of the grass family. It is that rare commodity a starchy high protein grain that can easily be raised and processed on a small scale. Though it is a fairly new crop in North America, it has great potential as a garden crop for the future when greater self-sufficiency may be the goal.

Nutritional content:
Quinoa is one of the most well balanced and nutritious of all grains. It contains from 7% to 22% protein, with a better balance of amino acids than almost any vegetable food. It even includes lysine which is missing from most vegetable proteins. It also contains vitamin E, several B's, calcium, iron magnesium, potassium and zinc.

The leaves are rich in vitamins A and C, as well as calcium and iron.

Soil:
pH: 5.5 to 7.5
Quinoa will grow well in any soil so long as it is well-drained and not too acid. However it will be most productive in a light fertile one.

Soil preparation: This fast growing plant likes nitrogen, so give it lots of compost or aged manure.

About Quinoa

Seed facts
Germ temp: 45 to 55° F
Germ time: 3 to 7 days
Viability: 5 to 7 yrs
Germination percentage: 70%+

Planning facts
Hardiness: Tender
Ease of growing: Easy
Growing temp: 50 (60 to 70) 90° F
Plants per sq ft: 1
Direct sow: 2 wks after last frost
Time to harvest:
 90 to 120 days seed
 40 to 60 days greens

Harvest facts
Yield per sq ft: 1 to 6 oz
Yield per plant: 1 to 6 oz

When: This crop is somewhat day length sensitive and grows best in the shorter days of late summer. It prefers cooler growing conditions than Amaranth and will even tolerate light frost. It doesn't like very hot weather and may not set seed above 90° F.

Planting: Quinoa is usually direct sown, because it germinates well in cool soil (it germinates best at 45 to 55° F). In fact if the soil is much above 60° F it doesn't germinate satisfactorily (I wondered why it didn't germinate in my greenhouse.) Plant the seed ¼″ to 1″ deep.

Spacing: The plants are spaced from 6″ to 18″ apart, depending upon the variety and the size of plant required. Some varieties can get quite tall (5 to 8 ft).

Care
Watering: Quinoa is a drought tolerant plant and can produce a good crop with as little as 10″ of water. More water results in bigger plants, but this doesn't necessarily translate into much higher yields.

Weeds: The plants need weeding when young, but after they reach about a foot in height they can take care of themselves.

Weeding the seedlings can present a minor problem, as they closely resemble the common garden weed Lambs Quarters and are hard to tell apart. It helps if you plant it in regular rows, so you can at least remove the weeds that aren't in the rows.

Mulch: This helps to conserve soil moisture and keep down weeds, which is helpful while they are young.

Pests: Flea Beetles and Aphids sometimes attack the plants, but generally these vigorous plants will just keep on growing and aren't greatly affected. When I first planted Quinoa in Western Washington it was plagued by leaf miners (which also attack Lambs Quarters). Birds don't usually go for the seeds because they are coated in bitter saponins.

When growing on a field scale Quinoa is sometimes affected by viruses or other diseases.

Harvest
The seed is ready for harvest after the leaves have died back. In some areas this may be after the first frosts. Gather the seed by bending the heads over a bucket and gently rubbing out the ripe seed. This is easily cleaned by screening and winnowing it.

The seed is not the only part of the plant that is edible. The young leaves can be used as a potherb like Spinach.

Storage: The seed must be thoroughly dry before it can be stored for any length of time

Preparation: The seeds have a bitter coating of saponins that must be removed before they can be eaten. This is done by soaking them in water for several hours, changing the water and soaking for several more hours. Agitating the water can speed this up. It has actually been leached by putting the seeds in a bag and running them through the cold cycle of a washing machine. Saponins are a kind of detergent and will foam up if agitated in water, so maybe you could wash some clothes at the same time!

Unleached seed may be several different colors but it all turns a pale yellow after rinsing. When you buy Quinoa at the store it has already been leached.

The seeds have no husks, so the leached seeds need no further preparation.

Seed saving: If you are growing Quinoa for seed, then saving seed for planting isn't very difficult. Just save some of the seed you have collected. It is generally self-pollinated, but some degree of cross-pollination may occur. If you want to keep a variety pure, you will have to isolate it from other varieties (and perhaps from related wild weeds). If you don't particularly care about purity just save seed from the best plants.

Unusual growing ideas
Ornamental: Quinoa is quite attractive and some varieties have found their way into the purely ornamental garden. They are quite tall though.

Varieties: There are now quite a few available, including some spectacular multi-colored varieties.

Cooking:
The Incas made beer from Quinoa

Quinoa is usually cooked by simmering one cup of grain in 2 cups of water for 15 minutes until it is soft. It can also be added to soups and stews.

The seeds can also be ground to flour and mixed with wheat flour for baking.

Related species: The *Chenopodium* genus has more than its share of good potherbs, they include:

Good King Henry
C. bonus henricus
This species differs from the rest of the *Chenopodium* potherbs in that it is a perennial. It is been cultivated for its tasty spring shoots, which are one of the first greens to be harvested in spring. It is a very low maintenance plant (like Asparagus) and deserves to be more widely cultivated.

Where: This Northern European plant doesn't like hot weather and in warm climates it does best in part shade. It is not a very productive plant and is better suited to semi-wild cultivation, rather than the intensive garden. It is ideal for the forest or wild garden, because of its shade tolerance.

Soil: Good King Henry likes nitrogen and does best on rich, moist soil.

Planting: This plant is perennial, but most people start it from seed initially. This can be planted directly in the garden in early spring (it is very hardy). It can also be started in the greenhouse and transplanted out after the last frost date.

Once you have some established plants, you can propagate it vegetatively. Just divide the plants while they are dormant.

Good King Henry is naturalized as a wild plant in parts of the east. If you can find it you can collect the seeds, or transplant some plants to your garden.

Care: This plant grows vigorously once established and spreads to form colonies. This makes it an ideal low maintenance food crop.

Watering: For best production keep the soil fairly moist at all times. It doesn't like to be dry.

Harvest: The leaves are at their best when they first appear in spring, though new growth can be eaten at any time it is available. The immature flower stalk can be eaten like Asparagus.

Seed saving: Good King Henry will produce seed with no help from you.

Unusual growing ideas:
Wild Garden: This is the ideal semi-cultivated crop. It can be planted in a suitable location and pretty much left to its own devices except for harvesting. Plant lots of individual plants and harvest a little from each, when you need it.

Cooking: The fleshy leaves are used in much the same way as Spinach (they also contain oxalic acid).

Beetberry
Chenopodium capitatum
Also known as Strawberry Spinach, because of its small red fruits. If you approach this plant with the word Strawberry in your head you will be sadly disappointed. There is no relationship, connection or similarity between this plant and the Strawberry. If you approach this plant with the word Spinach in your head you will be a lot happier.

Beetberry can be used like the related Spinach, as a potherb or raw in salads. It is a good addition to salads as the berries add color, as well as a rather bland green taste. Native Americans used the berries to dye skin, clothes and basket material. Beetberry self-seeds in my garden. I planted it three years ago and it is still reappearing.

Huazontle Try this
C. nuttaliae
This species was an important vegetable crop for the Aztecs. It is grown from seed in much the same way as Quinoa and may actually have the same ancestors.

The young plants can be used as a potherb like Spinach, but the tender flowering tips are the real star. These are gathered up until the flowers fade and are boiled or steamed for 5 to 10 minutes. They shrink quite a lot in cooking so gather plenty. These flowering tips have a lovely firm texture and delightful flavor. They are definitely one of the best green vegetable I have ever tasted. They are really, really good.

In Mexico the flowering tops are boiled for 5 minutes, squeezed into bunches, dipped in eggs and fried.

Giant Lambs Quarters
C. giganteum
This species is used like Huazontle and is equally good. I highly recommend it as a low work vegetable that self-sows readily and does well in warm weather.

I now have so many self-sowing Chenopodiums in my garden I don't know which is which. I just eat them all.

Radish
Raphanus sativus

Introduction: The Latin species name means "easily reared", because this is one of the simplest vegetables to grow. It is often one of the first vegetables a new gardener tries and is commonly recommended for children (though I can't imagine many children enjoy it very much).

The main virtue of Radish is that it is quick; some varieties may mature in as little as 3 to 4 weeks. Actually I would say that their only virtue is that they are quick, I am not a big fan of Radishes. They are not very nutritious and are way down near the bottom of my list of useful garden crops.

I actually prize Radish more for its tasty, spicy seed sprouts than as a root vegetable. The young leaves, flowers and green seedpods are all good in salads.

Nutritional content:
The root is fairly rich in vitamin C.

Soil
pH 5.5 - 6.8
Radish roots don't go very deep so the ideal soil is loose and well drained, such as a sandy loam. It should also be slightly acidic.

Soil preparation: Heavy soil should have 2″ of organic matter (compost or aged manure) added and should be cultivated deeply to loosen it. In very poor soil you can dig a special trench and fill it with a mix made from compost, sand and soil.

Like most root crops Radishes don't need a lot of nitrogen (don't give them fresh manure), but they do like potassium and phosphorus.

About Radish

Seed facts
Germ temp: 45 (85) 95° F
Germ time: 3 to 10 days
29 days / 41° F
11 days / 50° F
6 days / 59° F
4 days / 68° F
4 days / 77° F * Optimum
3 days / 86° F
Seed viability: 5 years
Germination percentage: 75+

Planning facts
Hardiness: Hardy
Ease of growing: Easy
Growing temp: 45 (60 to 65) 75° F
Plants per person: 20
Plants per sq ft: 16
Direct sow: on last frost date
Succession sow: every 3 wks
Time to harvest: 20 to 40 days

Harvest facts
Yield per plant: 1 oz
Yield per sq ft: 1 to 5 lb sq ft

Planning:
Where: In cool weather Radishes are grown in full sun. In hot weather they may benefit from light shade.

Because the roots are in the ground for such a short period, they are rarely planted in their own bed space. They are usually interplanted with slower growing crops, such as Brassicas or Lettuce.

When: Radishes are most easily grown in spring and fall, as they prefer short days (up to 12 hours long) and cool weather. Temperatures much above 70° F cause them to be very pungent. However if you know what you are doing, you can grow them through the summer, by planting different varieties, using shade and giving them lots of water.

Spring: Don't plant your first spring Radishes until the soil temperature reaches at least 45° F, which may be around the last frost date. If you warm the soil up with black plastic or cloches, you could get them going a month earlier than this (they are quite frost tolerant). You can then plant them in succession every 2 weeks until hot weather arrives.

Fall: Take a break until the hottest days of summer are over and then start your fall sowings. The roots that mature in the cool days of autumn are often the best.

Succession sowing: Radish roots are only in optimum condition for a short time, so it's best to only plant a few seeds at one time. Succession sow every 2 weeks.

Planting
Direct sowing: There is no reason to start Radish indoors, because it germinates easily in cold soil and the plants grow rapidly. Like most roots it doesn't transplant well anyway.

The seed is sown directly into the garden ½″ to 1½″ deep. A deeper planting may give you slightly larger roots, especially if you give them a slightly wider spacing (1½″). Bigger seed may also result in larger roots.

Spacing: Space the plants 1″ to 2″ to 4″ apart, depending on the fertility of the soil.

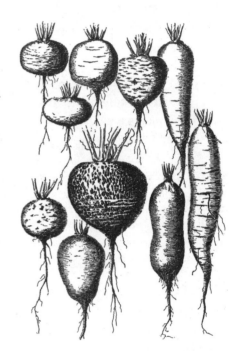

Care
Thinning: Proper thinning is absolutely vital if you are going to grow good Radishes. If the plants are crowded they won't produce useful roots. You can eat the thinnings in salads.

Weeds: These small plants don't compete with weeds very well, so should be hand weeded regularly. Don't use a hoe too near the plants as their shoulders are easily damaged.

Watering:
Radishes must have a steady supply of water, so keep the soil

evenly moist at all times. Too little water can result in woodiness and excessive pungency (often such roots are pithy and have marked growth rings). Too much water may encourage top growth at the expense of the roots.

Mulch: This keeps the soil cool, retains moisture and keeps down weeds

Major problems:

Though Radishes are one of the easiest crops to grow, beginners often have problems.

No root: If a Radish doesn't produce a swollen root, it is usually because the growing conditions weren't good enough. It simply wasn't producing enough food to have a surplus to store in the root and make it swell. This may occur because of competition from neighboring Radishes or weeds, low light levels, too high growing temperature or from insufficient water or nutrients.

Excessive pungency: Too high (above 70° F) or low (below 60° F) temperatures may cause the flavor to be excessively hot. Lack of water is another possible reason.

Woodiness: Insufficient water, or high temperatures (above 70° F) can cause the roots to be woody or pithy.

Bolting: Radish is an annual and will bolt when it has built up enough food reserves to produce seed. It may also be stimulated to flower by the long days of summer (another reason they are easier to grow in spring and fall). Crowding and other types of stress may also hasten bolting.

Pests:
Radishes are susceptible to the usual host of Brassica pests.

Cabbage Root Maggot: This is the big pest of the Radish. In fact they are sometimes planted to lure the little worms away from more valuable Brassicas. This pest is most problematical in spring and late summer. See **Cabbage** for ways to deal with this pest.

Harvesting

When: The rapid growth of Radishes can be a problem in that they quickly reach their prime and then pass it. It is important to harvest the roots as soon as they are ready. They will soon get over-mature if left in the ground. They will actually age more slowly if harvested and stored in the fridge.

Check to see if a root is ready for harvest with a little careful digging. They are generally best when still small (under 1″ diameter), as they often get woody as they enlarge.

If a root gets past its prime, you can just let it flower and go to seed. You can then eat the flowers and unripe seed pods, or you can gather the seed for planting or sprouting.

How: Uproot the plants by hand, and cut off the tops to prevent them taking moisture from the root.

Storage: The roots will keep for several weeks in a plastic bag in the fridge.

Seed Saving: Radishes are insect pollinated and will cross with any other variety, or with wild Radishes. It is so common in the wild around here that it would be

impossible to isolate them by the required ½ mile. They could be isolated by caging, though I'm not that motivated. I just allow the pods to ripen and gather them.

Unusual growing ideas
Pod Radishes: These are grown for their enlarged seedpods rather than their roots. These are fleshy and pungent and are a nice addition to salads. I actually rate them more highly than the roots. Rat Tail Radish is good, as is Munchen Bier.

Indoors: Radishes have been grown indoors in winter, in 6″ deep pots. They need frequent watering if they are to produce edible roots. You would have to be a Radish addict to bother with them though.

Trap crops: These easily grown plants are commonly planted as trap crops, to lure Brassica pests away from more valuable plants. If you plant more than you need, your regular Radish crop could perform this function.

Sprouting: Any surplus Radish seed can sprouted like that of Alfalfa.

Varieties: Crimson Giant Cherry Belle, Rainbow, White Icicle are highly recommended varieties.

Cooking: The roots are generally used raw in salads and sandwiches. They can also be cooked in soups or pickled.

The tender young leaves can be eaten raw in salads, or cooked as a potherb. The immature seedpods are good in salads and can also be pickled.

Radish, Winter

Raphanus sativus var *niger*

Introduction: Winter Radishes are most often associated with Japan, where a quarter of all vegetables grown are Radishes. However they were actually popular in Europe before the familiar small Radishes were introduced. Like the Turnip they were an important winter food for peasants. The roots get much larger than ordinary Radishes and sometimes reach 3″ diameter and 18″ long. They are called Winter Radishes because (like Winter Squash) they were stored for winter use.

Most of what was said about Radishes also applies to Winter Radishes, so I will only mention the differences here.

Soil
The soil needs to be more fertile than for Radishes and should be rich, loose and friable (ideally a rich, sandy loam).

Planting
When: If you plant Winter Radish in warm summer weather they will merely produce leaves and bolt, without producing a large swollen root. The plants enjoy the warm weather, but need some chill to produce large roots.

The plants need a minimum of 65 days to produce roots, so plant them in late summer, about 60 to 90 days before the first autumn frost is expected.

Spacing: Space the plants 6″ to 18″ apart, depending on soil and variety.

Sowing: Sow the seed ¾″ to 1″ deep and 2″ apart.

Watering: The plants need consistently moist soil for good growth. Abundant water after a dry spell may cause the roots to swell rapidly and split.

Seed saving: This is done in much the same way as Turnip.

Unusual growing ideas
Compact soil: Daikon Radish has such a deep penetrating root it is sometimes planted to loosen compacted soil, as an alternative to digging.

Harvest: The flavor of the root can be improved by frost, so don't harvest too early.

Storage: The roots can be stored in the ground under a thick mulch. If this is not possible they can be stored in moist sawdust, or sand, in a root cellar at 32 to 40° F. The harvested roots will keep in a plastic bag in the refrigerator for several weeks.

Varieties: Some varieties have very beautiful roots.

Tokinashi: It can be grown in spring or autumn and is mildly pungent. It matures in about 60 days.

Shogoin: This Turnip shaped Radish is usually cooked.

Sakurajima: This variety can get very big.

Cooking: The roots are peeled and eaten raw, cooked like Turnips, pickled (very popular in Japan), stir-fried and dried. The grated root is often used in sauces in Japan.

The immature seedpods are good in salads or pickled. The ripe seed is sprouted like Alfalfa.

Rhubarb
Rheum rhabarbarum

Introduction: Rhubarb was first grown in gardens for medicinal purposes, but then began to be eaten as a food. It became popular in northern Europe as a fruit substitute for desserts. Presumably this only happened after cheap sugar became available to sweeten it, as it is very sour. It was popular because it can be harvested early in the year, before any real fruit is available. It has fallen from grace in the past 50 years or so and is now becoming relatively unusual. It is quite an acquired taste, but many people come to love it.

Nutritional content:
Rhubarb contains vitamins C and K, as well as magnesium, calcium, potassium and manganese. It is also rich in fiber.

Rhubarb also contains oxalic acid, which can prevent the absorption of calcium. This is a relatively minor effect however and nothing for anyone with a reasonable intake of calcium to worry about.

Soil
pH 5.0 to 6.8
Rhubarb is a heavy feeder and prefers a deep, rich, moisture retentive soil with lots of organic matter. It is a perennial and will be in the ground for a long time, so you should incorporate lots of organic matter into the soil before planting. You might even double dig, to get some of that organic matter down deep. The soil needs to be well-drained, otherwise the roots may rot over the winter.

About Rhubarb

Perennial
Viability: plant may live for 20 years
Yield: 1 to 6 lb per plant
Plants per person: 2
Ease of growing: Easy

Planning
Where: Rhubarb is native to Siberia and so very hardy. It prefers cool moist summers (no higher than 75° F) and cold winters (below 40° F) with some freezing. When growing in cool climates Rhubarb needs a sunny site, where it won't get too much frost (which could delay early harvests).

I grow Rhubarb in a far from ideal climate of hot dry summers and mild wet winters, and it still does surprisingly well. In this climate it does best with light shade, as the large leaves can lose a lot of water on a hot day. It also benefits from a cooler micro-climate.

Rhubarb is in the ground for a long time, so choose a site where it won't be disturbed. It should be well away from shrubs or trees, whose roots might take nutrients away from it.

When: Rhubarb can be planted any time the roots are dormant, from late autumn to spring. Of course pot grown plants can be planted at any time.

Planting
This perennial is usually planted in large holes, which have been heavily amended with compost or aged manure. It is grown from crowns, which are pieces of root with growing buds attached. These are planted so the bud is a couple of inches below the surface.

Division: Plants should be divided every 4 or 5 years, to prevent them getting overcrowded. Divide the roots to leave at least one, and preferably two, buds on each piece of root.

Growing from seed: Rhubarb is surprisingly easy to grow from seed. It germinates readily and the seedlings grow rapidly. The problem with using seed is that the plants take several years to reach useful size. They are also quite variable, with some being inferior to their parents (or prone to bolting). Usually you select the best seedlings and propagate them vegetatively. You could even argue that the genetic variability is good.

Start the seed in spring in a flat in a greenhouse, or in the ground under a cold frame. They grow quite quickly and will need to be pricked out when they have 4 or 5 leaves. When they are large enough plant them outdoors in a nursery bed, taking care to water regularly during their first year. Plant out the best plants in their permanent positions the following spring.

Spacing: Plant the crowns 3 feet apart in each direction.

Care
Rhubarb is a very independent plant and needs relatively little care.

Weeds: Remove all perennial weeds from the Rhubarb bed before planting (this is one of the benefits of double digging). A mulch will take care of any annual weeds

Watering: In dry climates Rhubarb needs regular watering to keep it productive, otherwise it will go dormant in summer.

Fertilizing: Rhubarb is a heavy feeder, however the permanent mulch of aged manure or compost should supply all the necessary nutrients.

Mulch: Apply a 2″ layer of compost or aged manure annually. This keeps down weeds, conserves moisture and feeds the soil (which then feeds the plants).

Deadheading: Any flower stalks that appear should be removed promptly, to stop the plant devoting energy to seed production. If it does flower, don't let it produce seed as this would waste even more energy.

Forcing outdoors: In Northern Europe it was once a common practice to force Rhubarb. This would give an early crop, up to 6 weeks before the unprotected plants. This was done by covering the crown (it stayed in the ground) with a bottomless bucket (the lid was left on). Leaves, manure or soil was piled around the bucket to insulate it. The resulting shoots were pale and extra succulent from being deprived of light. After the harvest, the bucket was removed, a layer of mulch was applied and the plants were left to continue growing as normal.

Pests: Obviously any time you have a problem with a perennial plant it is more serious than with an annual. Rhubarb is relatively pest free, but you may occasionally have problems with Japanese Beetles, or Leafhoppers. Other potential problems include Anthracnose, Crown Rot, Foot rot, Leaf Spot and Verticillium Wilt.

My biggest problem has been with Gophers. These rodents will completely destroy a plant, which is a problem in a plant that takes so long to grow. In Gopher country the best solution is to plant them in wire baskets.

Harvesting

When: Leave the plants to grow for 2 years before harvesting.

How: Harvest by twisting the stalk, so it separates from the root. Gather 3 or 4 stems from each plant, after the leaves have opened fully and have reached full size. I prefer to harvest by just taking a few stalks occasionally. However some people harvest intensively for about two months and then leave the plants alone, so they can build up reserves of food. Never take more than half of the stems from a plant at one time.

Seed saving: Rhubarb produces seed readily if you allow it to; in fact the usual problem is stopping it. It doesn't often self-sow, but doesn't need to because it is a long lived perennial

Unusual growing ideas

Ornamental: Rhubarb has a strong bold shape, which makes it useful as an ornamental. Of course if you keep picking the stalks, it will often look less than attractive.

Wild garden: Rhubarb is a good plant for the wild or forest garden (plant in sunny clearings). It is a very independent plant and will often survive in abandoned gardens for years.

Varieties: There aren't many. Glaskins Perpetual, Crimson Red, Victoria

Cooking: Rhubarb is something of an acquired taste. as it is very sour and needs a lot of sugar to make it palatable.

Rhubarb crisp

1 cup whole wheat flour
1 cup oats
1 cup sugar
1/2 cup butter
4 cups chopped Rhubarb
2 tbsp cornstarch
1 cup water

Combine the flour, oats, ½ a cup of sugar and melted butter in a bowl and mix well. In another bowl mix another ½ cup sugar with the cornstarch, add a cup of water and stir until smooth. Pour this mix over the chopped rhubarb and then cover with the flour and oat mix. Bake for 40 minutes at 350° F, until the top is golden brown and the rhubarb is tender. Eat warm, with whipped cream or ice cream.

Rocket
Eruca Sativa

Introduction: Rocket has been in and out of fashion since Roman times. It is now fashionable again, under its Italian name of Arugala and is commonly found in commercially grown salad mixes. People tend to either love or hate its unique flavor. I don't like it very much, but some people find it irresistible.

Soil: I don't consider Arugala to be a very important crop and just plant it in any convenient vacant space. I don't do any special soil preparation for it, but it still does pretty well.

Planning

Where: This fast growing and compact plant doesn't take up much space, so is usually interplanted between slower growing crops.

When: Rocket grows best in the cool weather of spring and fall. In hot weather it gets very pungent and flowers as soon as it has produced a few leaves.

This hardy member of the Mustard family can be planted 4 weeks before the last spring frost. It is also a good fall or winter crop, though in harsh climates it may need the protection of cloches.

Succession sowing: Rocket matures and bolts quickly as it gets warmer. If you are to harvest for any length of time, you will have to make several succession sowings. Sow a few seeds every 2 to 3 weeks.

Planting: This annual is easily grown from seed, so is almost always direct sown. I just throw a few seeds in any small vacant area.

Spacing: I often grow Arugala as a cut and come again crop and space the seeds about 1″ apart. To grow it as a row crop you should sow the seeds 3″ apart in the rows, with 6″ between the rows.

Weeds: This plant competes against weeds quite well, because it practically is a weed.

Watering: In warm weather it is very important to keep the soil moist. This prevent it from getting too pungent and slows down bolting.

Pests: Flea Beetles are a common but minor problem, peppering the plants with tiny holes. I don't do anything about them, because these fast growing plants usually recover quickly.

Harvest: Harvest individual leaves as soon as they are of sufficient size (2″ to 3″), which may be only 2 weeks after transplanting. You can also harvest the whole plants, up until they start to flower.

Seed saving: Rocket bolts readily, so saving seed is easy. It is cross-pollinated by insects, but since there are few varieties available (and you are unlikely to have more than one), this isn't usually a problem.

When the seedpods begin to ripen, cut the whole plants and put them in a paper grocery bag to dry. When they are fully dry, crush them to free the seeds. Arugala produces seed abundantly and you can get a lot of seed from a few plants. I always have far more than I have use for.

Unusual growing ideas
Cut and come again salad mix: Rocket is commonly grown in cut and come again salad mixes, either in a mixed bed, or in a section by itself. I prefer the latter approach, as it is more vigorous than most salad mix plants and can take over.

Micro-greens: This is just a smaller version of the above. You plant the seeds ¼″ apart and harvest them when the first true leaves appear. This should be within 2 weeks.

Volunteer: Arugala self sows readily and can become a minor weed. Because of this I rarely plant it in its own bed. I just encourage it by scattering some of the seed I collect in suitable spots. As I write this it looks as good now as it has all year and it is almost Christmas.

Varieties: There are a few, but I can't say I've noticed much difference in any of those I have tried.

Cooking: If you don't like it raw, try it in soups, or steamed as a potherb. Cooking changes the flavor a lot.

Rutabaga
Brassica napus

Introduction: The Rutabaga is a bigger, hardier (because it contains less water) longer keeping Turnip. It originated in a garden somewhere in Eastern Europe, as a hybrid between Turnip (*B. rapa*) and Cabbage (*B. oleracea* var *capitata*).

This plant has long been an important winter food crop for humans and animals in cold northern climates. It came to Britain via Sweden, which is why it is sometimes called Swedish Turnip or more commonly Swede. The name Rutabaga is Swedish and apparently means Root-bag.

About Rutabaga

Seed facts
Germ temp: 40 (60 to 95) 105° F
Germ time: 6 to 10 days
Seed viability: 2 to 5 yrs
Germination percentage: 75+

Planning facts
Hardiness: Hardy
Ease of growing: Easy
Growing temp: 40 (60 to 65) 75° F
Plants per person: 5
Plants per sq ft: 1½
Fall crop: Sow 3 to 4 months before first fall frost
Time to harvest: 80 to 120 days

Harvest facts
Yield per plant: 1 to 2 lb
Yield per sq ft: 2 to 4 lb

I hated this food while growing up in England and long held a lingering animosity to it. However a few years ago I grew it for my wife and was very surprised. Like many crops, it was very different when harvested fresh from the organic garden and was actually really good. Not at all how I remembered it.

Soil
pH 6.0 - 7.0
Rutabaga likes a heavy rich soil that is not too high in nitrogen, but contains lots of potassium. The plants are so sensitive to boron deficiency that they can almost be used as a test for it. If it is deficient the center of the root may rot.

Soil preparation: Incorporate 2″ of compost or aged manure into the top 6″ of soil. Add wood ashes to supply potassium and lime if the soil is acid. Boron is normally supplied by the organic matter in compost.

Planning
Where: Like most cool weather crops Rutabaga needs full sun.

Crop rotation: Rutabaga should not be planted where another Brassica has been grown in the previous 3 years.

When:
Spring: Rutabaga is easy to grow if it has cool weather (60 to 70° F) and ample water. Spring sown plants tend to develop lots of leaves but small roots (excess nitrogen will do the same).

Fall: This crop does much better in its traditional role as a fall crop. Plant about 90 to 120 days before the first fall frost.

Planting
Direct sowing: Like most root crops Rutabaga doesn't like trans-planting, so is normally direct sown. Sow the seeds ½″ deep and 2″ apart initially. Thin out the excess plants in two stages, to reach the final spacing.

Spacing: Space the plants 6″ to 9″ apart, depending upon the soil.

Care: Weed when young, keep the soil moist, add mulch and they should be okay.

Pests and disease: The same pests that attack Cabbage may bother Rutabaga, but they are usually less troublesome. Root Maggots may attack early plantings.

Harvest: The roots are harvested when 3″ to 6″ in diameter. They are very hardy and can be left in the garden until needed, so long as it doesn't get too cold. They are improved by frost, but not by freezing, so must be protected from extreme cold with a thick mulch. They store well in the root cellar at 32 to 40° F.

Greens: If any plants remain in the ground in early spring, you can use their new foliage as spring greens (first year growth is generally tough and inferior to that of Turnip.) The flower buds can be used like Broccoli Raab).

Seed saving: This biennial is treated in much the same way as the Cabbage. It over-winters in the ground and flowers in the spring. It will cross-pollinate with Siberian Kale, so only one type can be flowering at one time. Stake the tall plants (the tops get very heavy with seed) and leave them alone. Save seed from at least 5 plants to maintain some genetic diversity.

These plants produce a lot of seed, far more than you will ever need for planting. You can sprout the seed like Alfalfa, to produce nutritious salad greens, or grow micro-greens.

Unusual growing ideas

Forcing: Any surplus roots can be used as a source of winter greens. They are potted up and forced like those of Chicory.

Varieties: Rutabaga isn't very popular in North America, a fact reflected in the lack of varieties. Best-Of-All, Marian, Virtue

Cooking: The roots are similar to those of the Turnip (though generally considered to be superior) and can be used in the same ways. They are good in soups, or mixed with potatoes (the two are often eaten together.) Some people like it raw in salads or even sandwiches.

Mashed Swede

1 lb Rutabaga
3 tbsp butter

The root is peeled and cut into pieces, put in boiling water and simmered for 15 minutes. It is then mashed with the butter to a puree. It is then put back in a pan and re-heated to dry off some of the excess moisture.

Salad Mix

Introduction: The best way to grow salad material in a small space is to grow the plants so closely together that they produce single leaves instead of hearted plants. The individual leaves are then cut as they reach suitable size. Rather than going out and harvesting an individual Lettuce, you then go out with a basket a few minutes before dining and graze along the salad bed, gathering individual leaves. I have had such success with this method that I now grow most of my salad crops in this way.

pH 6.0 to 7.0

Soil: The soil is called upon to produce a lot of foliage in a short time, so it should be fertile, moisture retentive and well drained.

Soil preparation: Incorporate a 2″ layer of organic matter into the top 3" to 6″ of soil. You might also add seaweed, wood ashes and colloidal phosphate.

Planning

How much: Plant 2 sq ft of mixed salad greens per person at each planting.

Succession sowing: This should be done in succession every 3 to 4 weeks until the weather gets very hot (or all summer in many cases).

When: The season makes a big difference as to what you can grow in a salad mix. You have to adapt your growing methods, and the kinds of plants, to the weather.

Spring and fall: Most traditional salad plants do best in cool weather, so these are the easiest and most productive growing times.

Summer: If you want to grow salad mix in summer heat, you have to be more resourceful. Put the salad bed where it will get light shade, or make a sunshade of shade cloth or wooden laths. Water daily to keep the entire area cool and moist, and to prevent the plants from developing very strong flavors.

For a hot weather, or long day, salad mix you will need to choose your varieties and crops carefully. Look for heat tolerant species and varieties. Bolting, the bane of summer salad growing, is less of a problem when you are growing in this way, because they have less time to do it. You also have many more individual plants.

Winter: In Europe salad greens were commonly grown under glass in winter and this can work well, as most of them prefer cool weather. You might use cold resistant varieties and grow them in a cold frame or under row covers. They will take quite a lot longer to mature at this time of year.

Your protected winter salad beds will be the perfect vacation resort for slugs and snails to spend the winter, so watch out for them.

Where

You don't need a lot of space to grow salad green in this way. In cool weather the plants will need full sun. If you want to grow them in hot weather you will have to give them some shade.

Spacing: Plant the seeds ½" to 1" apart in rows, with 3" between the rows. You can also broadcast the seeds at the in-row spacing.

Planting

Direct sowing: You can sow different kinds of seed into the same area of bed. In fact you can buy mixed seed packets, usually called Salad Mix or Mesclun, just for this purpose. The important thing is that the strongest growers don't overwhelm the weaker ones. Of course you should harvest judiciously to prevent this happening.

You can also plant each different variety separately, in its own short rows. This works well, because it allows you to compensate for different growth rates, as some plants grow faster than others. It also allows you to grow as much as you want of each variety

Care: The plants aren't in the ground long enough to need much attention.

Weeding: They will need weeding when young, to ensure that weeds don't take over before the salad plants are established.

Watering: The beds must be kept evenly moist at all times, so don't let them dry out. This is especially critical in summer.

Harvest

When: This is often known as a "cut and come again" method, because the same plants can be harvested more than once. You can start harvesting individual leaves when they are 2" to 3" tall, which takes about 3 to 4 weeks. The length of harvest depends upon the crop, variety and climate. Some plants can be harvested for several months, some for only week or two.

How: I will describe three ways you can harvest the small plants. You can use just one of these methods, or you could use a combination of all three.

You can cut whole small plants, leaving the bottom inch of stem behind to regenerate. This enables the plants to continue growing, so you can get a second (and sometimes even a third) harvest.

You can also pick the largest leaves from individual plants, to give you a longer harvest period.

Another alternative is to harvest entire plants and thereby thin overcrowded areas. By doing so you can slowly thin out most of the bed over time. The plants that remain at the end can be allowed to get bigger.

Foraging: To bulk up the salad and make it more interesting, you can go around the garden gathering various edible leaves and flowers. These can be gathered without significant harm to any plants and leave the garden looking untouched.

Throw in a few sprouts and edible flowers (see those separate sections) and you have a salad that not only taste great, but also looks spectacular and is highly nutritious.

Storage: Salad mix doesn't store well, so it's best to cut only as much as you need for the next meal. It will keep for a week in the refrigerator in a plastic bag, but this isn't ideal.

Unusual growing ideas

Hot weather salads: Many plants that bolt quickly in hot weather might still be grown as a seedling crop. For example Arugala, Lettuce, Mustard, and Peppergrass. Other useful plants that can tolerate some heat include Mizuna, Purslane, Amaranth, Siberian Kale and Some Lettuce.

Pests are very active at this time of year, so protect them vigilantly.

Pests and Disease: Slugs and Snails love salad mix and will eat the seedlings as they emerge. They can be hand picked at night, or perhaps you could surround the bed with some kind of barrier (such as a copper strip).

Birds also appreciate the tender succulent seedlings and they can also be a big problem in both cold and hot conditions. If so you may have to net the whole bed.

Seed Saving: Eventually any remaining plants will start to bolt. I sometimes allow a few of these to grow up and set seed, as this supplies an abundance of seed for growing next years salad mix.

Varieties: The ideal plants for a salad mix taste good, look good, germinate and grow quickly and don't bolt easily. The choice of suitable plants will vary according to the growing conditions. Finding plants that tolerate hot weather is more difficult than finding ones that grow well in the cold.

When choosing plants to use for as salad mix, you want a variety of flavors.

Bland: This is for the bulk of the salad. Lettuce is almost always the first choice, as there are so many kinds and they work so well. The best types of Lettuce are the Romaines, though leaf lettuce also works well.

Other bland green include Miners Lettuce, Mizuna, Spinach, Chard and Beet greens. Cornsalad is also good, but will probably need to be planted separately because it is quite slow growing.

Pungent: Mustards are the most commonly used, because they so fast and easy to grow. Arugala is also popular, if you like its distinctive pungent flavor. Kale, Green Onion, Garden Cress, Radish, Land Cress and Chinese Cabbages are all good as well.

Bitter: Chicory, Endive (the curly types add wonderful texture).

Sour: Sorrel

Succulent: Purslane is a great hot weather crop. Miners Lettuce does well in cool moist conditions.

Aromatic: Basil, Green Onion, Cilantro and Shungiku.

Tahini Salad dressing

4 tbsp tahini
Juice of a lemon
1 tsp mustard
1 or 2 garlic cloves (crushed)
2 tbsp tamari
1/2 tsp pepper
2 tbsp water

Mix everything together thoroughly and its ready.

Salsify
Tragopogon porrifolius

Introduction: This is an old European crop with thin pale edible roots. It is also known as Oyster Plant because these roots are supposed to resemble oysters in flavor. It is an easy plant to grow, as it is not that far removed from the wild plant.

Nutritional content:
The root contains calcium and potassium.

About Salsify

Germ temp: 40 to 85° F
Germ time: 12 to 16 days
Seed viability: 1 to 3 years
Hardiness: Very hardy
Ease of growing: Quite easy
Growing temp: 45 (55 to 75) 85° F
Time to harvest: 120 to 180 days
Yield: 1 to 5 lb sq ft

Soil
pH 6.5 - 7.5
Salsify needs the usual soil for root crops, deep, loose and fertile, but not too rich in nitrogen. It will fork in stony or freshly manured soil.

Soil preparation: Incorporate 2″ of compost or aged manure, along with wood ashes and phosphate rock. Lime if the soil is acid.

Planning
When: The soil should be at least 40° F before planting (this may be a month before the last frost.) The plants are improved by frost, so are usually planted to mature in fall.

Planting
Direct sowing: Salsify is very hardy, so is almost always seeded directly outdoors. Use fresh seed and don't sow it too thickly, 1″ apart and ½″ to 1″ deep is about right. When the seedlings are a couple of inches high, thin to their proper spacing.

Spacing:
Rows: 4″ apart in the row, with 12″ between the rows.

Beds: 2″ to 6″ apart in offset rows.

Care
Water: It is important to keep the young plants well watered. Once they are well established they are more independent, but should still be kept evenly moist for best growth.

Pests and disease: There are no serious problems.

Harvest: The roots can be dug anytime they are large enough, but their flavor is improved by frost and cold weather. They don't keep well once harvested, so it is better to leave them in the ground where possible. A mulch can help to protect them (cut off the tops) in very cold climates. They can be stored for several months in moist sand in a root cellar, at 32 to 40° F.

Tops: The tops and immature flower stems can be eaten when the plants begin to grow again in their second year. Use them in salads or cook like Asparagus

Seed saving: This is pretty simple, just leave the plants alone, and they will flower in their second year. They are insect pollinated, but there are so few varieties this isn't usually an issue. However they can also cross with Wild Salsify (which commonly occurs in some areas.)

Varieties: Mammoth Sandwich Island.

Cooking: Use raw or cooked, like Parsnip or Carrot. They should be cleaned well by scrubbing and then cooked in their skins. If you want to peel them it is easier after they have been cooked. The flowers and new spring greens can be added to salads.

Two other similar plants can be treated in the same ways:

Scorzonera
(Scorzonera hispanica)
This uncommon crop plant is also known as Black Salsify because of its black root. It is grown in much the same way as Salsify, except that it is a perennial and is sometimes allowed to grow for 2 years to reach a larger size. The root is eaten in the same way as Salsify. The flowers and new spring greens can be added to salads.

Spanish Salsify
(Scolymus hispanicus)
This species is even rarer than the above rarities. It is cultivated and used as above.

Seakale
Crambe maritima

Introduction: No one could call Seakale a popular vegetable, in fact you have probably never even heard of it. It is native to the sea coasts of Western Europe and was gathered from the wild for centuries before it came into cultivation. It's blanched spring shoots are something of a delicacy, but are quite easy to grow.

Soil:
pH: **7.0**
Seakale likes a light well-drained soil and may rot over winter if the soil is too wet. It doesn't like acid soil. Fertilize with compost, aged manure or seaweed (perfect for this maritime plant.).

Where: This coastal plant likes mild cool summers and mild winters. It needs full sun for best growth.

Planting
How: Seakale can be grown from seed, root crowns or root cuttings. The latter two methods are faster and only take a year to first harvest. However it is almost impossible to find Seakale roots anywhere in North America, unless you grow your own from seed.

Seed: The large seeds take 1 to 2 weeks to germinate, though they sometimes have difficulty getting out of the hard seed coat. Once they have germinated they are quite vigorous and grow quickly.

Outside: This hardy plant can be direct sown on the last frost date.

It is usually started in a protected nursery bed, and transplanted to its permanent location when a year old.

Inside: The only reason to start the seeds inside is so you can give them more protection. They should be transplanted when they have 3 or 4 true leaves, into a nursery bed (if outside) or into individual pots (if inside)

Spacing: Seakale is normally spaced 12″ apart in alternate rows.

Root cuttings: These are easier and faster than seed. The ideal cuttings are ½″ in diameter and 5″ long (cut the top end flat and the bottom slanted, so you know which way is up. These can be planted immediately they are taken in fall, or any time through to early spring.

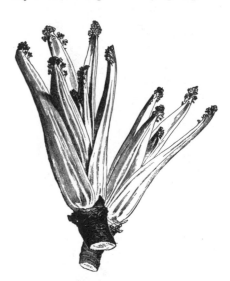

Care
As a recently domesticated plant, Seakale still has a lot of wild vigor and needs little attention once it is well established. It is a perennial and may provide harvests for 6 years or more, if you look after it well.

Watering: Water regularly in hot weather, to keep the soil moist.

Mulch: Use a mulch of aged manure or seaweed to keep down weeds and retain moisture.

Flowers: Remove any flower stalks as they appear, so they don't take energy from the roots.

Frost: Seakale doesn't like cold weather. In cold winter areas cover the plants with a thick mulch to protect them from freezing.

Pests: Seakale is rarely bothered by insect pests. It is vulnerable to Clubroot, which affects most plants in the *Brassicaceae*.

Blanching: Seakale is not really edible unless it is blanched. This is done just before the shoots emerge in spring, by covering the plants with upturned buckets. The blanched shoots should be about 6″ to 9″ long, with a small leaf at the tip.

Forcing: Seakale can be forced indoors at 45° F in much the same way as Chicory. This is better in that it is easier to control the rate at which shoots are produced. However it is also more work and the roots must be thrown away afterwards.

Plants for forcing are usually raised from root cuttings in a special bed. They are treated like Chicory.

Harvest: The shoots are gathered in spring when few other crops are producing. Harvest by cutting them off at ground level. If your plants are healthy you can take 2 or 3 cuttings in a season.

Seed saving: This is easy, just allow a few plants to flower and set seed. This will take energy from the roots however.

Varieties: The only variety I know of is Lily White. This gets its name because it doesn't have the purple-pinkish hue of wild plants.

Cooking: The blanched shoots are usually cooked like Asparagus. The flower buds can be cooked like Broccoli.

Other uses: The flower stalks are often used in dried flower arrangements.

Shallot
Allium cepa aggregatum group

Introduction: Some gourmets consider the Shallot to be the most refined of all the Allium family, as it is milder and more delicately flavored than the Onion or Garlic. It is the commonest kind of multiplier Onion, a group that also includes Potato Onions and Egyptian Onions. It produces a cluster of up to 10 or so bulbs, each up to 2″ in diameter and connected at their bases.

The Shallot has similar requirements as the Onion and is grown in the same way, though it is somewhat easier to grow. It works very well in small gardens, as it doesn't take up much space and is quite productive.

Nutritional content:
Similar to Onions.

About Shallot

Facts
Perennial
Yield: 1 to 4 lb sq ft (1 lb sets gives 5 to 7 lb bulbs)
Yield per plant: 2 to 8 oz
Time to harvest: 100 to 120 days
Ease of growing: Very easy
Growing temp: 50 to 75° F

Soil
pH 6.0 - 7.0
Shallots prefer the same kind of soil as Onions, well drained, rich, loose and moisture retentive. However they will do fine in a less than ideal soil.

Soil preparation: Incorporate 2″ of compost or aged manure into the top 6″ of soil, to supply nutrients and aid in moisture retention. The latter is particularly important if your soil is light and doesn't hold water well. You should also add colloidal phosphate to supply phosphorus and wood ashes or greensand for potassium. If the soil is very acidic then add lime.

Planning

Where: Shallots don't take up very much space, so it's easy to find a spot for them. Plant them anywhere there is vacant open space, where they won't be in the way. You can even plant them singly around the garden. Just remember that they need full sun.

When

Spring: The bulbs are quite hardy and can be planted up to 4 weeks before the last frost date. They do well in the long days of spring and early summer, and should be ready to harvest in mid to late summer.

Fall: In mild climates they can be started in fall at the same time as Garlic, but there is some danger that they may rot over the winter.

Planting

Vegetative: Because they are usually propagated vegetatively, Shallots are always planted directly outside. Plant them so the tip of the bulb just shows above ground level. If they somehow work their way out of ground (birds often have something to do with this), just put them back in.

Seed: Some varieties of Shallots can be grown from seed. They are treated in the same way as Onions.

Of course once you have raised them from seed, you can then propagate them vegetatively.

Spacing:

Rows: 4″ to 6″ apart in rows 9″ apart

Beds: 4″ to 6″ to 8″ apart They are sometimes planted 4″ apart and every alternate plant is picked for greens. However I prefer to use Egyptian Onion for greens.

Care

Weed: Shallots are vulnerable to weed competition, so must be weeded regularly. As I just mentioned a mulch helps to keep weeds down.

Water: Shallots are somewhat drought tolerant, but need evenly moist soil for best production. Don't let it dry out too much.

Fertilization: Foliar feed with compost tea when the shoots are about 6″ high. Feed them again about a month later.

Mulch: A light mulch may be applied when the shoots have appeared. This will help to keep down weeds and stop the soil from drying out in hot weather.

Unearthing: Shallots like to grow half out of the soil. If the

bulbs get partially buried, scrape away the soil to expose them almost down to the roots.

Pests and disease: Shallots are bothered by the same pests and diseases as Onions, but are usually relatively pest free. The commonest problem is for the bulbs to rot because the soil is too wet.

Harvesting

When: The bulbs are ready to harvest when the tops have died down, which is usually in July or August.

How: Pull the whole bulb clusters (you can almost just pick them up off the ground) and leave them to dry in a warm dry shady place. Don't break them up until you are going to use them (it may start them sprouting). Store as for Onions in a cold dry place (see **Onion**).

Storage: Shallots store very well and were once saved for use after the store of bulb Onions had gone.

Seed saving: Shallots can produce viable seed, but they aren't usually grown from seed. Normally you simply save some of the bulbs for replanting. You can re-plant them immediately if you want, or store them until spring. It may be a good idea to occasionally start with fresh bulbs, as they can become infected with virus diseases.

Unusual growing ideas

Greens: Shallots can be grown indoors in winter to supply green Onions. You can also harvest greens from outdoor shallots, though it's better to plant some specifically for this, rather than taking foliage from those you are growing for bulbs.

You could leave some in the ground all the time for use as greens.

Cooking:
Shallots work great if you only need a small quantity of Onion. The greens are excellent also.

Varieties:
There are a few different varieties of Shallot. The commonest are:
French - Have a pinkish skin.
Dutch - Yellowish skin, stronger flavored.
Frog Legged: One of the best flavored varieties.
Gray
Santa

Potato Onion
Allium cepa var *aggregatum*

Another good perennial Onion that deserves to be more widely cultivated. This one is a lot easier to grow than it is to find. It is similar to the Shallot, but produces larger bulbs, up to 3″ in diameter. It is cultivated in the same ways.

Shungiku
Chrysanthemum coronarium

Introduction: Shungiku is actually a species of Chrysanthemum, though not very showy. It is native to the Mediterranean, where it is known as Crown Daisy, but it is only commonly used for food in Asia.

Soil: This annual does well in most soil types, but (as usual) it gets bigger and more succulent in rich, moist soil.

Planning
When: Shungiku prefers cool weather, so does best as a spring or fall crop. It can be grown in summer in shade, but it won't last very long before it bolts.

Planting
Direct sowing: This plant can be broadcast or sown in rows like Spinach. I often sow a few seeds in a bed of mixed salad greens. You don't need a lot of plants as it is quite strongly flavored.

Spacing: Space the plants 6″ apart.

Care
Watering: Keep the soil evenly moist for best growth.

Weeds: Shungiku doesn't compete with weeds very well, so keep it well weeded.

Harvest: You can harvest whole, plants or you can pick single leaves from a number of plants (I prefer the latter). Gathering regularly may delay flowering. Pinch out any flower shoots as they appear.

Seed saving: This plant produces seed readily if allowed to flower. Just cut the ripe seed heads and dry in a paper bag.

Unusual growing ideas
Ornamental: This species is sometimes grown in the ornamental garden for its small, daisy-like flowers.

Varieties: I haven't seen any. It is sometimes sold as Garland Chrysanthemum.

Cooking: This species adds an interesting flavor to salads and I like it a lot. Apparently it has also been cooked as a potherb, or used as flavoring, but I haven't tried this.

Sorrel, French
Rumex scutatus

Introduction: This species was once much more popular than it is today, especially in Europe. Once established it will spread vegetatively and may self-sow, or even naturalize.

Soil: Sorrel will grow in most soils, so long as they aren't too alkaline. They don't need to be very fertile.

Planting: This plant is easily grown from seed, either started inside or direct sown. Once you have plants growing vigorously, you can get more plants by dividing the clumps.

Spacing: This perennial spreads vegetatively to form large colonies. Plan for a final spacing of 12″ to 15″ apart.

Care
Watering: Supposedly Sorrel needs quite a bit of water, but it has

done fine in my garden. There it is lucky to get watered more than once a week.

Feeding: For really vigorous growth you should give the plants a source of extra nitrogen, such as manure tea.

Deadheading: Remove the flower stalks as they appear, so the plant devotes more energy to vegetative growth. You don't want it to self seed everywhere.

Pests: I haven't noticed any pests of any kind. Maybe they don't like the sour taste.

Harvest: Pick leaves as they reach full size (they will still be tender). Harvesting is actually beneficial as it encourages further growth. The thin leaves wilt quickly after harvest, so gather just before you want to use them.

Seed saving: Sorrel can produce a lot of seed if given the chance. Usually the problem is stopping it.

Unusual growing ideas: Sorrel is too vigorous to be put in the intensive beds and doesn't need such rich soil anyway. Just plant it in the semi-wild garden and let it fend for itself. It is an ideal forest garden crop and could almost be used as a groundcover.

Varieties: None.

Cooking: The leaves are a nice addition to salads (they can even replace lemon juice or vinegar). They can also be used as a potherb, though they shrink a lot in cooking (like Spinach).

Spinach
Spinacia oleracea

Introduction: Spinach originated in Asia and reached Europe some time in the Middle Ages. It is one of the commonest leaf vegetable crops for cool summer areas and can be highly productive.

Many home gardeners ignore spinach, as it can be a problematic crop. It seems that no sooner does it reach any size than it bolts. This problem can be overcome if you know the plants habits however.

Spinach is one of the fastest yielding common crops. The harvest can start within a month of planting and it can be out of the ground within 2 months.

Nutritional content: Spinach is rich in iron, but this is very water soluble and easily leached out by boiling. It also contains vitamins C and A (beta carotene), folate, luteine and various useful phytochemicals.

Spinach also contains oxalic acid, which can make calcium somewhat less available in the body. Fortunately this is not a significant problem to anyone with a reasonable intake of calcium. It may also contribute to the formation of kidney stones, so anyone prone to them should probably avoid oxalic acid.

Soil
pH 6.0 to 7.0
A light, well-drained soil works best because Spinach is grown in cool weather and such soils warm up faster. The soil should be very rich in humus, moisture retentive

and contain lots of nitrogen and potassium. This plant is quite sensitive to pH (both extremes may cause deficiency), so adjust if necessary. It is quite tolerant of saline soils.

About Spinach

Seed facts
Germ temp: 35 (60 to 65) 75° F
Germ time: 5 to 22 days
62 days / 32° F
22 days / 41° F
12 days / 50° F * Optimum
7 days / 59° F
6 days / 68° F
5 days / 77° F
Seed viability: 2 to 4 years
Germination percentage: 60%
Weeks to grow transplants: 3 to 4

Planning facts
Hardiness: Hardy
Ease of growing: Temperamental
Growing temp: 60 to 65° F day
                        40 to 45° F night
Plants per person: 10 per planting
Plants per sq ft: 9
Transplants:
Start: 8 wks before frost free date
Plant out: 4 wks before last frost
Direct sow: 4 to 6 wks before the last frost date
Fall crop: sow 6 to 8 wks before first fall frost
Succession sow: every 2 weeks
Time to harvest: 40 to 60 days

Harvest facts
Yield per plant: 6 to 8 oz
Yield per sq ft: ½ to 2 lb sq ft

Soil preparation: Spinach likes organic matter, so incorporate 2″ of compost or aged manure into the top 6″ of soil (where most feeder roots are found). Spinach loves manure and can even thrive in soil containing fresh manure (ideally this should be incorporated the previous autumn).

Planning

Where: Spinach doesn't like heat and in warmer areas it should be planted in a shady site. For a fall or over-wintering crop it needs full sun. Each plant doesn't produce very much, so it is usually grown in wide intensive beds. Raised beds are good because they warm up quickly in spring and tend to be well drained.

When: More than any other common crop, Spinach doesn't like warm weather. It actually germinates best at only 50° F. It germinates more rapidly at higher temperatures, but at 70° F only about half the seeds will germinate.

Spinach bolts when exposed to long summer days, so is usually grown as a spring or autumn crop. It is much less prone to bolting in the shorter, cooler days and the leaves grow larger and more succulent.

Planting

Spring: You must sow Spinach early if you are to get a useful crop before heat or long days cause it to bolt. Start the first Spinach plants about 8 weeks before the last frost date and plant it out about 4 weeks later. You can also direct sow 4 to 6 weeks before the last frost date and in succession thereafter.

Autumn: Spinach does best as a fall crop, because the days are getting shorter and it doesn't bolt so readily. The soil must be cool enough for good germination however. Sow the seeds 4 to 8 weeks before the first autumn frost date.

Winter: In areas with mild winters, some varieties of Spinach can be grown as a winter crop. They are hardy down to 25° F and don't bolt in the cool, short days.

Spinach won't take hard frost unprotected, but it can be grown in harsher climates, if it is under the cover of cloches or cold frames.

The key to success as a winter crop is for the plants to get big enough before cool weather hits. They will then continue to grow throughout the winter. If they are not big enough, they will just sit there looking sorry for themselves.

Over-winter: Select a hardy variety and sow the seed about 6 weeks before the first fall frost. In mild climates they will survive the winter (though they may die back) and give a good early harvest as the weather warms. You can also sow the seed in fall, to germinate in the spring.

Transplants

Starting inside: Spinach doesn't like transplanting (it can cause bolting), but it can be started indoors in soil blocks or cell packs. You can even multi-plant it, to get several seeds per block. Don't get it too warm, otherwise it won't

produce well when transplanted outdoors. It is occasionally started indoors in late summer, to give it cooler conditions than it would have outside.

Direct sowing: Sow the seed ½" deep (¼" in cold soil) and 1" to 2" apart (either broadcast or in wide rows). Spinach sown directly into cold spring soil is slow to germinate, so some gardeners pre-germinate it first. Alternatively you could warm the soil with plastic or cloches. Some gardeners mark the location of the slow germinating seeds by sowing a few Radishes along with the Spinach.

Spacing: Spinach can bolt if overcrowded; so thin the plants carefully to 2" to 4" when they have all emerged. When the plants are 4" high thin them again to a final spacing of 4" to 8" (this time the thinnings will be big enough to eat).

8" (poor soil)
6" (average soil)
4" (good soil)

Care

Spinach must grow quickly to produce the highest quality food. This means giving it optimal conditions; as much water and nutrients as it requires and no competition from weeds or crowded neighbors (all these factors can contribute to bolting).

Bolting: Spinach will bolt when the day length is from 12 ½ to 15 hours, depending upon the variety (some are more sensitive than others). As with Lettuce, warm weather (above 75° F) may hasten bolting, but doesn't really cause it. Overcrowding and vernalization may also cause the plants to bolt.

Cool weather (below 65° F) may retard bolting, as can frequent harvesting of leaves.

When spinach gets ready to flower the top leaves become noticeably triangular and the stem elongates. Harvest as much as you can as soon as this starts to happen.

Water: Keep the soil evenly moist (not wet), otherwise it may bolt. Fortunately this isn't usually a problem in the cool weather preferred by Spinach.

Fertilization: Spinach likes nitrogen, so if the soil isn't very fertile, give the plants a regular feed of compost tea or liquid seaweed.

Pests: Leaf miners tunnel into the leaves and make them useless. Remove affected leaves and rub off the egg clusters. If they are very bad you will have to use row covers.

Flea Beetles, aphids, caterpillars, Anthracnose, Curly Top, Downy Mildew and Mosaic Virus may all afflict Spinach.

Harvesting

When: You can gather whole plants (harvest thin to begin with), or you can pick individual leaves (carefully) as soon as they are of sufficient quantity and size. Don't take too many leaves from any one plant and don't let them get larger than 6". Once the plants start producing you should harvest regularly and enthusiastically, Spinach doesn't usually stay in peak condition for very long, so take advantage of it.

How: Pinching out the leaves encourages new growth, so keep it cropped even if you don't need it. If the leaves get tough, try cutting the whole top off of the plant, leaving about 3" to re-sprout.

Storage: Use the leaves as soon as possible after harvest; they will only last for a few days in a plastic bag in the fridge. If you can't use them immediately then freeze for later use.

Seed saving: Spinach plants are dioecious (there are separate male and female plants) so all plants don't produce seed. Saving seed is easy; just allow a patch of plants to bolt (remove any plants that bolt earlier than the rest.)

The first plants to bolt are males, which have smaller leaves. You don't need a lot of males, but some are necessary for fertilization (keep 1 male for every 2 females). Spinach is wind pollinated and to keep it pure it must be isolated from other varieties by at least a ½ mile. Female plants may grow to 4 feet in height and produce a lot of seed.

Unusual growing ideas

Intercrop: When grown in ideal conditions, Spinach is very fast growing and makes a useful catch crop for interplanting between slower growing crops.

Salad mix: This fast growing plant makes an excellent salad mix crop, sown ½" to 1" apart. Individual leaves are gathered as they reach a useful size (anywhere from 2" to 5"). These are carefully pinched off (or snipped), leaving enough behind to enable the plant to regenerate. Spinach works very well when grown in this way, as bolting isn't as much of a problem. See **Salad Mix** for more on this.

Indoor Crop: Spinach is very cold tolerant and makes a good winter crop for the cool greenhouse or growing frame. If temperatures are high enough it may grow all winter without bolting.

Alternatives to Spinach: If the weather is too warm for Spinach, you will have to look at other options. Chard (particularly the variety called Perpetual Spinach) is very good, but I would look no further than Amaranth. Few crops are easier to grow and none taste better. New Zealand Spinach and Malabar Spinach are often recommended (maybe because they both have Spinach in their names), but I have had much better results with Amaranth.

Varieties: Spinach is sometimes divided into smooth and wrinkled leaf types. Many modern varieties are lower in oxalic acid, as well as being more bolt resistant. You will have to experiment to find the best types for your area.
Bloomsdale Long Standing, Melody, Monnopa, Oriental Giant F1, Giant Viroflay

Cooking: Spinach must be washed carefully to get all of the soil off the leaves. This is especially important with the curly leaved varieties.

The nutrients in Spinach are easily leached out by boiling water, so steam them, or cook with only the water that clings to the leaves after washing. The thicker leaved varieties are often preferred for cooking as they have more bulk.

I really like to use Spinach raw in salads. The smooth leaved varieties are considered superior for this, as they are also easier to clean.

Spanakopita

2 lb spinach
¼ cup parsley
1 oz dill leaves
1 cup crumbled feta cheese
½ cup ricotta cheese
4 tbsp olive oil
1 large onion, chopped
1 bunch green onions
4 cloves garlic, minced
2 eggs, beaten
10 sheets phyllo dough
¼ cup olive oil

Sauté the onions, green onions and garlic in olive oil until translucent. Add the spinach and chopped parsley and cook until wilted and then leave to cool.

Mix the beaten eggs, dill, feta and ricotta cheese and then stir in the onion and spinach mix. Oil and layer 5 sheets of phyllo dough into a 9" square pan, then spread in the spinach cheese mix. Fold edges over mix and then oil and layer the other 5 sheets of phyllo dough on top. Fold edges down into pan to seal.

Bake in preheated 350° F oven for 30 minutes until golden.

Sprouting Seeds

Seed sprouting is a logical extension of the garden, carried on indoors, even through the winter. It is a quick and easy way to provide highly nutritious salad materials, either as a supplement to garden salads, or as an entire meal. Sprouting is also a good way to use some of the abundance of seed your garden plants will produce if allowed to. In some cases these may be more useful than the original crop.

Nutritional content:
Sprouted seeds are some of the most nutrient packed foods we have. They are full of vitamins, minerals, chlorophyll, antioxidants, enzymes, phytochemicals and probably also things we don't even know about yet. Everyone really should eat more sprouts

Where: Anywhere, so long as it is sufficiently warm (70 to 80° F is ideal). If it is very cool they will take longer to grow. You don't even need sunlight; in fact some sprouts grow bigger if kept in the dark for most of the time.

When: Anytime. They only take a week or two to grow, which is faster than any other crop plants.

How:
The easiest way to grow sprouts is in a large jar (I like 1 gallon pickle or mayonnaise jars), with a piece of muslin, or cheesecloth, stretched over the mouth. This is held tightly in place with a rubber band.

Put the seeds in the jar, put the muslin cover on and half fill with water. Leave overnight to soak the seeds (some hard core people drink the soaking water), then drain. Rinse thoroughly with fresh water at least twice a day.

Another way to grow sprouts is in a sieve, or wooden frame with a gauze screen (some people have used old panty-hose). This is a good way to grow the larger seeds such as Sunflowers and beans. The seeds are soaked overnight and then spread out on the tray, one seed deep. They are kept moist by misting them with water several times a day. The bottom of the tray should be raised for ventilation. You can even stack the trays one on top of the other.

Many seeds can be grown on moist paper towels (some people use peat moss or even potting mix). Just spread the soaked seed on the paper towels and keep the paper moist. The seedlings will grow just as if they were in soil. In Britain this method is used to grow Peppergrass and Mustard sprouts. It is also a good way to grow Sunflower seed. Here we are getting into the area of **Micro-greens**.

177

Water: Seeds dislike frequent doses of highly chlorinated water and in some cases it can kill them. If you suspect this is a problem used boiled water (maybe water that has been left in the kettle after making a cup of tea). You could also leave the water overnight in an open container, to allow the chlorine to dissipate.

Harvest: You can start eating sprouts as soon as they are big enough to be worthwhile. In a warm place they may be ready in only 3 or 4 days, but most take a week or so.

Storage: Rinse the sprouts and store them in a plastic bag in the fridge for up to a week.

Varieties: The easiest sprouts to grow are probably Alfalfa and Clover, which is why they are the kinds most commonly found for sale. Mung Beans and Sunflowers are also easy and commonly available in stores. You shouldn't stop there however, there are many more possibilities than most people imagine.

Best
Alfalfa
Broccoli: very high in antioxidants
Clover
Fenugreek: A nice flavor, one of my favorites
Radish to spicy
Sunflower

Other seeds for sprouting:

Herbs
Celery
Chia
Dill
Fennel
Onion

Grains
Barley
Buckwheat
Corn
Millet
Oats
Rice
Rye
Triticale
Wheat

Pulses
Beans: Most beans contain digestive inhibitors and so should be cooked rather than eaten raw.

Adzuki
Mung
Pinto
Soy
Black Eyed Pea
Chickpea
Lentil
Peanut
Peas
Vetch (Vicia)

Miscellaneous
Cress
Flax
Hazelnut
Quinoa
Sesame

Edible weeds
The seed of almost any edible leaf plant can be used, if you can get it in sufficient quantity. Be aware that freshly produced seed may have a dormancy period and won't germinate well until this is up.

Amaranth
Dock
Lambs Quarters
Plantain
Purslane
Sorrel

Squash, Summer
Cucurbita pepo var *melopepo*

Introduction: The Squash originated in the Americas and have been cultivated for over 5000 years. Summer Squash are productive, fast growing and easy to grow, so they are a popular garden crop. They are actually something of a gardeners joke (though not a particularly funny one), for being so productive that it's hard to keep up with them. Just a couple of plants can produce more fruits than the average family can eat.

Nutritional content:
The fruits contain folate, potassium vitamin A and a small amount of manganese

Soil
pH 6.0 - 7.0
Summer Squash is a hungry and fast growing crop that produces a lot of biomass. To do this it needs a fertile soil, with lots of organic matter, so that it retains moisture, but is well drained. It doesn't do well on acid or saline soils.

Soil preparation: Squash have a very vigorous root system, which may go down 6 feet in its search for nutrients. Add 2″ of compost, or aged manure, to the top 6″ of soil, to supply nutrients and to increase the ability of the soil to hold moisture.

If the soil is poor you can plant into individually amended holes (you won't need many). You might also plant in hills, by digging a hole 12″

deep by 24″ wide and half filling it with compost. Return all of the soil to the hole to form a small mound or hill. Generally these should have a slight depression in the top to aid in water absorption - otherwise they are hard to water.

About Summer Squash

Seed facts

Germ temp: 65 (80 to 95) 100° F
Germ time: 3 to 10 days
16 days / 59° F
6 days / 68° F
4 days / 77° F
3 days / 86° F * Optimum
Germination percentage: 75+
Viability: 3 to 6 years
Weeks to grow transplants: 3 to 4

Planning facts

Hardiness: Tender
Ease of growing: Easy (if there are no Vine Borers)
Growing temp: 65 to 75° F
Plants per person: 1
Plants per sq ft: ⅓
Transplants:
Start: 2 wks before last frost date
Plant out: 2 wks after last frost
Direct sow: 2 weeks after last frost
Succession sow every month
Time to harvest: 50 to 120 days

Harvest facts

Length of harvest: 12 wks
Yield per plant: 15 to 20 fruits
Yield per sq ft· 15 fruits per plant

Planning

Where: Squash are large plants that take up a lot of room, but make up for it by being very productive. The vining types are very sprawling, but can be grown on trellises or cages to make them more space efficient. You might try growing them on the site of an old compost pile. All of the Squash must have full sun for good growth.

Rotation: Don't plant Squash where any other member of the *Cucurbitaceae* (Cucumber, Melon, Pumpkin, Winter Squash) has grown within the last 3 years.

When: These tender annuals originated in the tropics and love hot weather. They can't stand cold soil, so don't plant them until it has warmed up (ideally to at least 70° F). Use black plastic to warm the soil if necessary. If the weather is very variable at this time, plant them under cloches to keep them warm. The traditional method of sowing Squash in hills probably originated to help the soil warm up faster and to provide good drainage.

Succession sowing: You may want to make at least one succession sowing, 8 weeks after the first one, so you can replace declining plants. You can direct sow the second planting, as the plants will grow rapidly in the warm weather

Planting Transplants

Starting inside: Summer Squash is one of the easiest plants to grow from seed; you really have to work at it to fail. Early Squash are usually started indoors, because spring growing weather is often less than ideal and by starting indoors you have stocky little plants ready to put outside. This is better than having to wait for seed to germinate in cold soil.

Cucurbits in general dislike transplanting, so start them in individual containers. I like to use 4″ pots as they allow you some time before the seedlings must be planted out. If containers are smaller than this you may have to pot them up before planting out, which is an additional chore. Plant two seeds in each pot. After they have both emerged, you should remove the inferior one (pinch it off to avoid disturbing the remaining one).

Planting out: It's important to plant Squash out as soon as they have 3 leaves. Don't delay as they will quickly outgrow their pots and get root-bound. Plant them as deep as their first true leaves. If cold weather threatens to return, you can cover them with cloches.

Outside: In hot weather the large seeds germinate and grow quickly and soon produce vigorous young plants. Because of this there is little point in going to all of the work of starting them inside.

The most important thing to remember is to wait until the soil is warm enough (60° F minimum), if it is cold the seed may rot. Plant 2 seeds at each location and thin to the best one. If the soil is only marginally warm enough, you could pre-sprout the seed (take care not to damage it). Such extra effort is rarely worth it however; it's better to be patient.

Hills: The traditional method of growing Squash is in hills, small mounds in which are placed a half dozen seeds (plant ½″ to 2″ deep depending on how warm the soil is). These don't work so well in hot dry areas however, as they tend to dry out quickly. In this situation you can flatten the hills out, or make them into slight depressions to hold water.

Spacing: Squash grow into big plants that need a lot of space. In intensive beds they are spaced 24″ to 36″ apart, depending upon how large the particular variety gets.

You could plant your Squash down the center of the bed and fill in the rest of the space with a fast growing crop. I usually put them at the edge of the garden, where they have minimal impact on their neighbors. The vining types can then wander off into vacant space.

The hills (which are clusters of plants) are usually spaced at least 3 feet apart.

Care

Weed: Squash grow so rapidly that weeds generally aren't a big problem. However it's always a good idea to keep weeds to a minimum (if only to prevent them setting seed). A mulch works well for these widely spaced plants.

Watering: The soil should be kept evenly moist at all times, but particularly when they are bearing heavily. The best way to water Squash is with soaker hose, as wet foliage can easily lead to fungus diseases.

Fertilization: If your soil is poor give the plants a liquid feed of compost tea every 2 to 4 weeks.

Mulch: This is helpful with these widely spaced plants, to keep down weeds and conserve moisture.

Pollination: The first few Squash flowers to appear will be males and won't produce any fruit. These will soon be followed by female flowers, which have what look like a tiny fruit behind them. If these are fertilized, the fruit will swell within 4 or 5 days. If the temperature is very cool (below 50° F) the females may not be pollinated and the tiny 'fruit' will drop off. It is quite easy to hand pollinate (see **Seed Saving** below), but this is rarely necessary.

Pests: Depending upon where you live, Squash aren't much bothered by pests, or they may be so badly affected that they may be impossible to grow.

Squash Vine Borer: In my experience this is the number one pest of Summer Squash. Indeed it is one of the worst pests of a plant you are likely to encounter in vegetable gardening. Whereas many pests simply do some damage (often not serious), this one will kill the plant almost every time, unless drastic measures are taken. If you aren't very observant, by the time the damage is apparent the plant is wilting and close to death.

If a plant starts to wilt, the commonest course of action is to cut the plant open and pry out the worm like caterpillars (I don't like killing things but it's hard not to feel satisfaction when removing these). The borers give away their location by the sawdust-like frass that comes out of little holes in the stem. You might save the plant if you bury the stems in soil, so they can send out new roots. This is a very discouraging pest when it gets bad and can cause you to stop planting Squash. After digging out 8 or 10 borers the plant may be pretty well shredded.

Another course of action is to inject B.T into the stem.

It would be much better if you could prevent the borers from entering the plant in the first place. One idea is to lay a sheet of aluminum foil 'mulch' under the plant, apparently it is supposed to fool the parent moth so she doesn't find the stems. You might also wrap the stem with aluminum foil. I moved away from the area before I had a chance to try this.

Other problems: If you are lucky enough to save your plants from the vine borer, you may be faced with a variety of other pests, including Aphids, Cucumber Beetles, Mites, Pickleworms and Squash Bugs. Diseases include Angular Leaf Spot, Alternaria Blight, Bacterial Wilt, Downy Mildew, Mosaic, Powdery Mildew.

Harvesting

When: Harvest the fruit when they are 4″ to 8″ long, which should be about 4 to 6 days after pollination. Generally it's better to harvest them when still fairly small (4″ is good), though often they are still good when twice this size. If you pick them while they are small it's easier to consume all that are produced, so less are wasted.

Whatever the size you like it is very important to pick the fruit regularly and not let any mature on the vine. Those jumbo fruits take a lot of energy and can stop the plant producing altogether.

The male flowers can be used for food (leave enough to pollinate the females of course).

How: Cut the fruits from the plant with a sharp knife to minimize damage to the vine. Leave a small section of stem on the fruit to prevent moisture loss and so improve storage life.

Storage: The fruits are best used fairly promptly. They will keep in good condition in the refrigerator for 2 weeks, but by that time you will have many more new ones.

Seed saving

Squash are cross-pollinated by insects. They will not only cross with other varieties of Summer Squash, but also some kinds of Winter Squash. This means you have to hand pollinate them, or isolate by ½ mile. As with most Cucurbits you should save the seed from at least 5 plants to ensure enough genetic variability.

Hand pollination isn't as complicated as you might imagine. Go out in the evening and find some male and female flowers that are about to open the following day and tape them shut with ¾″ masking tape.

The next day you open a male flower (from a different plant) and remove its petals. You then carefully open the female flower without damaging the petals, brush the pollen-laden anthers from the male on to the pistil lobes of the female and then tape it closed again (to prevent further pollination). This procedure should work about 50 to 75% of the time. It works even better if 2 males flowers are used to pollinate each female.

You will soon know if this has worked because a successfully pollinated flower will swell rapidly (mark it carefully so it isn't accidentally harvested). If pollination wasn't successful the flower will soon fall off. You must then leave the fertilized squash to mature fully on the vine. This will slow down further fruit production, or may even stop it altogether.

When the fruit is fully ripe it will get woody like a Winter Squash. It takes time for the fruit to ripen fully, so allow plenty of time before frost - at least 60 days). You then clean the ripe seed, dry it thoroughly and store in a cool dry place.

Unusual growing ideas
Volunteers: You will often find healthy young Squash seedlings popping up in your garden (especially around compost piles). Unfortunately you don't know what they were pollinated by (though you may have an idea if you only grew one kind) and may end up with some strange and inedible fruit.

In mild climates some people sow Squash seed in the fall, in the belief that only the most vigorous and hardy seeds will survive until the spring.

Varieties
Most Summer Squash have a bush habit, though a few are vines (Long Green Trailing, Tender and True, Tatume). There is considerable variation in the kinds of fruit they produce, in both shape (crooked, straight, round, starburst) and in color (green, yellow, white). Squash are so vigorous that there is little point using hybrids.

Black Beauty, Bennings Green Tint, Golden Zucchini, Ronde De Nice, Summer Crookneck

Cooking
Squash flowers dipped in batter and fried are a delicacy.

Squash are quite versatile in the kitchen. My favorite ways of cooking Squash include frying in Tempura and making vegetarian 'burgers' from them. They can also be eaten raw in salads.

Veggieburgers
1 cup grated squash
1 cup oats
1 cup grated onion
Salt and pepper
Oil for frying
Herbs for flavoring

This is the basic recipe. Just mix all the ingredients together and shape into patties for frying. You can flavor them with a variety of herbs and spices according to your tastes and what you have available.

Squash, winter Pumpkin

Cucurbita species

Introduction: The Winter Squash belong in the *C. pepo, C. mixta, C. moschata* and *C. maxima* species. The Pumpkins are also in these genera, so when I talk about Winter Squash I also mean Pumpkins.

Winter Squash are not the most popular vegetables these days, but their yellow flesh is rich in vitamin A and they store well. They get their name because they were the Squash you ate during the winter. They can be used as a substitute for Sweet Potato and some people consider them superior. Their main disadvantage is that they need a lot of space.

Nutritional content:
Complex carbohydrates, Vitamins B6, A and C (beta carotene to especially dark skinned ones). They also contain magnesium, potassium, thiamin and lutein.

Soil.
pH 6.0 - 7.0
These are quite hungry plants and need a soil that is loose, fertile, moisture retentive and rich in organic matter. They dislike saline or acid soils.

Soil preparation: This is the same as for Summer Squash.

About Winter Squash

Seed facts
Germ temp: 65 (80 to 95) 100° F
Germ time: 3 to 10 days
16 days / 59° F
6 days / 68° F
4 days / 77° F
3 days / 86° F * Optimum
Germination percentage: 75+
Viability: 3 to 6 years
Weeks to grow transplant: 3 to 4

Planning facts
Hardiness: Tender
Ease of growing: Easy where there are no Vine Borers)
Growing temp: 50 (65 to 75) 90° F
Plants per person: 3
Plants per sq ft: ⅓
Transplants:
Start: 2 wks before last frost date
Plant out: 2 wks after last frost
Direct sow: 2 to 4 wks after last frost
Time to harvest: 90 to 120 days

Harvest facts
Yield per plant: 3 lb (5 fruits)
Yield per sq ft: 1 lb sq ft

Planning
Where: Winter Squash are sprawling plants, notorious for taking up a lot of room; so don't plant them in the middle of the intensive garden. They take a lot less space if grown vertically on trellises or cages, but then of course they cast a considerable amount of shade. Generally it is best to plant them in hills, on the edge of the garden and let them run off into unused space. The site of an old compost pile by a wire fence is perfect. Once established they can compete with almost any plant, so long as their roots are in good soil and they are well fed and watered.

Squash will tolerate some shade, so Native Americans traditionally grew them with Corn and Beans. This is a good space saving idea, as they produce almost as well as when growing alone. See **Corn** for more on this.

When: Winter Squash are quite frost tender, so can't be planted until all danger of frost has passed and the soil has warmed up (2 to 4 weeks after the last frost). Don't put them out before the temperature reaches 65° F daily (when Apple trees blossom.) Cloches can be used in the early part of the season to keep them warmer.

Planting
Transplants
Starting inside: Winter Squash are often started indoors, to get a few extra weeks of growing time, which can be important in cool climates. The plants dislike root disturbance, so must be started in soil blocks, cell packs or individual pots.

The naked seeded varieties of Pumpkin rot very easily unless given ideal conditions and so are usually started indoors.

Direct sowing: Direct sown Winter Squash grow fast in warm soil and will often catch up with indoor sown plants. Don't plant them out until the soil is warm enough (60° F minimum) or they may simply rot in the cold ground. You can warm the soil with black plastic to get them off to a good start and protect them until the weather gets warmer. You could also pre-sprout them before planting. You only need to plant Winter Squash once in a year, so do it properly.

Hills: Plant 3 to 5 seeds, an inch deep, in each hill and thin to the best two when they have all germinated. In hot weather the best 'hills' are actually slight depressions, so water moves towards the plants, rather than away from them.

Spacing: Winter Squash sprawl so much they are usually grown in hills. These are spaced 4 to 6 feet apart, depending on the variety and the fertility of the soil.

If they are to be trained to grow up supports they can be grown closer together, perhaps as close as 30″ apart.

Care

Weed: You need to keep the young plants weeded. Once they get going they are vigorous enough to look after themselves.

Water: Winter Squash are fairly drought tolerant, but do better if the soil is kept evenly moist, especially in dry weather.

Fertilization: If your soil isn't very fertile you may want to feed the plants monthly, with compost tea or fish emulsion.

Pruning: About a month before frost is due, pinch back the growing tips. This ensures the plants put their energy into ripening the fruit they already have and won't start any more. To get larger fruit you can remove some of the smaller ones.

Frost protection: These tender plants will be killed by freezing temperatures. If an early frost threatens give them protection.

Pests: They are bothered by the same pests as Summer Squash. Squash Vine Borers seem to prefer *C. pepo* species to the others.

Harvesting

When: Winter Squash must be ripe for optimal flavor and keeping qualities. It takes 2 to 3 months from pollination to full ripeness (4 months for Pumpkins).

The fruits are normally gathered after the skin turns dull and the dry stem snaps easily. For good storage properties the skin must be too tough to dent with a fingernail. If they are not fully mature they won't store well. The fruits must be picked before frost does any damage.

How: Cut the ripe fruit from the vine, leaving about 6″ of stem attached.

Storage: Cure for 2 weeks in a warm place (80 to 90° F) and then store at around 50 to 60° F and 60 to 70% humidity. They may last 6 months or more in storage, which is why they were once important for self-sufficient farmers.

Seed saving: This is the same as for summer Squash. It takes time for the fruit to ripen properly so allow plenty of time before frost (60 to 90 days.)

Unusual growing ideas
Three Sisters: Winter Squash are the third sister (the others are Corn and Beans) in this Native

American polyculture. See **Corn** for more on this.

Volunteers: Squash occasionally volunteer and produce healthy young seedlings. Unfortunately you probably don't know what they crossed with and may end up with a pretty strange fruit.

Screen: You can train the vigorous climbing varieties along a wire fence to make a deciduous screen

Giant fruit: To grow giant show Pumpkins plant several seeds in a hill made from almost pure compost and thin to the best plant. Feed weekly with manure tea or fish emulsion and only allow one fruit to develop on each plant. You could allow three to grow if you just want big ones for your own use.

Signature: You can scratch your name on a Squash or Pumpkin and it will get bigger as the fruit matures.

Varieties: Most Winter Squash are of the vining type, though there are some bush varieties also (these take up a lot less space). The Squash vary greatly in their eating qualities; some are rather bland, while others are excellent. I like Red Kouri and Delicata.

Winter Squash may belong to several different species:

Cucurbita maxima

Banana Squash
Hubbard Squash
Turban Squash
Small Pumpkins

Native to South America, these plants have very large rounded leaves, soft hairy stems and long vines. They can be distinguished from *C. moschata* because the leaves are rougher in texture and their margins are more ragged. Buttercup, Marina di Chioggia, Queensland Blue, Blue Hubbard, Red Kuri

Cucurbita moschata

Butternut Squash.
Crookneck Squash.

Another large spreading plant, the leaves of this species are softer than the above and more entire. The flower has large sepals.

Butternut, Chirimen, Musquee de Provence, Ponca

Cucurbita mixta (this may be a variety of *C. moschata*)

Cushaw Squash

This species resembles *C. moschata* but the leaf tips are more rounded and the fruit stem doesn't flare out as much.

Green Striped Cushaw, Tennessee Sweet Potato

Cucurbita pepo

Summer Squash
Golden Acorn
Spaghetti Squash
Table Queen Squash
Pie Pumpkins

This species contain the Summer Squash varieties as well as several interesting winter types. It is distinguished by the scratchy lobed leaves and the hard angular stem on the fruit. They are more vulnerable to Squash Vine borers.

Delicata, Royal Acorn, Table Queen, Spaghetti Squash (used like Spaghetti), Lady Godiva (naked seeded)

Immature Acorn Squash can be picked and used like Summer Squash. They don't store very well.

Cooking: The mature fruits were once an important winter food in some areas (which is why they are called Winter Squash).

Butternut Squash are commonly used to make commercial "Pumpkin pie" filling.

Squash flowers can be dipped in batter and fried.

The seeds are all edible and may be roasted for an hour at 250° F. The naked seeded types don't need shelling.

Sunflower
Helianthus annuus

Introduction: Sunflower is native to North America and was long grown by Native Americans. However it first became an important commercial crop in Russia, when breeders produced a variety with unusually large, oil rich, seeds. This use quickly spread throughout Eastern Europe until they were the most important oil seed crop grown there. It is now an important crop in its native land as well, though even today many commercial varieties are of Russian origin.

Many people think of Sunflowers as an ornamental, rather than an edible crop, but the seeds are highly nutritious.

Nutritional content:

Sunflower seeds contain about 20% protein, 20% carbohydrate, 40% fat (which is very rich in essential fatty acids), several B vitamins A, calcium, iron potassium and zinc.

About Sunflowers

Germ temp: 70 to 85° F
Germ time: 7 to 14 days
Seed viability: 3 to 5 years
Yield: 3 lb / 100 sq ft.
Time to harvest: 90 days

Soil
pH: 6.0 to 7.0

Sunflowers are very hungry plants and for good growth they need rich moist soil with an abundance of nutrients. They like phosphorus and potassium, but not too much nitrogen, as this may encourage leaf growth rather than flowering.

Soil preparation: Sunflowers are hungry crops, so enrich the soil generously before planting. Incorporate 3″ of compost or aged manure, along with wood ashes, colloidal phosphate and Kelp powder.

Planning

When: Plant Sunflowers 2 weeks after the last frost date, when the soil has warmed up to at least 50° F.

Rotation: Sunflowers have a reputation for exhausting the soil if continually planted and harvested on the same piece of land. Always leave at least 3 years between crops.

Planting

Indoors: Sunflower are often started indoors for an early start. The seedlings grow rapidly, so are best started in 4″ pots (to give them plenty of room). Plant 2 to 4 seeds in each pot and when all have germinated you can thin to the best one (or two).

Outdoors: Sunflower seeds germinate and grow so rapidly they are usually direct sown. Plant them ¼″ deep

Spacing: Space the plants 12″ to 24″ apart, depending upon the variety.

Care:
Weeds: The young seedlings can't compete with weeds very well, so weed them carefully. Once they get going they will soon outgrow any weeds.

Water: Sunflowers are thirsty plants and for maximum production they need a constant supply of water.

Mulch: In hot climates a mulch is useful to conserve soil moisture. It also helps to keep down weeds.

Pests and disease: Birds love Sunflower seeds and can be a major pest in some areas. Squirrels and Raccoons can also be a problem.

Harvest:

When: When the seeds are ripe the whole heads droop, and the seeds are fat and plump. Sample a few to see if they are fully ripe.

How: The easiest way to harvest the seeds is to cut off the whole heads. Dry them in the sun and then rub the heads against a screen (or against each other) to free the seeds.

Storage: Dry the seeds carefully if you want to store them for any length of time. They will mold if they are not fully dry.

Unusual growing ideas
Sunflower Lettuce:
Sunflower seeds can be grown indoors as a seedling salad crop. Soak the seeds for 3 hours and then spread them out, one seed deep, on trays of soil, peat moss or wet kitchen paper. Keep them in a warm place and mist daily. When the seeds begin to germinate move them into full light. The greens will be ready in 1 to 3 weeks (depending upon the temperature). Cut the plants with scissors when they are 3″ to 6″ tall, leaving about an inch of stem behind.

Smother crop: Their luxuriant and rapid growth also makes Sunflowers useful as a smother crop. They have been used to eradicate persistent weeds from fields.

Temporary screen: These tall growing flowers can be used to make a quick (and pretty) temporary screen. Try growing a Sunflower maze.

Fertilizer: Sunflowers use four carbon photosynthesis which makes them more efficient when growing under high heat and light intensities. This means they can grow very quickly and produce an abundance of organic matter.

They are sometimes grown as a green manure crop, which is incorporated just before flower buds appear (which is when the plants start to turn woody). They can also be grown to produce material for the compost pile.

Apparently even their hunger for nutrients has been put to use. The plants have been used to remove an excess of nitrates from the soil.

Seed saving: Sunflowers are cross-pollinated by insects, so you can only save the seed from one variety at a time (they will also cross with wild plants).

Gathering the seed is easy, except for the fact that birds and Squirrels will take every full kernel if you don't protect them.

Varieties: There are lots or ornamental Sunflower varieties, but most don't have large enough seeds to be very useful for food. The best edible seeded varieties include:

Skyscraper
Mammoth Russian
Snack Seed

Cooking: The raw or roasted kernels can be used just like nuts, eaten out of hand, in baked goods, granola and trail mix. Native Americans often ground the whole seed to meal for baking bread and thickening soups.

Edible oil: Modern varieties of seed may contain up to 60% oil. This can be extracted by pressing the crushed seeds, or you can do as Native Americans used to. They boiled the kernels in water and skimmed the edible oil off from the surface.

Sprouts: The raw whole seed can be sprouted like Alfalfa. Don't let the sprouts get too big, or they may develop an acrid taste.

Eating Sunflower seeds: If you are to grow Sunflowers for their edible seeds, you really need to learn how to eat them. Start by putting a seed vertically between your molars (chewing teeth) so the

seed holds in the indentations. Crack the seed gently, then use your tongue to separate the smooth seed from the rough shell. Finally you spit out the shell. This is harder to do than it is to describe, and it takes quite a bit of practice to get it down smoothly. Eventually you can have a store of seeds in one cheek, crack them on the other side of your mouth and spit out the shells in a continuous stream. If you get good enough you can start playing baseball.

Sweet Potato
Ipomoea batatas

Introduction: This species is native to South America and was introduced into Europe at about the same time as the Potato. Many of the first references to the potato probably mean this species.

Sweet Potato is a relative of the Morning Glory and should not to be confused with the Yam, which is a member of the Dioscorea family. It is an important food crop in many tropical countries, but can't tolerate any cold weather. In temperate regions it can only be grown as an annual.

About Sweet Potato

Planning facts
Perennial
Hardiness: Tender
Ease of growing: Fairly easy
Growing temp: 65 (70 to 85) 95° F
Plants per person: 5
Plants per sq ft: ⅔ to 1
Weeks to grow transplants: 8 to 12
Plant out: 4 weeks after last frost
Time to harvest: 100 to 160 days

Harvest facts
Yield per plant: 4 oz to 3 lb
Yield per sq ft: 1 to 3 lb

Nutritional content:
Sweet Potato is an important food plant from a nutritional standpoint. It is a good source of Vitamin C, as well as B6 and A (beta carotene). It is rich in potassium, pectin and also contains some valuable phytochemicals including lutein and zeaxanthin.

Soil

pH 5.5 - 6.5

The Sweet Potato can be grown on soil that is too poor for most crops, though (as is usually the case) better soil will give you a larger crop. The ideal soil for Sweet Potatoes is a rich, deep, sandy loam that retains moisture. It should be fairly acidic, as this reduces disease problems.

Soil preparation: No matter what type of soil you have, adding organic matter will be beneficial for Sweet Potatoes. It will lighten a heavy clay soil and help a sandy one retain moisture. Incorporate 2″ of compost or aged manure into the top 6″ to 12″ of soil. Double digging is beneficial to loosen heavy soils. Like most root crops they need phosphorus (add colloidal phosphate) and potassium (add greensand or wood ashes). They don't need a lot of nitrogen, as it encourages the growth of foliage rather than roots

The soil is sometimes made into 6″ high ridges for growing Sweet Potatoes, as these warm up faster than flat soil. Raised beds also work well.

Planning

Where: These creeping tropical vines need as much sunlight as they can get. They also need a lot of space, so should be planted where they can sprawl without interfering with other crops. In cooler climates they must be planted in the warmest and most sheltered spot you have.

When: Sweet Potatoes absolutely must have warm soil. Don't plant them out until the soil is at least 65° F and nighttime temperatures drop no lower than 60° F. If you have to gain extra time, warm up the soil with black plastic.

Planting

Sweet Potatoes are propagated vegetatively by means of shoots taken from the tubers, known as slips. Whole tubers aren't usually planted because they send out too many shoots that would eventually compete with each other.

Though Sweet Potatoes are usually fairly easy to grow, I have encountered a problem in obtaining planting material. In traditional Sweet Potato growing areas (the southeast) they can be purchased from nurseries and in most other areas they can be bought by mail order (these don't always arrive in the best shape, but usually do fine).

My problem in California is that you can't buy them locally and you can't buy them by mail order from another state because of quarantine restrictions. I have got around this problem by raising my own slips from tubers I buy at the store. This isn't always successful however. In some years it has worked great, in other years they have not sprouted at all. It all depends upon the tuber.

Starting your own slips: It is actually pretty easy to grow your own slips if you have some unsprayed tubers. The best source of tubers are those you have grown yourself, so it is a good idea to save a few for next years planting (reckon on 12 slips per tuber). You can also use tubers from the supermarket or health food store. These are often sprayed with a sprout inhibitor, but it is said that this eventually wears off. There is also some danger of introducing virus diseases when using them.

Start sprouting the tubers 2 to 3 months before you want to plant them out.

The usual way to sprout a tuber is to half bury it in a bed of damp sand or peat moss (some people cover it with plastic to retain moisture). This should be kept at a temperature of 70 to 90° F (the warmer it is the faster it will sprout). In 4 to 8 weeks it should produce a number of vigorous shoots with healthy roots on them.

Commercial operations sprout the tubers with bottom heat and you might want to try this. In the old days this was done in hot beds filled with fresh manure, covered with a few inches of sand or soil.

You can also suspend a tuber half in water with toothpicks (like an Avocado Pit). Just make sure the top (flat end) is upright. I haven't had any luck with this method, as the tuber rotted before it sprouted.

When the slips are large enough they are carefully detached from the tuber. If you detach the slip with all of its root attached it will recover faster, but you will transfer any disease from the tuber. If you cut it an inch away from the tuber it will take longer to recover, but you may leave any disease behind.

If it's still too cold outside, you might have to transplant them into gallon pots, or a deep flat.

Planting out: I prefer to plant the slips in individual holes. Make a large hole, add a couple of handfuls of manure, along with some wood ashes. Then bury most of the slip, leaving just the tip sticking out. If the weather is still cool, cover with cloches to keep them happy. In some areas you may have to use Cutworm collars to protect them.

Spacing: Sweet Potatoes are often planted in rows, as it is a lot easier to hill them up. Space the plants 9″ to 12″ to 18″ apart, in rows 36″ to 48″ apart.

Care

These plants are quite independent and don't need much care once they are established.

Water: Established plants are quite tolerant of drought, but the soil should be kept evenly moist while they are young. Once they are growing well you should just water them when the soil gets dry. Too much water isn't a good idea, as it encourages foliage growth rather than root growth.

Fertilization: It isn't necessary to feed the plants, unless the soil is very poor, in which case give them a feed of compost tea when the tubers are developing. Don't over-feed, as this can encourage lush foliage growth at the expense of the tubers.

Mulch: In cool climates a black plastic mulch is often used to give the plants extra heat. The slips are planted through slits in the plastic. An organic mulch may be used to keep down weeds and conserve soil moisture. Don't apply this until the soil has warmed up though.

Hilling: As soon as the plants are making good healthy growth, they should be hilled up as this can increase the final yield. Of course this is impractical if you are using black plastic mulch, or if they are not planted in rows.

Frost: Sweet Potatoes are very tender and any frost will kill the tops. If an early fall frost threatens, it pays to protect them with straw mulch, cloches or even sheets. This is extra work, but you may be rewarded with several more weeks of growing weather. The large plants grow rapidly towards the end, so there can be a big benefit in leaving them in the ground as long as possible. When a hard frost threatens, dig the tubers immediately. Don't wait too long, as any damage to the tubers will affect their storability.

Pests: A lot of pests may attack Sweet Potatoes; Cucumber Beetles, Cutworms, Flea Beetles, Japanese Beetles, Sweet Potato Weevils, Tortoise Beetles, Wireworms and more. They are also vulnerable to several diseases, including Black Rot, Fusarium Wilt, Internal Cork, Pox, Scurf Stem Rot and various fungal, bacterial and viral pestilences. One of the advantages of growing them in the north is that there are a lot less pests to deal with.

Harvesting

When: You can harvest and eat the tubers as soon as they reach a useful size. However if you want to store them you must wait for them to mature fully (the lower leaves will start to turn yellow and die back). Don't worry if a lot of the tubers are small, they will still taste good.

How: Dig the tubers very gently, if they are damaged they won't store well. Leave them to dry in the sun for a few hours and then cure them at 70 to 90° F, for two weeks. They can then be stored in paper lined boxes, in a warm, well ventilated place at 50 to 60° F (they may rot if it's colder than 50° F).

Seed saving:
Sweet Potatoes aren't propagated from seeds of course. Just save some of the best tubers for propagating slips. These should be stored as described above, but even more carefully.

Unusual growing ideas

Cuttings: If you have some plants, you can also propagate Sweet Potato from cuttings.

Indoor plant: Sweet Potato vines have been used as indoor plants, though I can't imagine they are very productive when grown in this way.

Varieties:

In marginal areas the choice of variety is important if you are to have success. In northern areas you will need to grow a short season variety.

Jewel
Georgia Jet 85 to 90 days
Centennial 90 days

Tomatillo
Physalis ixocarpa

Introduction: The Tomatillo is related to the Tomato and has fairly similar cultivation requirements.

Nutritional content:
The fruit contains vitamins C and K as well as copper, iron, magnesium, manganese, phosphorus, potassium. It is also rich in niacin.

About Tomatillo

Seed facts
Germ temp: 60 to 75° F
Germ time: 5 to 14 days
Seed viability: 4 to 7 yrs
Weeks to grow transplants: 8 to 10

Planning facts
Hardiness: Tender
Ease of growing: Moderate
Growing temp: 70 to 75° F day
                50 to 55° F night
Plants per person: 2
Transplants:
Start: 6 to 8 wks before last frost
Plant out: 2 to 4 wks after last frost
Direct sow: 2 wks after last frost
Time to harvest: 75 days from transplant
Yield: 2 lb per plant

Soil
pH 6.0 - 6.8
The ideal soil is a well-drained, moisture retentive loam, with lots of organic matter.

Soil preparation: Incorporate 2″ of compost or aged manure before planting.

Planning
Where: These sub-tropical plants need the same conditions as the Tomato. As much sun as possible and a warm sheltered site.

When: Tomatillo is usually started indoors like Tomato. However if you have a long growing season, or a fast maturing variety, it is possible to direct sow them.

Planting
Planting indoors: Plant the seed ¼″ to ½″ deep (they like to be covered.) You could pre-germinate the seeds and then plant them in cell packs or soil blocks. Transplant the seedlings when their first true leaves appear.

Transplanting outside:
Before transplanting outside you must harden the seedlings off, so they become accustomed to somewhat less than ideal conditions (see Tomato for how to do this).

Bury most of the stem when transplanting and roots will form all along its length. If the plants are very leggy you should pinch out the lower leaves before planting.

If the weather is cool at transplanting time, you can warm up the soil with cloches or black plastic.

Planting outdoors: The seed should be planted ¼″ to ½″ deep, after the soil has warmed up. Pregerminating the seed inside may help to speed things up. Direct sowing isn't a very efficient way to use precious bed space. It is much better to start the seeds in a nursery bed, and only put them in the growing beds when they are good sized transplants.

Spacing: Tomatillo plants can get quite big, so space them 24″ to 36″ apart each way.

Care
Generally Tomatillos are independent plants and don't need a lot of attention.

Water: Tomatillos are quite drought tolerant, but for best fruit production they should be watered regularly.

Fertilization: Give them a feed of compost tea or liquid Kelp when the flowers first appear.

Mulch: This is helpful to conserve moisture and keep down weeds.

Support: The taller varieties will benefit from some support. Tomato cages work well.

Frost: Protect the plants from an early fall frost by covering them with plastic or hay.

Pests and disease: They are vulnerable to the same problems as Tomatoes, but aren't usually as susceptible.

Harvest: The fruits are ready to harvest one to two months after flowering (depending upon the variety). When the fruit is ripe, the husk will turn yellow and will be completely filled by the fruit. Tomatillos will ripen off the plant, so you can pick the fruit while it is still green (so long as it fills the husk).

Seed saving: This is the same as for Tomato. The fruit is more variable however, so save seed from the best-flavored plants.

Unusual growing ideas: **Volunteers**: Tomatillo plants sometimes volunteer from fruits that fell to the ground. These will be just as good as their parents, so can be allowed to mature and bear fruit.

Varieties: There are few varieties available, but not many.

Purple De Milpa: This is considered to be one of the best flavored.

Cooking: The Tomatillo is important in Mexican cooking, for its use in salsa verde and other dishes. It is not usually eaten out of hand.

Salsa Verde

12 Tomatillos
1 medium onion
½ cup Cilantro
1 tbsp lime juice
5 cloves of garlic
¼ teaspoon sugar (optional)
1 to 2 finely chopped Jalapeno peppers
1 tsp salt

Chop all the ingredients and mix thoroughly in a bowl. That's all there is to it. It is better is left overnight before eating. It is used like Tomato Salsa in Burritos, as a dip and more.

Cape Gooseberry
P. peruviana
P. pubescens

These species are close relatives of the Tomatillo and are cultivated in the same way. Their fruit are sweeter than the Tomatillo though, and are often eaten as a dessert.

Harvest: The Cape Gooseberry comes wrapped in its own husk and may be picked before it is ripe. In fact it may fall from the plant before it is ripe, hence its other name Ground Cherry. Unlike the Tomatillo the fruit don't completely fill the husk.

These perennial species are significantly hardier than the Tomato, and will often survive the winter in milder areas. They are often more productive in their second year.

Varieties:
Goldenberry, Pineapple Cherry, Strawberry

Cooking: The ripe fruit is soft, yellow and quite sweet. It can be eaten raw, or cooked in preserves and sauces.

Tomato
Lycopersicon esculentum

Introduction: Tomato is native to South and Central America and was introduced into Europe in the sixteenth century. It took a long time for the Tomato to be accepted there as a safe and wholesome food. It first became popular in Italy, and is still closely associated with Italian food. Tomato is a tender perennial, but must be grown as an annual in temperate climates

The Tomato is the most popular garden vegetable crop in America. Probably more square footage of garden magazine space has been devoted to the Tomato than any other vegetable. It is popular because it is easy to grow, very productive (it is one of highest yielding vegetable crops) and because home grown fruit is generally much superior to commercial fruit. Few food crops have suffered as much as the Tomato in the search for agri-business perfection. Tomatoes are so easy to grow they even show up in office buildings and volunteer in cracks in sidewalks.

With the exception of the ripe fruits, all parts of the Tomato are somewhat poisonous (not to mention unpleasant tasting).

Nutritional content:
Tomatoes contain vitamin C and A (beta carotene) and a whole range of valuable anticancer (and other) phytochemicals (lycopene, lutein, zeaxanthin and more).

About Tomatoes

Seed facts
Germ temp: 60 (75 to 85) 90° F
Germ time: 5 to 14 days
43 days / 50° F
14 days / 59° F
8 days / 68° F
6 days / 77° F * Optimum
6 days / 86° F
Seed viability: 3 to 7 years
Germination percentage: 75%+
Weeks to grow transplant: 8 to 10

Planning facts
Hardiness: Tender
Ease of growing: Easy
Growing temp:
    70 to 75° F day
    50 to 55° F night
Plants per person: 10
Plants per sq ft: ½
Transplants:
Start: 6 to 8 wks before last frost
Plant out: 2 weeks after last frost
Succession sow: 6 weeks later
Time to harvest: 80 to 120 days
50 to 85 days from transplanting

Harvest facts
Length of harvest: 12 to 16 weeks
Yield per plant: 2 to 6 lb
Yield per sq ft: 1 to 3 lb sq ft

Soil
pH 5.5 (6.0 - 6.8) 7.5
Tomatoes aren't particularly fussy about soil, but generally the better the soil the larger the fruit. The perfect soil for Tomatoes is a deep, well-drained (they are prone to root rot in wet soils) loam with lots of moisture retentive organic matter. Early crops do better in light sandy soil because it warms up faster. They prefer a fairly neutral soil, but aren't very sensitive to pH.

Tomatoes are quite heavy feeders, using a lot of nitrogen (180 lb /acre), a moderate amount of phosphorus (21 lb / acre) and a lot of potassium (280 lb / acre). They have deep roots that may go down 5 feet, but most of their feeder roots are in the top 2 feet.

Soil Preparation:
Nitrogen: This is most important during the initial vegetative growth stage, though some is also needed for fruit set. If they get too much nitrogen they may produce excessive foliage instead of fruiting.

Phosphorus: Put a handful of bonemeal or colloidal phosphate in the planting hole, to supply phosphorus for early growth and good fruit set (a lack of it can delay maturation). I read somewhere that Alan Chadwick used to put a layer of phosphorus in the top 4″ of soil and another down 18″ deep to account for this (but that is getting a little too complicated for me).

Potassium: This is also important while the plants are young. Put a handful of greensand or wood ashes in the planting hole

Other nutrients: Tomatoes need calcium (dolomitic lime) and trace elements (organic matter and Kelp) right through their growth cycle. If you have added lots of well-rotted compost, or aged manure, to the soil before planting, this will supply all of the micronutrients they need.

Planning
Where: Tomatoes need a warm sheltered site and a minimum of 6 hours of sun daily, any less and they won't produce very well. Disease is more prevalent in moist and shady sites, so avoid them.

If the climate is cool, put them against a south facing wall or on a south facing slope. You could also grow them under cloches, or in the greenhouse.

Crop rotation: Don't plant Tomatoes where any other member of the *Solanaceae* (Eggplant, Pepper, Potato) has grown within the last 3 years.

When:
Tomatoes are very tender and have little tolerance for frost. They are usually started indoors about 2 to 3 months before the last frost date. The seedlings can be planted out a couple of weeks after the last frost date.

Generally determinate varieties need 6 to 8 weeks to be ready for transplanting outside. The rather slower indeterminate varieties may take 8 to 12 weeks to attain a suitable size. If you have a very long growing season you can direct sow them outside.

It is important that the soil be sufficiently warm (60° F minimum) for planting Tomatoes. If it is too cold they will simply sit there without growing and may even be permanently retarded. For very early plantings you might warm up the soil with black plastic and use cloches to protect the young plants.

Succession

Succession: Though Tomatoes will produce fruit for quite a while, they do have a peak bearing season and eventually get less productive (even indeterminate types). You might want to plant a succession sowing 8 weeks after the first (or direct sow some plants when planting the first batch out). However I usually just plant several varieties with different maturation times.

Cuttings for succession:

A quick way to get plants for a second sowing is to use cuttings. Pinch out some of the suckers from your favorite plants and root them in water. These cuttings will give you new plants much faster than growing them from seed.

Planting

Buying transplants: This is the easiest way to get Tomatoes, though you don't get as much choice as to varieties. You may also buy problems, in the form of disease or insect pests, so check them carefully before you buy.

The best transplants are about 8″ tall and stocky (never leggy). Don't buy plants with flowers, or tiny fruit, in the belief this will save you time. Premature flowering is actually a sign of stress.

The larger the plant, the greater the setback from transplanting, which is why smaller plants do better in the long term.

Transplants

Starting indoors: The seeds should be planted ¼″ or ½″ deep in flats, soil blocks or cell packs and put in a warm place to germinate. They germinate best at a tempera-ture of around 75 to 85° F during the daytime and 10° F lower at night.

When their first true leaves appear, the plants should be transplanted to individual 4″ pots. Plant them deeper than they were growing, as they will produce roots all along the buried stem. Temperature can also be slightly lower (65 to 75° F in the day and 55 to 65° F at night).

You must now give the seedling everything it's little green heart desires: water, humidity, warmth and all the nutrients it needs.

Once the roots have filled the soil in the pot, you must either plant them out or move them to bigger pots. Don't let them linger inside, as the roots will start to circle around and it will get root-bound. They may even start to flower, which (as I just explained) is not good

Hardening off: If you are planting Tomatoes out in cool spring conditions, they should be hardened off carefully. Do this slowly over a week, by reducing the amount of water they get and by leaving them outside for longer periods each day. This helps them to slowly get accustomed to the somewhat less than ideal conditions to be found outside.

In warm summer weather there is no need to harden them off. However you may want to keep them outside in the shade for a few days, so they don't get sunburned when planted out.

Planting out: The best time to transplant Tomatoes (or anything else) is on a cool cloudy day, if rain threatens even better. If you don't get cool cloudy days, then trans-plant them in the early evening, not in the heat of the day.

You can give Tomatoes a lot of attention while planting, because you don't usually plant very many. Dig a fairly large planting hole and amend it with a couple of handfuls of compost. Plant the seedlings so most of the stem is buried (pinch off the lower leaves) and they will grow roots along the buried stem.

Very large or leggy plants can be planted sideways in a shallow trench. They will produce roots all along the buried stem and will benefit from the warmth of the shallow soil near the surface.

Water well after planting and keep the plants moist until they are well established. It is a good idea to put the supporting stakes, or cages, in the ground at this time, to avoid disturbing the plants later.

If you have a Cutworm problem, wrap collars of aluminum foil or paper around the stem near ground level. A ring of wood ashes is also said to help.

Direct sowing: Sowing seed directly outdoors is only a practical proposition in areas with a very long growing season.

The seed should be planted ¼″ to ½″ deep, after the soil has warmed up. Pre-germinating the seed inside may help to speed things up.

Of course the problem with direct sowing is that the plants take up bed space from the moment they are planted, but don't give any return for months. It is much more efficient to raise transplants in an outdoor nursery bed.

Spacing: Traditionally Tomatoes are spaced 18″ to 36″ apart, in rows that are 36″ to 60″ apart. Intensive spacing puts plants at 18″ to 24″ to 30″ apart. The considerable variation in spacing is due to the difference in the size of the varieties and in the fertility of the soil.

Very close spacing of Tomatoes reduces the yield per plant, but may actually increase the yield per area, as you grow more plants. Sunlight isn't needed for ripening the fruit, so the foliage can be quite dense.

Determinate and indeterminate

Determinate plants only grow to a certain height and then flower and produce fruit. They produce one flower cluster on each side branch and then stop growing. They are then finished. These varieties are hardier, shorter (good for under cloches), earlier and produce a lot of fruit in a short time (usually 4 to 6 weeks).

Indeterminate plants never stop growing (at least theoretically). The side branches keep growing and can eventually turn into another stem, producing many clusters of flowers. They take longer to start bearing, but keep producing for much longer. They produce more poundage of fruit per square foot than the determinate types.

Care

For highest productivity Tomatoes need a steady supply of available water and nutrients. If you give them all they need, they will respond by flowering earlier and fruiting more profusely.

Watering: Tomatoes are quite drought tolerant and don't really need a lot of water. More water means more and larger (but less tasty) fruit, while less water means fewer (but better flavored) fruit.

You don't need to water these deep rooted plants very often, in fact keeping them dry encourages strong root growth. The time to give them water is when the fruit are sizing up. At this time give them water daily, or twice a week.

Don't get Tomato foliage wet, as it can invite the spread of fungus disease. Uneven watering may cause Blossom End Rot or cracking. Drip irrigation works very well with Tomatoes, as it keeps the soil evenly moist but the plants stay dry.

Dry gardening: Tomatoes were once commonly dry farmed in California, where they received no irrigation water (or rainfall) at all. Such plants are markedly sweeter than conventionally grown plants. This is well worth trying if you have a lot of space, but a limited amount of water for irrigation.

In a dry garden the plants must be spaced further apart than in a conventional irrigated garden. This eliminates competition with neighboring plants and gives their roots more space to forage for water. A mulch is also helpful, as it conserves moisture and keeps down thirsty weeds.

Fertilization: Give your plants a liquid feed of compost tea or liquid Kelp, after the first fruits are set. When the plants start producing fruit, you should feed them regularly.

Mulch: A mulch is useful to keep down weeds, conserve moisture and keep the fruit clean. It can also reduce disease problems by keeping soil off of the foliage. Don't put down an organic mulch until the soil is warm (when plants start to flower), as it could insulate the soil and keep it cool. In very hot areas mulch is useful to keep the soil cool.

Support: It isn't really essential to support your plants, they can just sprawl on the ground. However when plants are supported the loss of fruit to disease, rotting and pests is much less and one can grow more plants in a given area. As a result the harvest can be significantly larger.

Determinate varieties tend to be smaller and are often allowed to simply sprawl on the ground. Indeterminate varieties can get quite large and usually do better if given some kind of support.

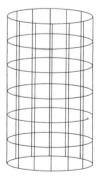

I tend to go for the easiest kind of support, because I value efficiency and getting the most results for the least effort. In my opinion this is the wire cage. Commercial Tomato cages are widely available, but not always big enough. It's cheaper to make your own, and you can make them any size you like. I use 6″ square concrete reinforcing wire mesh, to make cylinders 18″ in diameter. They can be any height you want (3, 4, 5 or 6 feet tall). In windy areas it is a good idea to fasten the taller cages to short stakes, so they don't get blown over.

You can also open up these cylinders and spread them across the bed like wire cloche frames. The plants will grow up through the mesh and sprawl on the top. In spring you can cover these with plastic to make a cloche for early growing.

The simplest and cheapest supports are Bamboo or wooden stakes. Their length is determined by the eventual height of the plants, plus 12″ or so, to go down in to the ground They may need to be 4 feet tall for some varieties, 6 feet tall for others. It's a good idea to put these in the ground while planting, to minimize future root disturbance. The plant can be tied to the stake with strips of cloth or wire ties.

Pruning:
Some people prune their tomatoes, mostly control freaks without enough to do. It basically consists of pinching out all the suckers (these appear in the axils of leaves) you don't want to grow into stems.

Pruning is most often done in cool climates to reduce the number of fruit produced and give them a better chance of ripening. It can also improve fruit quality by increasing the amount of light entering the plant and increasing aeration. It may hasten maturation by as much as two weeks and allows for closer spacing of plants.

Pruning reduces the area for photosynthesis, so means less fruit per plant (yields may be half that of unpruned plants).

Determinate plants should never be pruned, as it will reduce their already limited yields.

I don't bother with pruning, it seems like extra work I don't need to do. The most efficient way to grow Tomatoes is to use indeterminate varieties, unpruned, in cages.

Double stem: More fruit can be obtained if you allow one sucker to develop into a second stem (this is really training rather than pruning). You pinch out all suckers, except the one below the first flower cluster. This will quickly grow into a second stem. It can be supported by planting two flexible stakes together and spreading them apart at the top with a small stick. One stem is trained up each stake. A third stem could produce even more fruit, but this gets rather complicated.

Frost protection:
Spring frost protection: This is rarely needed, because you don't plant Tomatoes until the soil is warm. If a rare late frost threatens, it is not difficult to cover the low plants with row covers, mulch, plant pots or whatever is at hand.

Fall frost protection: This is important, as an early frost will usually kill unprotected Tomato plants. If you can help your plants make it through these first frosts there may not be another one for several weeks, during which time you can get a lot more ripe fruit. Almost anything can help them to survive a mild frost, old bed sheets, straw mulch, plastic sheet, cardboard.

Pollination: Most Tomato varieties are self-pollinated, so pollination isn't usually a problem. Often the first flowers fall off without bearing fruit, especially if temperatures go below 60° F, or above 90° F. In very hot weather you should water frequently to keep the plants cool. In cool weather you should put them under cloches.

Pests and disease: When I said Tomatoes are one of the easiest crops to grow, I could have added **if** you don't encounter a serious pest or disease problem. They have so many potential enemies, that it seems like it must be impossible to grow them.

Aphids, Cutworms, Colorado Potato Beetles, Flea Beetles, , Leafhoppers, Mites, Nematodes, Stink Bugs, Tomato Fruitworms and of course slugs and snails.

Diseases include Anthracnose, Bacterial Canker, Bacterial Spot, Early Blight, Southern Bacterial Wilt, Fusarium Wilt, Verticillium Wilt.

You can help to keep some of these problems under control by rotation. Be careful when watering as many diseases can be spread on wet leaves (use drip irrigation). Many modern Tomato varieties are resistant to Verticillium Wilt (V), Fusarium Wilt (F) and Nematodes (N).

Tomato Hornworm: These huge bizarre looking caterpillars can do a lot of damage to Tomato plants. I used to hand pick and kill them (usually with a stick as touching them didn't appeal to me). After a time I resorted to deportation from the garden, after I realized they turn into a spectacular moth (I know the deported caterpillars may well have died with no Tomatoes to eat, but I can't think of everything!) In recent years I haven't done anything, as Trichogramma wasps do the job for me. Their white egg cases can be seen on the motionless and unfortunate Caterpillars - I almost feel sorry for them.

Tobacco Mosaic: This serious disease can be spread by smokers who handle the plant after smoking cigarettes. It may also be brought into the garden on seedling Tomatoes. Prevent it by growing your own seedlings and not smoking.

Late Blight: This is the same killer that gets potatoes and is worse in cool humid weather. Spots appear on the leaves and then the whole plant turns black and dies (often overnight). You may be able to control it by removing infected plants immediately, but it's an indication that the plants don't like the growing conditions. Up in Western Washington I had whole beds of Tomatoes and Potatoes die almost overnight. They just didn't like the cool moist conditions (whereas the Late Blight did).

Other Tomato problems
Blossom end rot: Patches on the fruit turn black and rot. This isn't a disease and is usually caused by lack of water at some stage in development, or lack of calcium. It most commonly affects the first few trusses of fruit. Remove any affected fruit immediately (they won't be any use anyway), to reduce stress on the plant. Pruning may make this problem worse. For some reason indeterminate varieties are less commonly affected.

Sunscald: This is caused by too little leaf cover to shade the fruits and is most common on pruned plants. The simple answer is stop pruning. Another simple answer is to put the plants closer together.

Catfacing: This is caused by poor pollination and most often occurs in cool weather.

Splitting: This is caused by a sudden abundance of water, causing the inside of the fruit to grow faster than the skin.

Slugs and Snails: These can damage a good proportion of the fruit on unsupported plants.

Harvesting
When: The fruit will usually be ready to harvest 45 to 75 days after flowering (depending on variety).

The fruit takes 30 to 45 days to reach full green size (where it will ripen off the plant) and a further 15 to 30 days to reach full ripeness. They are fully ripe about a week after they turn red. The fruit won't usually ripen below 55° F, or above 85° F.

Sun isn't necessary for ripening, only warmth, consequently fruits will ripen even in the dense shade in the middle of a plant.

How: I'm sure you can recognize a ripe Tomato. Gather the fruit when it comes away from the vine easily. Their flavor is at its peak when they are fully ripe. They can be gathered earlier however, as they will ripen off the vine.

If frost threatens, gather any fruits that are nearly full size, even if they are still green and ripen them indoors in a warm place. They won't be as good as fruit ripened on the vine (they will also have less vitamin C), but they'll probably be as good as anything you could buy.

Storage: Never store Tomatoes in the fridge, or below 55° F as it spoils their flavor. They should keep for a week or two at 55 to 65° F.

Tomatoes can be peeled and frozen for storage (peel by dipping in boiling water), or you can freeze the puree.

Green Tomatoes can be ripened in a warm dark place. Just make sure the fruit don't touch each other and remove any that start to rot (check them regularly). There are varieties (i.e. Burpees Long Keeper) that are intended for slow ripening indoors. If you have a lot of green fruit, keep them in a cool place and bring them into the warmth to ripen as needed (it takes about 2 weeks.)

Seed saving: Tomatoes are usually self-pollinated so saving seed is easy. A few varieties have a high degree of cross-pollination (these usually have long stigmas that stick out of the corolla) and should be isolated for purity, either by distance or row covers.

To get the seed, simply squeeze it from the ripe fruit (eat the rest), add a little water and let it ferment in a warm place for a few days. Then scrape the scum from the top and rinse the seeds several times to remove bits of flesh. Strain the cleaned seed and dry it, first on paper towels and then in a warm dry place.

Unusual growing ideas
Volunteers: Tomatoes are commonly found as volunteers in the garden. If these are not hybrids and you have the room, you might allow some of them to mature for a late crop.

Cool climate growing: To
grow Tomatoes outside in cooler climates, you have to use one of the fastest maturing and cold hardy varieties, such as the Sub-Arctics or Siberians (which may mean sacrificing some flavor). Start them inside early, warm the soil with plastic and cover the transplants with cloches.

Early crops: This is pretty much the same as cold climate growing. Use an early, fast maturing variety, give it an early start inside, warm the soil with plastic and cover the transplants with cloches (or put a Tomato cage in place and wrap it with plastic).

Containers: Some Tomato varieties do well in containers, especially the determinate Cherry types. The bigger the plant, the bigger the container needed. You can also grow Tomatoes in grow bags, which are simply large plastic sacks filled with potting mix. Some varieties even do well in hanging baskets.

Cuttings: You can get extra Tomato plants by rooting suckers in water. This is a good way to multiply a single special plant you might have.

Greenhouse: Tomatoes are a great greenhouse crop and in cooler climates this may be the only way you can grow them. They can be grown inside from early spring until later fall. In Europe there are varieties bred specifically for greenhouse growing.

Varieties: For a long time modern seed producers focused on the needs of commercial growers (understandably because they buy their seed by the 5 gallon bucket). Their breeding work often concentrated on producing fruit that could withstand mechanical cultivation and harvesting (one of its more dubious achievements was in the infamous square tomato).

Home gardeners were largely ignored by these seed companies, so many gardeners started to ignore

them. They turned instead to the vast number of varieties that already existed, plants that have now come to be known as heirlooms. These are gifts to us from the gardeners of the past and are the common heritage of gardeners all around the world.

Probably no other crop has benefited as much from the recent interest in heirloom vegetables, as the Tomato. We now have a fantastic range of varieties, from 2-pound monsters down to the size of a pea. Determinate and indeterminate, early, mid-season, late, paste, black, purple, orange, yellow, long keeping ones. They are now even finding their way on to supermarket shelves.

The number of days to maturity mentioned on seed packets and in catalogs means from transplanting (so add 6 to 10 weeks to this).

There are also lots of good hybrid varieties out there. I avoid them though, because there are so many fantastic open pollinated varieties to choose from (and because saving Tomato seed is so easy).

Taste: My first criteria in choosing a Tomato is flavor. The flavor of different varieties varies enormously, some are almost tasteless and others are delicious. Why would anyone want to grow a picture perfect fruit that doesn't taste of anything? If I'm going to the trouble of raising a plant from seed, I want to have something special to show for it.

Climate also affects flavor, a variety may taste good in one area, but be relatively tasteless in another. In cool climates the large fruited types don't develop their best flavor, so stick to the small or medium sized ones. It really pays to experiment to find the best varieties for your area.

The number of Tomato varieties has exploded in recent years. Here is a tiny sampling of what is available.

Early:
Glacier (55 days), Beaverlodge Slicer (55 days)
Siberian (60 days) Stupice (65 days) Oregon Spring (80 days)
Early Girl (80 days)

Main
Beefsteak, Brandywine, Ponderosa, Marmande, Mortgage Lifter,

Sauce
Amish Paste, Principe Borghese, Roma, San Pablo

Cherry
Camp Joy, Chadwick Cherry, Gardeners Delight,

Unusual
Caro Red: Contains 10 times vitamin A of most Tomatoes.

Green Grape: Produces a small greenish fruit like a grape.

Cooking: Tomatoes are a very versatile food. They are good raw or cooked and of course are a basic ingredient of Italian cooking.

Salsa
This is quick and easy to make and very satisfying. All the more so because you can gather most of the ingredients from your garden.

8 Tomatoes
1 medium Onion
6 cloves garlic
½ cup Cilantro
1 or 2 finely chopped Jalapeno peppers
1 tbsp lime juice
½ tsp salt

Chop all the ingredients and mix together. Some people use a food processor, others prefer to hand chop. This is so good it is commonly eaten immediately, but it will be much better if left in the fridge overnight.

This is only a basic recipe and can be altered any way you like. You will probably want to vary the quantity of Pepper you use, depending upon personal taste and how hot your peppers are.

Turnip
Brassica rapa

Introduction: This cool season biennial was probably domesticated independently in two quite different places. Somewhere in the vicinity of Afghanistan and in the eastern Mediterranean.

In Europe the large swollen roots have been grown for centuries as food for animals and poor humans. They were scorned by the better off classes, as only fit for animals and still carry a slight stigma to this day. In Asia the Turnip is looked upon very differently and it is a very important crop in both China and Japan. In those countries a whole range of varieties exist.

Turnips are a fast growing and surprisingly versatile crop. The roots provide a substantial root vegetable, the leaves are nutritious greens, the flower buds can be used like Broccoli (they are popular in Italy under the name Broccoli Raab) and the seeds can be sprouted like Cress or Alfalfa.

Nutritional content:
From a nutritional standpoint the leaves are more nutritious than the roots. They are rich in vitamins A, C and K, chlorophyll and some important phytochemicals (including isothiocyanates).

The roots contain vitamin C, complex carbohydrates, soluble fiber, lysine and tryptophan.

Soil
pH 6.0 (6.8) 7.5
Turnips need to grow quickly for best quality. This requires a rich,

loose, well drained (but moisture retentive) soil. Brassicas in general do well on fairly neutral, or even somewhat alkaline soil. They don't like acid soils, as anything below pH 6.5 encourages the notorious Clubroot.

Like other Brassicas Turnips are vulnerable to boron deficiency, but this shouldn't be a problem if you add lots of organic matter.

About Turnip

Seed facts
Germ temp: 40 (60 to 85) 105° F
Germ time: 6 to 10 days
5 days at 50° F
3 days at 59° F
2 days at 68° F
1 day at 77° F * Optimum
Seed viability: 3 yrs
Germination percentage: 75%+

Planning facts
Hardiness: Hardy
Ease of growing: Easy
Growing temp: 40 (60 to 65) 85° F
Plants per person: 5
Plants per sq ft: 9
Direct sow: 4 wks before last frost
Fall crop: Plant mid summer onward
Time to harvest: 40 to 80 days

Harvest facts
Yield per plant: 3 to 16 oz
Yield per sq ft: 2 to 4 lb

Soil preparation: Like most root crops Turnips prefer a loose soil. If the soil is heavy, or compacted, it can be loosened by incorporating 2″ of compost or aged manure. Double digging is also very beneficial. A good practice is to plant Turnips on soil that was thoroughly dug and manured for a previous crop (such as potatoes).

Turnips don't require a lot of nitrogen (unless you are growing them for greens) as this encourages foliage growth rather than root growth.

Turnips like lime, as it supplies calcium and decreases acidity.

Planning

Where: Turnips need sun for good root growth. Leaf Turnips will do quite well in part shade.

Crop rotation: Turnips should not be planted where another Brassica crop has grown in the last 3 years.

When: Turnip is a cool weather plant and needs cold to encourage it to store sugars in the root, rather than make foliage. In warm weather the roots often become pungent, bitter and woody. This means that spring planted Turnips won't be as good as those planted as a fall crop.

Spring: Turnip can survive temperatures of 25° F and can be sown as soon as the soil can be worked in the spring (when it may only be 45° F). However it's generally better to wait until perhaps 4 weeks before the last spring frost. Very early plantings often take so long to grow in the cool weather, that later ones catch up with them. The first plantings may be done under cloches to speed up their growth. As it gets warmer the flavor of the Turnips will deteriorate.

Fall: Turnips do much better as a fall crop, as they have a longer period of cool weather. There are also less problems from insect pests. Fall Turnips are planted from July to September, so they reach maturity just before it starts to get cold.

Winter: In northern Europe fall planted Turnips were once an important winter crop.

It is possible to plant Turnips in the fall, for use as a Broccoli Raab or spring greens.

Succession sowing: You don't need many Turnip plants at one time. Sow a few seeds every 2 weeks, rather than a large number all at once. The exception to this would be a fall planting for storage, or over-wintering in the ground.

Planting

Direct sowing: Like most root crops, Turnips don't transplant well, so they are almost always direct sown. They can be broadcast or sown in drills. Sow the seeds ¼″ to ½″ deep and 1″ apart.

Spacing: Space the plants 3″ to 6″ apart in the intensive beds.

Care
The best Turnips are those that have grown rapidly, which can only occur if the plants have everything they need in the way of nutrients, light and water.

Thinning: Like other direct sown root crops, they need careful thinning and weeding. Use the thinnings in the kitchen.

Fertilization: Give the plants a feed of compost tea, or liquid Kelp, once they get going (not too much nitrogen though).

Water: Turnips don't need a lot of water, but it should be available constantly and not fluctuate too much. If the soil gets too dry, they can get woody and may even bolt.

Mulch: This is useful to prevent the soil drying out, to suppress weeds and to keep the soil cool.

Bolting: This common problem is by no means unique to Turnips. It happens to many biennial crops when they are exposed to temperatures below 50° F for two weeks and then it gets warm. The plant thinks winter has passed and so starts the flowering process. For this to happen the plant must have a stem diameter of at least ¼″.

Pests: Turnips are close relatives of the Cabbages and are vulnerable to the same pests (of which there are a considerable number.) Flea Beetles and Aphids have been the biggest problems for me.

Harvesting
Roots:

Spring roots should be harvested when they are still quite small, from 1½″ to 3″ in diameter (this may be within 6 weeks of sowing). As they get larger than this they usually start to turn woody.

Winter roots can be harvested when somewhat larger, as they stay in much better condition in the cold weather. They are at their best after their tops have been killed by frost.

After pulling the root you should cut off the tops (leave about 1″), so they don't draw moisture from the root. If the tops aren't too tough you can use them as a green vegetable.

Leaves: The tender young foliage can be harvested as required. Don't take too many leaves from a single plant as you can stunt the growth of its root (unless of course you are growing it for foliage). Take the tender new inner leaves from older plants (take care not to cut out the growing point however).

Storage: The roots should be stored in a root cellar at 34 to 40° F (if it's warmer than this they will eventually start growing). In milder areas they can be left outside under mulch, or in a clamp (see **Potato**). Some people say this is not a good idea as it may help Brassica pests to winter over.

The root can be cut into cubes and frozen.

Seed saving: Turnip is cross-pollinated by insects (that's why they have pretty flowers), so only one variety can be flowering within a half mile.

The commonest method of obtaining seed is to plant it in late summer, protect it over the winter (inside or outside) and allow it to flower in spring. It should be planted in blocks so insects are likely to visit many plants without going to other plants nearby. You collect the dry pods when they are ripe (they shatter easily so watch carefully), sift out the seeds, dry further and store.

In milder areas Turnips may self-seed if given the opportunity.

Broccoli Raab

In this country this Italian delicacy can be found in markets catering to Italian communities. It isn't a highly productive crop, but it is very welcome when it appears in early spring and the garden has little else to offer. It is grown pretty much like root Turnips.

Fall: The best time to plant Broccoli Raab is in late summer. If it gets very cold, cover the plants with mulch to protect them, as they may die if it gets too cold. In early spring the plants bolt and send up slender flower stems. These aren't nearly as large as Broccoli, but are used in much the same ways. The top 6″ to 8″ of stem is cut before the flower buds open and is steamed or eaten raw. The plant will then produce many usable side shoots.

Spring: Broccoli Raab can also be planted as a spring crop, started 4 weeks before the last frost, though it doesn't usually do as well. In cool climates it may be succession sown several times.

Forcing: Any surplus roots can be used as a source of winter greens. They are potted up and forced like those of Chicory.

Varieties: In England and Japan, where Turnips are very popular, they have special varieties for early planting and late planting, as well as some very dependable F1 hybrids.

Purple Top White Globe: The old standard.

Milan, Snowball.

Shogoin; A dual purpose crop grown for leafy greens or roots.

Seven Top: Important in the Southeast for Turnip Greens. It can also be used for Broccoli Raab

Tendergreen: This leaf variety is often thought of as a Mustard, but is actually a kind of Turnip

Cooking: Small Turnip roots (about 1½″ diameter) can be used as a substitute for Radish. They are actually milder and better flavored than most Radishes.

The flowers and immature seedpods are a tasty minor additions to salads.

Watercress
Nasturtium officinale

Introduction: Watercress is highly nutritious and has been regarded as a special food for several thousand years. However for most of this time it has been gathered from the wild, rather than cultivated.

The cultivation of Watercress is rather specialized, because of specific habitat requirements, but it grows easily enough if given the right conditions. It grows best in springs, ditches and shallow streams. In Europe it was once grown in special Watercress beds, created beside streams to take advantage of the slowly flowing water. It will grow in any wet soil, so long as it isn't too still or stagnant (which can cause the plants to rot).

Growing Watercress for yourself ensures that it is safe for use raw, which isn't always the case with plants gathered from the wild.

Nutritional content:
Watercress is continuously bathed in nutrients as they are washed from the soil. Consequently it is very rich in minerals, including copper, iron, iodine (perhaps the richest source of any land plant), manganese and sulfur. It is also a good source of vitamins A, C and E.

Watercress also contains the irritating mustard oil found in many members of the *Brassicaceae* and can irritate the kidneys if eaten in excess.

Soil: Watercress is accustomed to being bathed in nutrients as they float by, so needs a fertile soil.

Where: Watercress doesn't have to be grown in water, it can be grown on dry land. However care must be taken to keep it moist and it isn't as vigorous under these conditions. A good way to grow it is in shallow trenches (enrich the soil with lots of organic matter), which slows down the rate at which the soil dries out.

Watercress will do well in a shady place and won't need as much water if out of direct sunlight.

Planting: This plant is easily grown from seed (this is usually started inside), but it is faster and easier to get a bunch of fresh Watercress from a market and root it in water. All you have to do is put the plants in water and they will grow roots within a week or so. Of course plants grown from cuttings will all be genetically identical and so have the same degree of vulnerability to disease.

Watercress also transplants well, so you could take some from the wild and re-domesticate it.

Feeding: If the soil isn't very fertile you should give it an occasional feed of compost tea or liquid Kelp.

Watering: Watercress will need frequent watering if it isn't growing in water (every day in dry weather).

For good growth the soil must be kept moist all the time.

Pests: Commercial plantings are sometimes attacked by viruses, which is why it is often started from seed. Small home plantings are rarely bothered by anything, except drying out.

Harvest: When growing in water (with its temperature moderating influence) Watercress can often be gathered year round. Gather the plants by pinching off the growing tips, leaving the roots and lower leaves to continue growing. It is usually palatable at all times and stages of growth. Remove any flower heads that form, so the plant can devote its energy to vegetative growth.

Seed saving: Watercress produces seed easily, but this isn't really needed for propagation, as it is usually multiplied vegetatively.

Unusual growing ideas:
Given a suitable site, Watercress is a reliable, hardy and easily maintained perennial crop. It could be a valuable part of a cultivated freshwater ecosystem, providing shelter and food for numerous organisms. These in turn provide food for fish, birds and small mammals.

Pipe system. Get some 6" diameter plastic pipe and cut it lengthwise into 2 halves. Almost fill it with gravel and then plant Watercress in plastic containers filled with peat moss. Put the sections of pipe underneath an outdoor tap, so they can be watered easily.

Wastewater: Watercress can help to purify gray water, though of course you wouldn't want to eat it from this source.

Varieties: I have never seen any.

Cooking: Raw Watercress is good in salads, sandwiches and salad dressings. It is also good cooked as a potherb and in sauces, soups and stir fries.

Watercress sandwiches

These are perfect for impressing someone with your refined gentility.

4 cups finely chopped cucumber
1 cup watercress
¼ cup butter, softened
1 tbsp chives
⅛ cup mayonnaise
½ teaspoon salt
⅛ teaspoon ground black pepper
Whole wheat bread

Put the salt on the cucumbers and leave for 15 minutes. Then mix them with the pepper, chopped chives and butter.

Spread mayonnaise on 6 slices of bread and then a layer of chopped watercress. Spread the cucumber mixture on another 6 slices. Put them together, trim off the crusts and cut into triangles. I suppose you could argue they are cucumber sandwiches as much as watercress. Either way they are very good

Wheat
Triticum aestivum
syn *T. vulgare*

Introduction: Most gardening books don't even consider growing wheat as a garden crop and some of those that do reject the idea. Generally the reason for this is not that it's hard to grow, but rather that Midwestern wheat growers are so efficient and have such an ideal climate that somehow we can't 'compete' with them. In fact home wheat growing can be quite practical. I'm not suggesting that you grow it instead of more conventional crops, but if you have the space and inclination it could be an interesting and rewarding project. It could also be an important step towards food self-sufficiency.

The growing of wheat was once an important occupation for many Northern Europeans and it has entered into our culture in many different ways.

Nutritional content: The seed is rich in protein (though somewhat incomplete), as well as complex carbohydrates. They also contain iron, manganese, selenium, zinc, niacin, riboflavin and thiamin.

Soil
pH 5.5 - 7.0
To grow good wheat you need a good soil. It should be well drained, fertile and moisture retentive. The type of soil doesn't matter too much, so long as it contains plenty of nutrients.

Bed preparation: Wheat has deep penetrating roots, so a thoroughly double dug bed is ideal. Add a 2″ layer of compost or aged manure, as well as greensand or wood ashes (for potassium) and colloidal phosphate for phosphorus).

About Wheat

Germination time: 1 to 7 days
Seed viability: 5 years
Yield: 2 oz per sq ft
Time to harvest: days
Ease of growing: Easy

Planning

Where: Wheat needs full sun. Relative to other crops it takes up quite a bit of space, but not that much. A single 100 square foot bed could yield 10 pounds of grain, or even more. There is probably no point growing much less than this, except perhaps as a seed crop.

When: Wheat prefers cool weather for best growth and can be sown in autumn or spring.

Winter Wheat: This is grown in areas with mild winters, where the temperature doesn't go much below 20° F. It is planted in autumn and should be well established by the time cold weather arrives. Timing is important because it shouldn't be too advanced by this point. If the plants are too big they may lodge (fall over) the following spring and then they won't yield well. The plants go dormant over the winter, but start growing as soon as spring arrives and mature in early summer. The crop is out of the ground early enough that another crop can be planted (dry beans are good).

When grown as a Winter crop Wheat can get most of its water from winter rains and so doesn't require irrigation (which is a big deal around here).

Spring Wheat: This is grown where winters are too severe for Winter Wheat. It is planted in early spring as soon as the soil can be worked and matures in mid to late summer. It isn't as productive as Winter Wheat.

Planting

Raising transplants: Some people actually grow Wheat from transplants. Apparently it can increase yields by up to 50%, but it seems like a lot of work. I would only transplant if I had a small number of valuable seeds I wanted to multiply.

You can start the seed indoors in flats, about 6 weeks before the last frost. When the plants are about 2″ high they are transplanted outside. This should be about a month before the last frost date.

Direct sowing: This is the usual (more rational) way to plant Wheat. Broadcasting the seed onto the prepared seedbed is the traditional and most picturesque method, but it is quite wasteful of seed unless you are good at it. You don't want to have to thin your wheat. The most efficient way to plant is in rows with a seed drill, set to plant the seed to a depth of 1½″ to 3".

Spacing: Wheat doesn't like to be crowded. It's said you should be able to walk across a Wheat field and only stand on one plant with each step. This may seem rather thin, but the plants tiller freely, which means they send out additional stems. A spacing of 5″ is probably optimal in most cases.

Care

Water: Keep the soil evenly moist (this isn't usually a problem in cool weather).

Weeds: Because of the relatively wide spacing, weeds were once a big problem for wheat farmers and some weeds became synonymous with Wheat fields (for example the Corn Poppy). This isn't surprising when you realize how far apart the plants were spaced. It is a lot easier to keep a small area of the young plants well weeded and you should make sure you do. Older plants can usually take care of themselves.

Lodging: This can be a problem when winter Wheat is sown too early. If the over-wintering plants get taller than 6″ you can cut them back a little (it won't hurt them).

Pests and disease: One advantage of small scale growing is that your plants are unlikely to be seriously bothered by pests or disease. You should rotate your Wheat crop annually of course.

Birds and small mammals can be serious pests of Wheat, at both ends of the growing cycle. When it is sown and when it is ripening.

Hessian Fly is a serious problem for Wheat farmers in the east. You can avoid it by planting late (mid September to mid October).

Harvesting

When: Wheat is ready to harvest when the plants are turning yellow brown, but still have some green coloration. The heads start to droop somewhat at this stage. The seed can still be dented with a fingernail, but is no longer soft (it will harden further as it dries out).

How: For centuries the Wheat harvest was a major annual event for country people. It determined whether they lived well for the winter, or faced hunger and possible starvation. No wonder the annual harvest festival was a time to give thanks for a good harvest.

Wheat should be harvested later in the day, after the dew has dried out. If you are working on a small scale, you can cut the seed heads with shears and then dry and thresh them.

On a bigger scale the whole plants can be cut with a sickle (remove any weeds as you harvest), propped upright and tied into a stook to dry (a stook is a cone of whole plants with a hollow center). After the stooks had thoroughly dried they were made into a stack and left until threshing time.

Threshing is the process of freeing the seeds from the rest of the plant and was traditionally done with a flail. The threshed seed was then winnowed to remove the chaff. This was done by tossing it into the air, so the light chaff was caught by the wind and blown away. The heavier seeds fell straight back down.

The cleaned seed can be used immediately, or dried further for storage. Drying is a critical step, if the grains aren't fully dry (less than 13% moisture) they will quickly spoil in storage. Dry wheat should be stored in an insect and vermin proof container such as a metal bin.

Seed saving: Wheat is usually self-pollinated so it's easy to save the seed (you will be collecting it anyway). It isn't likely there will be many different wheat varieties growing around you anyway, unless you live near a farm.

Select seed from at least 10 of the best plants you have, to maintain some genetic variability. If you need more, you could just take a portion of the Wheat you just grew.

Your seed wheat should probably be stored separately from the bulk of the crop. It must be kept under optimum conditions if it is to remain viable for a long time.

Unusual growing ideas
Green manure: Wheat has also been grown as a green manure crop.

Organic matter source:
After you have harvested the grain crop, the straw is a valuable source of organic matter for enriching the soil. This is actually a significant bonus crop and makes wheat growing a more practical proposition.

Wheat Grass juice: See **Grass juice** for more on this.

Varieties:
Winter Wheat: These are the most useful varieties because they are in the ground over the winter, when it might otherwise be empty. When growing at this time they also use less irrigation water. They also tend to be higher yielding than spring wheat.

Spring Wheat: This is usually only grown where it's not possible to grow the Winter types.

Cooking: Wheat is most often ground into flour for making breads, cakes, pastry, tortillas and pasta. It can also be cooked for making cereals and even be popped like popcorn.

Herbs

I have already dealt with several annual herbs. In this section I am going to discuss the perennial herbs. I really like these plants, because they ask so little and give so much. They really deserve to be in every garden. If you don't have much space, herbs can even be planted around the garden as low maintenance ornamentals, groundcovers or foliage plants.

Chives
Allium schoenoprasum

Introduction: This is one of the best Onion flavored plants. It is often grown in herb gardens, but is so easy to grow and so pretty that it can be planted almost anywhere.

Nutritional content: Similar to other green onions.

Soil: Chives will grow almost anywhere, but does best in a rich, moist soil, with lots of organic matter.

Planting: Chives is easily grown from seed and will sometimes volunteer. It is often started indoors in flats or soil blocks and later transplanted outside. However it can easily be direct sown as well.

Vegetative propagation: Once you have an established colony, Chives can easily be propagated by division. The plants multiply quickly and may actually benefit from the occasional thinning.

Care: Chives is pretty drought tolerant, so doesn't need a lot of watering. It is quite low growing and somewhat vulnerable to weeds, so weed regularly.

Deadhead: Remove the dead flowers to prevent the plant devoting energy to seed production.

Mulch: In very cold areas protect it over the winter with a thick mulch.

Harvest: The leaves are at their best before the flowers appear, but can be used anytime they are available.

Storage: Chives doesn't dry very well, but the fresh leaves can be frozen. Fill an ice cube tray with clean chopped leaves and cover with water. Once they are frozen you can put the cubes in a plastic bag.

Seed saving: Just leave Chives alone to flower and it will make seeds. It won't cross-pollinate with anything.

Unusual growing ideas: Plant it as a low growing ornamental edging along paths.

Cooking: Chives is used to add a delicate Onion flavor to soups, salads, salad dressings, eggs, dips, sauces and cheese dishes.

Garlic Chives
Allium tuberosum

This plant is grown and used in pretty much the same ways as Chives. It is sometimes grown purely as an ornamental.

Lovage
Levisticum officinale

Introduction: This uncommon perennial is one of my favorite salad plants. Its flavor is often compared to the related Celery, but in my opinion it is much nicer (and nothing like it).

Soil: Lovage does best in a rich moisture retentive soil and sun or part shade.

Planting: Lovage can be grown from seed, but it is slow. Plant the seed when it is ripe in summer or early autumn. Seedlings will take several years to reach full size. A mature plant can be quite enormous, sometimes as much as 10 feet tall.

Lovage can be divided very easily. I initially bought a small plant, and as it got bigger I divided it. I also obtained seed from it.

Care: Lovage is an easy plant to grow and requires little attention. If you make sure the soil is kept fairly moist, that should be enough.

Mulch: This helps to keep the soil moist and keeps down weeds.

Harvest: Harvest the leaves, stems and seeds whenever you need them.

Seed saving: Just leave it to flower and produce seed, it couldn't be simpler.

Unusual growing ideas: Lovage is quite spectacular, if rather large, and is useful as an ornamental.

Cooking: I crave the young leaves and stems in salads, so rarely use them in any other way. They can also be used as a flavoring for soups and stews, in much the same way as Celery.

Marjoram
Origanum majorana

Introduction: Marjoram is a close relative of Oregano, but sweeter and more aromatic.

Where: This native of the Mediterranean thrives in full sun and grows without any attention in my garden. It is a perennial, but not very hardy (only to zone 6).

Soil: Oregano grows well in relatively poor soils, so long as they are well-drained.

Planting: This species is easily grown from seed, but it is slow. It's quicker and easier to buy a plant and then divide it as necessary. You can also grow it from cuttings. Space the plants 12″ apart.

Care: Marjoram is very drought tolerant, but will grow faster if watered occasionally. If winters are very cold you may want to pot it up and bring it inside for the winter. It does well on a kitchen windowsill.

Pruning: If Marjoram starts to get woody, cut it down to within a couple of inches of the ground. This will stimulate it to send up fresh new growth.

Harvest: Cut the tender shoots and leaves as you need them. They are best just before the flowers appear, so if you are going to preserve them, this is the time to harvest. They can be dried for winter use, or frozen as described under Chives.

Cooking: Marjoram is great in soups, sauces and salad dressings.

Mint
Mentha species

Introduction: The Mints are very reliable producers of tasty leaves, but can be used for a lot more than simply flavoring. Some types are extremely vigorous and if given suitable growing conditions they will put on an amazing amount of growth in a season.

Nutritional content: The leaves contain several valuable anti-cancer phytochemicals.

Where: Mints are not very concerned about location and will do well in sun or part shade, so long as they get enough moisture. They are notoriously invasive plants, spreading by means of creeping rhizomes. If your garden is big enough you might let them run free, but in most gardens it is safer to confine them behind a barrier.

Soil: These plants grow best in a rich soil, though almost any moist soil will do.

Planting: Though Mint is easily grown from seed, the flavor of a seedling won't necessarily be the same as the parent plant. It is better to propagate it vegetatively from root cuttings, as you can then be sure of what you are getting. Some kinds are distinctly inferior and the last thing you want is to have your garden choked by one of these. Space the plants one foot apart and thin every few years as they get crowded. You should only need one plant (or bucket) of each variety.

Control: It doesn't take a very talented gardener to grow Mint, probably the hardest part is stopping it from taking over the garden entirely. The best way to grow it is in a 5-gallon bucket with the bottom cut out, sunk into the ground to within 2″ to 3″ of the rim. This contains it very effectively. Don't think you can keep it under control by mowing, it will simply hug the ground and continue to spread.

When growing in confined spaces, Mint should be divided regularly, to prevent it getting too overcrowded. Replant a small part and discard the rest (be careful where, as it can re-root itself).

Care: This vigorous and independent plant doesn't need much attention. It does like moist soil however and won't be nearly so vigorous without it. In theory you could keep Mint under control by not watering it very much, but drought stressed plants don't taste very good.

Harvest: Mint is best harvested just before it flowers. After it flowers you can encourage fresh new growth by cutting it down to the ground.

Varieties: There are many different varieties and species of Mint to choose from, each with a different flavor. The golden rule when buying any mint is to taste it before you buy.

Spearmint is the most useful as a culinary flavoring. However I much prefer Peppermint as a tea. Apple Mint with its soft fuzzy leaves is good raw in salads.

Cooking: Uses in sauces, Indian cooking,

Oregano, Greek
Origanum vulgare ssp *hirtum*
Syn O. heraceloticum
Oregano Italian
O. majorana

These aromatic perennials are essential to Italian cooking.

Soil: Oregano doesn't need very fertile soil, but it should be well-drained.

Where: These species are native to the Mediterranean and love full sun. They both grow quite independently in my garden.

Planting: These plants can be grown from seed, but it is better to use a superior cultivar. I bought a plant of each type and then took cuttings from them. They can also be divided quite easily.

Oregano will grow quite quickly if given sufficient moisture. Space the plants 12″ apart.

Water: Oregano is adapted to a Mediterranean climate and suffers more from too much water than not enough.

Pruning: If the plant starts to get woody, cut it down to within a couple of inches of the ground. This will stimulate it to send up fresh new growth.

Pests: I have to admit to being completely oblivious as to whether it has any pests of not, I only pay it any attention when I am harvesting.

Harvest: Cut the shoots and leaves as you need them. It can be dried for winter use but is better frozen (see Chives).

Varieties: As with most herbs it is important to choose a good cultivar. Some are far superior to others, so smell and taste them before you buy.

Cooking: Oregano doesn't keep its flavor if cooked for too long, so should be added near the end of cooking. It's good with roast potatoes, as a topping for pizza and in sauces, stews, soups and vegetables.

Rosemary
Rosmarinus officinalis

This evergreen shrub is native to the Mediterranean and is perfectly at home in my garden. In fact I don't really feel qualified to give you much advice about Rosemary, because it grows itself with no help from me. It grows into a medium sized bush that can go without irrigation for months. It is completely ignored by deer.

Rosemary doesn't like extreme cold and can be killed by temperatures of 5° F.

Soil: Rosemary likes a well-drained soil and a sheltered position with full sun.

Propagation: I usually propagate it by layering, as branches will root where they touch the ground. Just pin them down to the ground, cover with soil and keep them moist. Once established the rooted branches grow rapidly.

If you need a lot of plants, propagate them by softwood cuttings taken in late spring. These should be 3″ long and have a small heel of older wood attached. Root them in a plant pot filled with peat moss, with a plastic bag as a cover. They should root within a month.

Containers: In colder climates Rosemary is often grown in containers and brought inside in the winter.

Harvest: You can gather sprigs of this evergreen any time you need them, even in winter. The flavor of the fresh plants is best, but it can also be dried for later use.

Landscape shrub: Rosemary is a useful evergreen landscape shrub. Its blue flowers are a magnet for bees,

Varieties: There are quite a few varieties, but they differ more in their habit (upright, prostrate) than their flavor.

Cooking: Use fresh or dried, in stuffings, stews, soups (pea is good) and vegetables. Add Rosemary sprigs to a barbecue, or remove the leaves and use as skewers.

Sage
Salvia officinalis

Introduction: Sage has been one of the indispensable culinary herbs since medieval times. Cooking wouldn't be the same without it.

You don't usually need more than 2 or 3 Sage plants. I grow more than this because my son grazes on it, sometimes defoliating whole bushes at one sitting.

Nutrients: Sage contains some valuable anticancer phytochemicals.

Soil: It will grow in any well-drained soil, but prefers a light, slightly alkaline one.

Where: Sage loves full sun, though in hot climates it will also grow in part shade.

Planting: Sage is easily grown from seed in well-drained soil. The seedlings will taste as good as their parents, but you won't be able to start harvesting until their second year.

I initially bought a small plant (a rooted cutting) from a nursery.

When that was big enough I divided it and also took cuttings.

Sage layers well, just lay a branch down on the ground and cover it with soil. By the end of the summer it will have rooted and can be detached. You can also bury an entire plant (except the tips) in soil. The more vigorous branches will all root.

Care: This is a very tough plant and once established it can be totally ignored, apart from harvesting. It is very drought tolerant and doesn't even need watering.

Sage doesn't like very cold weather and in very cold areas it may not survive the winter outdoors. In which case it should be potted up and brought inside for winter use (or kept dormant in a cool garage).

Pruning: Remove the flower stalks as they appear (unless you want seed) as this diverts energy from vegetative growth.

If a plant starts to get woody, cut it back hard, to encourage tender new growth. If a plant gets very woody dig it up, divide it, and replant the most vigorous parts (or just take cuttings).

Harvest: I just pick single leaves as I need them for cooking. They are evergreen and can be gathered year round in mild climates. In harsher climates you can pick whole branches just before they flower and dry them indoors (they dry well). Whole leaves can be frozen for winter use.

Unusual growing ideas: Sage has pretty blue flowers and can be useful as a drought tolerant ornamental.

Varieties: There are quite a few varieties out there: Golden, Tricolor, Berggarten (with big leaves). Unfortunately most of these look better than they taste. According to my son (who loves to eat handfuls of raw Sage leaves) none compare with the small, grey, often rather shabby looking, standard Sage.

Cooking: Sage is best fresh, but is also good dried. It is good with cheese, beans, soups, pâté, eggs, pasta, cheeses, sauces, soups and various vegetables.

Tarragon
Artemisia dracunculus

This is another important culinary herb. You should always smell and taste a plant before you buy it, to make sure it is a good cultivar. The best type is French Tarragon, which can only be propagated from cuttings, not seed.

Where: Tarragon prefers full sun, but in very hot climates it will also do well in part shade.

Soil: Tarragon likes well-drained soil. It is another herb I have planted and lost, only to find it several years later still hanging on.

Planting: Buy a small plant and propagate it from stem cuttings or division. Space the plants 12″ to 18″ apart.

Care: Tarragon is an undemanding plant that requires little beyond an occasional watering. It is quite drought tolerant and can even go dormant in summer if it gets neglected too much.

Harvest: Harvest the growing tips as you need them. If the plant gets woody then cut it down to within a couple of inches of the ground. It will send up vigorous new growth.

Storage: The leaves don't dry very well, but can be frozen to preserve their fresh taste. Do this as described under Chives.

Cooking: The leaves are used to flavor eggs, tomatoes, butters, vinegars, salads, mustards, sauces and soups (especially mushroom).

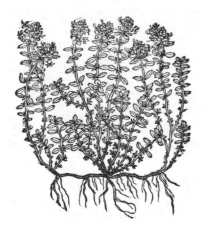

Thyme
Thymus vulgaris

Thyme is another kitchen essential.

Soil: Thyme will do well in almost any soil, so long as it is well drained.

Where: It does best in full sun, but will tolerate some shade.

Planting: Thyme is usually grown from cuttings, or by division, though it can also be grown from seed quite satisfactorily. I bought a small plant and divided it as it grew. I also took cuttings.

Care: Thyme is quite drought tolerant so only needs an occasional watering. If it starts to get woody cut it back to within a couple of inches of the ground and it will regenerate. You can also dig it up, divide it and replant the most vigorous pieces.

Ornamental: This low growing plant does well at the edge of paths.

Cooking: Thyme is good fresh or dried. It is a traditional ingredient of "Fines Herbes", and Bouquet Garni". Its warming flavor goes well with Winter Squash, soft cheeses, pâté, vegetables, and tomato sauces.

Edible Weeds

There are a number of tasty and nutritious food plants already growing in your garden; the weeds. Some of these are as good as anything you can grow and you should take advantage of them. Using them can even help to keep them under control.

As with any cultivated crop, these plants must be gathered at the right stage of growth and prepared properly,

Annual weeds

Intensively fertilized and watered beds, with their disturbed soil are just made for annual garden weeds. Of thousands of plant species from all over the world, these are the plants that are best adapted to life in the garden. Many of the same weeds can be found in temperate gardens right around the world, because every gardener strives to create the same conditions (rich, moist, loose, bare soil). Disturb a patch of soil and leave it bare for a week and annual weeds will appear. Within a month they will have completely covered every inch of soil.

Many of the commonest annual weeds are edible to some degree and some are very good. If you gather these while they are young, you will have some of the most nutritious and vibrant foods to be found anywhere.

Pigweed

(*Amaranthus* species)
This is one of the commonest summer weeds and is probably in most peoples gardens by July. They produce an abundance of long-lived (up to forty years) seed and can out-compete almost any crop plants.

The Pigweeds are close relatives of the Amaranth I have already described as a crop (see Amaranth). The wild plants are just as nutritious and tasty and can be used in the same ways. The only significant difference is that you don't have to grow them.

Wintercress

(*Barbarea* species)
Wintercress gets its name because it is extremely hardy and can grow right through the winter in mild areas. It is at its best in cool temperatures and can get very pungent in warm weather. I use it like Watercress, raw in salads or as a potherb. If it is too bitter to be palatable, the first cooking water can be thrown away and a lot of the bitterness will go with it. The unopened flower buds can be eaten raw, or cooked like miniature Broccoli.

Some species (*B. vulgaris, B. verna*) are so good they are cultivated as minor crops. They are a good example of a no-work vegetable, that even self seeds itself.

Shepherds Purse

(*Capsella bursa pastoris*)
This opportunistic little annual is naturalized all around the world. It has been so successful because it sets seed abundantly (it pollinates its flowers before they even open) and its seed may remain viable for up to thirty years. It is also very hardy and can survive temperatures as low as 10° F.

Unlike many members of the Mustard family, the leaves don't get very pungent or bitter, so can be used any time they are available. This plant is widely cultivated in Taiwan and China and can be found for sale in vegetable markets there.

In moist fertile soil the leaves get much larger than in the wild, often several inches in length.

The leaves are at their best before the flowers appear. They can be used in salads, or cooked for a few minutes as a potherb. They are good sautéed with onion.

The seed can be ground to flour and made into a condiment like Mustard. It has also been sprouted like Alfalfa (*Medicago*).

Lambs Quarters

(*Chenopodium album*)
A single Lambs Quarters plant will produce about 4000 seeds on average. Some of these seeds are able to germinate immediately; others must lie dormant for several years (they are an insurance policy for the plant). This is one reason why it is such a formidable competitor as a weed.

The leaves contain large amounts of vitamins A, C and several B's, as well as calcium, iron and phosphorus.

Caution: It is often said that one should eat Lambs Quarters in moderation. This is because it contains oxalic acid, which can inhibit the absorption of calcium. The danger of oxalates in general is over-rated, as they pose little problem to a person with a healthy intake of calcium. They may be a problem for people with a history of kidney stones however.

A close relative of Spinach, Lambs Quarters has been used as a salad or potherb for thousands of years. The young spring growth is good in salads, or as a potherb and is highly regarded by many wild food enthusiasts.

Mallows

(*Malva neglecta, M. rotundifolia*)
The Mallows are among the richest plant sources of carotene (which the body converts into vitamin A), containing as much as 16,000 i.u. per ounce. They also contain a lot of vitamin C and many minerals.

These hardy plants remain green all winter in mild climates, which makes them valuable winter greens in such areas. In China they are sometimes called Winter Amaranth, which gives an interesting insight into the importance of both species.

The tender young leaves can be used in salads, but are best boiled as greens. Older leaves can be chopped and cooked as a potherb, though you might want to change the cooking water once or twice. This is not necessary to remove any unpleasant taste, but to reduce their rather slimy quality.

The green seedpods have been peeled and used like Okra (actually a relative) to thicken soups and as a cooked vegetable. Their unusual shape and texture makes them an interesting addition to salads.

If you don't have them in your garden, but would like them, they are easily raised from seed. Once established they will self sow.

Miners Lettuce

(*Montia perfoliata*)
The plant got its common name because gold miners commonly ate it during the 1849 California gold rush. Before that event it was known as Indian Lettuce or Spanish Lettuce for similar reasons.

Miners Lettuce is a common weed on the west coast, where it grows in the cool weather of late winter and spring. It can be made into a weed elsewhere, as it is easily grown from seed and self-sows readily.

The mildly flavored and succulent leaves can be used as the base for a wild spring salad. They can also be used as a potherb, by steaming or boiling for a few minutes.

Peppergrass

(*Lepidium* spp)
All *Lepidium* species, native and exotic are edible and many are quite tasty. Like most members of the Mustard family they are best in cool weather and becomes bitter and unpalatable in hot weather.

The leaves contain up to 10,000 i.u. of vitamin A per 100 grams.

The tender young plants are good in salads and some species have been cultivated for this. Older parts can be used raw, if finely chopped. They can also be cooked as a potherb, though you may need to change the cooking water to reduce their strong flavor.

In Britain the seed has been sprouted indoors as micro-greens for as long as I can remember. Sprinkle a thin layer of seed on a wet paper towel and leave in a warm dark place for several days to sprout. When most of the seed has germinated bring them out into the light to turn green and grow. They are ready to eat when 2 to 3 two inches tall (in about a week).

If you can get enough of the seeds, they can be used to make a condiment like mustard (*Brassica*).

Lepidium sativum is cultivated as a dry land substitute for Watercress and is known, appropriately enough, as Garden Cress. It is easily grown from seed, in almost any soil, so long as the weather is cool. It bolts quickly in hot weather.

Purslane

(*Portulaca oleracea*)
One of my favorite edible weeds, Purslane is highly prized in Mexico (where it's known as Verdolaga) and other countries. In fact it is so esteemed that several improved cultivars have been produced. The succulent leaves and tender growing tips are an excellent salad plant. They are also equally good as a potherb. This is a low growing plant and can get quite dirty in wet weather. It will stay cleaner if it is mulched.

Wild Radish

(*Raphanus sativus*)
This is the garden Radish, escaped and reverted to its natural wild form. It is only of limited used as food, as it doesn't normally produce a swollen root.

The young leaves can be used like the Mustards (*Brassica*) as a tasty addition to salads, or as a potherb. In mild winter areas the whole plants can be eaten, cooked or raw, right through the winter. The flowers and unripe seedpods are also good in salads. The ripe seed can be sprouted like Alfalfa, or used as a condiment like Mustard.

R. raphanistrum - Wild Radish
Used as above.

Chickweed

(Stellaria media)

One of the commonest plants in the world, Chickweed is highly regarded as a source of wild greens. It is common, easily identified, mildly flavored, rich in vitamin C and in mild climates will provide food right through the winter. The tender growing tips can be used as a base for a salad, simply add pungent, sour and aromatic leaves to give more flavor. They are also an attractive garnish.

The young plants are a good potherb, though you will need to gather a lot, as it shrinks when cooked. The tops of older plants can be used in the same way, though you may need to discard the tougher stems.

Sow Thistle

(Sonchus species)

These useful food plants are more closely related to the Lettuces (*Lactuca*) than to other Thistles. They are nutritious (rich in vitamins A and C) and no species is poisonous, so any with tender foliage can be eaten.

The mildly flavored young leaves are a good potherb and can even be used for salads if their spines are trimmed off. Older leaves are bitter, but have been eaten after cooking in several changes of water (I am not sure they have any nutrients left after this much cooking though). They can also be blanched to reduce their bitterness, by covering with a bucket (or board) for a few days to exclude light.

The succulent flower stalks can be eaten until the flowers appear. Peel and eat raw or cooked.

Perennial weeds

These weeds more likely to be found in other parts of the garden, rather than the intensive beds, but they are worth knowing about.

Ground Elder

(Aegopodium podagraria)

This aggressive perennial spreads by means of creeping roots and by seed and is very invasive. It is also quite palatable, so if you can't beat it, eat it.

The young leaves, picked while still young and tender can be eaten raw in salads. They can also be cooked for 10 minutes as a potherb, or added to soups. Ground Elder leaves were once quite a popular food in parts of Northern Europe

Milkweed

(Asclepias syriaca)

This familiar weed contains a milky juice that is responsible for the common name Milkweed. This juice is also responsible for the toxic and bitter flavor that pervades all parts of the plant.

The bitter toxins in Milkweed are water soluble and can be removed by cooking them in at least one change of water. When prepared properly the plant is considered to be one of the best wild foods.

All parts must be carefully prepared before they can be eaten. The usual method of preparation is to drop the edible part in boiling water and simmer for a couple of minutes. This is then drained, more boiling water is added and it is simmered for another minute or two. You then drain them again, add more boiling water and simmer until cooked.

Most of the bitter principle remains in the first two lots of water. Never put Milkweed in cold water and bring to the boil, as this fixes the bitterness in the plant.

The tender spring shoots are used when 4″ to 8″ high. They can be eaten like as a vegetable, added to soup or fried in tempura batter.

The young leaves can be gathered from the top of the plant until the flowers appear and prepared as above.

The immature seedpods are probably the best Milkweed food. They are gathered when firm and only a couple of inches long and cooked as described above. They are mucilaginous (slimy) like Okra pods and can be used in much the same ways.

The Western *A. speciosa* can be used in the same ways.

Chicory

(Cicorium intybus)

Chicory has a history of cultivation dating back to the ancient Egyptians. It was introduced into North America as a food plant by the first white settlers and is now widely naturalized.

Chicory leaves are as bitter as those of Dandelion and almost as nutritious. They contain lots of vitamin A and C and many minerals including iron, potassium, calcium and phosphorus. The tender new spring leaves can be used in the same ways as the related Dandelion), as salad greens, or as a potherb. As the plants mature they become impossibly bitter. Blanching reduces their bitterness considerably (cover them with a plant pot or board) and this probably led to the forcing of the roots.

Thistles

(Cirsium species)

Thistles are available year round, are quite nutritious and are pretty good even when raw. The many species vary a great deal in habit and edibility so one must experiment with them to find the best.

The roots can be eaten year round but are best while dormant in winter. Locate them at this time by the rosette of leaves. I have dug roots in midsummer and found them tasty straight from the ground, however some species are bitter unless cooked in a change of water. They can be boiled, added to soup or baked.

The slow baked roots are very sweet as their starch turn to sugar and were a favorite of Native Americans. Bake them in a 350° F oven for 30 minutes. Native Americans dried and ground the baked roots to flour and baked a kind of bread with it.

The young spring leaves can be eaten as a salad plant, if you trim off the spines and chop well. Older leaves can be cooked as a potherb for 15 minutes, though you might have to change the cooking water once or twice to reduce their bitterness. The flower stems can be gathered before the flowers open, peeled of their tough skin and eaten raw or cooked (they are good in soup). For a quick snack, split the stems lengthwise and eat the succulent interior.

Evening Primrose

(Oenothera biennis)

The biennial roots are edible and can be gathered when dormant from fall to early spring. Locate them by finding the easily identifiable mature plants and then by searching for the leaf rosettes of young plants nearby. They are easy to recognize once you are familiar with them. The palatability of the roots varies with stage of growth (generally younger plants are best). Some are good enough to eat raw; others must be cooked in a change of water to make them palatable (peeling also helps).

The young leaves and crowns can be used like those of Dandelion (*Taraxacum*) and some species are even good raw. Older leaves are bitter, but can be eaten if treated like Dandelions and boiled in a change of water.

This species has been cultivated in Europe as a root vegetable. It was once known as German Rampion.

Hooker's Evening Primrose *(O. hookerii)*
This western species can be used in exactly the same ways as the above.

Great Plantain

(Plantago major)

Plantain is more often found in lawns and waste places, rather than garden beds (look for it on your paths).

In spring the tender, newly emerged leaves can be used in sandwiches and salads, or boiled as a potherb for 10 to 15 minutes. They are rich in vitamins A and C and quite nutritious.

Older leaves tend to be hairy and somewhat tough, but can be used as a potherb if you strip off the tough veins. They are better used in soups and stews (it may help to put them in blender for a few seconds). They may be improved by blanching. Just cover them with a board for a few days.

The related *P. coronopus* is sometimes cultivated as a salad plant.

Common Sorrel

(Rumex acetosa)

This species can be used in much the same ways as the cultivated Sorrel, I have already described. This hardy plant often stays green all winter and doesn't get bitter in summer, so can be eaten any time it is available. The arrowhead shaped leaves are a good minor addition to salads and can even be used in salad dressings instead of lemon or vinegar.

Sorrel is also a fine potherb if you change the cooking water once or twice, to reduce the sour flavor. Sorrel soup is a delicacy in France.

Sheeps Sorrel *(R. acetosella)*
This species is smaller than the Common Sorrel, but can be used in the same ways (the small leaves are a nice addition to salads).

Curled Dock

(Rumex crispus)

The Docks are familiar to almost everyone, as they are among the commonest and most widespread of perennial weeds. No member of the *Rumex* genus is poisonous, though they do contain toxic oxalic acid (cooking reduces this considerably) and many species are too tough, bitter or astringent to be edible.

This species is very rich in vitamins A (up to 7000 i.u. per ounce) and C. It also contains many minerals and is one of the best plant sources of iron .

In mild climates this hardy plant grows right through the winter and at this time it can be good. The tender young leaves are a nice addition to salads, or may be boiled as a potherb for 5 to 10 minutes. Older leaves are bitter, but can be made more palatable by cooking in a change of water for 10 to 15 minutes. If they are astringent you might add a little milk to the cooking water. The leaves don't shrink much in cooking, so you don't need to gather a huge amount.

Patience Dock (*R. patienta*)
Red Dock (*R. sanguineus*)
These perennial species are sometimes cultivated as potherbs.

Dandelion
(Taraxacum officinale)
Dandelions are one of the commonest perennial weeds in many gardens. I considered including it in the crop section, as it is such as good food plant and there are improved varieties available. I didn't for the simple reason that in most areas people don't need to cultivate it, they already have it growing for free. In my case I had to introduce it into my garden initially, but it is now naturalized.

Dandelion leaves are more nutritious than most common vegetables. They contain up to 14,000 i.u. of vitamin A per hundred grams, along with lots of Vitamin C and several B vitamins. They also contain many minerals, including calcium, chlorine, copper, iron, phosphorus, magnesium, silicon and sulfur. They are one of the richest plant sources of potassium.

Dandelion is only really good in cool weather and for most of the year it is too bitter for most palates. It is harvested in spring, from the time it first appears above ground, until the flowers stalks appear. It may also be good for a while in late autumn. In milder areas it may remain green and palatable all winter.

The young leaves can be used in salads, or cooked for 5 to 10 minutes as a potherb. If they get too bitter, change the cooking water at least once. Some people blanch the leaves by covering them with a box or a plank for a few days (just as they would with the related Endive or Chicory). This makes them less bitter and more tender.

Stinging Nettle
(*Urtica dioica*)
A weed of waste places, rather than the vegetable garden. The Nettle is famous (or infamous) for the sting in its leaves. It has a good reason for protecting itself as it does, as the young spring shoots are one of the most nutritious of all green plants. They contain more protein than almost any other green leaf, large amounts of chlorophyll, vitamin A, several B's, lots of C and D. They also contain an abundance of minerals including calcium, iron (one of the richest plant sources), manganese, phosphorus, potassium, silicon and sulfur.

The drawback to the use of Nettles as food is that they are only edible for a short time in spring. Not only does the plant get tough as summer progresses, but inedible crystal deposits form in the leaves.

Obviously this ferocious plant can't be eaten raw, you have to wear gloves to even handle it. However it only takes a few seconds of cooking to eliminate the sting and only a few minutes of boiling, steaming or stir-frying are necessary to produce an excellent potherb. The greens can be used as a substitute for Spinach in any recipe.

Other weeds
There are a lot more useful weeds out there. If you are interested in finding out more about them, I suggest you look at my book The Uses Of Wild Plants.

Complete plant index

Green Man Publishing

P.O. Box 1546

Felton

CA 95018

Greenmanpublishing.com

The Uses Of Wild Plants

Frank Tozer

This unique guide to the wild plants of North America describes the uses and cultivation of more than 1200 species in over 500 genera. A treasury of information on every aspect of plant use, it describes how wild plants were used for food in the past, how they can be used today and how they might one day become new crops. It is one of the most comprehensive guides to North American edible wild plants available.

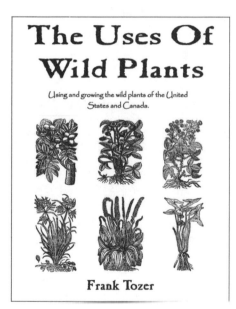

It describes how plants have been used to treat sickness, and how they can help to enhance health by providing superior nutrition. How they can be used for dyes, cosmetics, soap, paper, fuel, clothing, perfumes, glues, craft materials, and many other home, commercial and industrial uses.

Looking to the future, it shows how wild plants could help us to create an ecologically sustainable society, by providing new crops for food, medicine, fuels, renewable energy, chemicals and building materials. How they could help to clean our rivers and lakes, desalinate soil, remove toxic chemicals from polluted groundwater, recover valuable nutrients from waste, and maybe even reduce global warming.

For the gardener this book gives detailed information on the cultivation of the most important plants. It also describes their uses in the garden, homestead and farm, as new crops, fertilizers, fence-posts, fencing, hedges, mulch, screens, green manures, insecticides, groundcover, and for many other purposes.

ISBN: 0-9773489-0-3

$24.95

Green Man Publishing
P.O. Box 1546
Felton
CA 95018

Greenmanpublishing.com

The Organic Gardeners Handbook
Frank Tozer

Everything you need to know to create a low cost, low input self-sustaining intensive vegetable garden. A serious guide to the art and science of organic gardening, it covers the subject with a depth that is rarely seen in contemporary books. There are chapters on every aspect of organic vegetable gardening, soil dynamics, soil management, cultivation, composting, crop planning, raising seedlings, watering, harvesting, seed saving, greenhouses and much more. Whether you are a complete novice and need your hand holding through every step, or a veteran gardener with a permanent layer of soil under your fingernails this book will help you to become a better gardener. The Organic Gardeners Handbook is a companion to The Vegetable Growers Handbook.

ISBN: 978-0-9773489-1-6

$24.95